T0302144

The Most Important Asset

The principles of sound human resource management are generally understood, but too often practitioners believe the same policies and programs will work in all contexts. The effectiveness of any system is highly dependent on the context within which it must function. And due to globalization and increased workforce diversity, the contexts across and even within organizations have become more varied.

The Most Important Asset is a story about new graduates entering the human resources field, encountering and dealing with workforce management challenges and issues and developing their own professional competence through experience. Principles are presented and alternative solutions to problems are explored, providing the reader with a roadmap for analyzing situations and making decisions as to how to act. Placing the characters in different types of organizations provides insights into how different contexts call for different strategies. Alternative strategies for staffing an organization, developing its people, and defining, measuring and rewarding performance are used to illustrate how what is done should be compatible with the mission, culture, organizational strategy, and internal and external realities.

Robert J. Greene, Ph.D., is CEO of Reward Systems, Inc. and faculty for DePaul University, USA. He has over 40 years of industry, consulting and teaching experience. He is author of over 100 articles/book chapters, including *Rewarding Performance: Guiding Principles; Custom Strategies* and *Rewarding Performance Globally: Reconciling the Global–Local Dilemma*. Robert was the first recipient of the Keystone Award for achieving the highest level of excellence in the human resources field.

The Most Important Asset

Valuing Human Capital

Robert J. Greene, Ph.D.

Routledge
Taylor & Francis Group

LONDON AND NEW YORK

First published 2018
by Routledge
2 Park Square, Milton Park, Abingdon, Oxon OX14 4RN

and by Routledge
605 Third Avenue, New York, NY 10017

First issued in paperback 2021

Routledge is an imprint of the Taylor & Francis Group, an informa business

Publisher's Note
The publisher has gone to great lengths to ensure the quality of this
reprint but points out that some imperfections in the original copies
may be apparent.

British Library Cataloguing-in-Publication Data
A catalogue record for this book is available from the British
Library.

Library of Congress Cataloging-in-Publication Data
A catalog record for this book has been requested

Typeset in Bembo Std
by Swales & Willis Ltd, Exeter, Devon, UK

ISBN 13: 978−1−03−209619−3 (pbk)
ISBN 13: 978−1−138−30649−3 (hbk)

Contents

Figures

Tables

Acknowledgments

This book is the result of over five decades of experience in industry and consulting. This book is attributable to the contributions of many. My parents and my brother Richard during their lifetimes encouraged me by providing support and a nurturing family. My wife Dorothy and my son John provide that same kind of support today, while encouraging me to write and offering their perspectives.

A number of valued colleagues and friends acted as reviewers during the development of the book. Bruce Ferris began to press me to write this book before my first two books had been released. John Maxwell, Bob Butler, Ed Cassidy, Don Howard, Annette Howard, Howard James, Peter Ronza, Bill Seithel, Tom Taylor, Eric Wilson, Kathy McKee, Jim Buford, Jay Schuster and Patricia Zingheim provided constructive feedback and insights gained from their own professional experience in workforce management. A number of others provided me with the inspiration to do the best work possible. Dave Belcher, Wayne Cascio, Fons Trompenaars and Ed Lawler have set an example by sharing knowledge based on their innovative research. All of these people have earned my gratitude and friendship.

The opportunity to share knowledge with those who function as researchers, practitioners and consultants as a part of my consulting practice has enhanced my knowledge and understanding. Interaction with students of management has enriched my knowledge as well, and teaching has been a rich source of learning and personal development, as well as an opportunity to give back to the profession that has been so good to me.

My service as a faculty member for DePaul University in their MBA and MSHR degree programs, in the U.S. and internationally, has enabled me to develop a network of researchers and academics. The members of that network have helped me to increase my understanding of the concepts and principles underlying sound workforce management.

My involvement with World at Work and the Society for Human Resource Management over the last thirty years has provided me with the opportunity to define the body of knowledge in HR, develop a certification program, design and teach professional development programs and speak at their conferences. This has given me exposure to thousands of HR practitioners and enriched my understanding of the issues they deal with.

All of my experiences have resulted in a firm belief that the most important asset for any organization is its people.

1 Preparing for the real world

"Without an organization's people, nothing of value happens"
Robert J. Greene

Three students ready to remake the business world. That is how Don, Annette and Rob saw their mission. Their qualifications would soon include both the Master of Business Administration (MBA) and the Master of Science in Human Resources (MSHR) degrees. They had been exposed to all the leading theories and best practices over the last few years as students. There was no doubt that the business world needed their help.

They all had copies of their favorite *Dilbert* cartoon that had the pointy-headed boss announcing, "I used to think employees were our most important asset. I was wrong—they are eighth." When asked what was seventh the answer was "carbon paper." How people managing organizations could place such a low value on the people who made their technology and machines actually do something useful was a mystery to the trio, and they were determined to help change minds about the criticality of the workforce.

The trio had attended a presentation by Lester Thurow, a visiting academic, during which he had made the case that people are every organization's most important asset. He stated, "the only sustainable advantage is a workforce that is competent to do what the organization needs to succeed and that is committed to doing it . . . all other assets (capital, technology, infrastructure) can be obtained by competitors under pretty much the same conditions. And a competent and committed workforce cannot be bought . . . it must be built and sustained." This message really resonated with the three and they became advocates. They were missionaries looking for a challenge, and they saw bringing rigor to management decisions relating to the workforce as their job.

In their classes the three "people advocates" took their share of scorn from their more "scientific" and "business-oriented" classmates. Those with engineering undergraduate degrees working on MBAs had difficulty with courses that fell under the "behavioral science" category, thinking that to be an oxymoron. And the finance majors thought the metrics used by human resource practitioners were too subjective to be taken seriously. Besides, HR majors

advocated expenditures on things like training, which every financially liter-
ate person knew generated short-term costs (reducing profits) while creating
nothing that could be recognized as short- or long-term assets . . . or at least
not assets that could ever be shown in the financial statements. When the
trio pointed out that there was an increasing acceptance of the importance of
"intangible assets," the financial types often brushed it off as wishful thinking. When performance management was described as a critical management
activity by the MSHR candidates, the operations majors pointed out that
the leading quality gurus said 95% of defects were caused by the system and
that there was no need to try to measure individual performance differences
when the system was in control . . . they were just too small and insignificant.
Several of their fellow students had asked them what led to the decision to
get a second degree in Human Resource Management—wasn't the MBA the
ticket to success?

When the three of them had begun their MSHR degree programs, they
had been extensively interviewed about their backgrounds and why they chose
HR as a specialized discipline. Don had received his undergraduate education
at an elite private university, as had Annette. Annette had considered becoming
a doctor or a psychologist, since she had always had a desire to help people. She
attributed her interest in HR to that orientation, since she felt that some of the
"hard" disciplines undervalued the importance of people in making organizations successful. She was a humanist to the core and was optimistic, sometimes
to a fault. When people marveled at computers, she pointed out that the real
marvel was in the imagination of the designers of the software and the hardware, not in the machines. It was that perspective that caused her to consider
the human capital in organizations to be the most important asset and to focus
on managing that asset well. She understood that finance and technology and
all of the other assets were important as well, but without a competent and
dedicated workforce, she believed no organization could truly be successful.

Don wasn't sure about what sparked his interest in HR but thought part
of the cause was the quality of a couple of the faculty members he had for his
undergraduate courses in organizational behavior and psychology. He was a
pragmatist and realized that organizations were above all else collections of
people who banded together to serve a customer base with goods and services
they wanted and/or needed. He had a deep respect for financial management
and understood how difficult it was to do it well. And Don had worked in
a manufacturing plant for a couple of summers during undergraduate school
and recognized how much skill was required to produce high-quality physical goods, having ruined a good bit of material when trying to shape it into
something useful. When spending several weeks in the model shop as a vacation replacement, he had marveled at the ability of skilled model makers to
work within extremely close tolerances and to do so quickly without turning
expensive metals into junk. And his last summer job had been at a national
research lab, where he came to understand what advanced technology was
and how exciting it could be. He had cleaned up report drafts created by

design engineers that documented their explorations and discoveries and had come to appreciate the value of following the scientific method when creating new knowledge.

Rob was a bit older, having broken up his undergraduate work with a two-year stint in the military, which he viewed as an obligation for someone lucky enough to be a citizen of the U.S. His rather direct approach to interpersonal dealings had resulted from his service experience with a special operations unit, where you often did not have time to say much, but when you did speak, you told the unvarnished truth and did so succinctly. As a result of his manner, people often overlooked that under the surface he was very thoughtful and actually a bit of an intellectual

He had spent a few years in industry before attending graduate school. His first job was with a large, highly respected pharmaceutical firm, which had selected him into their executive development program. He followed that with a job in a smaller manufacturing firm, where he could assume a great deal of responsibility early in his career, as a management systems person. But a great opportunity came up with a consulting firm. It had not taken him long to realize he was not cut out for climbing the ladder in highly structured organizations. He had stopped preparing a number of reports at his first employer, thinking they were meaningless to anyone, and when no one complained, he assumed they were no longer a part of the routine. But his boss had spent over thirty years in a highly structured organization and found this approach to be unacceptable. Rob had thought that way of thinking to be misguided, so becoming a part of the consulting profession looked like a better way of life. Living by his intellect and being able to apply his ideas was very attractive to him. His orientation to application was at least partly attributable to the fact that most of his graduate work was done on a part-time basis while working, except for the last year, when he focused on the MSHR degree to add to his MBA. Rob decided if he had children and they showed a penchant for business, he would recommend they do their graduate education while working, which would allow them to apply at work what they learned in school and apply in school what they learned in their work.

Although the three of them differed in many ways, they found they shared high standards, which they imposed on themselves and on others. What sealed their friendship was serving as a team in the business policy capstone course in the MBA program. The course used a computer model to enable teams to compete in running a company. The teams made decisions, which were then run through a model that calculated the results of those decisions. Their team had done reasonably well in the early stages, but they all agreed that they needed to pay some attention to making workforce decisions as well as marketing and operating decisions. They devised incentive compensation plans at the company-wide level, the group/unit level and the individual level to provide the motivation to perform at high levels. When their programs were run through the model. they got virtually no credit for them. The professor was focused on operational issues and had not programmed in any logic that supported effective workforce management. The trio took on the teacher and convinced him to alter the model. After all, the idea that you just had to market well and design and produce products well appeared absurd to them. In fact, the discussions with the teacher would have resulted in multiple technical fouls if they had been debating with a basketball official.

When they were working as a team, it became clear that the left-side grey cells were dominant in both Rob and Don, while Annette was more influenced by the grey cells on the other side. Rob and Don were "cut to the chase . . . run the numbers," while Annette suggested that every strategy had to be executed by people, not computers, and that it was important to consider those people when deciding what to do. In fact, Annette had been the one to lobby for the incentives they created during the business policy course exercise. Rob and Don accepted the idea because they had studied motivation theory and believed you can use legal bribes to get people to perform well. During one of their "philosophical combat" sessions, Annette called a timeout and announced she had written a poem the night before and would like them to reflect on it.

The Right Path

Here I sit
Left side grey cells firing

                                        Activate the right-side cells
                    And I become whole brained
                        The reverse path
                produces the same result . . .
                So we all can play!

She had expected both of them to smile and acknowledge that they got it. Instead, Don blurted out, "so you think the two of us are half-brained?" Annette cringed and wondered if there was any hope for him. Rob was not much better. "Swell, when I go to my airborne division reunion, I will tell them I am getting in touch with my softer side." Annette realized that physical assault was a childish response, so she smiled and figured sooner or later the message would seep through the granite blocks they carried on their shoulders.

So, a common foe at school bound them together and they emerged a team going forward into the future. They all thought their school underestimated the importance of people. But when they saw a survey of the top twenty-five U.S. business schools, they found this wrongheaded view was prevalent. The survey results summarized the course content of the required curriculum in each school. The average number of finance/accounting courses required for an MBA was 2.1. The average number of HR courses was less than 1. So, they sarcastically concluded, in order to manage well, you only need to count well—no need to be good at managing the workforce. They were not pleased with the reality that workforce management was held in low esteem in many top schools. But at least their graduate school offered the MSHR degree and had two HR-related courses as requirements for the MBA degree.

Whether due to conviction or just stubbornness, the three made their course selections based on the belief that the management of people was the key to managerial success. Annette was in the process of getting serious with recruiters from a high tech firm about a position with them. Don was looking for a public sector organization he could help. And Rob was convinced that consulting is where one could make an impact on multiple organizations. They were ready, but was the world out there ready for them?

They all met one evening and decided that throughout their careers they would remain committed to helping organizations effectively utilize their most important asset—their people.

2 Entering the real world

Annette, Don and Rob all had obtained positions shortly after graduation. Annette landed an HR generalist job with a software design firm. Don accepted an offer with a major metropolitan water utility, also as an HR generalist. Rob began as a consultant in the HR practice with a professional services firm. Both Annette and Rob had received very attractive starting salaries, accepting the reality that they would not have much of a personal life for a few years, if ever. Don's role came with a starting salary somewhat below those of his two colleagues, but it was accompanied by a very generous benefits package, a lot of time off and the expectation that the work schedule and demands would leave adequate time to achieve "work–life balance."

The mission statements of their organizations were: "make those shareholders really rich (Rob)," "make the employees rich (Annette)" and "serve the citizenry by providing reliable, safe and affordable water (Don)."

They began regular get-togethers soon after they had jobs and incomes. During their first gathering, they compared the total rewards packages that they had received. The consensus was that they were very different but roughly equivalent. But both the HR function and the employees were viewed very differently in their organizations. Annette accepted that the employees of her organization were not viewed as its most important asset, trailing leading-edge software by a considerable margin. Rob found that his firm recognized they needed consultants in order to bill clients for time but that individual consultants were seen as replaceable parts of a revenue machine. Don felt that management of the utility viewed employees as being at least as important as customers, based on the fact that the total rewards package was so rich and that work-life balance seemed to be as important as productivity. Since turnover in their respective organizations was 30% (Annette), 50% (Rob) and 1% (Don), this metric suggested they were employed in very different contexts, with widely varying views of how the organization felt about the importance of its employees.

There was a lot more that was different as well. The strategies and programs used by their organizations to attract, retain and motivate their employees bore little similarity. When members of senior management in their organizations were asked what the best index of organizational performance was, the answer differed: "stock price escalation (Rob)," "profit and revenue growth (Annette)" and "staying within the operating budget while providing quality services to the populace (Don)." These differences in the way performance was defined led to very different HR strategies and programs. They also represented value propositions that were attractive to different types of potential candidates for employment in the three organizations. Annette recounted the striking comment made by Edward Lawler when he was speaking at a conference she had attended: "no matter what you do some people will hate it . . . just make sure they are the right ones." The course that the three had taken on staffing management reinforced that concept—organizations got the workforce they asked for by the way they structured their value propositions as a potential employer.

The three neophytes decided to pretend they were consultants (Rob was, but in name only at this point), evaluating the contexts that existed in each of their firms. They would then use that understanding to assess how each of the organizations managed their workforces.

The software firm

Annette was amazed that she was made eligible to participate in the annual incentive compensation starting her first day. There was also a discussion of her future eligibility in the firm's stock plan. On top of the generous starting salary, the total rewards package was almost overwhelming. The firm was still private, since the plan to go public had been put on hold given the impact of a serious economic downturn on initial public offerings. The price of the stock was tied to an annual valuation of the firm, which aligned everyone's interests and focused them on growth and profitability. Although she was not a revenue contributor, her HR role made her a part of the professional cadre of the firm, and management acknowledged that high levels of performance in her role would contribute to firm performance, albeit indirectly. Life was good and she immediately began looking for a better apartment.

The benefits package was on the lean side, but Annette realized this reflected the strategic focus of the firm. A flexible benefits program was in place that allowed employees to customize their programs to fit their needs. For example, if some employees did not wish to take all three weeks of vacation they were eligible for, they could "sell back" days at 1/260th of the annual salary per day, and use those funds to upgrade the health insurance coverage or some other benefit. The defined contribution plan was of particular interest to her. The plan provided a 50% matching contribution, based on the employee's contribution, up to 6% of salary. But it also provided for an increased match based on the firm's profitability each year, which could go to 100% of the employee's contribution in high-performance years. There were no automatic "sick days" accrued. If you were sick, you did not drop in to infect everyone else. If you were not sick, you came to work. And there was no vacation carryover from year to year. Management had asked themselves the question, "why do we provide vacation time?" The unanimous answer was "to let employees replenish themselves." But they also realized that if the vacation was deferred, there was no replenishment going on. This made it obvious to them that vacation carryover made no sense and just created accounting liabilities and something else to keep track of. Looking at the total package, Annette found it both reasonably competitive with prevailing practice in the private sector and very reasonable considering the firm's culture and strategy.

The firm's staffing strategy was of immediate interest to Annette, since one of her first responsibilities was recruiting new candidates. Management made it clear that the strategy was to hire the smartest people who also fit the organization's culture, with less emphasis on their having specific skills. Most hires were new college graduates, except for isolated cases when mid-career people with skills that were immediately needed were brought on board. The firm did of course consider its current needs and attempted to hire people with the appropriate level of experience. However, the firm considered the need for experienced hires to be a failure of their replacement and succession planning programs. As a result, managers who repeatedly attempted to hire experienced people were counseled on their failure to do adequate workforce planning. They were also reminded that every mid-level hire reduced the perception on the part of current employees that they would have adequate career progression opportunities. The executive team had evaluated the research on what the cohort of people entering the workforce most valued, and they realized that continuous development was at or near the top of their list.

The development strategy was also of interest to Annette. She had been taught that staffing and development strategies should be aligned with each other, particularly since new graduates entering the organization would require significant investments in their development. One of her professors in school had suggested that there were three alternative strategies for finding someone to fill a particular role: (1) hire someone who was "job ready," (2) hire someone who was capable of learning what was needed and invest in their development or (3) change the nature of the role or outsource it (generally when there was a shortage of people who would allow the organization to adopt either of the other two strategies). And a total cost computation should be made. For example, if less expensive recent graduates were hired, the cost of developing them should be factored into the cost of that strategy when it was compared to hiring up-to-speed people at higher salaries.

The executive team had attempted to ensure that both short-term skill building and longer-term development were emphasized. Since the firm's core competence was in software, it had developed extensive online skill-building programs that were available to all employees at all times. There was also a generous tuition reimbursement plan in place, as well as a program for ensuring high-potential employees were offered growth assignments. In the past, there had been instances where development was pushed aside as a priority in order to enhance short-term financial performance, but the new CEO vowed to ensure that a philosophy of emphasizing long-term optimization, rather than short-term maximization, governed workforce development.

The public utility

Don had a revelation soon after starting work. The workforce management context in the public utility differed substantially from private sector organizations, a concept that was not addressed in their courses in school. He had found a superb text on HR in the public sector[1] shortly after joining the utility. When studying that book, he realized that his school's faculty appeared to have overlooked many of the differences between the for-profit private sector and the not-for-profit and public sectors. He soon found that budgets controlled what could be done each year relative to pay adjustments in the public sector. And the utility's retirement program was a part of the state system, which meant it was largely out of the utility's control. He was concerned when he learned that the liabilities created by the plan provisions were not funded and the legislature could pass on the burden of paying benefits to future legislatures. This had made it easy to create generous retirement benefits, which offset the lower base pay rates. But this had over time created enormous liabilities, and the state did not have the resources to meet them when revenues declined due to economic downturns. Don was surprised to find that policy makers did not seem to worry, since dealing with reality could be left for someone else to face in the future. And the paid time off and health care benefits were dramatically richer than the prevailing practices in the private sector. This fact had been disguised because the utility's competitive position on benefits was measured only against other public sector entities.

Don did not understand how this approach could continue forever. The implications of having a very rich retirement program were creating other problems. People were retiring in their mid- to late-50s with generous incomes, supplemented by a generous retiree health insurance program. The obvious downside of this practice is that experienced people who were critical to providing services were leaving, since they had an incentive to retire early, due to the way the pension plans and retiree health plans were restructured.

As he was taught to do in his graduate courses, he had done an analysis of prevailing practices from a total rewards perspective and presented it to Margie the HR director and her direct reports. He had recently read a piece in *The Economist* that reported on the relative levels of compensation between the public and private sector. It contended that when actual time worked was used in the calculation, the average public sector employee was paid 17% more than the average private sector employee, and when benefits were compared, there was an additional 30% gap. This seemed to Rob to be a ticking time bomb, since the taxpayers were forced to write the checks to pay for all this. Even if *The Economist* calculations were off by half, they still could be a public relations disaster if there was an economic downturn and the ratepayers suffered as a result of economic conditions. Even though the utility's finances were separate from the city and county, the organization could easily become a target for citizen discontent.

Don confidently entered the conference room for his first meeting on strategy and made recommendations that included: (1) freezing the defined benefit pension program and replacing it with a defined contribution program, (2) raising premiums for retiree health programs to 100% of the cost, (3) increasing the employee share of health care insurance costs to 25%, (4) limiting vacation and sick day carryover from year to year and (5) reducing time off and vacation benefits to levels more in line with current practice in the private sector.

The reaction by those present at the meeting made it obvious that he should either modify his views or find another employer, probably in the private sector. Annette and Rob had found his recommendations to be justified when he had reviewed them at one of their coffee sessions, and since they were among those who were picking up the tab for all the current programs, they were enthusiastic about changing the strategy. But since the two of them did not offer to pay his rent and other expenses, Don found their support heartening but lacking in economic feasibility. If he were to stick to his recommendations, he might be in the market for a new income source.

Don also found that the utility had no clear staffing and development strategies. When someone was needed, a recruiting effort was launched. This seemed to him to reflect a disregard for the importance of effective workforce planning, which was to him a prerequisite for long-term workforce effectiveness. Waiting until a critical spot was vacated could well expose the organization to the risk that important work would go undone while replacements were trained.

The tuition reimbursement plan in effect at the utility covered just about everything, whether or not it was job related. But managers believed it was an employee's responsibility to manage their careers, as well as how each employee chose to use the support the utility made available for both skill building and developmental programs. This led to some employees becoming almost full-time students while others did not avail themselves of developmental opportunities. Since there was no payback for spending one's weekends and evenings on personal development, many employees received training only when their managers sent them to programs, and these were almost always focused on current skill needs. In the Operations Division, many of the employees needed licenses in order to work with water and waste water treatment plants and systems. As a result, they typically focused on the specific courses required for their next level of license. Although the training leading to licensing was necessary, it consumed the development budget, which meant that employees wishing to move into management would not have had any training in how to manage until after they had been placed in management roles. Margie had joked that this was sort of like the city issuing badges and guns to new police recruits and only sending them to the academy when it was convenient. When pressed, she admitted the city should then be held accountable for the mistakes made by those not properly trained.

After the meeting during which Don had made his revolutionary recommendations, Margie the HR director asked him if he could join her for lunch. Steve, the operations and maintenance director, was in attendance as well. Don was pleased to have this opportunity, suspecting that Margie would side with him and bring Steve around. Things did not go quite that way. Steve started by saying, "I congratulated Margie on hiring you. When I participated in the interview panel, I was impressed with how much your graduate studies had provided you with some contemporary approaches to managing employees and with an understanding of the principles underlying sound workforce management. After you had cited that book[2] that included the research support for using goal setting and feedback to improve motivation and productivity, I got the book and read it. I quickly realized that I lacked some of the behavioral science background to fully interpret some of the research, but it was helpful to know what was supported and what was not. Yet, what really struck me was the way the author pointed out the criticality of process—the way in which the principles were applied. He made it clear that the context within which programs would be applied had a huge influence on their effectiveness, as did the involvement of everyone in developing the strategy and implementing it. It was consistent with my philosophy of 'what works is what fits.'"

"But," Steve said, "did you get the message about the importance of *context* from the book as well?" "Uh oh," thought Don, "maybe this is not going to be a conversation I would like to have on tape to replay during my performance appraisal session. The word 'but' normally spells trouble." Steve continued with a lesson in reality: "Our utility is in the reliability business. We have an elaborate, far-flung system for purifying and distributing water and for processing waste water. If we commit errors in the water treatment plant, we can make a lot of people sick, and in fact if we don't follow procedures after fixing a leak in the field, that can have the same effect. The citizens of this community rely on us to do it right every time. Over the long run, we are charged with finding adequate sources of water and maintaining an infrastructure to be sure we can purify and deliver it. Finally, we must provide high-quality service at a reasonable cost. Our mission is similar to the police and fire departments in the city in many ways. And efficiency often takes a back seat to competence. A fire station is staffed not at the bare minimum level, but at a level that makes it possible to deal with the most severe crises a very high percentage of the time. We have the same type of pressure to be responsive, although to a lesser degree. Now, how do you think this all might explain some of the HR programs we have in place?"

Don thought a good bit about that and realized that the majority of their employees were directly involved in the processing and delivery of water. And because of the complexity of the water and waste water systems, both of which were somewhat unique to their utility, there might be a greater emphasis in retaining people for a much longer time than a software firm or consulting firm may find to be critical. "So, having people who know where the pipes are really buried, rather than what the engineering records show, might be important?" he quipped. "Yes," said Steve, "and have you considered that the fact that most of my people have been here a long time might be a plus, even though it makes my workforce more expensive?"

Don began to see it might make sense to pay a great deal of attention to employee benefits and pension plans, since if they were very attractive, they would appeal to applicants more interested in staying with the organization for the long haul. "Steve, I can see that for the plant and field people, but surely it is less critical for people in the office," he offered. "Well," said Steve, "the dispatchers need to know the geography, our system and how our field crews work. Customer service reps need to understand our rate structure and how customers are billed. The IT people deal with many systems tailored to a utility. So, who is it that is not critical? I agree that new engineers or entry-level field crew members are under direct supervision and that people early in their careers do not dream about how great life will be when they are old and drawing a pension. But since laws and regulations force us to offer similar benefits to everyone, that does not weaken the case for encouraging longevity. And given the laborious processes involved in letting people go and in hiring new people, I consider low turnover to be a blessing, although sometimes a mixed blessing."

"OK," said Don. Now his tendency to debate and to prevail, learned well in graduate school while chasing grades, prompted him to attack on another front. "So then, why is it that we have our pension plan and retiree health benefits designed the way they are? It seems to me that when two-thirds of our key people are eligible to retire in the next few years, that we have erred in creating incentives for them to leave at 55 rather than stick around to 65, which would benefit the utility greatly?" "There you have me," responded Steve, "we have really dug a hole for ourselves. I agreed with your recommendation to charge full fare for retiree health, as long as we phase it in for people already getting that benefit. While you were talking in the meeting, I created a plan—charge 100% of the premiums to all future retirees and start currently retired people at 50%, increasing by 10% per year for 5 years. That could still be taken as reneging on a promise, but at least we would probably not end up in court. The pension is another thing that needs attention. I support a normal retirement age of 65 to receive full benefits, but I think we could accept 60 with 30 years of service as well, a 'rule of 90' rather than a 'rule of 75' for full benefits." "What about time off—vacation and sick leave?" asked Don, sensing he was on a winning streak. Steve admitted he had never thought about challenging the idea of vacation carryover and wanted to give it more thought. And as long as the sick leave was changed in a way that would not leave people who were actually ill without adequate income, he was good with that as well.

Margie chimed in to make sure Don took away the underlying theme in the discussion. "Due to the recent economic downturn, there are a lot of angry people out there ready to light their torches and start up toward the public sector castle. But their perception of privileged status for those of us who are supported by their tax dollars is not one based on an understanding of all of the reasons. Human resource management systems must fit the organizational context and must contribute to a currently effective and continuously viable workforce. You have a tendency to accentuate the theoretical without perhaps appreciating the practical issues associated with implementing new concepts. No, we are aware of the growing angst on the part of the public, and we need to change some things that may be out of line. But how long do you think it is going to take to right the pension benefits issues? Let me make one other contribution here. We have historically set our base pay levels using surveys that included both the private and the public sector—and in fact dominated by private sector organizations. But when we compare benefits, we only use public sector organizations as comparators, and that is the wrong thing to do. It was partially responsible for the confrontation with our Board over things like the level of employee contribution to health care costs and even whether employees should be contributing to their pensions. So, we have not been asleep and are aware we need change, but at a digestible rate."

Don responded sheepishly, "I realize I came on like Attila the Hun in the meeting and also like someone who just got here and did not know the terrain. So, Margie will be my sounding board for bringing forth recommendations. I know we are one of the most respected utilities, so you all could not have been doing much wrong. I have also come to appreciate that changing some things will be like turning a heavy ship rather than like doing a ninety-degree in a hydroplane. So, thank you for this counseling and I go away happy that some of what I said is something you are considering." Don thought this would be an interesting encounter to report to his two friends at their next meeting.

The consulting firm

Well, if Rob had been anxious to find work, he certainly found work. On the first day, which was supposed to be orientation, there was a crash project. Rob was to find out that consultants don't often have "whenever you get to it" projects. The senior on a live project found out Rob was a bit of a quant jock. So Rob's first day started at 5 a.m., when he woke up anxious and excited, and his office presence did not end until 1 a.m., when the project report was emailed to the client. And after that everyone went out for a libation to celebrate, taking him to the next 5 a.m. As the consulting team shared war stories about the project and detailed their acts of heroism, Rob was feeling a bit sorry for himself, having been up 24 hours. But since one of the consultants was flying out that afternoon and facing 25 hours on planes on his way to Singapore, he was upstaged. There were plenty of assurances that this was not a normal day. A colleague who fancied himself a stand-up comic offered that sometimes they were able to go home before midnight. But at least Rob did not have to sit through mundane and/or touchy-feely new employee orientation sessions. It would have been nice to know where the cafeteria was when the dinner hour had passed without nourishment, but this all seemed like great fun, and boredom did not seem to be a probable risk.

In contrast to the first day, the rest of the first week was quiet, much like the calm after a hurricane. So Rob did get an employee orientation session, although he suspected it was something the HR director did in between storms. He was realistic enough to know programs like these would be delayed if there was billable time on the table. It was clear to Rob that the total rewards package offered by the consulting firm was very different than what Don had at the utility, although fairly similar to what Annette found at the software firm. Rob presumed it was a private versus public sector distinction. But Rob's direct compensation consisted of less salary and more performance-contingent incentives than Annette's did. And the incentives were primarily based on individual performance. It seemed the firm had carefully thought out what type of results they were willing to pay for and what they wanted consultants to focus on. As a new consultant, most of Rob's performance rating was based on the percentage of his time that was billable to clients and on the quality of his work. He would find that the performance metrics changed as he became more experienced, with new business development becoming more important. This all seemed very reasonable since he depended on others to assign him work now, and only when he had the experience and opportunity would he be expected to generate new business.

The philosophy underlying the employee benefits programs offered seemed very similar to what Annette found at the software firm. The flexible benefits program enabled someone without family responsibilities to stick with the basic health care package, while allowing those with growing families the opportunity to increase medical coverage. Since these employees could not afford to take a lot of vacation, they could sell vacation days back and use the funds to cover their significant health care expenses. And the defined contribution plan allowed older employees to divert a larger share of their current income to the time after they had retired.

The long-term incentive program particularly intrigued Rob. A consultant career ladder was in place that included five levels, from associate to managing consultant. At each level there was a stock ownership requirement, ranging from 50% of salary for associates and 300% of salary for managing consultants. Consultants were given time to acquire the required level of owned stock, principally by having one-half of their annual cash incentive award go to stock purchases. They of course could buy stock as well to allow them to acquire it at the current price with the expectation that the stock would appreciate. The firm had gone through an initial public offering three years ago and the stock had performed very well. Everyone seemed convinced that 15% per year appreciation was reasonable to expect over the long run. This seriously disagreed with what Rob had learned in his economics classes about long-term investment returns and was certainly unrealistic based on recent experience in the equity markets. But he was willing to roll the dice with the firm on that portion of his total rewards package.

Rob had a school friend who worked for a public accounting firm who described the single-minded focus on attaining partnership. "Six years of hell leading to the potential of salvation (partnership)" is the way it was described to Rob. When asked what happened to those who did not make Partner for whatever reason, he was shocked to learn that even those employees who were highly profitable for the firm were let go. Of course, the accounting firm attempted to do this gracefully and tried to find a slot for the excommunicated in client firms, which would provide them with allies in retaining and building business. After several tries at trying to figure out the wisdom of running off people who made money for the firm, Rob gave up and figured there must be some rationale he was unaware of. So when interviewing with the consulting firm, he made sure he understood their philosophy, which was to keep anyone who was making money for the firm, assuming behavior that fell within the bounds deemed acceptable by polite society and regulatory agencies.

One of Rob's concerns was his personal growth and development. Although there was a tuition reimbursement plan in place, signing up for courses that cut into work time for extended periods was risky. Since project work can result in highly variable workloads, Rob was never sure how busy he would be in a month or two, and he had heard horror stories from other consultants who spent days offsite at training programs and were then forced to spend the nights working on client work rather than sleeping. There was also the danger of being thought to be someone with a greater concern for their own development, rather than carrying their fair share of the workload, if the person signed up for a part-time evening program.

Rob chatted with the recruiter who had brought him to the firm shortly after his arrival. He realized he was more curious about hearing which of his many virtues had been the most attractive to the firm than about understanding the firm's staffing strategy. He noticed that people who came to the firm were at all stages in their career, and there were even some people who had retired from organizations yet still wished to keep a foot in the game. The recruiter said the firm tried to balance the skill mix when recruiting. If the firm needed to develop business in a practice area they had not been active in, the recruiters would try to find a few high-visibility people with an established reputation and rich networks. They would hire experienced managers to be practice leaders and include staff development in their performance objectives. For example, Rob had been attractive to the firm because of his graduate training in human resource management, and he was assigned to the human capital practice. The firm already had experienced HR people who had been brought in to provide the practical knowledge that was a requirement in their HR consulting practice. And since the firm wanted to take a lead in the e-HR field, it also had brought in people experienced in designing and implementing human resource information systems. By pooling all three types of consultants into teams, the firm offered a full-service package.

Bruce, the firm's HR director, was a veteran of many years of HR work in a number of high tech firms. He seemed a sage advisor and was forthcoming with information on how the HR function handled workforce issues.

Rob enjoyed asking him what it was like on the front line "in the old days" but soon came to realize that not that much had changed drastically when it came to what constituted sound human resource management, and even relative to what employees wanted and valued. Bruce had some reservations about consultants giving advice on workforce management to client organizations when their own experience was limited and/or when what they knew was learned in school from people who had no practical experience. But Rob showed humility and openly admitted that he had a lot to learn, thereby winning Bruce over and providing himself with an inside track to advice on how to manage people.

Comparing their organizations

As Don, Annette and Rob exchanged their evaluations of the rewards packages offered by their respective employers, they realized that each had its own logic in place. Rob had a favorite principle he had heard from several sources: "what you measure and reward you will most surely get more of." And a brilliant piece of advice had been offered by George Odiorne: "If your people are headed in the wrong direction, don't motivate them." Both of these bits of wisdom were consistent with the research on motivation that they had studied in their organizational behavior courses and did not seem manipulative, but rather businesslike.

Another lesson learned in their studies was that any workforce management strategy should be derived from a deep understanding of an organization's context. A model from one of their textbooks[3] became their basis for deciding the soundness of their own organization's human resource management strategies. That model explained the relationships between the forces that shaped the organization's context and that could be used to guide the development of a "good fit" HR strategy. Mission, culture, and internal and external realities all had an impact on what type of strategy would be feasible and the structure that would be effective in executing that strategy.

Figure 2.1 Aligning strategy to fit the organizational context

Adapting to the real world

As the first year of employment passed, Don, Annette and Rob continued their regular get-togethers. As they compared notes on the human resource management practices existing in their organizations, it had become apparent that there were differences across occupations, even within each of their organizations. How employees were recruited, selected, placed and developed differed based on the type of employee and how critical they were to the organization. How employee performance was measured and rewarded differed based on the nature of the work, the nature of the people doing the work and the impact the type of work had on the performance of the organization. They had looked at this as an interesting idea when in school but did not realize how important it was to ensure that HR strategies and programs were a good fit to each part of an organization.

When they had studied job evaluation in school, the professor had used an example of how different types of organizations valued occupations differently relative to each other. The example was a professional services firm that had started as a public accounting firm and then later created a division that did consulting in information technology. In the traditional audit division, business accountants were viewed as more valuable than IT personnel, while in the consulting business, the reverse was true. The principle the professor derived from this was that the most important occupations in any organization were those that were *central* to its core capabilities *and critical* to its performance. Using another example, a hospital would be likely to value an RN in critical care higher than an IT staffer, even though the market rates reported in surveys suggested that IT people were paid more than nurses. This created a dilemma, since the accepted principle was that pay rates should be both internally equitable and externally competitive. The three of them struggled with this contradiction, since it existed in their own organizations.

Don began to realize that this dilemma could present itself even within an occupation. The utility had a large number of engineers, with degrees in several disciplines. Most were civil engineers, a number were mechanical engineers and a few were electrical engineers. He had been told by Margie that over the years, the disciplines had taken their turns being "hot." Supply/demand imbalances often made the supply of one discipline scarce, thereby raising the average hiring rates in the short term for that discipline relative to the others. When he asked the engineering director how the utility handled it, the answer was vague at best: "We ride it out. . . it corrects itself every two or three years, since students with a year or two of school left can change majors to chase the big bucks." That was less than intellectually satisfying as an answer, but it seemed practical and Don could not think of a better explanation for the variation over time.

Riding home with Eric, the IT director Don got an earful about the late 1990s, when the Y2K panic was in full bloom. The utility had hired people with network skills to make the conversion from the legacy mainframe systems to client network systems but had to offer very high salaries in order to attract enough people to deal with the crisis, due to the skill shortages. Don suggested that there must have been a realization that there really would be a year 2000 for several decades and that waiting until 1999 to deal with the conversion seemed a questionable planning technique. Eric gave him a "you just don't get real life" look but proceeded to point out that the worst mistake made during this crisis was that the organization treated it like a permanent condition rather than a one-time project, which resulted in destroying internal equity relative to the IT employees who had to keep the old system running until the conversion. As a result of this error, once the conversion was complete, the utility was left with a lot of overpriced people they had hired, and the poor morale among long-service employees who felt their value had been ignored.

What Don took away from these two encounters is that relative internal values can change depending on the circumstances, and that external values can also change depending on supply–demand conditions in the labor market. He pointed out to Annette and Rob that no one prepared them for that in school. Their course work had them doing job evaluation and market pricing exercises and then using single factor linear regression to create a pay structure—a Newtonian approach in a quantum world.

Annette admitted she had been a little resentful of the way her firm differentiated between the software developers (techies) and people in staff functions. It seemed a bit of an aristocrat–peasant dichotomy. But she began to realize the central and critical test was valid and the organization could not do without those who created the products that produced their revenue. In theory, the firm could outsource much of the building management, accounting and human resources work without hollowing out its core capabilities. But turning HR strategy over to outsiders was not acceptable to Annette. If HR did not excel in formulating strategies and designing programs that attracted, retained and motivated the workforce the organization needed, there would be a negative impact on performance. And no vendor of outsourced services would know enough about the culture and internal workings of the organization to develop strategies that would lead to success. Outsource repetitive transactions? Sure. Outsource critical strategy formulation? No. Yet, she realized she was a little biased and also had come to know that every manager fancied himself or herself as an expert in staffing, development, performance management and rewards management. They just followed their impeccable instincts. This led them to believe that having an HR function in-house was not all that critical. Annette was confident they were mistaken.

Rob joked about the classless society he lived in. He suggested that even if you were an office assistant, if your numbers looked good you were golden (but, of course, these folks did not have numbers anyone cared much about). But Rob also despaired that the firm did not do a good job of forecasting future demand or the relative profitability of their various consulting disciplines. Whatever was selling today attracted resources, and promising new entrants were usually directed to the hot areas, rather than allocating them based on a longer-term perspective. And the firm promoted consultants through their career ladder based on present and past results, which increased the cost of delivering work in specific practice areas. If the market demand shifted to other expertise areas and those areas currently in vogue flamed out, the firm ran the risk of being left with a lot of high-priced people who could not be rented out, at least not at profitable hourly billing rates.

Rob was also troubled by the way project-centered practices made it difficult to balance marketing, doing the work and developing the consulting staff. When people were fully billable, they did not have time to market and they certainly were not going to detract from their revenue results to take courses to prepare themselves for future assignments. The pattern seemed to recur: work flat out, finish the work, market full time to find new work, work flat out and so on. The trouble with the pattern was that even if the firm knew that another practice area was heating up, there was no feasible way to develop the current staff so they were ready to shift gears, at least not without negatively impacting current financial performance. Rob found that Bruce and the HR staff had been unsuccessful in selling a workforce planning model that would enable the firm to take a longer-term view of what it would need to stay successful. This was not unique to their firm. The pressures of rolling out numbers to the Wall Street analysts that supported the stock price was too great to risk lower profitability, even in the cause of sustained success. That was a lesson for Rob about being publicly traded—the analysts and the investors had votes, and in some cases their votes could exercise a veto over the strategy.

So, although the trio did not seem powerless to influence the direction their organizations took relative to human resource management, it had become apparent that their powers were severely limited in some areas. That did not discourage them but rather made it clear that they would have to continuously make their case when they had something to offer.

Notes

1 Buford, J. and Linder, J., *Human Resource Management in Local Government*, 2002, Southwestern, Cincinnati, OH.
2 Latham, G., *Becoming the Evidence-Based Manager*, 2009, SHRM/Davies-Black, Boston, MA.
3 Greene, R., *Rewarding Performance: Guiding Principles; Custom Strategies*, 2010, Routledge, New York.

3 Making sense of the real world

Yet another year had passed and the three neophytes had grown both in knowledge and understanding of how things really worked. Annette was called into a meeting that had executive management and the HR staff present. There was an announcement made that a consulting firm had been retained to examine the firms' HR strategy. And it was the firm Rob worked for. She was not sure what if anything she should say about her long friendship with Rob, but she was certain it would not be wise to tell the consultant to be sure to assign Rob to the project. She did not have to—his name appeared on the staff assigned to the project in their proposal document. Apparently, Rob's firm had a great track record when it came to evaluating HR strategies. This was going to be great, thought Annette, a little weird since her old chum was on the other side of the table, but great.

During the first meeting between the consulting team and the HR staff of Annette's organization, the focus was on the business strategy. The software firm had committed to a focus on e-commerce, encompassing both systems for other business and systems for consumers. Of particular interest was the development of new features that appealed to relatively unsophisticated buyers when they tried to do their shopping online. Once the strategy was clear, the project manager for the consulting team asked the client to describe the workforce that would be required to execute the business strategy. When the required workforce was defined, the participants would move on to developing a human resource strategy that would build and sustain a viable workforce. Annette asked Rob to present a model that described the process of deriving HR strategy from an organization's context. All agreed that it would be premature to attempt to lock in on an HR strategy until all the characteristics of the firm's context had been considered.

Since the mission of the firm had already been developed and widely accepted, the next step was to define and evaluate the culture. Rob cited Edgar Schein's definition of culture, which is "how organizations deal with issues of external adaptation and internal integration." The HR staff chimed in to describe how things were done in the software firm, how priorities were set, how resources were allocated, what behaviors were expected, what was not tolerated, and so on. It became apparent that if new technology was to be invented, rather than existing technology improved, that people must be willing to take risks and deal with uncertainty. There had been a history of punishing mistakes in the firm, but the present CEO changed that when she was hired a few years ago. Designers were told to balance risks and rewards. A big gamble that required significant resources must have a large potential payback. And her track record so far seemed to be in line with that philosophy. It helped that the major shareholders were believers in dedicating reasonable amounts of resources to bets on the future. In fact, they would be concerned if it appeared that everything was being managed for short-term maximization rather than long-term optimization. Once the culture had been discussed, the next step was to evaluate the internal and external realities faced by the organization, particularly those that should influence the strategy.

The firm was sitting on a war chest of cash that had been accumulated during the recent profitable years. The consultants suggested they discuss whether an acquisition would be a preferred path to new technology or if management felt it more prudent to develop it internally. The CFO and CIO were asked into the meeting to address this question, and Carla, the CIO, was ready with a quick answer: "develop, don't buy." Her rationale was rooted in the belief that first-rate designers wanted to be challenged and needed the prospect of creating new knowledge in order to stay motivated. "I would rather give them a piece of the profits created by new technology rather than using those funds to buy what others claimed to be the new frontier. It is just too difficult to test someone else's design, to see if it can do what is needed and whether it fits in with our other proprietary technology." Kim, the CFO, agreed and added, "We are not experts at knowing when something is what we need and what we should pay for it. Besides, there are many studies that show that most mergers and acquisitions don't live up to expectations, generally due to cultural issues and people conflicts." Once this was agreed on, the next step was to decide how the organization should be structured.

Organization charts often elicit the perception of bureaucracy and rigidity, but Howard, the project manager for the consulting firm, pointed out that they can be a valuable tool for deciding on the optimal structure and in defining appropriate management roles. The current chart disclosed that Carla had all software people reporting in to her, whether they were the inventors, the refiners or the mechanics who handled breakdowns. With eleven direct reports, she spent most of her time in 15-minute meetings with them, scheduled weeks in advance on their electronic calendars. When asked how her direct report managers referred to her, she smiled and said, "old what's her name." The organization's strategy was focused on invention, so it became clear to all in the meeting that the structure was not an ideal fit to that strategy. Carla asked for some time to arrange meetings with her key managers to see how he could be converted from a bottleneck into a more strategic leader.

Rob, being a performance and rewards management wonk, asked how the firm defined performance at each level: organization, group/unit/function and individual. But Howard, the project manager, intervened, stating that before

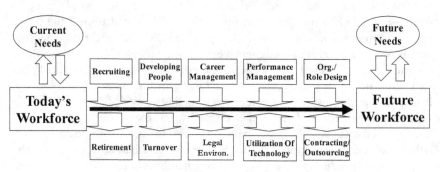

Identify sources of supply and losses, calculate net gain or loss and determine if human capital will be adequate in the future.

Figure 3.1 Assessing workforce viability: today and in the future

they addressed those issues, it was necessary to build a workforce planning model that would ensure the firm had the right workforce today and that it did all the things necessary to ensure the workforce sustained its viability in a changeable environment. He presented a model to be used as a starting point (see Figure 3.1).

The first step, cautioned Howard, required that the firm be honest in its assessment of how well the current workforce met current needs. The knowledge and skills present in the current workforce should be compared to what is needed in order for the organization to meet its current objectives. The anguish associated with moving people out and in to rebalance the workforce should not be a consideration initially. "My experience with many organizations is that the skill mix of the current workforce does not match the mix of work very well. For example, low turnover is usually celebrated, and it should be if it is due to the right causes. But too much longevity can lead to a concentration of senior people that does not match the mix of work. If there is a considerable amount of relatively routine work you end up using highly skilled people to do things that people who are less skilled could do as well—or better. Underutilized people will tend to be disinterested and unchallenged, and they will also be too expensive to use for this level of work. You need to think about this carefully, since managers will tend to over-hire, playing it safe even when the organization needs to bring in new grads and to develop people that will contribute to balancing the work and the workforce mix."

Annette was struck by this insight, as was Rob. He thought to himself, "maybe I did not learn everything I needed to know in kindergarten—or even in graduate school." He also had a flashback to Bruce's concerns that his own firm had not been able to get behind an aggressive workforce planning initiative. The group was in agreement that an assessment of the current workforce and how well it matched the mix of work would be the first step, and assignments were made. Then Howard asked everyone to assess the type of workforce they believed the firm would need one, two and five years out. This should be done by projecting where the organization would be at those times in the future, based on the long-term business plan. "Wow, in this chaotic environment? I sometimes worry about next Thursday," exclaimed Julie, the HR VP. "The way around that is to continuously scan the environment, update your scenarios and revise your projections," answered Howard, fully expecting this reaction.

"The next step is to evaluate each of the sources of supply and losses of needed skills and then to develop workforce management strategies to produce the best results given the realities," said Howard. "Look at it as if the firm was a water distribution system supplying a city." "Don should be there," thought Rob. "There are sources of supply (rainfall, rivers) and there will be losses (leaks, users along the way). And if the needs of the ranchers, farmers and city folks change, then capacity planning should reflect that." Some of the boxes in the model had both + (increased supply) and − (increased losses) signs, recognizing that laws/regulations, technology and the use of outside parties to perform work could change the internal staffing requirements in either direction. There was general satisfaction with the model, and assignments were given to small subgroups.

The staffing function was assigned to look at recruiting strategies and probable turnover levels, as well as the supply/demand conditions in the labor markets. The human resource development function was assigned to examine the firm's capabilities in training and developing people. Annette was to lead the assessment of the performance management system and to evaluate how the firm's structure was likely to change. The CIO was charged with assessing technology usage and trends. A line management group was asked to assess the use of contractors and outsourcing vendors, particularly when skill needs spiked in a certain area but were only expected to exceed staff capabilities for short periods.

Two weeks later the HR staff and the consulting staff met again to report on their findings and recommendations. The team responsible for evaluating the current workforce against current and near-term future requirements presented a case for reducing the percentage of hires who were new graduates and increasing the percentage that brought frontline experience from government and industry. This strategy was to be in effect for only a year or two, and the focus would be on people who had installed and even designed large-scale software systems for government agencies. There was going to be a lot of business forthcoming from government agencies, which would need to replace their aging systems.

Annette jumped in, "But let's not let this approach weaken the ties we have created with the best schools or we will lose ground to competitors and have trouble being a preferred employer when we do need more new grads." Mushira, a member of the consulting team, offered a suggestion: "Why not go to the graduate programs that are part-time, for people who are working, and look for people who have the experience you think you need while also getting the graduate-level technical knowledge?" Annette realized that Mushira had been in some of her classes in school and made it a point to thank her for that idea and to get better acquainted.

Beverly, the HRD representative, offered suggestions for doing more online training, to enhance the skills of current software personnel and to keep them abreast of new technical developments. She proposed that marketing be approached to see if they could run some focus groups with large customers, to identify where they were headed with technology and thereby identify the subject matter that would be most relevant for training.

Gregg, the employee relations representative, reported on the sources of potential losses, to include both retirement and turnover. The retirement volume was small and those who retired were not the traditional "done working, live on social security and my savings" kind of people. Most planned to leave full-time employment and to do contract work as it suited them. It was suggested that this presented an opportunity for the firm to find out where people were in their career planning and when valuable people who wanted to change their status in the near future were identified, there should be a plan to utilize them when possible. For example, they could be offered contracts to develop concentrated training for new grads and less experienced people on a part-time basis for a couple of years after they left full-time employment. They could also be brought in as contractors as needed, since they would not be receiving pension plan benefits. The ER representative reviewed a model for evaluating turnover that they used. The model broke down turnover numbers into different types (see Figure 3.2).

The employee relations department had been tracking the turnover and found that fully half of it was initiated by the firm. The performance standards were necessarily high, and, given the policy of hiring new graduates in

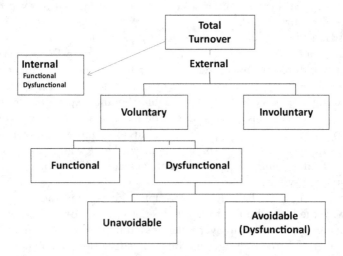

Figure 3.2 Evaluate turnover: is it too high? What are the implications?

large numbers, a significant number of involuntary terminations should be expected. They had then evaluated voluntary turnover, to see what percentage was actually beneficial. Surprisingly, about half of the voluntary turnover was due to the people recognizing that the high-pressure project work was not attractive and/or that they were not suited to a design that required a great deal of invention. So, the 30% total turnover figure was more like 7–8% when only dysfunctional voluntary turnover was counted. And there had also been a number of cases within that category that were not avoidable. People relocating, family issues and other external factors explained a lot of these instances. Mary quipped, "We had three dudes who were *Lord of the Rings* fanatics and decided they should live in New Zealand for a time, while they were young. Since we did not believe an office was needed in Wellington and since that kind of mindset does not bespeak a committed employee, we decided we could live with that loss."

Annette had read an insightful book on "the creative class"[1] that identified that some professionals picked locations rather than specific employers when making career decisions. She felt that the firm could brand itself as a "best place to work" organization and offset the fact that they were not located in one of the "hot" locations. The organizations that selected the best organizations had criteria they used in the process, and she planned on doing a self-assessment to see how they stacked up and to identify areas they needed to improve.

Annette had done a good bit of analysis of the career management and performance management systems and reported that they seemed to be functioning well and that very rarely did people complain about lacking career growth opportunities. Of course, everyone ranked their performance higher than it actually was on a relative basis, but that tendency was a common human trait. When studying organizational psychology, she had been exposed to research on human tendencies, many of which were relevant to the work she was now doing. Some of these tendencies were:

- illusions that things were more positive than they were;
- more rapid acceptance of information that was consistent with current beliefs;
- egocentric interpretation of information;
- over-discounting future outcomes relative to short-term outcomes;
- avoidance of short-term certain costs even when potential long-term gains are large;
- bias toward omission of negative information;
- favoring the status quo over change;
- overemphasizing information that is vivid.

The longer she had reflected on these cognitive tendencies, the more she realized how important it was for all managers to understand them and to realize how they impacted workforce management. In fact, it was equally important for employees to understand them as well, so that they can appreciate that their reactions to information and policies may not be totally rational. So, in addition to requiring an HR course in every MBA degree program, there should also be a course on organizational psychology/behavior. She made a note of that so she would be ready to make those recommendations to all the graduate school deans who approached her for advice.

She also felt that there was a need to actively communicate these tendencies to employees in a way that enabled them to broaden their perspective and better appreciate why there seemed to be a disconnect between how they believed they were performing and the appraisal ratings they received. This was particularly challenging for employees who worked in teams or groups that were highly interdependent. There is a tendency for people to attribute success to their own efforts and to attribute poor results to uncontrollable external causes. The more she reflected on these cognitive distortions, the more she realized it probably was not possible to abolish them, and the best an organization could do is to be sure there is a continuous effort aimed at increasing understanding of our predispositions and that it did not make us bad people. Her analysis showed that the rewards package was viewed by employees as equitable, competitive and appropriately structured, which was good news. Normative data from a large number of organizations demonstrated that the median score of employee satisfaction with rewards was "somewhat dissatisfied." When she finished, the group decided to close the meeting, after identifying future steps.

After the meeting, Annette asked Mushira if she had time for a cup of coffee and the two of them went off to the "in-house dining facility." She clued Mushira into the fact that no self-respecting software firm would have anything as industrial as a cafeteria. Annette said that she and her two friends had always wondered why Mushira and Hari (another fellow student) were so quiet in classes. Mushira was from the Middle East and Hari was from Indonesia, but they spoke flawless English and that should not have been the reason. Mushira offered, "We always were amused at how much the American students wanted to talk during class, taking time away from the opportunity to learn from someone who knew something, rather than listening to someone who enjoyed talking. We also thought it disrespectful."

Annette remembered reading about the cross-cultural research Trompenaars had done[2] and realized people from different cultures really did have differing views about how a classroom should operate. "It also seemed to us that breaking the class into teams to work on cases was overdone, since we did not agree with Socrates that people had all the relevant knowledge and it was only necessary to draw it out. People without the necessary expertise are unlikely to produce great revelations, and, even if they did, it was a less efficient way to learn than having the expert impart the knowledge."

"Well, we differ somewhat on that," Annette pointed out, "but I do agree that students were allowed to fill the air with speculation and unsupported ideas a lot more than was necessary. But faculty members find that informing people that they did not know as much as they think they did really does have a negative impact on student evaluations."

Annette started to be concerned about how some of the training the firm had done for new software developers had been received by employees who had come to the U.S. from other countries for graduate school and had stayed on to work. Perhaps the firm should take a long, hard look at the way they handled training and even communication. After all, the point was to have messages accepted, which required sensitivity to employee views about the appropriate way to do things. When she shared this concern with Mushira the response was, "remember Trompenaar's 3 Rs of cross-cultural management: (1) recognize differences, (2) respect people's rights to hold different views and (3) reconcile the issues those differences create." The two agreed to stay in touch and Annette asked Mushira to give her Hari's contact information as well.

Notes

1 Florida, R., *Rise of The Creative Class*, 2007, Basic Books, New York.
2 Hamden-Turner, C. and Trompenaars, F., *Riding the Waves of Culture*, 1993, Irwin, Burr Ridge, IL.

4 Assessing organizational context

Don was called into a meeting to fill in for Margie, the HR director, who was at a conference. And lo and behold, sitting in the conference room, in addition to the general manager, CFO and operations director were Howard and Rob, the representatives of Rob's consulting firm. The utility had retained the consulting firm to see how the organization could reshape its human resource management strategy and programs to better fit the workforce it would be relying on for the next few decades. There had recently been turndowns by sought-after recruits, and many of them seemed to be due to the fact that every employee's pay rate progressed each year at a specified rate. The step structure used by the utility had a series of steps for each grade, and annual step increases were relatively automatic. The utility had tried to recruit engineers who could reshape the infrastructure and design new control systems to increase efficiency. But when candidates found that all employees, no matter how good or how bad their performance, got the same pay adjustments, many of them decided to go elsewhere.

Don had already told management that anyone who did accept the pay system was probably looking for a safe job that did not demand much ("What you measure and reward, you will surely get more of"). But he slapped himself mentally, remembering the wisdom Bruce and Steve had given him about fitting the environment and motivating people to behave in the manner you wanted them to. Admittedly, the time-based step structure approach encouraged people to stay once they were at or above the middle step, which was set at average market pay levels. And they did have a lot of senior people. He had done an analysis and found that 40% of the employees were at the top three steps of their ten-step ranges, which would make it very hard for them to match their base pay rates if they were to seek another employer. "Retention incentive," thought Rob. He also winced when he thought what the cost of that practice was.

Howard agreed that the pay philosophy would need to be examined carefully, but he suggested they first should do an assessment of the culture of the utility and then evaluate how it branded itself as an employer. He pointed out that working for a utility lacked sex appeal to many potential candidates, even though the work was meaningful and impacted the lives of the citizenry of the area. Everyone agreed this would be a good place to start. He presented a questionnaire that the firm could use to evaluate its culture. Rob was very proud of this questionnaire, since he had developed it as a class project in school. He relied heavily on the research Trompenaars was doing on cross-cultural management issues, but he had also woven in the work of others to produce an assessment instrument that incorporated the best research in the cultural anthropology field. They would administer the questionnaire to each member of top and middle management and to a random sample of other employees. The results would be tabulated by Rob, and he would present a summary of the results to the management team in two weeks.

CULTURE QUESTIONNAIRE

1. PERFORMANCE IS DEFINED AS:

(1)---------------(2)----------------(3)---------------(4)---------------(5)

**(1) ORGANIZATION
   MEETING ITS GOALS**
* business plans must be met
* superiors evaluate performance
* sound internal systems critical
  and must serve organization

**CUSTOMER
   SATISFACTION (5)**
* customer must be satisfied
* customer evaluates performance
* service levels/processes must be
  acceptable to customer

2. PERFORMANCE IS DETERMINED BY:

(1)---------------(2)----------------(3)---------------(4)---------------(5)

**(1) ACTIONS OF
   INDIVIDUALS/UNITS**
* effort/resources applied
  determine results
* outcomes under organizational
  control
* there is no "try"—only "do"

EXTERNAL FACTORS (5)
* uncontrollable forces determine
  results
* people should accept/adapt to
  conditions
* efforts should focus on doing
  the best
  given the realities that exist

3. PERFORMANCE IS TYPICALLY ATTRIBUTED TO:

(1)---------------(2)----------------(3)---------------(4)---------------(5)

(1) A FEW KEY INDIVIDUALS
* focus is on individual results
* belief in self-determination
* a few people determine
  performance
* performance is on competitive
  basis and relative rank is
  "score"

**ALL EMPLOYEES/UNITS/
   FUNCTIONS (5)**
* focus is on group/unit/team results
* belief in shared destiny and that it
  takes everyone to succeed
* contribution to effectiveness of
  unit/others is considered part
  of performance

4. ORGANIZATIONAL LEARNING IS:

(1)---------------(2)---------------(3)---------------(4)---------------(5)

(1) VALUABLE BUT NOT CRITICAL
* critical knowledge/skills already in place
* training should be focused on current needs
* learning is needed only at the individual level
* knowledge belongs to individuals and goes with them if they leave
* new challenges can be met by hiring people with required skills/knowledge
* values fully specified and acceptance expected

CRITICAL TO FUTURE SUCCESS (5)
* environmental change mandates continuous, rapid learning
* learning is rewardable
* transfer of knowledge must occur within and across groups/units
* intellectual capital/property is a critical asset of the organization
* assumptions continually surfaced, debated and adjusted as needed

5. PERFORMANCE IS THOUGHT OF IN TERMS OF:

(1)---------------(2)---------------(3)---------------(4)---------------(5)

(1) SHORT-TERM MAXIMIZATION
* annual shareholder returns critical
* efficiency is stressed
* annual report is scorecard
* annual results determine rewards
* blame for errors assigned
* reporting of errors encouraged:— information is basis for learning

LONG-TERM OPTIMIZATION (5)
* creating long-term value critical
* sustainable methods are stressed
* long-term measures used
* rewards given for long-term as well as short-term performance

6. INFORMATION IS:

(1)---------------(2)---------------(3)---------------(4)---------------(5)

(1) TIGHTLY MANAGED
* communication is downward
* "need to know" controls access
* generated/used by specialists
* policies/procedures provide direction
* too much information thought to confuse

COMMUNICATED WIDELY (5)
* communication in all directions
* broad, unfiltered dissemination
* potentially created by anyone
* sharing is valued/rewarded
* individuals/groups given access to everything and are expected to decide on its value/use

7. MANAGERS ALLOCATE RESOURCES BASED PRINCIPALLY ON:

(1)---------------(2)---------------(3)---------------(4)---------------(5)

(1) IMPACT ON OWN UNIT'S IMPACT ON OVERALL
* units seen in competition
* contribution to overall organization not emphasized
* managers balance interests of unit
* managers promote unit interests against interests of organization

PERFORMANCE ORGANIZATIONAL PERFORMANCE (5)
* units share based on value added
* contribution to overall result is key

8. THE OPERATIONAL PHILOSOPHY IS:

(1)---------------(2)---------------(3)---------------(4)---------------(5)

(1) MINIMUM RISK
* insure adequate resources on hand at all times
* avoid shortages at all cost and minimize errors
* staff to meet workload peaks
* use only permanent workforce to provide critical skills/knowledge

BALANCED RISK (5)
* consider cost of resources when deciding what to have on hand
* plan to operate under conditions of shortages/limited supply
* staff to allow for slack but ensure levels are cost-effective over time
* ensure critical skills/knowledge are readily available

9. PLANNING IS:

(1)---------------(2)---------------(3)---------------(4)---------------(5)

(1) BASIC TO PRESCRIBING TACTICS
* future tactics determined
* plans changed only when required
* top down planning process
* tactics linear/sequential
* plans internally driven
* leaders focused on results vs. plan

A TOOL FOR SETTING DIRECTION (5)
* focus on environmental scanning
* interactions determine direction
* bottom up formulation of approach
* constant attention to possibilities
* plans dynamic and co-evolve with the environment
* leaders focused on preparedness for the unexpected

10. SOUND MANAGEMENT IS THOUGHT TO BE:
(1)----------------(2)----------------(3)----------------(4)----------------(5)

(1) CLOSE CONTROL/
   SPECIFIC
   DOWNWARD
   DIRECTION
* develop specific policies
  and procedures
* define specific work
  assignments
* make decisions at high
  level
* identify who produces
  results/failure and
  reward or punish
  accordingly
* focus on managing the
  known/expected
* deference is to rank

PROVIDING LEADERSHIP (5)
* articulate values, vision and
  culture
* identify objectives
* encourage initiative
* look for reasons for results/
  failure and use to improve
  performance
* prepare for managing
  unexpected
* deference is to expertise

11. HUMAN RESOURCES ARE MANAGED AS IF THEY ARE:
(1)----------------(2)----------------(3)----------------(4)----------------(5)

(1) COSTS
* outlay on development
  minimized
* hire/release based on need
* focus is on job assignment
* job/task-specific training
  stressed
* blame for errors assigned
* rewards based on short-
  term results

ASSETS (5)
* ROI on HR maximized
* focus on career management
* value = human capital
* learning stressed
* rewards based on value
  created over long term

12. REWARDS ARE BASED ON:
(1)----------------(2)----------------(3)----------------(4)----------------(5)

(1) INDIVIDUAL
   CHARACTERISTICS
* loyalty/seniority
* effort/conformance to
  policies
* competencies possessed

OUTCOMES PRODUCED (5)
* performance in job/role
* results compared to goals
* relative contributions

13. HIGH LEVELS OF PERFORMANCE IN THE FUTURE WILL REQUIRE:

(1)---------------(2)---------------(3)---------------(4)---------------(5)

(1) INCREASED EFFICIENCY, QUALITY AND RELIABILITY

* reliable delivery of high quality at reasonable cost is key to success
* doing things better is major concern
* heroes reliably execute and generate continuous improvement

CONTINUOUS, DRAMATIC INNOVATION AND REVISIONS TO MISSION (5)

* mission is continually evolving
* culture must be continuously reshaped
* doing *new* things is critical
* heroes are those who invent new and re-invent existing products

14. DECISIONS SHOULD BE BASED ON:

(1)---------------(2)---------------(3)---------------(4)---------------(5)

(1) VERIFIED AND OBJECTIVE FACTS RELEVANT TO ISSUE

* all relevant data should be accumulated and analyzed to identify patterns
* rational models should be employed
* decision should be based on analysis
* most correct solution should be selected

INTUITION AND PERSONAL KNOWLEDGE (5)

* decisions based on feel of the situation
* feelings about what will work are applied
* personal experience in similar situations should be considered
* alternative approaches should be tried

Howard suggested a meeting be held with the GM and executive staff to go through a branding exercise once the cultural assessment was completed. The purpose of the meeting would be to identify the advantages of working for the utility and to honestly portray the "not so good" aspects of working there. "The talent war rages on, even when unemployment is up," Howard pointed out. "If the management mindset is focused on cost control, rather than meeting skill needs, the staffing strategy will be ineffective. There will always be a shortage of top-notch people in any occupation, and organizations that recruit in bursts end up with the short straw." Howard also alerted the management team that they would need to go through a workforce planning exercise to ensure that the utility could sustain workforce viability. Rob thought to himself, "Aha! A reuse of the model that we recommended to Annette's software firm." He realized that this was not one of those "We have a hammer, so we have to pretend everything is a nail" tap dances consulting firms sometimes do. After all, the concepts underlying a sound thought model and process should work in any organization, no matter who participated and whether the critical issues differed.

Two weeks later, Rob had summarized the results of the cultural questionnaire exercise and had identified several things that needed discussion, including: (1) the degree of agreement on what the current culture is, (2) the degree of agreement on what the culture should be, and (3) what actions were necessary to close the "is–should be" gaps.

The assessment of the culture prevailing in Don's utility identified the following gaps:

1   Performance should be defined more in terms of satisfying the customers, while still staying within the budget.
2   The performance of the overall organization should be considered by managers when making decisions, rather than only considering how their unit will be impacted.
3   Managers should balance risk with costs when making decisions.
4   Employees should be viewed as assets to invest in, not just a line item in the budget.
5   Pay levels and pay actions should be earned through performance, rather than being an entitlement that is based on time spent on the job.

These findings identified a number of undesirable realities. Departmental fiefdoms existed, causing managers to focus on making their goals, no matter what impact it had on other departments or the overall organization. Operations and maintenance managers were indifferent to the costs of holding large inventories because they had been trained to avoid stock-outs during emergency situations. Investment in training was insufficient, since the costs of training went against each unit's budget and no credit was given for developing people, particularly for progression to greater responsibilities in other units. Finally, pay adjustments were granted annually that equaled the cost of living or increases in average market wage levels, whichever was greater. The increases were viewed as an entitlement and were given to everyone in the form of general increases, in addition to the time-based step increases.

Don remembered a discussion he had with the manager of their warehouse during the cultural evaluation, prompted by the manager being chewed out by his manager for having too much inventory on certain parts. "What would you do in my position?" Ed had asked Don. "The water main hemorrhages in front of the major department store downtown on a Friday night, just before their biggest weekend sale of the year. By the way, the mayor's brother-in-law owns the store. I get a call that the repair crew had gone to the warehouse to get the parts they needed, and lo and behold, they were short a few, since there had been a major repair job that week at the airport and the replacements for what they used had just been ordered Thursday. Do I tell the crew that the parts won't be in until mid-week and they should ask the store owner to be understanding? No, I don't think so. So, I don't run out of anything." Don attempted to capitalize on the high finance he had studied in school and asked Ed, "Do you know what excess inventory costs is?" Ed thought for a minute and said "No." Don realized no one had bothered to educate employees about such matters, and as a result, people took the reasonable approach, which was to protect themselves against the disaster scenarios. That was something he made a note of, since several of his professors had suggested it was shortsighted not to teach employees your business. They would be better businesspeople and their decisions would be more aligned with the organization's objectives. The old adage, "If you think training (education) is expensive, cost out the alternative," ran through his mind.

During the meeting where these results were reviewed it was agreed that HRM systems needed to be changed in a way that would facilitate reshaping the culture. These included: (1) changing performance criteria to include satisfying customers and positively impacting the effectiveness of other employees and other units, (2) directing and funding training out of a corporate budget account, (3) hiring people experienced in satisfying customers, (4) teaching employees about the economics of the business and how they impacted results and (5) modifying the base pay system to reward merit rather than just length of service. It was also decided that HR should be at the center of this process and should be the function with "culture management" in its job description. "Unfortunately, culture typically just happens—responsibility for it falls into a black hole, being the concern of no one," lamented Howard. "Unless the culture becomes a priority for the executive staff and unless one function is assigned the responsibility for monitoring it, there is a high risk of the culture falling out of sync with the environment and becoming dysfunctional."

The branding exercise was next on the agenda, and the GM and her direct reports gathered to participate in a dialogue about making the utility a preferred employer. Rob summarized their discussions as they went along. It was decided the summary would be reviewed in focus groups of selected employees to test its validity.

Before they identified the good and the not-so-good things associated with being employed in the organization, the group participated in a brainstorming session to identify the external and internal realities they were facing. They compiled these realities into a table that summarized their views (see Table 4.1).

The majority of participants were surprised to find that the current pay plan was the same as the one used by the city, even though the utility had become a separate entity with its own board three years ago. Margie said the plan could be changed—that would be a consideration as they progressed through the consulting study. There were also questions about the consent decree mandating an enormous investment in infrastructure over the next ten years and what

Table 4.1 Current realities

Internal	External
Aging workforce	Tight labor market for critical skills
Using city pay plan	Ratepayer resistance to rate increases
Union must buy into any changes	Demands imposed by infrastructure overhaul
Need to staff up for infrastructure projects	Public perception of excessive benefits
Strong entitlement culture	Perception that utilities are not desirable employers

implications it would have. Margie said that the major impact was the need to bring in a large amount of engineering talent, both through hiring and through contracting with engineering consulting firms.

The next item was making a commitment to tell potential employees the whole truth and nothing but the truth about working for the utility. Of course, as they changed the culture, some things would change, but the current internal and external realities would be shared with candidates openly and honestly. Research had shown that a "realistic job preview" was one of the most effective ways to reduce unwanted turnover during the first 18 months of employment,[1] which was important since it took time to bring even experienced engineers up to speed on the utility's unique systems. The realistic preview required that all the realities be presented to candidates, including things that might be viewed as negative by some. This honest approach not only began the relationship on an ethical basis, but it served to inoculate people against unpleasant surprises when they encountered the not-so-good parts of their jobs.

This was an approach that Rob was most interested in—the honest assessment of what was good and what was not so good about working here. He expected a lot of input here and a lot of disagreement. It certainly was reasonable to expect that different types of employees (by level, by department, by occupation) would view things differently. One of the "good" items Rob wanted to elaborate on was that there was important work being done in the utility. What they did and how well they did it had an impact on the quality of life in the metropolitan area. Don chimed in that a few of his friends worked at organizations that tried to motivate employees to "make the shareholders really rich." He pointed out that most employees were not shareholders and did not even know any, so it seemed unrealistic to believe that this objective could be motivating. How could employees show up every day, willing to give their all, in order to promote the financial well-being of strangers?

Don also took the lead in pointing out that the benefit package was really much richer than the typical package in the private sector and that job security was much greater. He had asked a number of people in focus groups if they agreed with that and was somewhat disappointed that most employees did not think the benefits were all that special. Don had learned in his formal training that you had to have benefits that were viewed as adequate, but that you got very little credit for benefits that greatly exceeded those offered by other employers. It was true that 50- and 60-somethings would value the rich pension and time-off programs. But the utility was currently most worried about attracting capable 20- and 30-somethings. And new graduates placed a much lower value on benefits, since they believed that they were immortal and old age was so far in the future that they figured the medical community would find a cure for aging before they had to face it. Don believed that if they were forced to cut people costs, he would suggest they start with trimming benefits rather than cutting pay or headcount. There was little added to the two lists by employees. But a group of employees got so into the process that they suggested the organization run a "the best thing about working here" contest, and the winner would get a 3-day weekend. That he made a note of.

The whole truth

The good stuff

- Important work is done that impacts people's lives.
- Job security is provided.
- There are career growth opportunities.
- There is investment in developing employees.
- The workforce functions cooperatively.
- There are great benefits.
- Equal opportunity exists.
- Fair practices are followed.

The not-so-good stuff

- There is limited upside compensation opportunity.
- Culture often impedes dramatic innovation.
- Errors can cause severe consequences.
- There are civil service rules that constrain effective operation in many cases.
- It is not a sexy industry.
- The structure is bureaucratic.
- There are rigid personnel policies that often preclude the best actions.

Don and Rob talked during a break at one of the sessions, and Rob told Don about some of the recent research on promoting employee engagement. There was a lot of evidence accumulating that showed engagement to be a key to organizational citizenship behavior (going beyond what was required on one's own initiative). And this "over and above" behavior had a significant impact on organizational effectiveness. They developed a series of questions that could be used in a questionnaire to find out whether the conditions favoring engagement were present and to what degree.

Engagement questions

1   Do you recommend the utility as a good place to work?
2   Are you proud to tell people you work here?
3   Does your job provide you with a sense of accomplishment?
4   Are you willing to extend effort beyond what is expected of you?
5   Do you understand how your role is related to the utility's mission and objectives?
6   Do you understand how your unit is expected to contribute to overall performance?
7   What would make this a more satisfying place to work?

They decided there should be focus groups for discussing engagement issues, and once the responses to the questions were finalized, they planned to use this information to communicate to employees about plans to increase engagement and to request feedback on these plans. Although they worried that they might induce employee fatigue, Don pointed out that employees had not been asked about much in the past, and it had been his experience that when he did ask, the response was bright eyes and enthusiasm, not rolling eyes. Although they knew there were employees who would be cynical about these attempts at open communication, they were willing to risk it in order to open the channels with those who were not given to cynicism. Rob pointed out to Don that they would have to be sure to get back to employees frequently throughout the assessment process, sharing what had been suggested, which of the suggestions were being considered and why some others were not. "Employees need to know their input was valued and they must be given a chance to make a case for their ideas if you want them to continue to be engaged and to support the decisions," said Rob, reinforcing the recommendation.

After the focus groups had been conducted and all the opinions were in and counted, the management and consulting teams concluded that if they took the cultural assessment seriously and followed through to begin to reshape the culture, that it would be a giant step along the yellow brick road. Oz was still far away, but the progress made thus far was encouraging.

The biggest item on the agenda going forward seemed to be an overhaul of the pay system. Losing good candidates because they viewed the way in which performance was (not) rewarded was a losing game, and they realized they needed to change it. The first step was to identify feasible options and to evaluate the advantages and disadvantages of each. They realized they needed to keep the process of reshaping the culture aligned with revising the rewards strategy. If they were to reinforce positive contributions and discourage dysfunctional behaviors, they knew that both the performance management and rewards management strategies and programs must support it.

The utility had actually been using performance appraisals for some time. Rob was amazed to find that most were done reasonably well as he pulled random samples of past appraisals and reviewed them. The factors used for non-management personnel were productivity, quality of work and dependability/adherence to organizational values. Rob told Don that he had seen a trend toward adding a factor that measured an employees' contribution to the effectiveness of others and of the unit. Since work was increasingly interdependent, this factor put *how* people achieved results on their radar screen, alongside *what* they achieved. "This simple revision has been shown to have a positive impact on cooperative behavior," Rob told Don, "and it does not cost anything. How much more could you ask for?" Don took the suggestion seriously and made a note to revise the format used for appraisals.

They both remembered their professor for the compensation course in school had said not much had changed over many years relative to the benefits of paying for performance. He had a well-worn copy of David Belcher's *Wage and Salary Administration* text and said the principles cited in this classic book that was the leading text for several decades were repeated in the latest texts on the subject. Don had heard Bruce say that David Belcher was one of his long-time friends and that he was one of the best at listening to others and learning how things really worked in the field. "So much for *leading-edge* practices" Don thought. The fundamental principles endure.

Note

1 Cascio, W. and Aguinis, H., *Applied Psychology in Human Resource Management*, 6th Ed., 2005, Pearson/Prentice-Hall, Upper Saddle River, NJ.

5 Facing a down economy

Although the economy had been on steroids for 7 years, the current year seemed to be different. As the year progressed, there was increasing evidence that something was afoot. And so, it was. The news kept getting worse, and by early the next year, some economists began to think that perhaps the new reality had been a temporary reality. More and more businesspeople began to think that it was possible that a dot-com-like collapse could reoccur. Since it had taken the stock market 5 years to come back from the turn of the millennium debacle, this was troubling news. And when businesses began to have trouble with credit lines and revenues started to plummet, the scramble was on to react in a way that would minimize the damage.

As the economy worsened, the downsizing tsunami began. Scrambling to cut costs to offset drops in revenues, one organization after another cut their employee headcounts. Annette's firm saw an immediate drop in revenue, since organizations who were contemplating upgrades to their IT capabilities decided that could wait until their costs and revenues were realigned. Rob's consulting firm saw projects frozen or cancelled. There was some work for the HR consulting practice as organizations pondered how they could cut their people costs without devastating their ability to serve customers or spend all of their time in court defending themselves against wrongful discharge suits. Don's utility suffered little immediate impact. In fact, engineers let go by other firms, some of them thought to be elite employers, began to apply for the job openings the utility had. Unfortunately, most of the applicants were not ideally qualified for the slots available. After several years of talent wars, a period of increased unemployment could have been viewed as a great opportunity. But it also could create a dangerous situation if managers took advantage of the situation now, only to have employees who were just waiting for the economy to improve so they could depart for more fertile fields. Given the length of the current projects central to infrastructure renewal, any rapid turnover of the new hires could really hurt.

During a caffeine replenishment session, the trio wondered why experience had not taught executive management that downsizing was rarely the best choice when cost cutting first became a necessity. They had all read with great interest the award-winning book *Responsible Restructuring*,[1] which analyzed the results of a broad array of downsizing efforts. Wayne Cascio, the academic who had authored the book, had presented at an HR conference and made a compelling case that most organizations went about deciding how to restructure workforce costs in the wrong way. He had pointed out that the message sent to employees by making downsizing their first cost cutting initiative was "you are our most disposable asset," not "you are our most important asset." And the vast majority of downsizing efforts had not produced the desired results, according to his extensive research done on the 2000–2002 initiatives.

Since Don was in the process of going through the branding process at the utility, he realized that downsizing would send an unwanted message to potential candidates for employment. Luckily, the utility was pretty well insulated from the immediate pressure to cut costs, but he thought that if ratepayers lost their jobs and began to have difficulty paying their bills, they might well begin to question why the utility was able to be an island of employment stability. He thought the reasons they would come up with might not be all that positive and that pressure on the board might ensue. Again, that conversation with Margie and Steve came back to him. He himself had been critical of all the utility offered, without thinking through the underlying reasoning. He made a note of this issue, to bring it up at their next session with the consulting firm. But when he thought about ways to cut costs while retaining service levels, he realized that all direct compensation was in the form of wages and salaries. And there had never been freezes or cuts, since step-rate progressions were automatic, producing even higher fixed costs.

He joked with himself that he would tell Anthony, the employee relations manager, that they could use the consultants to break any bad news, since staff members had to live there on a permanent basis and liked being popular. And when the going gets tough, consultants leave town anyway. He puffed up his chest and said to Annette and Rob, "I think I will once again bring up some of those ideas about reducing benefits to reasonable levels that got such a frigid reception before." They both joked that they would split his rent and fixed expenses if the reaction was as negative as it had been the first time he bravely identified the elephant in the room. He had forgotten to tell them he had learned a lot from the Margie and Steve counseling session and that he was going to have Steve and other members of senior management have their say. After all, Steve admitted some things ought to change.

Annette suspected her firm would freeze hiring for a time if business stayed slow. And since their professional workforce was fairly young, they would not be harming themselves in the longer run by slowing the flow at the entry level. Besides, most of their work required experienced people and there was little maintenance work that was used to acquaint new graduates with their systems. But if the revenue downturn was substantial and persisted for some time, there would have to be other actions taken to shift costs downward. Thankfully, there was a significant component of variable compensation in their direct compensation package, and incentive awards would drop. Since there was not much to cut in the indirect compensation programs, that was not a fertile field for initiatives. "Who said lean benefits packages have no redeeming features?" she planned to ask her colleagues. So, she made a mental list of her ideas for cutting costs, putting them in order of priority. They would be having a staff meeting in two days and she wanted to have her thoughts organized.

Rob worried most about the senior management of his consulting firm immediately mandating across-the-board cuts if cuts were forthcoming. The staff in the HR consulting practice was booked solid, and he suspected that a lot of organizations would need creative ideas for reducing costs without endangering the viability of their workforce in the long run. This meant there would be even more consulting work in the HR practice. Other practices would no doubt be adversely impacted by the economic downturn, since many of the assignments had been generated when business was so good that client companies were struggling to find things to spend all of their money on. He thought he had better suggest to Howard that the consulting staff of the HR practice meet to talk about strategy and to prepare a plan for senior management that was economically feasible and that sustained their viability as a practice. But he did think that some of their consultants were not contributing at the level that would be satisfactory in leaner times and that there should be a thorough performance assessment of the staff members to see if some people should be let go. There were consultants in other practice areas that had skills that could be valuable in the HR practice, so perhaps the wisest thing to do would be to do a firm-wide assessment so that valuable people were not victims of being in the wrong place at the wrong time.

The following week, Don and the utility's HR staff met before their scheduled meeting with the consultants to determine if there should be modifications to the timeline for the consulting project or if it should be called off. Don, not able to contain himself, blurted out, "Wait a minute, we are caught off guard by this economic reversal because we had not done long ago what we are in the process of doing now." He startled everyone with the volume level and the emotion evident in his response. "Maybe I should cut back on pumping iron at the gym and do more yoga," thought Don, who was normally much more subdued.

Anthony smiled and supported Don. "I have just added damage control to my job description," he said, "and we don't want to look like we are in a desperate reactive mode, with no plans for managing this with a well-thought-out strategy. We are a few years late with the cultural assessment and with the branding initiative, but we all are convinced it is the right thing to do, so let's continue before things get worse and we have no choice but to batten down the hatches."

Everyone seemed to agree that there could be short-term benefits coming out of the two initiatives, and they dedicated themselves to presenting a unified front to management in favor of continuing them. Besides, they would still have to hire a number of engineers to get the consent decree work started, or else pay huge fines for failing to meet the timeline. Don pointed out that if they looked more like a people-friendly organization than their competitors, recruitment efforts might be made easier. Anthony nodded and added that there were some very good people who had been put out on the street and there would be more coming, so now was the time to take advantage of an ample supply of qualified candidates.

Annette's next meeting with the consultants and HR staff of the software firm did not go so well. Senior management had developed a bunker mentality and announced they were planning staff reductions. "The value of the firm must be protected," said Kim, the CFO, "and if our numbers look bad for a quarter or two, it will have an adverse impact." "Sure," said Carla, the CIO, "let's cut off all development of new products and reduce the quality of services of our existing products. As long as we keep our numbers looking good, we can be finding other jobs and cashing in our stock holdings when we leave."

Annette thought that Carla was being a bit caustic but also thought Kim was being totally unrealistic. Propping up the stock price would not help the people who had been downsized, since any profit they would realize on exit would have to pay their mortgage and put food on the table until they found new jobs. And they probably would be unenthusiastic about coming back to work at the firm if the downturn was short-lived and they were invited back. Besides, the cutback in those responsible for providing high-quality support to customers would have a further negative impact on the bottom line in the short to mid-term, particularly since competitors would be shaving their margins to get what business there was. But before she took on Kim, she better have a better plan.

Annette called Rob late that evening and called for a powwow. Rob arrived with a low-throttle setting, since he had been getting up early to run and his bedtime had been close when Annette called. "OK," he asked, "what's the emergency?" Annette laid out the challenge and asked Rob if they could come up with strategies for cutting costs without impacting their capabilities of their current workforce, today and into the future. Stimulated by this challenge and by the fact that the server had mistakenly given him regular coffee rather than decaf, Rob went down the list of alternatives.

"First, how much of your annual direct compensation costs are in variable pay plans?" Annette was ready for that and said that the performance-sharing plan based on firm results was about 10% and individual incentive awards were averaging 15%. "And what percentage of payroll did management say they had to cut?" asked Rob. "About 20%," responded Annette. "And your problem is what?" was Rob's response.

"I know cutting all incentive plans seems to be a simple fix, but our salaries are set below market averages, and without incentives, we will not be competitive" responded Annette, somewhat defensively. "Do you take me for an idiot not to realize the numbers work out if we freeze all variable plans?" Rob quickly shifted his tone. "No, Annette, I am fully aware you are not lacking in cognitive skills and that you are capable of doing simple calculations, but going to employees and laying out the economic realities should result in acceptance that the firm needs to do something. After all, you can ask them if they relish the thought of three people doing the work of five, particularly since you have high performance expectations."

After musing a bit on that challenge, Annette realized one of the problems was that they had never taken the time to share performance numbers with employees, so headcount cuts would probably be viewed as a management ploy to have them pay for a situation they did not create. And they probably would not believe things are as bad as they were. She made a note to commit to launching an effort to teach their employees the business. She started to tell Rob it was too late to gain immediate acceptance of the incentive plan freezes because of their failure to involve employees in the economics of their business. But she realized that this was something they had to sell, even if it was only partially accepted. And he could not be responsible for dealing with this. "Well," she said, "the best thing about doing this is that it will clarify that the 10% performance sharing bonus is not automatic, even though it has been paid every year since dirt was invented, and it will force management to make a serious effort to begin sharing the business realities with everyone. And the cut in individual incentives can also be explained by pointing out that the firm cannot lower standards just because the current conditions were not the doing of the employees. If the billable time is down, the billings are down. And if the billings are down, so is realized revenue, and revenue pays the bills. This all can be handled if we do our jobs well. I am still worried about falling below prevailing market levels however."

"Wait a minute," retorted Rob, "do you think your competitors are prospering? Your analysis of competitive levels is based on last year's industry compensation survey and that is not the reality today. If your competitors are doing as well as they did before, you better ask yourself about your strategy and why you are underperforming relative to them."

"When did you get so intelligent?" asked Annette. "That is really a good point and we need to make an estimate of what the competitor compensation levels are likely to be when the overall software market is down by 30%. The survey tells us that the other firms use variable compensation extensively as well and their payouts will probably be down." She did realize that there was still the challenge of explaining why the performance sharing plan would not pay out for the first time, and this would be an opportunity to make it clear that the plan was indeed variable.

"I am so thrilled with the advice you have given me that I will pay for the coffee," announced Annette. After calculating that the payout represented about 0.1% of the billing rate for an hour of his time, Rob told Annette that he looked forward to many of these sessions—it would allow him to adopt a much richer lifestyle. Rob did suffer from a tendency toward sarcasm.

Note

1 Cascio, W., *Responsible Restructuring*, 2002, Berrett-Koehler, San Francisco.

6 Evaluating alternative HR strategies

Things were not getting better for the software firm, for the utility or for the consulting firm. The excesses of Wall Street and the banks had resulted in a real crisis as the euphoric spending behavior of governments came to look absurd and as the crisis went global. Countries rescheduling their debt and manipulating their currencies made matters even worse, since the majority of U.S. organizations did a substantial percentage of their business outside the country.

Two large software projects in Europe were cancelled, knocking a hole in the revenue projections for Annette's firm. As unemployment soared, the citizenry became angry, first at the financial community for causing all the troubles and then at the public sector for seeming to believe nothing was wrong that had anything to do with them. Don had no trouble seeing the storm clouds headed in their direction. And in the minds of many CEOs, expenditures on consulting joined advertising expenses as a luxury to be enjoyed when there was prosperity and something to be cut when there was a mess like this. The trio decided to get together for a Saturday session, and everyone brought their laptops and files that were relevant to the challenges they were facing.

The first thing they decided on was that their firms were hardly choosing to do what was the best (least bad?) thing when it came to sustaining workforce viability. The issues facing each of them were somewhat different, but cutting expenses was the dominant theme. The business strategy gurus claimed that "growing the top line" was a better approach to rebalancing revenues and costs, but just how to do that was a puzzle to all three of them. Certainly, the utility could raise rates, but the criticisms that would be directed at the board would be plentiful and spiteful. The software firm was more worried about maintaining sales volume, and given the intensifying competitive pressures, it was delusional to consider raising prices. Besides, the sales force was pulling out all stops just to keep sales from falling faster than they were. Finally, the consulting firm recognized its services were considered optional by executive management of their client firms and delaying or canceling projects had no short-term costs for them. So, growing the top line seemed to be for someone else to work out. Back to managing costs better.

"Let's start from scratch," suggested Don. "We get a directive from management to cut workforce expense by X%. Our first step is to identify our options, the next is to assess the plusses and minuses associated with each, and finally, we recommend the best option." "OK," said Rob supportively, "I am a consultant and that is what I am trained to do. I will act as if I was consulting my own firm as well as the utility and the software firm. Actually, I guess I am, although on somewhat different issues. The first option typically considered is a headcount reduction. But making the current workforce more effective may be a better solution. If the organization can get more for the same cost, this could tip the balance in favor of sticking with the people on board. For example, instead of cutting overhead in a staff function such as HR, existing staff could be used to develop current employees. Restructuring work schedules, using part-time employees to meet peak workloads, and outsourcing non-core activities that are not being done well could be implemented."

He continued: "If downsizing truly seems to be the only feasible option, the organization should carefully consider what cost savings might actually be realized. For example, firing ten staff members earning an average of $50,000 per annum does not immediately save $500,000; it takes a full year to realize that amount. And those savings will be reduced by a number of required payments. The obligations relative to severance pay, accrued vacation/sick leave, pension obligations and other liabilities that will come due upon severance will add to immediate expenditures. Our future unemployment compensation tax rates may also be impacted. Incurring these costs may be unwise if the downturn in revenue is not expected to last for an extended period.

"When considering downsizing, it's also important to consider the impact of downsizings in the past. We are familiar with Cascio's research on the outcomes of the 2001–2002 downsizing adventures. Outcomes included reduced morale and employee engagement, without the desired improvements in financial results. His findings bring into question the assumption that lowered payroll means more profits. Another consideration should be the potential increase in legal liabilities due to litigation that downsizing may create. If the cuts have a statistically significant adverse impact on a protected class, this could trigger discrimination suits." Don broke in, wanting to contribute the results of his deliberations on the issue. "As organizations evaluate what actions they should take, they should also keep in mind whether a subsequent upturn in the economy will require staff additions, perhaps even before all the severance payments have been covered by reduced payroll costs. Some employee changes may be warranted based on individual performance and the organization's workforce needs going forward, but there should be an emphasis on removing unnecessary or underperforming employees."

"OK," offered Annette. "Given these realities what are the options and how do they compare?"

The three of them worked up a table that listed the options and their probable outcomes (see Table 6.1).

They agreed that including reducing base pay rates is a difficult action to take if employee morale and engagement are major concerns. Some employees

Table 6.1 Evaluating alternative actions

Action	Employee impact	Employer impact	When appropriate
Reduce base pay	Drop in income; lower morale	Reduces payroll, beginning immediately	When it is the only alternative to firing people who might be needed in the future
Freeze base pay	Income does not increase with inflation.	Prevents further increase to fixed costs	When there is an uncertain future; when it will not cause loss of critical skills
Split pay-increase budget into increases and cash awards	Does not reduce income, and good performers may prefer it to base pay reduction.	Slows escalation of fixed-cost payroll; may motivate better by rewarding better performers with cash	When fixed costs must be controlled; when more motivation is needed
Replace future base pay increases with incentive potential	Positive for high performers; negative for poor performers	Enables restructuring of costs over time; ties costs to resources	When there is a need to change strategy; when measures of performance are clear; when short-term cost reduction is not required
Replace cash awards with equity program	Impact is based on market performance.	Shifts costs to equity markets	When a stock price increase is believable
Increase employee participation in health-care costs	Reduces net income; acceptance will depend on the current sharing formula.	Saves growth in costs; whether employees will accept it depends on the current sharing formula.	When employee share is less than 25% of cost
Move from defined benefit (DB) to defined contribution (DC) plans	Increases investment return risk	Decreases investment return risk	When total rewards will remain at or near competitive levels
Tie DC contributions to performance	Increases focus on organization performance	Increases employee focus on performance; may reduce morale among employees who prefer known retirement income	When performance is measurable and the formula for producing rewards is competitive and accepted by employees

will view a base pay reduction as a breach of contract, since they have established a standard of living based on the expectation that the base pay will always be there and that all rate changes will be increases. This is a key consideration for all companies, but especially at those public sector organizations that use time-based step systems to regulate base pay progression (such as Don's). Since step progression is written into some public sector organization policies, it is very difficult to freeze progressions without policy changes and without challenges by those affected. Despite these concerns, an organization in danger of running out of cash may be forced to implement pay cuts. In such situations, having executives more impacted by the pay cuts and making those cuts public can help promote a sense of fairness relative to sacrifice. For example, senior executives could take 10% cuts, middle management and professionals, 5%, and lower-paid employees smaller or no cuts.

A more moderate approach would be to freeze base pay. While this takes away something employees have come to expect (and even believe they are entitled to), they certainly would prefer it if the only other alternative is base pay reductions. The problem with this approach is that it only impacts the growth in costs and does not provide a short-term reduction in costs. Further, freezing base pay rates might not have any impact for close to a full year. Most organizations use a single focal date to make salary adjustments, and if that date has already occurred, the freeze option can only be effective the following year. Another key factor in freezing base pay is the impact of this strategy shift on turnover among those with critical skills and knowledge. Such turnover will depend largely on what other organizations do. It is very difficult to call those organizations that are competitors for critical skills and ask them for detailed information on their plans.

Any base pay freeze could be accompanied by implementing a variable pay opportunity, to be realized if the organization is able to perform at a level that warrants incentive awards. This approach may seem fair from the employer's perspective, but employees will not see it that way if they believe that exceeding performance targets is a major challenge and perhaps an unachievable one, given the economic conditions that precipitated the strategy change. And if performance does not meet targets, direct income levels will not increase.

These approaches can still make it difficult if employees base their expenditures on a certain expected income stream, and one that increases steadily. One strategy being used by more organizations is to maintain the basic structure of merit pay systems that are in place, but to reward employees with a combination of base pay increases and cash awards. For example, if the organization had originally budgeted 4% for base pay increases but now finds it necessary to cut the budget to 3%, this can be done by splitting the budget into base pay increases and cash awards. Cash awards would be limited to those whose performance was rated at the highest one or two levels. The advantages of this approach are: (1) fixed cost payroll increases at a slower rate, (2) cash awards are allocated based on performance, increasing motivation to perform and (3) it sends the message that increases to income can be less than those of the prior year if performance does not warrant an increase in that year. The most extreme version of this approach is to use the entire budget for cash awards. This has the advantage of providing performance incentives without having to design and implement an incentive plan.

Don pointed out that making variable compensation a part of the total direct compensation package would present major challenges at the utility, since metrics like profitability did not exist for use in evaluating performance. Annette and Rob both agreed that this approach was much more feasible in their organizations. Don also understood that using variable compensation for the first time is a major step, and strategic issues must be considered. Is the organization going to stay with incentives? Will management accept and stand behind the metrics used to measure performance? Will the necessary training and communication be forthcoming initially and on an ongoing basis? Will incentive plans measure and reward things that employees can impact? Will there be an adequate line of sight so employees see the connection between how well they perform and the metrics used to determine incentive awards? Will incentives be based on performance at the organization, unit or individual level, or on a combination of those levels? All these issues must be examined before this option becomes a realistic one.

All three of them simultaneously asked, "What about benefits?" They certainly agreed that when it comes to evaluating reward strategies, all benefits programs should be addressed: what their objectives are, how they are designed and who pays for what. This is important because the cost of benefits programs had been rising at a rate that far outstripped direct compensation escalation ever since the 1940s, when benefits began to expand as a result of wartime wage freezes. As a result, many employers who had traditionally paid all or most of the costs associated with benefits programs had begun increasing the share of the costs borne by employees. In fact, benefits surveys indicate that a reasonable and competitive approach is to have the employer pay 70–75% of health care costs and the employees the other 25–30%. "We have a problem getting employees to accept they should pay anything at all for health care," Don offered. "And when we talk about retirement plans, things really get ugly. Our people feel it is an inalienable right to retire at 55 if you have enough service— with an adequate income to sustain their standard of living. Despite the fact that they will live longer after retiring than they worked, they somehow think taxpayers should be happy to provide this benefit to them." Annette reminded him about the advice Margie and Steve had given him and he realized he was off the deep end, accusing people of having expectations he was not sure they had. Annette and Rob also reminded Don that the employer had made all the decisions on what programs to offer, so how is it the employee's problem all of a sudden? "Drat," replied Don, "maybe I ought to go decaf all day."

Annette and Rob had lived in the defined contribution world since day one of their employment, so the notion of a guaranteed pension benefit seemed unrealistic. Their employers required employees to make contributions in order for the organization to contribute. If people did not care enough about their retirement to plan for it and contribute to it, that was their choice. Matching 50–100% of the first 6% of employee contributions should represent an adequate employer contribution to employee well-being in retirement. A three-legged stool concept had prevailed in the U.S. for many decades. It meant that your retirement was made secure by the aggregation of (1) social security, (2) contributions to a retirement fund (by both employees and employers) and (3) personal savings. The contributions and the savings were the key to controlling one's destiny after stopping work.

Over lunch they turned to yet another benefit issue, paid time off. It was puzzling to all of them why the purpose of this benefit is not well-thought-out. It seemed that organizations should question whether what they were doing—at significant cost—made any sense. For example, vacation schedules most frequently award the most time off to those closest to having a whole lot of time off—that is, those close to retirement. Also questionable is allowing vacation carryover when the primary objective of providing vacations is to allow employees to experience a change in pace and regenerate their energy stores on a regular—not delayed—basis. And sick leave that is accrued by formulas can cause a disconnect between the amount of leave taken from the amount related to actual illness. Annette and Rob pointed out that Don's utility offered a lot of time off, some of which seemed misdirected. Canceling vacation carryover seemed to be a no-brainer, even though it would not cut costs in the short run. And budgeting sick time also seemed to be a strange practice with no real benefit. Admittedly, public sector organizations did not have to consider the accrued liabilities created the way private sector employers did. They all agreed that it was necessary to integrate short-term and long-term disability plans to ensure that those who really were ill were covered if the accrual of sick days were to be stopped. And all three realized that changing any of these plans would trigger an intense emotional reaction.

The trio unanimously supported the notion that benefits programs must also take into account changes being made in the direct compensation strategy. For example, raising employee contributions to health care costs while freezing or reducing base pay levels can produce a double hit to employee income. The impact of doing both simultaneously may be thought by the organization (and employees) to be overly severe, forcing a choice between the two. On the other hand, if employee contributions do not represent an adequate percentage of the cost of health care, why not increase the contribution in lieu of cutting base pay? The economic impact on employees is the same and it actually begins the process of increasing the employees' share of costs, while avoiding morale damaging pay cuts. "Wow," Rob blurted out, "that would make a good article. Pursue your long-term objectives while considering the impact on employees. There's a concept everyone can get behind." Rob had been told that consultants should write articles, since they enhance one's reputation, as well as giving back to the profession. He put that on his mental things to do list.

Now that they had worked their way through direct compensation and benefits, they thought it wise to consider what other cost reduction strategies might be available. Being people with two graduate degrees, they were able to conclude that having lower headcounts would result in lower costs. But their knowledge of how poorly headcount cuts generally worked out, they thought just cutting numbers was not the answer. Don had been an avid student of re-engineering when it first burst on the scene, but he had been knowledgeable enough about history to recognize this was nothing new. Yet the effectiveness of key business processes often deteriorated over time as contextual changes made current practices less effective. But although this made a case for periodically going through a re-engineering exercise, 70% of initiatives failed to meet expectations. Several studies found the biggest oversight by organizations attempting to re-engineer was not ceasing to do things that were not necessary. "Why," said Don, "would people do things they did not need to do anymore?" The answer, of course, was that they had been doing them and no one had told them to stop. Don recognized that as a near universal tendency.

"Annette, how much payback is there in attempting to redesign key processes like new software development?" Don asked. Annette knew where he was going but put an abrupt stop to this line of inquiry. "How would I know? I do my word processing, spreadsheets and presentations with software that is in the can, with no clue how the stuff materialized. And I am reluctant to challenge Carla's management ability by asking if maybe she could do things more efficiently in the software design function." Don acknowledged they were just HR types and they were wise to be careful in suggesting that it was not necessary to cut pay or benefits, or to lay people off, since the answer was to have managers manage better. But he did think HR had something to offer when decisions about the size and the structure of the workforce was determined.

"Bruce told me about one of the great mistakes made in staffing an organization he worked for," offered Rob. "He saw the panic about Y2K compliance result in firms treating a one-time project like a permanent condition. Virtually all organizations that had used two-digit date fields for the year were forced into making a decision. They had to modify their IT systems to work in 2000 or they had to replace the legacy systems with new ones, which were typically network-based. But they waited too long to make their decision and were forced to compete for skills in labor markets where supplies of qualified people were desperately short. Instead of hiring contractors or outsourcing the projects, they paid inflated salaries for new hires. The crisis passed and many of them were left with highly paid, underemployed people on their payrolls. They had also demoralized or driven off many of the IT folks who did not have the network skills, due to the inequities created by the inflated salaries for new hires. It was a classic case of a bad staffing strategy, and I wonder if there are pockets of overpaid, underemployed people in our organizations that could be a source of savings." "I have heard that same story before," interjected Don. "Reggie, our IT director, said our utility had made all of those mistakes and paid the price for a long time. Guess HR failed in a lot of organizations during that crisis." "Maybe no one would listen to them," responded Annette.

"Ever notice that most line managers can control their enthusiasm over having HR telling them how to organize and staff their functions?"

Don thought about the engineers they had been hiring to handle the infrastructure projects and wondered if there was a parallel to the Y2K debacle. After all, many of the projects required specific skills for as little as three to six months and hiring experienced (aka highly paid) engineers could be a cause of ballooning payroll costs. The engineering director had resisted using consulting firms or contractors, saying that they charged the utility three or four times their salary and were therefore far more costly than regular employees. "What if each segment of these huge projects causes us to hire a few engineers we won't need in the future? How much excess staff can we end up with?" Don had asked out loud in a meeting with the director. "And when people start comparing salaries, as they will, won't we spend all of our time trying to explain the pay relationships?" Don knew the engineering director preferred not to hire new graduates or early career people, since they required training and supervision, even though if properly utilized they could do much of the less complex work at a lower pay rate. He promised himself that he would talk with Margie to see if they could explore the staffing strategy with the director. It could be a disaster if they had to cut budgets and lay people off while bringing in engineers from the outside. Of course, they could not train accountants or Water treatment plant operators to do engineering work, but they certainly could bring in early career people and supplement their limited knowledge with contractors on a selective basis. That way they would have employees in place for the long haul that were a part of creating the new infrastructure and systems.

All three of their organizations had been struggling to find the best strategy for dealing with the economic downturn. Don, Annette and Rob had all been involved in the decision-making processes, although they sometimes felt like voices crying in the wilderness where no one could hear. In discussions with each other, they finally admitted that their bias toward focusing on the employees had caused them in some cases to be less than businesslike. They also at times forgot about the reality that they all had multiple constituencies to satisfy. No actions could make all constituencies happy, but they had to try to achieve an optimal balance between business considerations and employee considerations. So, their decisions should be driven by the context within which their respective firms were operating, and which would be different from each other.

The utility's current realities

Don's utility had seen continued drops in revenues. On top of its inability to get rate increases that would provide the revenue needed to continue all its projects, the ratepayers were slower in paying their bills. And the last several quarters, the weather pattern had been cool and wet, which reduces water usage and further impacts revenue. So, something had to be done to reduce costs, if for no other reason than to send the message to its board and the citizenry that it was doing what should be done, given the circumstances. After deciding which infrastructure projects could be put on hold or slowed down and how the finances could best be handled, it became Margie's turn to offer cost-cutting measures. "The employees know things are not good," she had told executive management, "but we have not done a great job of getting the message across that things are far worse than not good. We have to begin communicating realities continuously and completely to get them on board with what we are facing. And though some will be delusional and hang onto a *nothing-to-do-with-me* mindset, the vast majority should begin to realize where we are and what is necessary."

The software firm's current realities

Annette's firm was facing reduced revenues, which could be expected to persist for at least a year. Although short-term projects involving upgrades to already installed systems would be continuing, they were not the large-fee projects required to change the financial picture. Several large projects had been cancelled or put on hold. There were proposals for other large projects pending, but the timeframe was such that revenues would not begin materializing for three to six months, even if the firm won those projects. So, unless something was done to reduce costs, there would not be money to pay the bills. Unfortunately, most of the cash outflow was in the form of pay and benefits, and the employees were not likely to accept IOUs. A hiring freeze had been implemented already, and the only exceptions were individuals who would be critical to the success of any new projects that were landed. Further headcount reduction would be necessary, even after all individual and organizational incentive plans were frozen.

The consulting firm's current realities

Rob recognized that employees looked to their stock holdings as being their major source of long-term financial security, and if they could not show numbers each quarter that were at least minimally acceptable, the stock price would suffer. There were, after all, some employees who had been there from the start and who were fairly close to retiring, or at least changing what they did. Being on the road for a number of years can age one quickly and can also create a longing to have more of a family life and to be able to become more a part of one's community. Rob knew that he wanted to teach some day and did not want to wait until he lacked the energy to do it well. So, even though the shareholders were a critical constituency to be considered in their decisions, employees were the only real asset the firm had. They leased computers and offices and owned virtually nothing, save some intellectual property. If the employees became less capable or less willing to provide the services they had become known for, there would be little left to liquidate. So, Rob realized that great weight should be given to the likely impact on morale, engagement and turnover of the decisions they made about how to cut costs.

The decisions finally were made about cost reduction strategies that related to the workforce. Each of the three organizations had used somewhat different processes, which involved different parties.

The utility's strategy

Don was pleased with some of the decisions that senior management had made working with the board. The board members had been getting criticism from all sides, the mayor (who had appointed some of them), the citizenry, and even their friends at social gatherings. "Enough," said Kathy the utility's public affairs director, in a firm tone. "I have to deal with the board and they are not happy campers. You all need to do something."

The first step was to significantly increase employee contributions to health care coverage, for both active and retired people. The contribution for active employees had amounted to 15% of total costs and this was raised to 20%. Retiree health care premiums were raised to 50% of the cost for those already retired and would be raised to 75% and 100% over the next two years. All new retirees would pay 100% of their retiree health costs.

This saved enough to enable management not to impose unpaid furloughs, but there would be no adjustment to the pay structure and no step increases for the current year. Additionally, any overtime for non-exempt employees would have to be approved by the operations and maintenance director in advance of the hours being worked. And some of the outside consultants working on long-range projects were directed to freeze their work. Management had spent a lot of time in employee meetings sharing information about the financial situation with employees. Don had developed scenarios for the next three years and employees were informed that there was a possibility of staff cuts and revisions to the time off policies, particularly vacation carryover and budgeted sick leave.

Although this would be a lot for employees to accept, there was little choice and Don encouraged management to involve employees in making choices where possible. The employees may be willing to sacrifice current benefits to reduce the necessity for staff reductions, or at least to delay them until the work could be reorganized so that smaller headcounts did not severely diminish service levels and/or put unreasonable demands on people going forward. By making the employees a part of the decision-making process, management could at least demonstrate that they were aware of the impact of actions on employees and that they were concerned about their welfare.

Don had bounced ideas off Annette and Rob, who listened with one ear because they were concerned about their own organizations and what they were going to have to do. Rob had suggested to Don that he poll members of the board and samples of ratepayers to determine what their perceptions were about the rewards package offered by the utility. They agreed that the generous retirement benefits that could begin at a relatively early age were a source of public criticism and that a study should be done of alternative fixes. They could of course freeze the defined benefit pension plan and offer future hires a defined contribution plan, but that seemed a bit extreme as an initial step in the reform process. Yet the board seemed willing to consider this option, given their desperation level.

One of the most important initiatives decided upon was the strengthening of the performance management process. Across the board, staff cuts never seemed to get rid of the right people and often left some units still over-staffed, while others were rendered incapable of functioning at the desired level. The process for identifying poor performance and for either improving it or removing the poor performers would be studied and policies and pro-cedures developed to ensure that every employee was performing at least at a fully satisfactory level.

The software firm's strategy

It was decided that each employee would receive a comprehensive perfor-mance appraisal on the same date, and those whose appraisal was not at least fully satisfactory were put on the list for termination consideration. Managers were charged with evaluating the nature of the performance deficiency and with evaluating the likelihood that performance could be brought up quickly. The firm often put people in over their heads to see if they would stretch and survive, so some of the poorer performers may be the victims of a temporary gap between their capabilities and what they were being asked to do. Annette was given the responsibility for ensuring that the performance reviews took place and that the rating distributions were compared across managers. This was an attempt to calibrate raters, so they were using standards of the same or similar relative difficulty. She promised herself that she would make a pitch for training in performance management once the financial situation improved somewhat.

Each product area was evaluated to see if it was profitable and what staff reductions would be necessary to raise the performance of those that were not. Staff reductions would begin in product lines where capacity exceeded current revenues and those projected for the next two quarters. Once all excess staff conditions were fixed, the decision had been made not to reduce staff else-where, at least not until sales declines made them unprofitable.

The firm-wide incentive plan was frozen until such time as it was restruc-tured. It had become an automatic source of cash for everyone, irrespective of organizational performance. Although executive management realized that having a "shared destiny" plan reduced the perception that everyone was in competition with everyone else, this plan had run on autopilot. Management had every intention of redesigning it so that performance standards would be set at a stretch level and that no fund for payouts would be created until those standards were met or exceeded. The individual incentive plans were kept active, although the expectation was that most employees would be unable to meet even the threshold level of performance at which awards began to accrue. Employees understood this and accepted that if management lowered the standards to what was possible in the short run, that there would be inadequate profit to cover cash needs.

Since the employee benefit package was relatively conservative, the decision was made to leave the current programs in place, although employee contributions to health care coverage would be increased, both to increase the percentage of total cost paid by employees and to absorb rate increases in the insurance. Annette planned to challenge their insurer if they imposed significant rate increases, since she had noted from their proxy that they were making record profits and their management personnel were receiving very large incentive payouts. She did not buy that they suddenly had become brilliant managers and that the profitability increases were attributable to them, rather than solely to rate hikes.

The consulting firm's strategy

Rob was a little startled at how upset the thought of staff reductions made him. Being a no-nonsense product of the paratrooper mentality that he had acquired while serving, he figured he was tougher than that. Graduate school was pretty tough also—you worried about your own grades. And consulting was a dog-eat-dog kind of world, or at least so he had heard. But in the military, you counted on everyone else and you looked out after them. He was also surprised at his anger at management for staffing at levels that were delusional. But as he thought about the binge people had been on relative to buying real estate and running up their debt balances, he realized that the American optimism had two sides, and the dark side was visible now.

When he and Annette talked on the phone that night, they were amazed at how similarly their two managements had decided to proceed. The consulting firm would evaluate all practice areas and begin trimming staff levels where the revenue did not support the payroll. And the incentive plans were frozen for the time being. There was a pool set up for awards that could go to individuals and teams accomplishing extraordinary things. Management had worried that some people would do brilliant work but yet not be rewarded because the firm was not doing well at that particular time. "Could always tell them their timing was bad," thought Rob, but he figured that was a poor motivational strategy. And although there was a tight control imposed on base pay increases, there was still a small budget to fix inequitable pay ratess to ensure good people did not leave.

The structure of the benefits programs was to be left alone, although employee contributions to pay for health care insurance would be increased, much like the approach taken by Annette's firm. Rob shared Annette's view the insurance provider was supporting profits with rate increases, but it was hard to tell how much justification there was for increases. There were new medical breakthroughs being announced all of the time, but often they resulted in slight extensions to longevity at huge cost. Rob promised himself he would avoid engaging in a debate about how cost-justified some of the late-life procedures were, or that cost should be an issue when human life was involved.

The Three Musketeers decided to have a little celebration to commemorate the third anniversary of their graduation. Their professional society had its annual conference in Las Vegas, and they figured this was an opportunity to learn from others, share what they knew and to take advantage of other recreational opportunities that presented themselves. They booked five days at a top-rated hotel and promised themselves they would leave behind the dreary economics their organizations were facing. Each of them of course thought, "fat chance of that—the discussions will restart on the flight out."

7 Learning from others

There is something about looking down The Strip at night from a high-floor window that awakens the soul. Don admitted this was the first time he had seen the place lit up, except when he watched CSI on his high-definition, large-screen TV. "Wow," he said, "I wonder what the light bills are for these places." Rob had a client in Vegas who gave him an inside view of the entertainment palaces. "Believe me," said Rob, "they do not worry about the utility bills." "Maybe," Don responded, "but wait until they run out of water and have to truck it in. That might penetrate their psyches."

Despite the atmosphere dictating flippant behavior, they decided to get to work evaluating the challenges they all faced. Meeting in the coffee shop, they started by pooling the information they all had gathered on the probable future of the economy in the short run. Actually, they labeled their "information" as speculative guesses by economists and consultancies. They were educated guesses, but no one knew what the margin of error there was in the projections. Most knowledgeable experts figured the economy had bottomed out but that it was probably going to look like a "U" when the past, present and next few years were plotted. The question was how wide the bottom (horizontal) part of the U would be. Certainly, there was little or no job growth, and orders that would result in revenues within the next several months were few. So, what should their counsel be to their respective managements? If they were overly optimistic, the focus on cutting/holding costs would be lost and that could prolong the gap between revenue and costs. If they were overly pessimistic, they could keep the reins on hiring too tight and constrain their ability to ramp up as the economy improved.

The *Salary Budget Survey* conducted annually by World at Work[1], an association for rewards practitioners, was the most comprehensive source for determining what companies were doing relative to budgets for compensation adjustments. But a strange thing had happened the last 2 years: the actual expenditures had ended up being much lower than what had been projected prior to the start of each year. This meant that optimism prevailed when budgets were being created but that cold reality depressed the expenditures that were actually made. It is not unusual when the economy keeps heading downward, they all concluded. So, what should they tell their CFOs when asked about budgets for the forthcoming year? Rob was not technically the compensation manager for the consulting firm, but Bruce, their HR leader, was wise enough to get the opinions of the consultants practicing in their human capital line of business.

"Well, here we are, on the firing line," offered Annette. "We struggled to get to the table where the big decisions are made, and now that we are there and they are listening to us, we realize what pressure there is to be right in our projections. Don't know if I thought that through when seeking the invitation." Her apprehension about stepping up to the plate was only temporary, and both Rob and Don knew that. They went to the convention center to attend seminars, hoping to find some answers.

As the conference progressed, the trio observed that the very senior people speaking at the conference were the ones who seemed reluctant to provide clear-cut answers, and that they did not pretend they had discovered the answers to every attendee's most pressing problem. Some speakers talked about the critical importance of culture and how it impacts everything management does. Others suggested there were numerous strategies that might address any issue and that the "good fit to the specific context" test would guide the decision maker in selecting the right one for their organization at that particular point in time. The speakers that came on like zealots used the 3D approach: (1) dichotomize the alternatives, (2) demonize the one they did not prefer and (3) deify their recommended approach. The sorts of evidence they presented to support their recommended approach seemed questionable. For example, some pointed out that all of the articles appearing in the literature showed that a particular approach always was successful. Rob laughed at this, reminding Annette and Don about what one of their favorite professors had asked: "Who would write about their professional failures? And what percentage of the times an approach was tried did the favorable articles represent?"

There was a speaker who warned against using extrinsic rewards to motivate people, lest they destroy the intrinsic motivation of employees. But the trio recognized that the research supporting this contention was lab rat in nature, meaning that it had not occurred in real work settings involving real work. "But given the scarcity of funds right now, I wish we could tell people we were preserving their intrinsic motivation by not giving them rewards," said Don. They all realized that claiming something controversial or contrary to prevailing beliefs was probably a good way to sell books and speaking engagements, but it certainly was not sound science. They all agreed that both types of rewards were necessary in order to motivate and satisfy people. If extrinsic rewards were a form of manipulation, they could certainly have a negative impact. And extrinsic rewards for doing miserable and unrewarding work often did not work—or it took an unconscionable amount of money to overcome the realities of the work/workplace. Don's dad had received a bonus once that he complained about because the supervisor grudgingly threw the check in his direction, behaving as if it were coming out of his pocket. "Our family will never forget that evening's discussion about bonuses around the dinner table," Don offered.

Rob attended a session led by a field investigator for the Equal Employment Opportunity Commission, mostly because it was where an attendee he had struck up a conversation with was heading. "Why are you going to that session," asked Rob. "Because I want to know as much about the thought process and analytical procedures investigators use." replied James. "You can do the same analyses on your own as a form of self-audit and anticipate what an investigator is going to conclude before the drill is with live ammunition." Good thinking, thought Rob. He also realized that in his consulting work he should be aware of the legal/regulatory challenges practitioners face.

The speaker started with a slide, asking the audience what they would conclude from it (see Figure 7.1).

"This is a plot of the average salary for all jobs with 70% or more male incumbents (M) or female incumbents (F) in an organization. The trendline represents the market average pay at each level. I suggest there are two troublesome patterns here. What do you think they are?" One attendee suggested that the male-dominated jobs tended to be at the higher levels in the organization. "Why would that be the case, and is it a pattern that exists in your organization?" responded the speaker. The attendee knew that this indeed is what its plot would look like but rose in her defense by saying, "But this is due to historical conditions, and we are working hard to dissolve any glass ceiling." "You should not be defensive about this kind of relationship—it is pretty common," said the speaker, attempting to get to his real point. "What would be telling is to do the same plot based on conditions five years ago and see if you are making progress." Rob realized that was an insight he should tuck away for future use, since many industries had long histories of senior positions being filled with men.

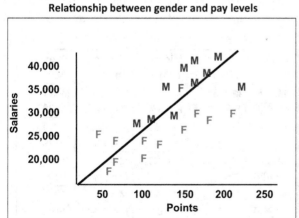

Relationship between gender and pay levels

F = Average pay rate for female-dominated jobs
M = Average pay rate for male-dominated jobs

Figure 7.1 Example of audit results

"What is the second potential issue?" asked the speaker. "The average salaries in the female-dominated jobs tend to be below the market average, while the male-dominated jobs tend to be above," called out Rob. "Right," answered the speaker, "so the CEO gets to go directly to jail without passing Go and collecting $200, right?" "Not necessarily," retorted Rob, "the average salaries might be a function of how long the incumbents have been in the jobs. In fact, if women are recently being brought into jobs that have traditionally been male-dominated jobs, the company will need some time to get its salaries up to the market averages." Rob really found this discussion to be illuminating and promised himself to add it to his repertoire of tools for evaluating pay level differences across employee categories based on gender, race, age and the like. He also realized that this was the type of visual that HR could use in board meetings to get across some of the challenges the organization was facing and the fixes that were being recommended to remedy problems before a regulator suggested how they do it.

"Now, another challenge for all of you to think about," the speaker continued. "How can you tell if your pay adjustments are equivalent by gender? Most organizations have a policy that says base pay increases will be determined by two factors: performance rating and the position of the employees' pay rate in their assigned pay range. That about capture your policies? OK, the vast majority of you. Now, how many of you break that down by gender, or race or any other protected class distinction? Look at the analysis in Figure 7.2.

"This is a real organization that had never done an analysis like this. I ran it for them and made it clear I was not suggesting that this was proof of gender-based discrimination in determining pay increases, but the compensation manager was a decent sort, and I wanted him to dig down to explain this troublesome pattern. What he eventually found was that when he analyzed this by job grade level, he found larger increases were given to people in higher grades and that most of the incumbents of those higher grades were males.

Performance Rating	Below Min	Lower Third	Middle Third	Upper Third	Over Max
Outstanding	M & F To Min	M = 8% F = 6%	M = 6% F = 4%	M = 5% F = 2%	M & F None
Significantly Exceeds Standards	M & F To Min	M = 6% F = 5%	M = 5% F = 3%	M = 4% F = 1%	M & F None
Fully Meets Standards	M & F To Min	M = 5% F = 3%	M = 5% F = 2%	M = 4% F = 2%	M & F None
Does Not Fully Meet Standards	M & F To Min	M = 3% F = 0%	M = 2% F = 0%	M = 0% F = 0%	M & F None
Unacceptable	M & F 0%	M = 0% F = 0%	M = 0% F = 0%	M = 0% F = 0%	M & F None

Figure 7.2 Analysis of base pay increases by performance rating and position in range

He concluded that the analysis showed status discrimination, not gender discrimination, and that this needed to be presented to management to determine if this was something that needed to be addressed. He also realized there was pretty poor implementation of the guidelines that all managers were supposed to be using and began to formulate a plan to do some communication and training to improve that.

The speaker summarized by saying "So every statistical finding of difference does not mean there is illegal activity, but if you do these analyses internally and proceed with a Sherlock Holmes investigation to uncover the causes, you won't be on the defensive if an outside regulator does the analysis and confronts you with it." Rob wondered if all regulatory people were this reasonable and dedicated to helping organizations fix what was wrong. He doubted it but hoped they were in the majority. He also recognized that all he had learned had been the result of serendipity, and it was a good idea to take the initiative to understand how others might view practices and to ensure the organization was not unprepared to demonstrate it was acting in a legal fashion.

It was becoming obvious to all three of the attendees that all the great information they were accumulating at the conference was just that, information. It needed to be turned into wisdom, which required that they apply an understanding of their specific context when deciding whether an approach that worked well in another organization would work well for them. The dangers of emulating "great" or "great to work for" companies had become apparent to them, unless of course they were able to factor in contextual differences when considering adoption of a strategy or program. While studying the evolution of Western management, they had been made aware of the tendency to jump from one quick fix to another, resulting in inconsistency and confusion about what might contribute to resolving the important issues. That did not mean that change was not necessary in order for the organization to co-evolve with its environment, but that the costs of change should be realistically assessed and compared to the benefits expected. Chris Argyris,[2] one of their most respected intervention strategists, had often warned "Don't fall in love with change . . . it too has costs."

So, when the conference was over, the three returned to their organizations to attempt to apply some of the ideas they had been exposed to. Since their serial adventures in the casinos had not made them independently wealthy, it seemed they would have to work for a bit longer, so they might as well do something productive.

Rob got a bit of a shock when he returned to work. The political maneuvering had resulted in the staff reductions being based more on who was connected and who had been profitable, rather than an assessment of the practical needs of the organization going forward. The reduction targets were suspiciously similar across departments, uncorrelated to real needs. Since Rob was not on the hit list, he should have been able to stay out of the fray, but a lunch with Bruce caused his temperature to rise. "They caved in to pressure from the practice leaders and took the easy way out," Bruce offered. "I think I have just been motivated to begin the process of retiring from work and to focus on finding a slice of paradise on the Oregon coast." Rob thought about attempting to counter this mindset with "we need you" appeals, but realized that would be attempting to run someone's life who probably did a pretty good job of doing that himself.

Bruce did offer a bit of advice to Rob, with good intentions. "You are not the person with the responsibility for managing the firm's intellectual capital; you consult with client organizations and give them the best advice you can. If your own organization does not do what you would recommend it do, then you must back off and make your decisions about continued commitment based on your own situation. Of course, I could recommend you as my replacement, but I fear you would go all out in an attempt to change the decisions that have been made and then find you cannot support management. Not a good place to be."

Bruce was right and Rob felt this was the time to talk with Howard to get an assessment of just how good a fit he was to a large consulting firm. He was not sure that he had enough experience to be an effective solo consultant, and he knew his network was pretty weak to support him, particularly during an economic downturn. He thought about making inquiries about teaching at a university that had a part-time MBA program with a concentration in HR. Without a PhD, he would have little chance of getting a full-time appointment, and he could not live comfortably on an adjunct's fees. He concluded it was time to get back to work and to forget about trying to formulate the firm's HR strategy, but at the same time to begin exploring options. The stock price had fallen as revenues had sunk, and his economic position did not enable him to consider drastic actions.

Annette had a somewhat better homecoming than Rob. Recruiting had been totally frozen, and there was no plan to invest in college relations any time soon. As a result, her biggest concern was how she could best focus her efforts to produce positive results. Certainly, the workforce planning initiative they had started with Rob's consulting firm would be one area she would stay focused on. As she sketched out some ideas, she had a call requesting her attendance at a meeting. In addition to the HR staff and Howard and Rob from the consulting firm, Carla (CIO) and Kim (CFO) were there, accompanying two people she did not know. Then the big news was released. There was a huge software project in Singapore that was theirs for the taking if they merged with a local firm that had been servicing the government agency funding the project. The new project was too large and diverse for the local firm, but when the capabilities of Annette's firm were merged with theirs, it was a good fit to the project requirements. "We are going global," thought Annette, not without some trepidation.

Notes

1 *Salary Budget Survey*, World at Work, Scottsdale, AZ.
2 Argyris, C., *Intervention Theory and Method*, 1970, Addison-Wesley, Boston.

8 Expanding horizons

Annette was informed that she would go to Singapore to do an assessment of the workforce management programs being used by their new partner organization, as a part of the due diligence process. She knew that people issues were one of the top reasons for merger/acquisition failures and that due diligence often consisted solely of looking at unfunded pension liabilities and open lawsuits.

That night she got out Trompenaar's book[1] that contained his research on cross-cultural issues. It became apparent that cross-cultural issues should be a critical consideration, since there seemed to be significant differences in the cultures prevailing in the U.S. and Singapore. Avoiding stereotyping, she noted that in aggregate the Singapore culture was more collectivist and accepting of deference to authority than the U.S. culture, and there was a common belief that external factors often significantly affected results. Much of this orientation was due to the high percentage of Singaporeans who were of Chinese derivation. The Singaporean culture tended to contrast sharply with the individualistic, low-power distance and internal control (can do) values that she had been socialized to accept. She knew that there would be variation within each of the groups, and it is possible that a member of one group that represented an outlier might behave more like a member of the other group. But she had read a lot of supporting research that alerted her to the fact that there would be differences they should be aware of and that they should address in some way. She also surmised that there would be less variance among the creative software designers, who were inwardly focused on their work, than there would be across the sales and customer service workforces. "Yipes," she thought, "this will be stimulating but also fraught with peril."

Rob told Annette this would be an opportunity for both of them to get a more significant grounding in cross-border alliances, and it had been announced that Rob would represent the consulting firm in the development of the HR due diligence plan. Unable to help themselves from having an opinion on everything, Don and Rob jumped in and began to "help" Annette out with developing a due diligence plan. Annette had brought home organization charts from both firms. She found the Singapore organization's chart was a bit on the abstract side. The job descriptions were also different across the organizations and Annette realized she would have to have an assessment made by the two CIOs (soon to be one CIO?) as to what the combined workforce would ideally look like once the merger was complete. It had been made clear at the announcement meeting that the merger was not an attempt to gain efficiency through staff reductions, but rather to expand the staff in numbers and skill variety. "Well," thought Annette, "that will reduce the chances that I will be named ogre of the year after working as the layoff coordinator."

Don found little had been decided during his absence to attend the conference. Although there had been indications that management was ready to consider significant modifications to the benefits package, the momentum seemed to have diminished. The rate increases for employee health care contributions had been made, but when alterations to time off programs and an evaluation of the retirement plan were brought up, they did not seem to get anyone's attention. And the move to implement a rigorous performance management system also seemed to have died. Don knew that there had been no history of cutbacks; everything was always up and the issue was merely by how much. "Well," he thought, "if the board thinks that will hold off the wolves, it is their decision, but I sure hope the investigative reporter that recently nailed the city for their do-nothing approach does not show up at our front door." He was a little sad that Annette and Rob would be doing something that was both challenging and positive in nature while he tried to keep some momentum behind improving the utility's strategy for restructuring workforce costs.

Annette had laughed at the movie *Lost in Translation* but now wondered why she thought it to be comedic and unreal. It was 2 p.m. in Singapore, but she felt like it was three hours after her bedtime, which it would have been had she been home. Now she realized why the health club at the hotel was open at all hours. After breakfast, Rob and Annette jumped on the subway and came out of the station in the building where the offices of their potential partner were located. They were shown into the office of the director, who offered coffee.

"The real strength of our proposal to get the project was that we have a diverse group of people who understand the local culture and who possess skills in aggregate that enable us to do all the design and implementation work in house," offered Hari, the director. "Since the systems we will be developing will be used by a broad range of citizens and also by government staff, we must apply an in-depth knowledge of what people expect and what they will accept as appropriate. We must create a team that consists of representatives of all functions, as well as staff from both of our organizations." Annette immediately began to wonder if some of the U.S. staff would be required to live in Singapore for extended periods and how their compensation packages would be fashioned. One of the first things that she wanted to analyze was the relative pay levels across the two firms, sensing this would be the source of conflict if things were out of line.

Joined by Hari's assistant Anthony, they began to discuss potential cultural differences that might have an impact on how well mixing the staffs would work. Hari was a fan of Trompenaars' research on cross-cultural management, and since Annette was also familiar with that research, they decided to use that as a basis for predicting compatibility. "We here are similar to other Asian countries in some ways and different in others," Hari offered. "For example, we are similar to Hong Kong and Japan in our belief in applying rules across the board, not as dogmatic as the U.S. but more so than China. We tend toward a collectivist mentality. A few other Asian countries are less so, but they are not as individualistic as the U.S. is. We believe that many things are out of an individual's control, not as much as China, but all the major Asian countries fail to buy into the U.S. "can do" mentality, which suggests every outcome is up to the individual." "I have always been amused that U.S. HR people tend to lump all Asians into the same cultural profile, expecting them to behave in the same way," noted Hari. They all agreed that their assessment needed to be more refined than that.

After further discussion, it seemed to everyone that cross-cultural differences were probably significant. Yet, since the way software development was done, the importance of teamwork and mutually supportive behavior was well accepted by staff members already. The local software staff had learned that their individual skills and knowledge were insufficient to get the whole job done and that they needed others in order to be successful. And since there would be no need for administrative people to be brought over from the U.S. operation, there would be no major obstacles to workforce effectiveness. "It would be wise to set up team-based incentives at the start," counseled Rob. "We need to drive home the message that rewards will be based on product performance. And to encourage cooperative behavior, there should be a more egalitarian distribution of rewards than U.S. personnel would readily accept. On the other hand, we need to keep the merit pay system in place to ensure individual performance and contribution does not get overlooked."

Hari then mentioned that they would probably have to staff up in Singapore and might recruit some of the software developers in India and China. "There would be different cultural challenges if we decide to bring these people on board," Hari cautioned. "That is probably the understatement of the decade," responded Annette. "Mixing staff from India, China, Singapore and the U.S. could present some real challenges, particularly with regard to performance and rewards management."

After their evaluation of the staffing needs, the four of them agreed that no more than a handful of U.S. personnel would be required to spend extended periods in Singapore. Given the effectiveness of working asynchronously via the internet, the movement of people would be minimal. They decided that it would be unwise to alter the compensation arrangements of U.S. staff members, except for their participation in project/product-based incentive plans. "Whew," sighed Annette, "that is a relief. The material on expatriate compensation that we studied in school gave me a headache, and although we will still have to develop a few policies to manage the movement of people, this is

- **Eastern/Southern**
  - Communitarian
  - Hierarchical
  - Particularistic
  - Ascribed Status
  - Person-focused
  - External Control
  - Intuitive/Holistic

- **Western/Northern**
  - Individualistic
  - Egalitarian
  - Universalistic
  - Achieved Status
  - Task-focused
  - Internal Control
  - Analytical/Reductionist

Figure 8.1 Cultural contrasts: impact all HRM strategies

not so scary now. We will let the CFO worry about how they handle stock holdings and other such items during the merger."

The next morning, Annette reviewed some of the research on country differences with her peers,[2] the cultural dimensions that had been found to have the most impact on how people responded to different types of performance management systems and to different direct compensation programs. She showed them a chart that contrasted Eastern/Southern cultural tendencies with those more prevalent in Western/Northern countries, pointing out that this was generic and individual countries often showed significant variation on individual characteristics (see Figure 8.1).

"The most impactful factors on performance and rewards management will be the individualistic versus collectivist, the internal versus external control and the equality versus hierarchy dimensions. The U.S. averages place it at the individualistic end of the comparative scale, while India averages are close to the collectivist end of the scale, with China somewhat less collectivist but still much closer to India than to the U.S. I think Singapore would fall somewhere between the U.S. and the other two. On this dimension, we are definitely dealing with big differences. When we reward performance, we have to decide the level at which we define and measure performance. The U.S. staff will expect a strong emphasis on individual performance, while others will believe that it takes everyone to produce a result and that the level should be at the overall project or project segment level." Hari and Anthony felt that if the U.S. staff members were kept on U.S. programs, that the differences between the staff members from the other three countries might not be large enough to warrant putting them in different incentive plans. Annette made a note of that and said she would take it back to corporate for review.

They agreed that the next dimension that will have an impact is internal versus external control orientation. "The U.S. averages are near the internal control end of the scale. The tendency is for Americans to have a 'can do' mentality," Annette suggested. "They believe they should be given goals and then be measured on how well they meet them. External factors are seen to have more of an influence on one's ability to produce results in China and India, the averages for those countries being at or near the external control end of the scale. Given those tendencies, a rock-hard tie of performance ratings and rewards to measured results may not be viewed as completely fair by anyone except the Americans." Hari said that he felt they could convince the non-U.S. staff that performance measurement would be done in a manner that considered external factors impacting results. He also pointed out that this would be a further argument for keeping the U.S. staff members in a separate plan.

"The last cultural characteristic that might impact us is the egalitarian versus hierarchical dimension. The U.S. is nearer the egalitarian end of the scale, while China is at the hierarchical end, with India in between but closer to China. This should probably impact how we structure the project teams. The U.S. staffers will expect to operate like a herd of cats, with authority going to those who have the knowledge and skill, rather than whomever happens to have a title. This could be very frustrating to the others, and they could view the U.S. approach as being tantamount to anarchy." Hari recognized that this would be a potential problem, particularly if the project leaders on most of the segments were U.S. staffers, since they would "lead" in the manner most comfortable for them. This could lead to a great deal of frustration on the part of the Chinese staffers, and Hari promised to meet with the management of the software design division to alert them to this issue and to work something out that might work when they were staffing the project. He promised the U.S. software management people would be involved in that process.

Anthony, who had been quiet throughout the discussion, finally spoke up. "Are you Americans different from everyone else on everything, and is this deliberate?" "It is not deliberate," responded Annette, "but much of it is due to the open frontier mentality that prevailed throughout much of the country's history, and in the minds of many, it still prevails. We are not unique, in that there are other Western countries that share similar tendencies. But the U.S. is certainly very unlike many Asian countries. During the years when Japan was doing so well economically, the business schools were all trying to teach Japanese techniques to the U.S. students, but they completely overlooked the fact that Japan was much more culturally homogenous than the U.S. and differed substantially on most of the cultural dimensions. As a result, processes like quality circles did not produce the same result in the U.S. that they did in Japan. If more attention had been paid to the differing cultural contexts, the results would have been better. This challenge we face when creating a cross-cultural workforce is not unique. My favorite book on the topic, *Rewarding Performance Globally*[3], told the story of a U.S. multinational trying to sell a one-size-fits-all program, and the story was not pretty."

Later in the day, they evaluated the job classifications and pay levels of the software staffs of both firms. They found a significant difference in the way people were classified. The U.S. software employees were matched to a career ladder that used specific criteria for classifying individuals. In addition, there were two branches in the ladder: one for individual technical contributors and one for managers (of projects or people). The ladder was well-established, and the U.S. people more or less accepted the methodology.

"Do you train internally to enable people to progress through the levels of this ladder?" asked Anthony. "We try to develop our people," responded Annette, "but our accounting system treats training as a current expense, which reduces profits, and the benefits of training never show up as an asset on the financials. This makes it difficult to get budgets when money is tight, so we often vary training investments based on the current numbers." "Please excuse my abruptness," said Hari, jumping into the conversation, "but that is crazy. Just because an asset, such as a more qualified workforce, is intangible, your management views it as less valid than something you can record on your books?" Annette just smiled and responded, "That is why we hope that the valuing of intangible assets will become more recognized. Investment analysts are already beginning to factor such considerations into their evaluation of companies, so perhaps it just takes management realizing that the intangibles really can impact the valuation of the organization positively. But you do invest in your people here, and I hope you will continue to do so."

It was decided that the career model would be applied to the Singapore software staff and that any current pay rates that were inconsistent within the staff would be corrected once the classification was completed. It was also decided that they would create a separate ladder for project planning and administration specialists, since the project being started would require support activities that would be critical to success and that required much more specialized skills than existed in the current staff. The Project Management Institute (pmi.org) had fully developed certifications at several levels, and both Hari and Annette committed to researching the project staffing needs further and to decide how much they would invest in further training and certification.

Rob suggested they establish a framework for the project incentive plan that would be developed. Since they would be using project management

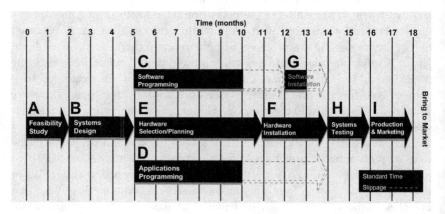

Figure 8.2 Fitting rewards systems to project-based performance management

modeling to manage the project, the potential awards should be tied to actual results versus the plan, both at the segment level and overall.

The overall project management model would be the basis for determining overall incentive awards, and performance criteria and standards would be developed for each segment. Staff participating in each segment would be eligible for awards based on segment performance, which would make the award potential proportionate to each person's participation in the overall project. It was also decided that there would be an incentive based on the acceptance by the customer of the product and on the performance compared

Segment	Milestones	Standard Time/Slippage	Performance Criteria	Eligible
A	Present feasibility study to management	2 mos./0	Quality of study	Project staff
B	Complete systems design	3 mos./0	On-time completion/ quality/cost	Systems staff
C	Complete software programming	5 mos./ 2 mos.	On-time completion/ quality/cost	Software staff
D	Complete applications programming	5 mos./ 4 mos.	On-time completion/ quality/cost	Applications staff
E	Complete hardware selection/planning	6 mos. /0	On-time completion/ quality/cost	Operations staff
F	Complete hardware installation	3 mos./0	On-time completion/ quality/cost	Operations staff
G	Complete software installation	1 mo./1 mo.	On-time completion/ quality/cost	Software staff
H	Run successful systems test	2 mos./0	On-time completion/ quality/cost	Project staff
I	Produce/market system and deliver to market	2 mos./0	On-time completion/ quality/ productivity	Project staff

Figure 8.3 Performance standards

to quality standards. This would provide an incentive for people not to cut corners in the short term and to focus on the overall success of the project.

For each segment, there would be milestones defined and metrics established that captured cost versus planned cost, completion versus scheduled completion, technical performance versus technical standards established, and customer satisfaction. All further work would be contingent on the outcome of the feasibility study. If the project required more resources than would be more than offset by the benefits, it would not be approved. They would have to be careful to appropriately evaluate the performance of the feasibility study team and to be sure they understood success had nothing to do with the go or no-go finding. If team members thought someone wanted to do the project and that their feasibility study was just an exercise to build a case for doing the project, they would hardly be neutral. But they could also examine multiple approaches and justifiably conclude that with the appropriate modifications to the original specifications, that it might be beneficial to go ahead, but with a redefined scope and objectives.

When Annette arrived home, she felt she had grown professionally and was gratified that the cross-cultural research she had viewed as fascinating but largely theoretical had turned out to be so practical. It seemed the prominent behavioral scientist Kurt Lewin was right in saying, "There is nothing more practical than a *good* theory." While meeting with the CIO, she reviewed the new classification scheme and the proposed project incentive model, and they both agreed that there would be no need for extensive expatriate compensation packages. They also agreed to explore the creation of the project planning and administration career ladder for the U.S. staff. Since the travel of the U.S. people would be handled as extended business commuting, it would not necessitate revisions to their current compensation plans.

They pledged to ensure there were face-to-face meetings at the start of the project and frequently during the life of the project. Asynchronous electronic communication does not provide the basis for building a professional relationship, and they felt it was important to build a sense of shared destiny among project staff members.

Notes

1 Trompenaars, F. and Hampden-Turner, C., *Riding the Waves of Culture*, 1993, Irwin, Chichester, UK.
2 Trompenaars, F., *Riding the Waves of Culture*, 1994, Irwin, Chichester, UK.
3 Greene, R., *Rewarding Performance: Guiding Principles; Custom Strategies*, 2010, Routledge, New York.

9   You win some, you lose some

Don was worried about getting some traction in controlling workforce costs in the utility. Inertia had really set in, and the good intentions relative to pruning costs seemed to have evaporated. A new deputy general manager had been brought in from the outside, starting rumors that the GM was going to retire earlier than people had surmised. The new deputy had been brought in from a for-profit private sector organization that ran utilities on operating contracts, and the first meeting with the HR staff gave Don some hope. The newcomer was taken aback by the lack of a credible performance management system and the time-based step rate pay program. After a long discussion, there was agreement in the room that there needed to be staff reductions in some areas but that there should not be across-the-board reductions, which would perpetuate staffing levels that were not matched to the workload. The strategy agreed upon was that HR would begin to develop a credible performance management system so any terminations would be based on performance.

Progress had been made on the cultural realignment initiative, and the new deputy fully supported the direction being taken. In fact, she made cultural reshaping the theme of each of her staff meetings, driving home the message that they needed to set priorities and behave differently on many fronts. Recognition awards were now to be based on exceptional instances of customer service, available to all employees who touched the customer as well as those supporting them. And contributing to the effectiveness of others and to that of the unit was to be considered in the new performance management system. Finally, the pay system was to be evaluated and alternatives considered that would have two characteristics: (1) there would be less fixed liability that increased every year (which step increases created) and (2) increases would be based more on performance. So, the initiatives begun with Rob's consulting firm were to continue. This relieved Don, since he had assumed that not much would come out of their earlier decisions. The branding initiative was working well and was having a positive impact on recruitment efforts. It had also cheered up many of the employees—the process of recognizing what was good about working at the utility had changed their perspective and made them realize there were pluses and minuses in all organizations.

Don began to revise the performance appraisal form and, in doing so, con-cluded there were two formats needed. One would be used for management and professional people and the other for the operating and administrative sup-port people. The format for managers and professionals was focused on two considerations: (1) how well the person did their day job and (2) how well they performed relative to established objectives for the current performance period. Also included was an in-depth evaluation of the person's current capabilities and what might be done to increase the employee's value to the organization. This information was to be used in providing them with career development opportunities but was kept separate from the appraisal of performance during the last measurement period.

The format to be used for the rest of the employees was more based on performance on the job, using evaluation factors. Those factors used for all the covered employees were: (1) productivity, (2) quality of work, (3) depend-ability and adherence to organizational values and (4) contribution to the effectiveness of others and of the unit. Additional factors were added for some jobs where considerations such as safety were an important part of the job. Don realized the appraisal would require a couple of rounds of usage before the results could be used as the basis for status changes and pay actions, but given the pace of change people were used to, this was probably not an issue. He also realized that communication and training would have a major impact on the success of the new system. People had to understand why this was being done, what personnel actions it would impact and who was responsible for doing what.

After a series of meetings with managers and employees, Don was encour-aged. The new deputy had called senior staff together and delivered the critical message: "We are not voting on whether to do this, and it is clearly not in any-one's best interests to be anything but fully supportive." One addition that Don had made to the appraisals for management employees was that a significant part of their appraisal was based on how well they managed the performance of their employees. It had been made clear that late or superficial appraisals were unacceptable. And everyone was made aware of the fact that appraisal rating distributions would be evaluated across raters to ensure managers were using equivalent performance standards.

Don had gotten the budget to develop training modules for managers and for employees that would make clear the roles each party would play and the process that would be followed. The training for managers was based on the frame-of-reference concept that included groups working together to align their performance standards. Finally, the process for evaluating rating distribu-tions across raters was agreed upon. Supervisors would meet as a group with their manager, and the ratings would be calibrated to ensure they were fair across raters. Then managers would meet with their directors, and this would be continued up to the top.

It was critical that this process did not stop at any level and that division directors receive written appraisals just as everyone else did. If that were not mandated, people who did not receive appraisals could legitimately ask why it was so important for them to do appraisals for their direct reports. It was decided that forced distributions would not be used, but rather that division directors would meet to ensure that if their rating distributions differed that all parties accepted them as appropriate.

The pay system was next. The downturn had forced the utility to suspend step progressions for the first time. None of the step schedules had been adjusted either, since labor market conditions were such that increases of any type were not warranted. A change in concept was needed. Since any step schedule adjustments resulted in automatic across-the-board increases, it was necessary to disconnect range adjustments from pay increases in the new pay system. The new system would adjust the ranges based on labor market rate changes to keep them competitive. Automatic, time-based pay rate increases would be discontinued and performance on the job would become the driver of pay actions. The proposed system would follow a process that involved budgeting increases:

1 determine the funds available for pay adjustments;
2 price jobs in the marketplace and adjust pay ranges to keep them competitive;
3 develop guidelines that would tie pay adjustments to: (a) employee performance and (b) the position of the employee's pay rate in the pay range;
4 have mangers submit performance appraisal ratings;
5 calculate the proposed increases based on the ratings using the guidelines, modifying the guidelines if the results varied from the budget established;
6 provide managers with the increases proposed; and
7 enable managers to adjust the pay actions by moving dollars around; this would help to ensure that adjustments would be in relative internal alignment, while staying within the allocated budget.

The philosophy underlying the guidelines is that those who are paid below the midpoint of their salary range (the proxy for market value) and who perform well should receive the largest percentage increases, while those at or above the

Performance Rating	Lower Third of Range	Middle Third of Range	Upper Third of Range
Outstanding (10%)	$$$$	$$$	$$
Exceeds Standards (30%)	$$$	$$	$
Fully Meets Standards (55-60%)	$$	$	None
Does Not Fully Meet (0-5%)	0 - $	None	None

Figure 9.1 Pay increase guidelines

midpoint and who perform at lower levels should receive small or no increases (see Figure 9.1). The practical impact of this change in philosophy would be significant, since longevity had driven increases in the past. The new system would base rewards on both individual contributions and the current rate of pay. Those at the top of their range would now be expected to perform at high levels in order to receive an adjustment.

The transition to the new system would no doubt result in resistance from those who are already high in the range, but their expectation that they should get increases similar to those in the lower part of the range on a percentage basis was unrealistic and economically unsustainable. Whether the change would prompt more retirements among senior employees was not clear. But if better performers were still rewarded and those not performing as well were not rewarded, perhaps the right people would be motivated to exit the organization. Don had recommended that those at the very top of their range receive moderate cash awards if their performance was rated as "exceeds standards" and larger cash awards if their performance was rated "outstanding." This would recognize the best performers without further compounding fixed costs.

Don was getting a big kick out of this development work, particularly since he really believed it would benefit the utility and that it would address an important issue. By responding to the board mandate, it made it easier for them to defend their oversight activities to the public. Don believed this would justify the disruption these changes might create.

It would also be made clear to everyone that although the performance and pay systems were the same for everyone, that the measures used to define performance below the organization-wide level reflected the role of each of the functions. The Operations Division captured, treated and distributed the water, fulfilling a major responsibility of the utility. Finance set rates and made sure the utility had the capital necessary to operate. Planning looked into the future and ensured the citizenry would have an adequate supply of water. Engineering designed the systems that turned plans into reality. Information Technology provided systems for capturing, analyzing and distributing data. HR helped the organization build and sustain a viable workforce that was competent to do what was needed and committed to the mission of the utility. "We all count and we all contribute, each in our own way," thought Don, smiling.

Rob and Annette suggested to Don that he was too smug and contented and that if he got a high level of intrinsic rewards out of his job, he could do with less money. But Don felt the two of them should give him some of the lordly sums they were raking in. They responded that perhaps the benefits package he got more than made up for the cash part. After the extended debate about who was doing the best, they all agreed that they were all doing alright.

Without throwing cold water on the love-in, Rob felt he must let it be known that he was very unhappy with the across-the-board cuts his firm had done. He fine-tuned his message to a succinct set of questions: "How can we opt to reduce staff by the same percentage across the board when we don't know which practices are overstaffed and which are understaffed? Was this decision the result of cowardice by senior management—afraid to make an honest assessment of staffing levels versus staffing needs? Or just pandering to the practice heads, to avoid telling anyone they needed to cut?"

Don suggested that Rob cool his tone and reminded him that he was not a part of the decision process and was not certain that such a review had not been done. "But the perception is that it was a cop-out," responded Rob. "Managers should realize that perception is reality to people, and if they do not explain the rationale behind decisions, they will not get the buy-in they need in order to have decisions have the desired effect." Annette suggested that Rob was correct and that he should include that principle in his first book on workforce management. They all joked that they were collectively writing that book every day and at some point in time, they should sit down, organize what they had learned and share it with the rest of the world. But they agreed they needed to build reputations before anyone was likely to read it.

Don got a phone call, and, seeing that it was his manager Margie, he took it. "Don," said Margie, "I have some good news and some bad news, and you get to choose the sequence of disclosure." "OK, give me the ugly first," answered Don. "We won't be working together anymore," Margie said slowly. "So, what is the good news," asked Don, somewhat taken aback by this pronouncement. "You are the new director of HR for the utility if you will have the job," continued Margie, "I have taken the position of HR director for the city.

Don promised himself he would set out a plan when he formally accepted the job. He would not issue a mandate but thought it important to make it clear what he hoped to accomplish and how he thought that it would help the organization. He felt he already had the support to develop a sound performance management system and to replace the base pay system with one that recognized performance rather than longevity. So, perhaps he should ask for permission to begin reshaping the retirement programs. That last one would not be a deal breaker, but it might help his cause if a commitment to consider it was expressed early on.

10 Considering new career frontiers

As the result of a conversation Rob had with a tenured faculty member at one of the better business schools in the city, he had been asked to teach an HR course as an adjunct faculty member. It would be held on five consecutive Saturdays, with each session taking up a full day. "Well," Rob thought, "I wanted to find out what teaching was like and whether it was right for me, and here is a chance to try it without conflicting with my work schedule." It was true that he might have to drag himself in from out of town late Friday night after being gone all week and then get up to teach on Saturday, but that was better than trying to leave an evening during the week open. And he also dreaded the thought of facing a classroom full of people who had worked all day and now faced the challenge of keeping their energy level up at least at a level that resembled consciousness. So, night classes were never something he wanted to teach.

Rob accepted the offer to teach the course, and when he was given the syllabus that the department chair had used when she had taught the class the prior term, he realized the topics more or less paralleled the issues he had faced in his work life since graduation. He immediately thought about getting Don and Annette on board as unpaid consultants, which would give him the perspective of an HR person who deals with the issues on a daily basis. And they were cheap.

When he arrived at work a few days later, Bruce caught him and asked for a powwow. Bruce informed him that Howard, the head of the intellectual capital practice, had read the riot act to the CEO about the inappropriate strategy that had been adopted relative to staffing the professional practice areas. Howard had been told to get back to work and to implement the decisions that had been made. Howard had told the CEO that rather than doing that, he was departing to form another consulting firm that would actually have some competent leadership and that would be driven by business considerations, rather than by what was easy and/or politically acceptable. Bruce said this had resulted in the CEO deciding to dissolve the human capital practice rather than worrying about finding a new leader who was more obedient and dealing with the associated disruption. Rob would receive 6 months of severance, which was generous given his short tenure, but he was expected to be off the premises by the end of the week. "This is a classic case of poor leadership," said Rob, "and I think I will use it in my class." Bruce just shook his head and wished him good luck but also gave Rob the address and phone number of his new digs on the Oregon Coast. He also made it clear Rob was welcome at any time to visit and stay as long as he wished.

"OK, I have 6 months to find another income source," thought Rob. He certainly would talk with Howard about some sort of alliance, but Howard would be starting from scratch with the clients he had personally serviced, and it was not likely that he needed to create a lot of overhead in the short term. When Rob did talk to Howard, it was made clear that Rob would be welcome as an independent consultant and that there probably would be a good bit of work for him, even in the short term. That was comforting, since the party collecting Rob's rent and all the suppliers of utilities were probably still going to expect timely payment.

That evening after class, Rob was caught by the department head. "You are doing a great job and really have a knack for teaching," said Charlotte. "Have you given any thought to working on your PhD so you could teach full time?" Rob admitted that the thought had occurred to him. He had been writing a few articles and speaking at professional conferences and was beginning to think he was pretty hot stuff. But he had seen a number of smart people who began to believe their press and who fell into the trap of pontificating continuously without regenerating and updating their knowledge. "I would love to do that," responded Rob, and he went on to explain what had just transpired relative to his employment. "This could be ideal," said Charlotte, "you could do contract consulting while you take the courses you would need part time. But one question: Do you have a thesis topic in mind? There are too many ABDs (all but dissertation) around, doomed by the fact that they never could get a thesis topic approved and/or could never do the research and finish it." Rob responded without even thinking. "The impact of organizational context on the effectiveness of human resource strategy," he blurted out, scaring himself, since he was not sure when this critical decision was made.

"Can you structure a hypothesis and do research to support it?" queried Charlotte. "Yes, I would use three substantially different organizations to demonstrate that the effective HR strategy for each must be a good fit to the context within which they operate," responded Rob. "OK, let's get the paperwork started. It will probably take you about 2 years if you can stay with the courses and work on the dissertation at the same time. I believe I can get you a research fellowship that would cover your tuition and pay you a small monthly stipend. If you live in a luxury high-rise overlooking the lake, you might have to consider a basement flat, but that will depend on how much contract consulting income you can generate. You might be able to live on street level."

Rob more or less floated out of the discussion, as if in a dream. "Well not too much has changed in my life lately," he chuckled. "Wait until Annette and Don get a load of this," he thought. He called Howard, filled him in and encouraged him to bring in lots of work so he could maybe afford an apartment with a view—maybe only of the street or a parking lot. Yet, if he amortized the six months' severance over the two years and added that to his monthly stipend, he realized it would not take much consulting income for him to retain his current living arrangements. "Might have to brew my own coffee more often," he acknowledged, but that was doable once he got a really good coffee pot, a gold foil filter and the best spring water available.

"So, what do you think—have I gone off the deep end here?" Rob asked Annette and Don. Don supported the direction Rob was taking and told him so in a serious manner. "Follow your heart; the head often takes you to a wrong place," Don offered. "You both know I am willing to sacrifice a lot just to make you call me Doctor Rob," the aspirant to PhD status threw out. The looks he got suggested the probability of that happening was low.

Don was facing challenges settling in as Margie's replacement. Some of the veterans in the line units viewed him as an OK guy and pretty smart but also very wet behind the ears and lacking in utility knowledge. He felt that was manageable and he would rather earn their respect by showing them he knew he must understand the business and the organization's mission and culture to be able to recommend viable workforce management strategies and programs. He had told Steve, the operations and maintenance director, that he appreci-ated the lecture Steve had given him a while back when he was all puffed up by the theory he had learned in school. It made him realize that organizational change cannot happen faster than the rate at which the organization could digest that change. He recognized that some of the reluctance to throw out the old and roll in the new was attributable to beliefs that change was mandatory in order to be successful. He admitted to himself that the utility was still operat-ing far better than the typical utility in the industry, when measured on things like rate increases, customer satisfaction and the occurrence of service outages or quality problems. Steve had cautioned him that the seasoned veterans were not unrealistically confident that they were doing everything right, but that the metrics led them to believe it would be foolish to implement changes if there was not good evidence that they would result in improvements.

Don asked Alice the deputy director to approve an employee task force, consisting of managers and senior-level professionals, to explore how the pay system would be modified. She supported the initiative and promised that senior management would support it. Don said he expected the executives and board chair to be at the kickoff session to make sure people knew this was not a conceptual discussion about whether the pay system should be changed but rather a dialogue about how it should be done and when. With that support committed, Don asked the division managers to nominate representatives to serve on the task force, after they had been informed by the senior executives that this was a go.

The first meeting went well, and since everyone knew they were working on a project that was going somewhere, rather than participating in a fanciful exploration of how things could be made better, they had all been in enough of those meetings. Some of the members felt a little trapped in the middle between employees they knew would resist any change and management, which was committed to change. But Don made it clear that they should be open about the nature of the resistance they anticipated and should honestly portray the probable difficulties that resistance might present.

Don had brought Rob in as a contractor to help with the project and had asked him to talk about the outside world and what was going on there. Rob pointed out that the annual survey done by the industry association clearly showed that the number of utilities using time-based step increases had dropped by half in the last decade, leaving a minority of utilities with step plans. He also talked about the reasons why so many utilities had changed their systems. And he recounted that the board chair had decided they could no longer tolerate an escalating payroll that went up automatically each year, no matter what was happening in the labor markets. To ignore competitor trends would signal arrogance and unrealistic beliefs that the utility was somehow subject to a different set of rules than the rest of the world, which would be an indefensible position for the board to stand behind. After hearing all of this, the members asked to be educated in how alternative pay rate determination systems operated so they could evaluate how they would work here.

The decision was made to adopt a merit pay plan, similar to the one that Don and management had tentatively agreed upon. The plan would use guide charts that specified the amount of pay adjustment, based on where the employee was paid in the pay range and the performance rating. All performance appraisals would be submitted prior to the development of guide charts, and the budget for adjustments would be approved by management and the board prior to finalizing them. Once the budget was set and the guidelines agreed to, managers were provided with a list of recommended adjustments. Then each manager was allowed to vary the adjustments somewhat, once approved by the division director. Since the performance appraisal system had been revised a few years ago and rating distributions were in line with what would be expected, management felt confident that it could support this type of pay system.

A few of the senior managers were not convinced merit pay was the best thing for the organization, since it could cause individuals to behave competitively rather than cooperatively. Don had looked at the research about merit pay and found merit pay programs provided the motivation to perform if pay was viewed as being tied to performance. It was necessary for employees to accept a merit pay program as equitable, competitive and appropriate in order for them to accept it, and that did present challenges. And since contributing to the success of the unit and of other employees had become an important rating factor, it should be possible to make employees understand that cooperative behavior was required.

Don was ready to celebrate this major accomplishment. He was confident that the new pay system would provide more motivation to perform well and that it would treat everyone fairly. Those he expected not to like the system were the people who probably were the ones they least cared about losing.

And those who hated any kind of change would probably get over it after a while. "Yes," he thought, "now onto overhauling the system." "Taking a few weeks of vacation in the near future would probably be good for me," he said to himself in the bathroom mirror. He was certain that this step would be the best way to balance his life.

11 Life in the (not so?) real world

Rob was really into his course work and had begun to become active in both the Academy of Management (AOM) and the Society for Industrial and Organizational Psychology (SIOP). AOM was the organization most academics belonged to, while SIOP was for both organization development practitioners and academics. As he began to read the journals published by AOM (prompted by the fact that they were useful in his course work), he felt like a stranger learning a new language. He had been an observer at an informal get-together in the business school lounge that ended up in a debate about why practitioners did not use the research the academics toiled laboriously to carry out. The debate was started by a study that showed that practitioners did not read the journals that the research was published in, which meant they did not know about it and therefore were unlikely to apply it. Rob took a chance and weighed in as a practitioner, pointing out that although he found the journal articles fascinating intellectually, he often did not see the application of what was being researched. And on top of, that the language used and the form of presentation made the journal articles pretty much inaccessible to people lacking graduate-level training.

Several of the faculty got on their high horses and defended the way they did things. Rob found out that the only way you get tenure is to publish in the "A" journals. And the only way you publish in those journals is to conduct your research and present your material by the rules—the rules used by journal editors. Before stating his dislike of everything about the concept of academic tenure, Rob thought he better make sure who had control over his doctoral program and his potential career as a faculty member. But he did feel it appropriate to point out that he had just read a journal article and the first page contained eleven words in two sentences. The rest were citations in parentheses with one too many names in each. "Why can't you use footnotes like everyone else, so people can actually read the material?" asked Rob. The answer obviously was that the style guide mandated the current format. And the number of citations was an indicator of how rigorously the author had done their literature search. "Sorry to tell you, but none of that cuts any ice with someone who is not in the academic world and would like to be able to extract useful information without all the obstacles," said

Rob, increasingly oblivious to giving offense and more committed to saying what he believed.

Rob also had a problem with the way things happened in the research community. What was researched seemed to be decided independently of what practitioners needed to know. An HR practitioner would like to know if implementing incentive compensation programs had been shown to increase performance in a particular kind of organization. But if that practitioner searched for support of that proposition she might end up with 50–100 very specialized studies that had been done, each one dealing with some of the relevant determinants of incentive plan effectiveness. Rob thought it would be sensible to aggregate studies, organizing them around a central theme deemed relevant by those who would find it useful. There were things called meta-analyses, which combined multiple studies to produce more robust results, but they were not very helpful if they did not address the issues about which one was concerned. He had also read about systematic reviews, a concept that involved combining all types of relevant evidence to provide guidance on key issues.

Denise Rousseau had made "evidence-based management" the theme of her Presidency of AOM,[1] and after reading some of her articles on the topic, Rob felt this was the way to build a bridge between the research and practitioner communities. Evidence-based medicine had been developed mostly in England and was being used increasingly in the U.S. Rousseau had suggested applying the principles to decision making in management. Rob made a note to read everything he could find on this topic because its value seemed to be so self-evident and consistent with everything he had been taught. There were also books being written on the subject, including one entitled *Becoming the Evidence-Based Manager* by Latham.[2] Rob was familiar with this book and fully subscribed to what it presented and to the message to managers to use evidence more.

More and more, Rob realized that he would be most comfortable with people that maintained a presence in both the academic and practitioner communities. And he also began to realize that much of the valuable research was being done by practitioners and by consulting organizations. Even though their results would never make it into an AOM journal, the value of what academics scorned as anecdotal evidence (based on people's opinions) was just too great in Rob's mind to reject. He was shocked to find out that writing a book or an article aimed at practitioners in some academic institutions might actually be viewed as a negative, rather than something credit would be given for in consideration for tenure. Rob accepted that a lot of the books that were published were filled with advice unsupported (or even contradicted) by research evidence, as were many of the articles in practitioner magazines. But he felt practitioners might be intelligent enough to decide what constituted evidence and what was just peddling magic cures for problems.

Rob attended a SIOP annual conference and went to an all-day session on evidence-based management, led by panels of academics, practitioners and consultants. He really bought into the concept of bridge-building between those who did the research and those who would benefit from knowing about it and applying it. He had played that role somewhat when functioning as a consultant but realized that rather than building a case based on research, he often advised *what to do* without providing the *why it should be done*. During his graduate studies, he had read an article by Sara Rynes that had become a classic[3]. She had administered a thirty-five-question True/False test to over 1,000 HR practitioners at all expertise levels on what the research on various HR-related topics had determined. For example:

> Only 18% correctly answered False to the statement: "On average, encouraging employees to participate in decision making is more effective for improving organizational performance than setting goals."

> Only 18% correctly answered False to the statement: "On average, conscientiousness is a better predictor of job performance than is intelligence."

> Only 35% correctly answered False to the statement: "Surveys that directly ask employees how important pay is to them are likely to overestimate pay's true importance in actual decisions."

The median correct score was 20 out of 35, which was pretty depressing. After all, guessing should enable one to score 17–18. Rob committed to ensuring that students and clients knew what research could tell us about the probable success of alternative HR strategies and programs so they would not make promises to management that were unlikely to be realized. He had known about one of the biggest misunderstandings prior to reading the article: that increased job satisfaction does not necessarily lead to increased productivity, but it did tend to improve unwanted turnover and absenteeism. By knowing this, practitioners would sell strategies based on realistic expectations. They could be confident that positive results would come out of increasing satisfaction but would not be promising something that may not result. So, building this bridge would enable practitioners to benefit from research, but how could these two communities be aligned? He volunteered to serve on a SIOP committee exploring this issue and hoped that ways could be found to influence researchers to research topics practitioners were interested in and to convince practitioners they needed to extend the effort to know what the literature contained.

As Rob listened to the presentations of some of the renowned researchers talk about their work, he became inspired but also realized this is not what appealed to him. He very much wanted to analyze research results and search for ways to apply it to practical problems. Yet he doubted that doing the original research would be his forte. "That might be a problem if I am in an academic position seeking tenure," he thought, "but do I really care? I believe so strongly that tenure is an obsolete concept that I really don't want to make that my objective in teaching." He did realize he would be swimming against the current if he wanted to make teaching his principal focus, since it was unlikely he could change the system and gain credit that would be equivalent to A journal publications. So, maybe he had better prepare himself for making both consulting and teaching his game, even though that might mean never ending up on the faculty of one of the very top schools. He also realized that there might be opportunities teaching for one of the professional associations that had certification and development programs.

While at the conference, Rob did make some new acquaintances that had the same interest in seeing evidence being used more in making decisions. "It is not that practitioners ignore all types of evidence when they grapple with issues," suggested Mushira, who Rob had been surprised to find in attendance. "They just too often try to mimic what has been successful in other organizations and different contexts without determining why they succeeded. Benchmarking is a useful tool, but in order to be certain that what worked somewhere else will work the same way here is to ensure the contexts are nearly identical . . . or to adjust for contextual differences. When specific strategies or methodologies take over the literature and get labeled best practices, the promoters forget to mention under what conditions they are good practices. Even good research studies that are internally valid often do not spell out the conditions under which the results are generalizable (externally valid). I just wish the zealots would splash some cold water on their faces and be more realistic about where these supposed best practices will turn out to be the best—and even where they might be the worst."

Rob agreed with Mushira's points, since he had seen "new" techniques take over the literature, just like the latest fashions sweep across the globe, for perhaps a season before they fade out. He had not seen an article about broadbanding or competency-based pay for some time and wondered why if they were in fact miracle drugs that would cure all ills for all organizations, which was pretty much how they were marketed a few years ago. Rob knew that the U.S. was viewed as "fad central" by practitioners in many parts of the world. One of his students from an Asian country had pointed out that another word for "new" was "unproven." And Rob had discussed some of the techniques that were currently hot with Bruce a while back, and Bruce pointed out that most of them had come on the scene in cycles, usually wearing different clothes, but the same in substance. Bruce noted that the practitioner magazines would go out of business if something had to really be new in order to be written about. But in order to get something published, it had to be made to look new or be sold as the answer to the challenges presented by current conditions.

Several of the people in the chat group defended the brick by brick research approach, even if it involved doing many studies which were individually focused on a very narrow hypothesis. They pointed out you needed a lot of bricklayers to make a cathedral, especially if you wanted it to stand up over time. Rob agreed with that but again realized his calling was not that of a bricklayer. Maybe he was lazy and perhaps he was trying to take a shortcut to fame. He hoped that was not the case and that he could serve the profession by working on that bridge that would transport research findings to the practitioners who could and should apply it.

When the chat group broke up, Rob and Mushira went to grab a quick lunch at the deli in the lobby of the hotel. It turned out that Mushira was still with the consulting firm and had found a slot for herself in the practice that applied IT solutions to administrative processes. "I really did not want to go through a job change and probably will be going home in a year or two," she confided. "The firm is in a bit of a mess now, but you can still continue to work in specific areas as long as the client work is sufficient to support you. I would much rather be in a human capital practice, since it is so much more stimulating and it typically has much more impact on workforce effectiveness. But how often in life do you get exactly what you want?" Rob got Mushira's contact information and they promised to stay in touch. Mushira had respected Howard and liked working under his direction, so she made it known that if her firm shook itself apart, she might be interested in doing contract work with Howard and Rob.

When getting back to his studies, he was pleased to find out that writing articles for practitioner publications was viewed positively by his school. The department chair and the dean both felt these application-oriented articles made a contribution to the field and that it was a positive for the school if faculty took the time to do it. Of course, it was assumed that the author recognized that A journal publications were the track to tenure and promotion and that they also needed to be a focus. But after discussing the possibility of exploring the idea of how to build a bridge between the research and practitioner communities, he was reminded that most journal editors could control their enthusiasm for attempting to reach out to practitioners through their journals. So, anything he worked on would most likely find its way into print in practitioner publications. Rob was alright with that, and since he would probably be consulting as a primary or certainly secondary source of income, articles in practitioner publications made good sense as a marketing tool. He wondered if he should publish under different names in the two worlds. But he did think it would be wise to approach Howard about co-authoring articles on topics that were relevant to practitioner needs.

Notes

1 Rousseau, D., *Academy of Management Review*, Vol. 31, No. 2 (2006).
2 Latham, G., *Becoming the Evidence-Based Manager*, 2009, SHRM/Davies-Black, Boston, MA.
3 "HR Professionals' Beliefs About Effective HR Practices," S. Rynes, A. Colbert and K. Brown, Human Resource Management, Summer, 2002.

12 Stepping into new roles

Annette had been working on the integration with the firm in Singapore but was called into the office of Kathy, the CEO. "I am asking you to take the job of VP of human resources," Kathy began. "We have had a bit of a problem with the leadership in that area conflicting with the executives leading the other functions, and I think you have the personal style that will allow these critical relationships to improve." Annette was now having a bit of conflict within herself. Should she ask what happened to her (ex) boss? Would she actually be a better fit in the job?

"I have the confidence that you have progressed professionally in a relatively short time and that you would find this to be a good career choice," Kathy continued, trying not to come off like a used car salesperson. "And I have discussed this with several of my staff, who share my belief that this is a good move." "Wow," thought Annette, life comes at you fast.

Cautiously, Annette began to question Kathy about the expectations and what kind of latitude she would have in building a staff. "Your show, you run it," was Kathy's response, cutting right to the chase. "OK, sign me up," said Annette, being a big fan of short responses when the stakes were high.

Annette knew a good bit about staffing and had been involved in employee relations and employee development a good bit. But she knew very little about performance and rewards management, at least the technical side, and she knew she would have to rely on their outside legal counsel to keep her alert to what she needed to do on keep the CEO out of jail. New laws seemed to pop up every day and there had been threats of litigation relating to employment and pay discrimination in the past that she knew little about. But she had Don as an unpaid advisor and she could get Rob pretty cheaply if she was clever.

While Annette was absorbing the changes she would be facing, Don had been knee-deep in compensation issues. He worried most about the benefits area, since he was not sure he had a lot of support for moving aggressively to reshape the utility's retirement programs. But they had to stop motivating employees to do exactly the opposite of what the organization needed. The list of retirement-eligible employees was frightening, since it included many of the people with the critical skills that were in short supply in the labor market and who were difficult to attract. He could always go to the board and emphasize the public relations peril they were in if ratepayers got up in arms about rate increases and decided to carefully examine the reasons for increasing costs. He promised himself to tread carefully, ensuring executive management was convinced as well, and to avoid looking like he was going around them and taking the issue straight to the board.

Meanwhile, the third member of the trio was dealing with the challenges of teaching. Since Don and Annette had shown interest in Rob's teaching, he invited the two of them to participate in one of his Saturday classes, which he planned to be a discussion of how organizational context impacted the appropriateness of any HR strategy. He planned to have the three of them talk about the experiences they had with their respective employers and to explore how various factors impacted strategy effectiveness. Although the Saturday gig would require some preparation, and both Don and Annette knew they would be facing long weeks, the date was a couple of weeks out and it sounded like fun. They accepted the invitation and set a date to meet and review what each of them had prepared on their respective organizations and the lessons learned by each of them.

Annette came to work on a Monday morning to find there was a raging battle over the perceived lack of fairness in the way one of the key managers dealt with her people. The manager had apparently agreed to give an employee every other Friday off to participate in a professional development program that ran on alternate Fridays and Saturdays for twelve weeks. It was agreed that the employee would work on Saturday when the class was on Friday that week. Although it seemed harmless enough and fair to the employee and the organization, the other employees in that unit were upset that it messed up their schedule for group sessions, which were held each Friday for the entire afternoon. The group sessions were to discuss what each of the staff had done that week on a major software development project and to integrate their efforts so the project could stay on schedule. This one instance started a discussion about managers making deals with employees that varied from defined policies. One of Annette's favorite books was written by Denise Rousseau, the prominent organizational psychologist, and dealt with this very issue.[1] The book was followed by an article she had read that provided a decision-making outline to guide managers when they considered variations from established policy. The guide was in the form of questions that could determine the appropriate course of action relative to requests for deals.

Decision-making guide

1 What is the policy? How clear is it? Is it accepted by other managers/ employees?
2 How much does the request vary from policy?
3 Does it fit the culture? What are the norms relative to consistency?
4 What has been done in the past that is similar or that varies from the policy?

5   Who else will know about the variation?
6   Is the variation controversial? Does it violate laws/regulations?
7   What is the likely reaction by co-workers? How would they vote if asked?
8   Can the employee be as productive and effective if the deal is made?
9   How common is the variation in other organizations?
10 How competitive is the labor market? What would the impact be if the person is lost?
11 How legitimate is the request? Is it a real need or just a preference?
12 Is this the first request by this employee or the next in a long line of requests?

Annette knew there was a need to communicate to managers just what a policy was: fixed rule, guideline or the starting point for negotiation. There was also a need to train managers to think through the implications of making different arrangements with individuals, particularly the impact on productivity and on the other employees. It was very easy for employees to believe there was favoritism driving decisions to vary from policy, particularly if the decision was made in stealth mode. On the other hand, if the manager were to involve HR initially to ensure the policy was fully understood and that the reasons for the policy were clear, the fallout from making the decision could be anticipated. There was also a need to communicate the reasons to the other employees. Rousseau had pointed out in her book that very often other employees would view flexibility positively, since it reflected a willingness to consider employee needs. Of course, there would be others who would find out about the deal and wonder what kind of deal they might be able to cut.

Annette thought the worst situations were those when there was a poor understanding of what policies are and/or why they exist. This often leads to management decisions that happen below HR's radar. And managers may know the policies but decide they are wrong, resulting in a quiet violation of the policy without an appropriate review of the implications. What is needed is a recognition by managers that the actions of any one of them can impact other managers throughout the organization, as well as employees, when they learn of the deals being made. And problems are further exacerbated when other employees are not told the "what" and the "why" of the decision and when they do not have any input into the decision.

Although the furor raging over this Monday morning incident would probably die down, Annette was worried about how policies should be viewed and applied. The deals that would have to be made with employees who went over to Singapore to work on the project would almost certainly present challenges. She had taken a course in global workforce management, and one of the things she learned was that cutting individual deals on individual travel would soon spin out of control as people compared their arrangements with others. If the decisions were made by different managers, the possibility of inconsistency was magnified exponentially. "Well," she thought, "this is another item to add to my list for immediate attention." She called the training manager and asked that he develop a training session on workforce policies, to include clarification of what the policies were, an explanation of why they were necessary, what process should be followed when considering a variance from policy and what managers should consider when formulating recommendations.

Don was having a busy Monday at the office as well. The naysayers were conjuring up disaster scenarios that would occur if all people did not get the same base pay increase. Some thought they should try to form a union, others were claiming that individual relationships would drive pay actions rather than actual performance, and others just did not want to deal with any change. It was true that some of the managers and supervisors still needed training and a lot of support if they were to appraise performance appropriately. The biggest challenge was getting them to tell poor performers what they had been doing for years was no longer acceptable and that there would be financial implications of not performing. Don remembered the words of Ed Lawler: "No matter what you do some people will hate it . . . just make sure those are the right people."

Don was good with poor performers resigning and with employees paid at the top of their pay range getting small or no increases. But was senior management prepared to stand up to the complaints that would certainly come from the weakest managers that they were being set up as the bad guys? There were also a few managers that complained they did not want to put their people in competition with each other, which Don had countered by pointing out they were being compared to performance standards and not to each other. But he recognized that years of weak management and a long history of managers being allowed to do their own thing was difficult to overcome. If he lost the unwavering support of executive management, the new performance and pay management system would fail and the wrong people would win, and he realized that this was an issue that might cause him to think about exiting the organization.

Rob's life seemed to be the simplest one among the three of them. He had his studies and his teaching but at the moment did not have to worry about internal politics, unreasonable employees and the rest of the stuff no one likes having in their laps. "You going to build yourself a hiding place in academia after you get your papers?" Don asked. "Actually, Howard just called me and he has talked with both of your CEOs and probably will be using me to do some consulting in your organizations," Rob responded, relishing the thought of being a sage advisor to these new HR executives. "I am between terms at school, both taking and teaching classes, so I have a lot of time to tell you about all the things you are doing wrong or are not doing at all." Actually, Rob did not like the role of preacher and was reluctant to assume he knew more than the people he consulted with. He found he sometimes was expected to know the solution to a problem and ran the risk of losing status if he honestly admitted he did not have a ready response. Teaching also had some of that pressure to be all-knowing, however, and he had promised himself he would find an appropriate balance between playing expert and joining others as an equal in addressing difficult issues. In some cultures, the manager is expected to know the answer to any question asked by a subordinate, even if it was something made up on the spot, but that made Rob totally uncomfortable.

He had done a seminar in Indonesia and found that none of the attendees would jump in with their ideas. Being the brilliant strategist, he began presenting outrageous premises to agitate them and get them to respond. But instead, they wrote down what he said! Given the unintended consequences of that failed strategy, he floundered around until finally figuring out the only way to engage the people was to get them debating each other. He had heard about deference to the "expert" up front but had severely underestimated the impact on the willingness of attendees to engage in a dialogue. In the U.S., you often could not shut the self-anointed experts up, but at least it made for engaged participation. Rob did realize that his school had programs in Eastern Europe, the Middle East and China and that he would have to review the research on cross-cultural differences if he were asked to teach in those locations.

Annette and Don had asked Rob what Howard was going to recommend for their organizations. There had been projects started on several fronts when Howard and Rob were with their prior employer, and they were not aware of what senior management was willing to proceed with. Rob promised to get back to them on that as soon as he had gone through the project plans with Howard. He asked if Don and Annette wanted to join him for dinner the next night. One of his students worked for a nonprofit organization out West that provided additional educational services for special needs children who needed more than their public school system could provide. She was commuting to finish her last course for her degree and Rob was very impressed with her. Of course, Don and Annette fantasized about a budding romance, so they could not resist poking their noses into Rob's private life. After all, he needed a little help realizing how empty his life was and believed they were ideal counselors. They "generously" accepted the invitation.

The next evening the foursome met at a restaurant that was part of the chic crowd repertoire. Sharon was a delightful person and connected with Don and Annette instantly, so much so that Rob was having a tough time getting a word in. Sharon surprised Rob by saying she was going overseas to work for a nonprofit in a developing country as soon as she completed his course and graduated. She asked if they knew of anyone who would be interested in working for the nonprofit she would be leaving. They were creating an executive director position and were seeking a person who could do fund-raising, administer the organization and maintain the culture of service. Rob wondered if Annette was biting her tongue. He was well aware that deep down she would rather be of service to people in need rather than strangers looking for a high return on their investments. Both Don and Annette promised to think about possible candidates, since they had been so impressed with the mission and the culture of Sharon's employer.

The following day, Don got a call from a recruiter who asked him if he would be interested in a senior management position at a professional association that served utilities. It was disclosed that the association was head-quartered in the same major western city as Sharon's nonprofit organization. "This is one of those Alfred Hitchcock or Twilight Zone moments," he realized. But the more he listened, the greater his interest. The job would be to manage the HR function for the association but also to create professional development services related to workforce management that would be offered to member utilities. "Now that would be interesting—and extremely challenging—given the lack of focus on people issues in the utilities I am familiar with," he thought. He promised he would give it some thought, and when he hung up, he called Annette. "Why don't you take that job at the nonprofit and I will take the job at the association," he proposed. "Why don't you stop drinking at lunch," she replied. But Don insisted it was not such a crazy idea, given the contiguous locations of the two organizations. And they both loved mountains and outdoor activities, which were limited in their current location. "Let's at least explore this," pleaded Don. Annette agreed, although reluctantly. Both of them avoided thinking about the fact that relocation would move them many miles from Rob.

That evening, they shared that they would pursue the two possibilities or at least get more complete information and see if they would be a good fit in the eyes of the leadership of the two organizations. Moving west would be an exciting change, although it would change a lot of their daily lives. Since they had not bought a home and since the rental market was tight, they figured there would be no great barrier to terminating their leases, as they both had with their prior residences. But at this stage of their careers, they would also have to consider their opportunities where they were. Since they both had received promotions very recently, they would be challenged for at least a few years in their current roles. On the other hand, they probably were both as high in their organizations as they were likely to go, since neither would be considered for the top job given their backgrounds. They both agreed that at least their lives were not dull.

Note

1 Rousseau, D., *I-Deals*, 2005, M. E. Sharpe, Armonk, NY.

13 New challenges in new roles

Don talked to the recruiter about the association job and Annette asked Sharon to put her in touch with the management of her employer, which she did. After details and resumes were exchanged, a strange thing happened. Don began to realize that the association job required more of the skills that Annette possessed. And Annette found out that the nonprofit had all the dedicated service providers they needed, but that they needed a combination of an administrator and fund-raiser, which were things that Don was better at. That evening they talked on the phone and decided they would each put the other in touch with the organization they had each been considering.

Interviews with the two organizations the next day went very well, and it looked as if Annette and Don were inclined to make the career changes. When they collaborated, they realized that early on that Don could help Annette determine what utilities needed and that Annette could help Don understand how the services provided by the nonprofit could benefit children. She had taken a number of courses on child psychology and pedagogy and had always been interested in how children learn and how they react to challenging situations. "I can be Don's unpaid consultant on the nature of the services provided," she thought, and that gave her a great deal of satisfaction. She knew she could not allocate enough of her time to fund-raising when she was so focused on the well-being of the kids. They called Rob and set up a meeting later that day.

When the three met the discussion centered around careers. They wondered if they had wasted some of their time in their graduate education, focusing on human resource management. But they reminded themselves that there was little recognition that every organization succeeded through its people. And what they had learned about managing people was valuable no matter what roles they eventually would play in the business world. They believed that associations and charitable organizations needed to be run like businesses just as for-profit private sector organizations must. Part of Don's frustration at the utility was that no one seemed to recognize that it needed to be managed in a business-like fashion, with accountability to the multiple constituencies. So, they satisfied themselves that they were in the HR business, although perhaps not assigned to the HR function.

And they began to accept that they had selected the right education to prepare them for what they would be doing. "The longer I think about what it means to be a human resources management practitioner, the stronger my belief that we have been and will continue to be in the field," offered Rob. "Whatever our roles, we find ourselves relying on people to get things done and realizing that not much can be accomplished without them. Doing a poor job of selecting people, developing them, defining and managing their performance and rewarding them reduces our chances of success. We all have heard the protests that calling employees 'human resources' diminishes and depersonalizes them, but I don't get that. They are resources that are critical to the functioning of organizations. Calling human resources 'intellectual capital' or 'talent' does not change anything. We could even go back to personnel management without changing anything significant. Maybe we should reconsider the use of the term 'asset' when we talk about the people, since the accountants have captured that term and the use of it implies we can book the value of employees. But asset has a much broader definition, and although some assets are intangible, they still are valuable resources for organizations."

Don suggested that Collins had it right when he pointed out that the nature of the leadership an organization relied on had a lot to do with the effectiveness of the organization.[1] "What we see too much of these days is the CEO who pretends to be the key to success, defining the mission, formulating the strategy and driving its execution, Alexander the Great single-handedly leading his followers to victory." Collins described the Level 5 leader who looked a lot different than that and made the case that this was the type of person who allowed everyone else to use their capabilities to make things happen. Annette supported that idea by pointing out that most of her role models for leadership did not nominate themselves as worthy of acclaim—the people who worked with them were the ones who did.

Rob had always wondered how so many shelves in bookstores could be filled with works purporting to provide the recipe for good leadership, even though the diversity of organizational contexts mandated that multiple leadership styles were appropriate, and the right style would be determined by what would fit a specific context at a given point in time. One of Annette's favorite tee shirt slogans was, "Hey, wait up . . . I am your leader," which had been used by a civic leadership program to get the point across that you were not always out front, having all the ideas and dictating all the solutions to problems. They all concurred that each of the many styles of leadership had a time and a place, the effectiveness of any style depending on how well it fit the context. And there was a difference between the type of leadership needed from a CEO, which often included line management that was directive in nature, and the type of leadership needed from a chief human resources officer (CHRO), which was more often thought of as leadership based on persuasion. They had all been in staff functions since their careers began and they fully appreciated that the HR function was much more about leadership than management, despite the human resource management title most often used for the function.

So, Rob would be doing research on what organizations can do to increase the viability and effectiveness of their workforce and teaching students the conceptual foundation of people management as well as transmitting the research lessons to them. Don would be running an organization that had both employees and volunteers delivering key services to those in need. And Annette would be creating professional development programs that would help organizations better manage their human resources. When they defined their roles this way, they realized they were still in HR and they were proud of it.

Rob explained his dislike for much of the best practices research that was prevalent in studies done by consulting firms, largely anecdotal and based on correlation rather than causation. He was well aware that just because very successful organizations used specific strategies more often than unsuccessful organizations, one could not conclude that using those strategies *caused* them to be successful. It was equally likely that being successful made strategies affordable (e.g., paying their employees more than prevailing market rates). He did not want to change the world but only make a small contribution to the knowledge pool relating to formulating effective HR strategies and programs. And he decided to offer a seminar at his school on the impact of organizational context on HR strategy, which he anticipated would bring together people working in a broader range of organizations. Although a dialogue with attendees would not produce empirical evidence that was quantifiable, Rob felt anecdotal information like this could lead to additional insights that would be useful in formulating appropriate HR strategies.

Annette had told Don about an article written by a friend of hers in a large health care organization. It was from the newsletter of the American Society of Directors of Volunteer Services,[2] and her friend had been given a copy of it by the retiring volunteer services director, who lamented that she had never really acted on the idea. The article suggested that although volunteers were not paid employees, they brought skills to the organization that were typically underutilized. For example, a skilled IT person might volunteer ten hours a week and be assigned to the information desk in the lobby as a greeter, since that was the slot that was available. And other volunteers who were not competent to do simple computer work were difficult to assign, since the slots they could fill were limited in number. The article suggested using the IT volunteer to run training courses for other volunteers that would teach them computer skills that would increase their value to the organization. This would make the IT person far more valuable and at the same time provide work that would leverage his skills and increase the satisfaction he derived from volunteering.

"Don, you should evaluate your volunteers early on to see if having them teach each other would make them a more valuable resource to your organization," Annette proposed. "Since I am the boss, I guess I can invest in training people who are technically not employees if it increases their capabilities," Don responded. "In the past, I had enough trouble getting adequate resources to train employees to do their jobs well. I am always suspicious of something that looks like a free lunch, but this may be. It will require a lot of thought and planning, but it will not require a cash outflow, which will keep the accountants off my back. I just realized my available human resources are not just employees and paid providers of professional services, and those volunteers need to be developed and the value of their contributions recognized and appreciated."

Annette began to realize that the strategy of developing volunteers would have a great deal of relevance in her new role as well. She would be identifying and recruiting successful people managers from the industry to develop and conduct the seminars she planned to offer to their members. Don could attest to the fact that many utilities underemphasize the impact of their workforce management practices. And yet, many of the most pressing challenges they faced were related to managing their people effectively. In fact, one of the top three issues, as identified in an industry research study, was dealing with a mature workforce that would have to be replaced in order for them to fulfill their missions. With a significant percentage of their employees eligible to retire currently, or in the next few years, these organizations were in danger of not having enough time to develop their people, so they could do what needed to be done. And it would be HR programs that would enable them to do workforce planning, succession analysis, effective recruiting and employee development in a manner that would address this critical issue. So, HR would have to rise in prominence in the industry, but Annette felt Don's association should be the primary source of expertise, as well as the vehicle for disseminating it, while HR provided guidance on people issues.

So, the trio had entered a new phase in their careers, focusing on developing people as well as disseminating sound human resource management practices. It was hard to believe that they could be paid well for doing something they loved to do and that they had been trained to do.

Notes

1 Collins, J., *Good to Great*, 2001, Harper Business, New York.
2 Greene, R. and Betz, P., "Managing Volunteer Human Resources Effectively," Volunteer Services Administration, May–June, 1993.

14 Learning the value of applied research

Rob had completed the required courses, and he had been working on his dissertation. He planned a trip to the annual Academy of Management conference, where most academic jobs were filled—and where many hearts of aspiring academics were broken. Since he would soon be ABD (all but dissertation), he was clear to look for an academic job. He wanted to stay local to be close to Howard and the prospect of consulting work, but he also realized consultants usually don't get any work in their home city and therefore spend more time in airline terminals and on planes than just about anywhere else.

One of the things he promised himself was that he would attempt to find a school that valued teaching and that he would not be influenced by the higher salaries paid by the research-oriented schools and those who sought the big names. He was planning to focus on teaching, with consulting being the secondary activity, at least for a few years. Yes, he would write, but it would be for practitioner journals. He really wanted someone to actually be able to do something with the ideas he put forth rather than impress fellow academics with his cognitive prowess. He certainly did value the high-quality research that was published in the academic journals, and he used the findings derived from those articles to further his own knowledge. But he fancied himself a bridge builder between the research and practitioner communities, and there was a need for publications that focused on bridging. And since he had little interest in tenure, he accepted that he might have to change employers every few years.

When he got to the conference, he marveled at the number of sessions he desperately wanted to attend at any given time. While reviewing the listing of open academic positions, he noted that there were a couple from schools that were on the west coast, one or two of which were biking distance from the ocean. He pondered the wisdom of locating near the ocean, since his two best friends had the mountains covered and they could crash in each other's place, alternating locations to fit the ski and beach seasons. "Pretty unprofessional," he thought, chastising himself for acting like a footloose 20-something. But he got over the guilt attack, and while talking to one of the ocean-accessible institutions, he hit it off with the interviewer. The school was just realizing the importance of having HR courses in its MBA curriculum and wanted to develop an MSHR within the next few years. That really got Rob's attention, and he agreed to visit the school in the near future. Howard would just have to build airfares into Rob's consulting assignments. And if the consulting assignments were not plentiful, he could always set up a grass shack on the beach and ride his bike to work. But he soon got over that silly fantasy.

When Rob returned from the conference, he conducted the seminar he had planned on the impact of context on HR strategy. The seminar was well attended, and even more importantly, the diversity of organizations represented was even greater than he could have expected. He started off by asking attendees to work in small groups to determine how similar their HR strategies were, and if they differed, in what way. They were then to figure out what it was that made strategies that were successful different across organizations.

One of the groups contained representatives from a health care organization, a banking/finance organization, a durable goods manufacturer and a retail organization. They had done an excellent job of explaining why they used different staffing, development, performance management, rewards management and employee relations strategies, and that the causes of the differences were due to contextual differences. One of the first factors they identified was how their respective organizations defined performance, what made them successful. Since the health care organization was the only not-for-profit organization, its definition of success differed from the two that were for-profit, but principally in the metrics they used to measure performance. Rob had already identified the likely impact of these differences in his dissertation draft that dealt with the three organizations he knew so well (the prior employers of the Three Musketeers). But all of the members of the group had put forth the nature of the work and the nature of the workforce as key considerations when developing an overall HR strategy, as well as the variety of occupations employed.

Of particular interest to Rob was how they explained the reasons behind their competitive postures relative to prevailing labor market pay rates. The manufacturing company representative pointed out that they paid much higher wages than surveys indicated to be the market averages for similar jobs and provided rich benefits as well. This company was very successful and was the world leader in food processing equipment. Rob had become sick of hearing how you could not manufacture in the U.S. anymore unless you paid very low wages and/or did not provide benefits, so this organization really intrigued him. Its HR executive explained to him that the company made equipment that was recognized as being of much higher quality and as being more durable than competitor products, and the premium prices it charged did not reduce sales, even in developing countries. One of the other members of the group had suggested that the manufacturer could be even more profitable if it paid lower wages and cut benefits, but the representative of the company confidently responded that the quality of the product would not be sustainable if they lowered workforce costs, so they would have to lower prices due to the lower quality.

Rob thought of Cascio's comparison of Walmart's Sam's Club and Costco.[1] The analysis pointed out that though the two organizations had similar characteristics, they had very different philosophies regarding human resource management. Costco paid considerably more than Sam's Club and made a larger percentage of their employees eligible for benefits than did Sam's Club. The Costco CEO justified spending more on employees to shareholders by demonstrating their lower turnover more than paid for the costs. Cascio's analysis had convinced Rob how important it is to ensure the HR strategy is appropriate for each organization. "So much for benchmarking based on surface similarities," he thought.

Another useful insight that came out of the group sessions during the seminar was that although an organization used a tool like merit pay throughout the organization, it might be administered differently for different types of employees. The retail organization representative had pointed out that although many of their employees had limited discretion in their jobs, others could have widely differing impacts on operating results. Rob had attended a SIOP program by John Boudreau, where he used an example from Disney World to illustrate two key points. One was that the impact of some employees was very different than that of others in the same job, based on performance differences. He used a diagram to show the performance–impact relationship (see Figure 14.1).

Boudreau had pointed out in a recent book that even though the Mickey character is "more important" than the park sweeper, there is a bigger difference in impact attributable to performance for sweepers. The Mickey character has a handler, and there is a detailed specification that controls how that character behaves. On the other hand, the sweepers act as the customer relations representatives in the park. They wander the assigned region, ensuring it is clean at all times. But they also observe patrons, and if someone seems

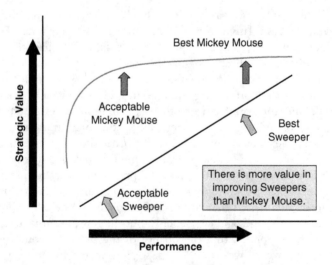

Figure 14.1 How much variation is possible?

lost or has to find a drink or facilities for a child, that sweeper is to shift gears and become the customer service representative. The difference between a poor incumbent and one that performs at a high level is therefore much larger than the difference between an adequate Mickey and an outstanding Mickey (a difference that is hard to produce, given the limited discretion). This principle can be generalized to other types of roles. The possible performance ratings for an employee following specific procedures with limited discretion might be "acceptable" and "unacceptable." The ratings for a software designer might number four or five, with significant differences generating a wide range of rewards.[2]

When the seminar ended, Rob decided he would build some of what had come out during the dialogue between people from different contexts into his courses when he began teaching and would where possible use some of the results as supporting anecdotal data in his dissertation.

Notes

1 Cascio, W. and Aguinis, H., *Applied Psychology in Human Resource Management*, 6th Ed, 2005, Pearson Prentice-Hall, Upper Saddle River, NJ.
2 Boudreau, J. and Ramstad, P., *Beyond HR*, 2007, Harvard Business Press, Boston, MA.

15 Recognizing that HR is everyone's job

Settling in at their new organizations, Annette and Don found they had a lot to learn. The psychology courses Don took did not seem to help him in convincing potential donors that the work they did was important enough to warrant their generosity. And the administrative stuff included becoming intimate with the financials, not something he had ever warmed to. There was not much traditional HR stuff to do, since there was a relatively small full-time staff and most of the people had been there a long time and seemed to do what they did competently. So, he buckled down and spent some evenings going back through the materials from his finance courses, as well as spending time at work with the CFO, figuring out what his responsibilities were in that area. He had asked Beth, the office manager, to start organizing programs that would build the skills of the volunteers, and she took to the task immediately, thinking it a brilliant strategy. "That was my HR contribution of the month," thought Don, rather sadly. And yet, in the back of his mind, he began to realize his job was mostly human resources management—not the HR in capital letters kind, but rather about creating a culture and a structure in a way that enabled people to discharge their designated responsibilities well and to contribute to the fulfilment of the organization's mission.

Don began to realize that he had to merchandise the organization better to potential donors if the needed financial support would be forthcoming. During a discussion with Rob, the branding project they had worked on together at the utility came up, and Don wondered if he could brand his organization with the desired effect. Rob suggested he call Sara and John, two acquaintances who were highly skilled at branding, to see if they could help him create an image that would have the organization stand out among the nonprofits competing for significant corporate and private foundation support. He brought them in, and they had a session with Don's key direct reports to define what was special about what the organization did. Sara and John had suggested they get testimonials from influential people about the value of what they did, including heads of the school systems they serviced and political leaders who had publicly supported organizations providing special services to those in need. "Well, here I go again, doing things that are not in my experience," he thought, but he experienced a great deal of satisfaction as the strategy began to bear fruit.

This working out of classification brought to mind common charges that "staff" people (such as HR practitioners) were not capable of handling complex "line" responsibilities. The finance folks had gained recognition as being critical to organizational success and it was about time HR got the same recognition—when they earned it.

Annette also found that her HR-related duties would not consume all or even most of her time. The staff was not that large, and, like Don, she found most incumbents had relatively long service and seemed to be competent in running their areas of responsibility. The problem with associations is that you have a few people in each of a large number of somewhat separate functions. They had a substantial technical publishing function, they ran conferences, they provided a wide range of services to members, they represented the industry in dealings with state and national government and they coordinated research on a wide range of topics of interest to utilities. No one function was very large, which meant that it was critical to have competent incumbents in each role. They hired more senior people, since they did not have the luxury of training people to do what they needed done, except for some of the support positions that did not require all fully-up-to-speed people.

Annette soon recognized that the culture was a major factor in determining how effective the association was. People needed to share all that they knew and to support peers. Knowledge management was a topic Rob had been interested in, and he had written a paper on the subject. His major message was that IT was a necessary but not sufficient prerequisite for effective dissemination of knowledge. Just because people *could* share their knowledge did not mean they *would* share that knowledge. Since in many organizations employees compete with each other for fixed-sum pay increases and incentive funds, there was often a disincentive to share one's best tricks with peers, even though it would increase organizational effectiveness. So, the culture would have a major influence on the degree to which valuable know-how was disseminated throughout the organization. And, as she, Don and Rob had all recognized, if no one was responsible for ensuring the culture was appropriate, it just happened, often to the detriment of the organization. She promised herself to add that to her job description.

She put out a call to the senior HR practitioners in member utilities to volunteer for an HR council, which would identify workforce issues and develop a strategy for helping practitioners in the field deal with them effectively. She was overwhelmed with the response. "Boy," she thought, "did I identify a need on the part of people to be involved and to contribute." The logistics of getting volunteers together represented a challenge, since utilities were spread out, with no concentration even in large metropolitan areas. And face-to-face meetings would probably be necessary, at least at the start. Another challenge, but since there was so much enthusiasm and a plethora of candidates, she felt she was onto something good.

Annette called Rob and asked him if he would be willing to do a seminar on current trends in HR for the members of the newly formed HR council, to kick off the professional development program for the association. Rob was enthusiastic about doing the seminar, and when it was over, he and Annette shared their surprise at how much knowledge had been generated and shared at the session. They had videotaped the session and decided to make it available on the association's website. The hope was that the program would stimulate utilities to recognize the need to continually assess the effectiveness of their workforce management strategies. It would also be likely to result in good attendance at the workshops on HR topics that were under development. Don had come over for lunch the day of the seminar and was so taken with the discussions that he spent the rest of the afternoon there. They had all three gone out for dinner after bidding farewell to the council members and unanimously proclaimed Annette's program a winner.

Rob had gotten a call from the school on the west coast to schedule a visit, and when he visited the west coast school, his decision to join its faculty was made on the spot. He would start teaching in the MBA program in the fall and he would also begin to help faculty members develop the MSHR degree program. One of the first things Rob wanted to do was to change the human resource management course required in the MBA program so that it focused more on the management of people and less on the technical characteristics of programs that practitioners in the HR function would have an interest in. Subjects like the role of the HR function in developing staffing and selection programs, designing performance appraisal and compensation systems and complying with employment laws and regulations belonged in courses that students pursuing the MSHR degree would find appropriate and useful. Since the MBAs took courses with titles like financial management, marketing management and operations management, perhaps the title of the required course related to HR should be workforce management. A subtle difference perhaps, but worthy of consideration since his informal sample of MBA students told him they agreed they needed to know about managing the workforce but had little use for HR stuff.

He decided to develop a white paper based on his dissertation and to use that paper as the basis for course instruction. He would use both his dissertation analysis and what he had learned by conducting the seminar for people from differing organizational contexts. He decided that there would be a paper required in the course, and in that paper students would be charged to: (1) define their own organization's current human resource management strategy, (2) evaluate the effectiveness of the strategy by citing examples of where it was effective and where it came up short and identify what factors are impacting effectiveness and (3) recommend changes to make the current strategy more effective and explain why they would improve its appropriateness and effectiveness. Since many of the students would work in a variety of organizations during their careers, Rob felt it was important for them to realize that how well strategies and programs fit the context within which they would have to function would largely determine whether they contributed to organizational success.

As the central theme of the white paper, Rob used the model he had borrowed from *Rewarding Performance*[1] and that he had used as the basis for his consulting assignments ever since. The model identified the factors that would impact the effectiveness of an HR strategy and provided a guide to defining an organization's context. He had used the model for each of the five organizations included in his dissertation and felt confident that it was an effective way for any manager to understand what made any HR strategy a good fit to the context. Rob told students to methodically define their own organization's/unit's context, using the elements of the model, and to comment on why alternative strategies would fit or not fit the organization/unit. This analysis would provide a basis for determining what changes would make the strategy more appropriate and effective. He also planned to turn the white paper into a guide for HR practitioners and to offer it to his professional association to use in their professional development programs.

The White Paper

Aligning HR Strategy with the Organizational Context

A human resource management strategy must contribute to producing the desired results at the individual, group and organization-wide levels. In order to accomplish this, executive management must ensure workforce viability and effectiveness by:

- defining, evaluating and shaping a culture that is appropriate;
- designing an organization structure and employee roles that fit the context;
- formulating staffing and development strategies that produce the workforce required;
- formulating performance and rewards management strategies that motivate that workforce to work towards organizational objectives;
- integrating all strategies and programs that impact workforce management in a manner that is fair, competitive and acceptable to employees.

Once an effective strategy has been formulated, a model can then be created to evaluate how well policies and programs support the strategy. The model must be used in a dynamic fashion. If any of the contextual characteristics change, the HR strategy should be reassessed. The degree to which the HR strategy is made specific will also depend on contextual characteristics. During stable periods, it may be well-defined. In times of uncertainty and/or rapid change, it may be in the form of a general direction, to be in sharp focus only when a direction is clear and new objectives are defined. This demands a dynamic strategy that is

(continued)

(continued)

administered by continuously assessing the environmental and internal realities and by reallocating resources in a manner that keeps the organization on its desired course. To ensure alignment with the context, several key characteristics of that context must be defined.

Vision/mission

The *vision* of an organization defines the organization's desired future; the desired end state it is focused on producing. The *mission* of the organization defines the role it intends to play in producing that end state. The vision statement serves as a "magnetic north" that can guide the organization. It can provide a purpose for its existence and define what it needs to accomplish in order to be successful. The mission statement defines the role of the organization in making the vision come true. How the mission is defined provides signals to potential employees as to what the organization deems to be of primary importance and enables candidates to determine whether what the organization does and what the benefits are to employees are a good fit to their needs and priorities. It should align the efforts of all employees.

Private sector organizations typically define their mission in terms of the products/services they deliver and the market segments they deliver them to. In some cases, they define their constituencies and the obligations they owe to each of them, although U.S. organizations tend to put shareholders/investors at the top of the priority list, sometimes to the exclusion of the others. Since they finance their activities primarily through the equity markets, they must ensure that every effort is made to keep the stock price at the highest level that is achievable.

Not-for-profit organizations also identify their products/services and their customers in their mission statements but typically identify a social good that their activities serve as well. Many of them rely on donors to support them, so it is necessary to ensure their mission is well understood and deemed to be worthy of investment. The mission must also be viewed by employees and potential employees as being consistent with their values and worthy of their best efforts.

Public sector organizations tend to focus on the segment of the public that they serve and their mission statements are most often focused on the services provided to that segment. Due to the nature of their services reliability and quality are most often emphasized, although cost effectiveness is a consideration, since the consumers of their services must deem their value to warrant the expense. As with the not-for-profit sector, the mission must be viewed by employees and potential employees as being consistent with their own values and worthy of their best efforts.

Culture

The *culture* of an organization defines how its members see the world. It is a function of their beliefs, values and priorities. Edgar Schein defined culture as how an organization resolves problems of external adaptation and internal integration.[2] A formal articulation of the desired organizational culture can help to align all constituencies.

It is important for each organization to define and evaluate its culture to determine if it is optimal, given its vision/mission and the realities it operates within, as well as the nature of the culture(s) of its workforce. The definition of the culture will help employees and potential employees determine whether the way things are done and the values that are emphasized will fit their values and their preferred way of working. The culture will impact the way employees are treated, how their contributions are measured and what types of rewards will be forthcoming.

Private sector organizations vary substantially in the types of culture they embrace. Some will value contributions by employees that are sustained over time, while others will focus on what people have done this year and the impact it has on current results. What they emphasize will have a profound impact on how they recruit and select new employees, how (and if) they invest in their development and how they define and reward performance. The culture will also largely determine the employee relations environment and the manner in which employees are expected to relate to each other and to management.

Not-for-profit organizations can also have widely varying cultures. There is typically a greater emphasis on providing services to a defined population than there is in private sector organizations. Employees may be expected to focus on satisfying the parties who provide the financial resources to the organization, much like the way for-profit organizations concern themselves with satisfying shareholders/investors. Providing a high return on investment is not measured in numeric ROI terms, but rather in terms of efficient use of resources and how well the eventual beneficiaries of the organization's efforts are served. The culture will impact the relative attractiveness of the organization as an employer and will typically appeal to a different type of person than would a for-profit organization.

Public sector organizations are in many ways similar to not-for-profits in that they provide services and are measured based on how efficiently they provide them. The usual public sector organization culture tends to emphasize longevity and loyalty more than private sector organizations and how performance is defined and rewarded often is different. This cultural characteristic tends to result in a larger portion of the total compensation received by public sector employees to delivered in the form of benefits, rather than in current income, and programs are often designed to encourage a stable workforce.

Environmental realities

The SWOT model addresses organizational realities by identifying internal strengths (S) and weaknesses (W), providing the guidance to ensure the strategy employed builds on strengths and minimizes the

(continued)

(continued)

impact of weaknesses. External opportunities (O) and threats (T) must be recognized and the organization's resources employed in a manner that exploits opportunities and minimizes the impact of threats. Organizations in the same industry will find their strengths and weaknesses will probably be unique to each of them, at least to some degree, since they represent internal realities. But they may share many opportunities and threats, which tend to be external realities.

The *environmental realities* faced by an organization at a given point in time should impact its strategy. The economic, market, social/political, legal and competitive conditions will play a major part in determining what constitutes a feasible approach to accomplishing organizational objectives. Failure to perform regular environmental scans and to consider the impact of the current realities on the organizational and human resources strategies can be a recipe for disaster. The environmental realities must be identified and their impact assessed. A summary of environmental forces identifies the critical realities faced by the organization and assesses their impact on both strategy and on how operations are conducted. It is important to ensure that how an organization defines, measures and rewards performance is reasonable when externalities are considered.

Private sector organizations must compete to survive. In order to attract the required financial resources, these entities need to: (1) be sufficiently profitable and provide an adequate cash flow, both current and long-term, (2) provide a competitive return on investment to those who provide funding and (3) be seen as viable over the long term. The degree to which private sector organizations are regulated by laws or governmental agencies varies widely, and these can have a significant impact on how they conduct business. The competition for people with the skills required for success is most often with other private sector organizations.

Not-for-profit organizations also compete, for resources and for people who can help them achieve their objectives. Very often their resources must come from parties who are impacted by economic conditions, making their willingness to contribute variable. Because of the variable revenue stream, these organizations must be careful not to incur fixed-cost liabilities that are affordable when times are good but a burden when they are not. Full-time staff members are virtually all fixed cost; payroll and benefit costs are more difficult to reduce than they are to increase. They also may be subject to strict regulation, through laws or agencies overseeing their work, an example being the health care industry. Whether these realities pressure these organizations to make greater use of volunteers, part-time workers, contractors or outsourcing will depend on the nature of the work being done and its criticality to fulfilling the mission.

Public sector organizations rely on taxes and levies to provide their resources, and these resources can be highly variable, controlled by legislatures, funding agencies and even citizen votes. In that respect, they are like not-for-profits, since they may have limited control over their funding levels. These organizations live in a fishbowl, and numerous constituencies make judgments about the appropriateness of their human resource strategies and programs. Even though the public does not want fires to rage out of control, it is difficult for them to understand that staffing levels must be set based on the probabilities of events occurring, rather than being based solely on efficiency and cost.

Organizational realities

The *organizational realities* existing at a given point in time will also have a critical impact on what the HR strategy can be, how it can be executed and what performance levels are achievable. The characteristics of the organization and its business(es) will be dynamic, as will the resources it has available. As organizations grow, it becomes increasingly critical to formulate policies and systems that will enable the growth to be controlled. The human capital requirements are particularly relevant to the human resource management strategy. It does little good to build a state-of-the-art microchip plant if the available workforce does not have the knowledge, skills and abilities to operate it effectively.

Private sector organizations must consider how and how well they are capitalized and how broadly they compete geographically. They should also identify their strengths and weaknesses and how they can achieve high levels of performance given these realities. A start-up organization will have different operational and financial needs and will require a different type of workforce than a mature organization. Small organizations will face different challenges than large organizations, and there will be differences in the contexts between complex, multidisciplinary businesses and single-product/service organizations. All of these internal realities will impact the type of workforce needed.

Not-for-profit organizations will face many of the same kinds of internal challenges as private sector organizations, as will *public sector organizations*.

Strategy

Once the vision and mission of the organization have been established, the culture defined and the environmental and organizational realities identified, the next step is to formulate a strategy that will enable the organization to achieve its objectives. Successful organizations concern themselves with both *comparative advantage* and *competitive advantage*. *Comparative advantage* is determined by evaluating what the organization is best at and where it should focus its resources (e.g., build high-quality products that customers will purchase, based on quality rather than on price versus be a low-cost provider of lesser quality products). In order to test the feasibility of a strategy, the core

(continued)

(continued)

capabilities required for successful execution of the strategy must be defined and the existing capabilities assessed. Many strategies are not implemented because organizations are not capable of doing what is needed, so it is critical to realistically assess the feasibility of adopting a strategy.

Once core capabilities have been identified, the next step is to decide how they will be deployed to produce a *competitive advantage*. One of the critical prerequisites for producing motivation and alignment in the workforce is a clear definition of what is needed and a clear understanding by each person/unit of how they must act to facilitate attainment of the organization's objectives. Many organizations seem to think a viable strategy is "to be better than everyone at everything." It is unlikely that all other organizations are so inept that such an approach is possible. This kind of strategy can cause resources to be applied in a dispersed fashion, often rendering the organization ineffective at everything. But it is also wise to be the best at something that matters.

Private sector organizations develop strategies for generating adequate profits and cash flow in the short-term and keeping their share price at acceptable levels if they are publicly traded. They also are concerned about market share and growth rates when assessing the appropriateness of their strategy. But the bottom line is satisfying investors that the organization is a good investment in the short and the long run. Treacy and Wiersema contend that organizations must compete in one of three ways: (1) operational excellence, (2) product leadership or (3) customer intimacy. Although they need to be acceptably proficient in all three, they must be a leader in one in order to gain competitive advantage. The strategy pursued will significantly impact the type of workforce required, the optimal culture and the best HR strategy. An operationally excellent organization focuses its employees on efficiency, reliability and low costs and rewards them for performing well on these measures. An organization that competes through product leadership will require innovation and will seek to employ those who are capable of creating new things. Product leadership organizations will often define performance using measures of innovation and will reward those who maintain its product leadership. Organizations striving to compete based on customer intimacy will seek people who are skilled in developing strong business relationships and will define performance in terms of customer retention, share of wallet and/or customer satisfaction.

Not-for-profit organizations will employ strategies that enable them to provide services to the targeted market segment in a manner that convinces investors that they are worthy of support. They will tend to employ people who are service oriented and who accept rewards that usually are based more on organizational than individual performance.

Public sector organizations are similar to not-for-profits, except that their strategy must be satisfactory to the public they serve and to the legislators or tax/ratepayers who provide their revenues. Many types of public sector entities must ensure they are prepared for uncertain demands and must therefore emphasize readiness and responding to peak demands rather than efficiency.

Structure

The *organizational structure* is directly related to strategy execution. The structure is the architecture of the organization and must be reflected in the human resource management strategy, since it defines the roles of functions/units and employees and also the relationships between the parts of the organization.

Structure is a major consideration in the development of the HR strategy, much as an architect's plans prescribe the type of materials needed and how they must come together in order for the entity to function appropriately. It should have a major impact on how the organization defines and measures performance.

Private sector organizations will create structures that enable them to effectively deliver products and services and to operate profitably. Structures must be malleable and responsive to changing demands placed on them by customers. Within a given organization, many different types of structures may exist, prompted by the differing nature of the staff functions and the operating units. Team structures may be used in functions such as R&D, while other functions may define and reward performance at the individual level.

Not-for-profit organizations tend to organize around the specific services provided or around customer segments. Team-based structures are often used and employee roles tend to be more fluid, with the primary job being defined as doing what is necessary to produce the desired results at the aggregate level.

Public sector organizations commonly use hierarchical structures. Since their mandate is to provide services reliably and because specific direction comes from the top of the hierarchy, this type of structure fits the context. The structure will appeal to some people and not to others, which means each organization must be clear about its structure and its culture if it is to get and keep the right kind of employee.

Human resource management strategy

The organizational context and the strategy utilized by the organization must be considered when defining human capital requirements. The human resource management strategy must be designed to produce a workforce that can execute the organization's strategy and do so effectively in the organization's context. The strategy must enable the organization to staff operations with the right kind of people, develop those people so they are able to do what is required, define and measure performance in an appropriate manner and reward individuals and units based on results

(continued)

(continued)

realized. Organizations define their HR strategy by describing the strategy in each of the functional areas while at the same time ensuring that the functional strategies are well aligned with each other.

The HR strategy helps to define an organization's value proposition. It becomes its "brand" as an employer. The HR strategy must define how people will be selected for employment, how they will be developed and how their performance will be defined, measured and rewarded. From the organization's perspective, the HR strategy must establish how its human capital will be deployed to support its strategy and to meet its objectives.

The integration of the components of an HR strategy can best be illustrated by an example. A mature organization with a long history of sustained success had maintained an HR strategy that was based on the following functional strategies, which were aligned with each other:

- *Staffing*: Fully qualified candidates were hired when the demand dictated.
- *Development*: Minimal investment was made in development; specific skill training was conducted when current needs dictated doing so.
- *Performance management*: Current results compared to established standards determined the performance rating.
- *Rewards management*: Pay levels were at or above market. Base pay rates and adjustments were directly tied to current performance. No equity or long-term programs were utilized.

The culture of the organization was one that supported treating employees as bundles of skills who were rented for the duration of the need for those skills. Security was viewed as an individual responsibility. This strategy worked until there was a spike in demand for the products provided by the organization and by its competitors. This led to a huge increase in the demand for critical skills, creating a shortage of supply. The organization was unable to fill orders. Leasing temporary help, using contractors, enticing people out of retirement, substituting capital equipment for labor and other initiatives moderated the shortage but at great cost. Once the year-long demand surge passed, the organization rethought the viability of its HR strategy into the future. A new HR strategy was formulated that contained the following components:

- *Staffing*: People with the innate ability to grow were recruited into entry-level roles.
- *Development*: The investment in training and developmental assignments was increased, accompanied by a commitment to continuously develop people. Workforce planning was initiated so that future needs could be forecasted and met.
- *Performance management*: The singular focus on current results was moderated by an increased focus on employee competence, with

more emphasis on breadth of capabilities. Development plans were linked to performance appraisals.

* *Rewards management*: The competitive pay posture was modified to position base pay levels at prevailing market levels and to provide incentives that delivered above market direct compensation levels if organization and individual performance warranted it. Base pay rates were tied to skill acquisition for some jobs. Long-term incentives were used for management and cash profit sharing plans for everyone.

The new culture viewed employees as valuable assets that warranted investment. By investing in people, the objective was to promote retention, so the organization could not be held hostage by ups and downs in the external environment.

This organization moved from one HR strategy that had a long history of success to one that would produce better results in the changing environment. Both were internally integrated, and rather than changing one thing (such as pay) to respond to a need, the organization rethought all parts of the strategy to ensure that they would not work against each other. The ultimate folly is to change the parts independently—the result could be hiring for A, developing for B, defining performance as C, rewarding D, all the while hoping for E.

Aligning HR strategies across the organization

Increasingly, large organizations are composed of a number of businesses, which they may desire to manage as separate entities. For example, when an organization acquiring another in similar lines of business, but with a customer base that is loyal to the acquired organization's "brand," the acquiring organization may leave management in place and let that business set its own direction. Conversely, if the acquisition is aimed at merging the two organizations in order to gain economies of scale, integration and homogenization may be the order of the day.

Very diverse organizations may continue to operate their different businesses separately. But management may wish to formulate and administer a single overarching human resource management strategy, at least for management and professional personnel. There may be a belief that people who are moved across businesses gain a broader perspective and that those who succeed wherever they are moved are the leading candidates for progression into executive management. This approach can raise issues of internal continuity within the businesses and in some cases make it very difficult to design and operate performance and rewards management programs that are a good fit to local contexts.

Mergers and acquisitions present very large challenges relative to HR strategies. It is important to define the contexts existing in each of the merged organizations and to select one of three approaches: (1) one of the HR

(continued)

(continued)

strategies can be selected as the new common strategy, (2) the HR strategies can continue to be different from each other or (3) a new HR strategy can be formulated, adopting the best features of the pre-combination strategies. Perhaps the most difficult challenge with any of these is dealing with cultural differences.

An example of difficulties that can arise is an insurance company that acquired another insurance company. The combination was a dream from a business perspective, at least on paper. The customer bases and the product lines were both complementary and synergistic. It was obvious to decision makers that the merged organization would be a much stronger entity on both the customer and product dimensions. However, culture was considered only after the decision had been made. The acquiring entity was staffed at relatively lean levels, had competitive base pay levels and aggressive incentive programs and had a very "what have you done for us lately" attitude relative to performance. The acquired entity was an overstaffed, happy family organization, with pay levels that were substantially below market and with performance being defined as staying with the organization for another year. The contrast could not have been more challenging if someone had deliberately chosen opposites. An appropriate and effective HR strategy was the key to a successful combination, and it took 3 years for the transition to the new strategy. Some people left voluntarily and some involuntarily, but the organization survived the transition because they laid out the culture, strategy and structure they wanted going into the future and formulated an HR strategy to fit that context.

The bottom line

"What works is what fits" is the guiding principle relative to formulating and executing a human resource management strategy. The fit to the overall organizational context and to the parts of the organization should be the primary consideration when selecting a strategy. Emulating strategies used by successful and/or admired organizations should be done only after careful analysis of the contexts within which the organizations operate. One organization's success can be another's disaster due to contextual differences. And once implemented, the HR strategy should be continuously evaluated to determine if it should be modified to stay aligned with the current context. How effectively an organization builds a viable workforce and sustains its viability will significantly impact its ability to succeed.

Notes

1 Greene, R., *Rewarding Performance: Guiding Principles; Custom Strategies*, 2010, Routledge, New York.
2 Schein, E., *Organizational Culture and Leadership*, 1985, Jossey-Bass, San Francisco.

16 The five-year reunion

Annette, Don and Rob were satisfied with their professional lives. They every so often joked that Don and Annette should attend some of Rob's HR classes so they did not become disconnected from their HR roots. But they had come to realize that most of what they did was related to and guided by what they had learned through their formal education.

A latecomer to their group, Kathy had been an academic since completing her formal education and had become a sort of fourth Musketeer. She had become convinced that researching topics dealing with people and workforce management was her calling. Kathy initially had felt like an outside observer when the three HR specialists collaborated. But given her training in organizational behavior, she was sympathetic with the notion that HR was as critical as any function within organizations and had become an avid student of the discipline. Because of her curiosity about their experiences in graduate school, she accepted an invitation to attend the five-year reunion the others would attend.

When the four of them arrived at the reunion, a group had formed and someone kicked off the dialogue with a question. "What is the most important principle relating to effective workforce management you have recognized," Mushira asked Annette. "Easy, what works is what fits," jumped out of Annette's mouth before she realized that was her answer. She elaborated, "When I changed organizations, I found that effective workforce management required changes to strategies and programs; no one strategy seemed to work in all contexts. And when Rob, Don and I compared notes we found the same enormous impact of context on the effectiveness of any approach." "Well, I guess that is some sort of universal principle because I would have to say that is what I discovered as well," responded Mushira. "When you are in consulting, you have to recognize that being an expert with a methodology does not justify you treating everything as if it were something that methodology can address. We built a knowledge database in our firm, and we often found that querying it produced conflicting answers for different organizations. Our colleagues had used different tools for each organization, even though on the surface they were the same type of organization, based on industry and customer characteristics. And we came to realize the enormous impact organizational culture had on the success of any strategy."

A few of the classmates had kidded Rob, Annette and Don about not being able to get a real job and about going into HR as a last resort. The fact that all three of them could easily shrug off such comments told them that they had become confident they had made the right choice. Several of their classmates did admit that their most intractable problems involved "soft stuff" issues and that their avoidance of courses in human resource management and behavioral science had left them a bit short on concepts for dealing with people issues.

Erin, one of their classmates, had risen to the top production job in the Asian region, with numerous plants in several countries. He was forthcoming in relating his new-found appreciation for the global workforce management course he had been required to take as a part of the MBA program. "Glad they added that," he admitted, "or I would not have been exposed to cross-cultural management issues and would have shot myself in the foot a lot more times than I did." He related how the application of Trompenaar's three "Rs"[1] had saved him many times. By *recognizing* issues when they were present, *respecting* the right of others to hold different beliefs and *reconciling* the issues different belief structures created, he had been made much more sensitive to treating people as they would like to be treated, not as he would like to be treated.

"I now believe the golden rule only holds within a single culture. The global platinum rule is to treat people the way they would like to be treated, since what you would prefer may be irrelevant. And I am a much better people manager as a result of recognizing that." Kathy had just taught a course on cross-cultural management and was gratified that more of the managers she was encountering were beginning to appreciate the value of cross-cultural research and that they were attempting to apply it.

Don provided another perspective. "I learned while working in a public utility that many of the problems faced during an economic downturn are addressed without giving enough thought to the long-term implications of the strategies an organization pursues. In the case of the utility, they continued enhancing the benefits package during good times, only to find they had created expectations that benefits could only be improved. When combined with automatic step rate progressions of base pay rates, the fixed cost of the workforce became overly inflated, and when there was pressure to reduce costs, the only thing that seemed plausible was a headcount reduction. Across the country, governmental entities have built up enormous and unsustainable liabilities, and they are being forced to do things that will negatively impact service levels and employee morale. The bottom line is don't do anything in the short term you will not want to continue into the future."

All present agreed that most organizations, public or private sector, attempted to deal with economic upturns and downturns as if they would persist forever, which of course they knew was delusional. "Thanks for cheering us up, Don— but we are at a party," responded Mushira.

As the evening progressed Rob, Annette and Don mingled with people they had barely known in their classes. While in school, they had come in to their evening classes stressed from work and had hunkered down, trying to digest the hurried consumption of a delectable product from the vending machines. Kathy, one of Don's close friends, bemoaned the fact that she often viewed class discussion as a contest, which caused her to behave competitively. She had believed that withholding your best answer until offering it would gain both attention and credit and that this was the winning strategy. But this caused everyone to focus on what they were going to say next, rather than listening to others from whom they might actually learn something. "When I bemoan that behavior, I recognize that the same behavior recurs in many of the meetings I go to now," she admitted. Don suggested that most of them were guilty of that at least some of the time, if they were completely honest. The reality is that in many organizations interactions are competitive and career advancement is like a tournament, leading to these dysfunctional tendencies. Annette had read the book *Dialogue*[2] and said she had really tried to incorporate some of the concepts into her own interactions. "Yes, but you have always been good at interaction," interjected Rob, "that is the advantage of being a female."

Despite their friendship, Annette almost pointed out how stupid and sexist that comment was, but she tried to apply the principles of interpersonal relations she had studied and instead suggested everyone could learn how to engage in effective dialogue. "Very little of the capacity to engage in dialogue is genetic," she said, "although sometimes the roles males and females play in their early years predispose males to be more competitive. We all need to learn how to use dialogue by understanding the theory underlying it and practicing it until it becomes habitual. But many believe that being open will put one at a disadvantage relative to aggressive competitors." Don decided that what he needed was another glass of good wine, which would make a lot of this seem less threatening.

Kathy had noted Annette's mention of the book *Dialogue,* and she said that there was a fascinating insight she had found in the book but was not sure it was valid. The author suggested that there are three different forms of language people use: (1) action oriented, (2) affect (feeling) oriented and (3) meaning oriented. It was suggested that sometimes HR practitioners had a difficult time communicating with line managers because they typically spoke from an affect-oriented perspective, while the line managers tended to use action-oriented language. This often led to HR people believing line managers were singularly focused on results without any regard for people, while the line managers thought the HR people just did not get it from a business perspective. "Is this valid?" Kathy asked Annette. "I am going to have to think about that for a good while," Annette responded, "but my first reaction is to believe there is some truth to it—crossed communications often occur and I do not fully understand the cause of these frequent disconnects."

A group joined their discussion, and a number of the people snidely suggested that with the advent of the internet, they had begun to suspect that actually meeting face to face was illegal. They had been going around the circle one by one, talking about what was on their minds and what concerned them. The internet issue was brought up by Rob. "I saw the movie *Up in the Air* and was really shaken by the subject matter. I had studied research on downsizing[3] that demonstrated how often it failed as a strategy. So, when the movie started, I thought to myself that any organization who brought in outsiders to fire their people were lower on the intelligence ladder than those who used downsizing as a first response to drops in revenue and who used it often. But when the fire-for-hire organization experimented with performing the firings over the internet, I thought this must be a joke. The possibility that any organization could value its employees so little and could treat them as if they were not worthy of human contact at such a perilous time in their lives really overwhelmed me and I began to think about the overuse of the internet."

"So how about the organizations who decide to outsource human resource management to an outside provider?" interjected Alicia, a marketing specialist. "I am not an HR specialist, but I think I know a bit about strategy formulation and implementation. And to turn your strategy for building and sustaining workforce viability over to a contractor who will never know enough about you to do it well is just plain ridiculous. Sure, turn over transactional work, such as payroll and benefits claims processing, and use service centers for routinized processes, but get out of the workforce management business? What do the managers do, manage the internet, rather than the people?"

"Sounds like you are not all that enthusiastic about that concept," replied Don. Kathy chimed in and suggested that behavioral research was still in the formative stage on the topic but that there was evidence that interpersonal transactions that were solely electronic, and often asynchronous and at a distance, were impeded by a lack of familiarity and trust between the people who were communicating. "That is not to toss aside the huge benefits of using IT tools," she said, "but I doubt hiring people or firing people would ever be successful if done over an electronic connection between two machines."

Nina and Eddie, two classmates who had been international students, jumped in to offer a contrasting opinion. Nina, who was from Mumbai, and Eddie who was from Hong Kong, believed the potential of electronic communication was being sold short. Nina began. "We have each formed software firms in our respective countries that provide interactive tools we believe overcome some of the challenges you have pointed out when attempting to build cohesive and effective global teams. In each of our countries, we face the challenges of having people who are not co-located work together on a continuous basis. Eddie's staff is split between Dalian, Beijing, Shanghai and Chongqing—there are some real distances to cross there. And my staff is in Bangalore, Mumbai, Delhi and Kolkhata. Those distances are also very great, and sometimes travel is so difficult people are willing to go to great lengths to avoid it by working together electronically." Eddie nodded and pointed out that the cultures in both countries were much more collectivist than the U.S. was, making the lack of face-to-face contact even more challenging. Rob and Don exchanged cards with them and promised to stay in touch so the discussion could continue. Rob was particularly interested, since his global workforce management course dealt with cross-cultural team effectiveness.

After a few hours of dialogue, the bartenders got bored due to the lack of business and closed up, but the chat group had found another stimulant: talking about how organizations must recognize that a competent and committed workforce is the only sustainable competitive advantage an organization has.

"For a bunch of general management geeks, you all are starting to sound like HR people, or at least managers who have an understanding of which assets are really important and in need of effective management," said Rob, more or less closing the evening. "We HR types are going to leave here very encouraged." "Yeah," responded Aaron, who was running a start-up business, "but don't forget that the required money, technology and infrastructure have to be there so people have something to do." The evening ended with good feelings and a sense of accomplishment.

Notes

1 Trompenaars, F. and Hamden-Turner, C., *Managing People Across Cultures*, 2004, Capstone, Chichester, UK.
2 Isaacs, W., *Dialogue*, 1999, Currency Doubleday, New York.
3 Cascio, W., *Responsible Restructuring*, 2002, Berrett-Koehler, San Francisco.

17 Want to trade jobs?

Don and Annette both had second thoughts about how well suited they were to be leading their respective organizations presently. Don had joined the non-profit as the CEO and Annette had taken the job of executive director of an association serving utilities. Ironically, they had both been the leading candidates for the job the other had taken, but at the time, they were a better fit to their current organizations. Rob had assumed that Don would take the association job, given his background with a utility. And he knew Annette had always wanted to help children and assumed she would be a natural for the non-profit. But he had realized that their decisions were sound, given the needs of the two organizations.

"I remember vividly reviewing the work on contingent leadership that suggests no one style will fit every organization at all times; what works is what fits the current context," Annette said with a real intensity in her voice. "And both Don and I were right for the roles we have when we took them." Don nodded affirmatively and his serious expression tipped Rob and Kathy off that they were both having real struggles. Don responded by pointing out that he was right for the non-profit when he assumed his current leadership role. It had been run in a chaotic fashion, which had left it in dire financial straits. "Too many folks were joining the organization because they believed so deeply in its work and focusing on providing the maximum amount of benefit to the children serviced, without concerning themselves with the financial implications. And they raised money from a large number of believers, which resulted in inadequate funding because the individual contributions were small. I have refocused the fund-raising on corporate sponsorship and foundations and have restructured our decision making so that it is more business-like. But now that we are fully funded, we need someone in the top job who is a champion of the cause and who can lead in a manner that increases the base of people committed to what we do."

"The more I think about it, the more I think that is someone like me," responded Annette. "And our association now needs someone with more of a focus on formulating a strategy that will work going forward and on effective management." Don responded, "Yes, someone like me."

"Simple—why don't you just switch jobs?" interjected Kathy. The silence was prolonged. Both Don and Annette realized that the leadership needs of their organizations had changed while they had not, causing a misalignment. "Well, maybe it is time for us both to step out of our roles, but I don't know about just switching jobs," responded Annette. "Do either or both of you have a logical internal successor?" asked Rob. They both responded "no" at the same time. Don admitted that he had been so focused on restructuring and on putting in more effective management systems that he had not given much thought to who would carry the torch next. And Annette sadly said, "I have really been derelict in getting some help on succession planning, since it is not something I have a lot of knowledge about. And there was no one who was fully qualified to do the tough stuff, so I did it." Rob was careful not to make his observation an indictment but offered, "There rarely is, that is why development is so hard. You have to trust people to take on stuff when there is a risk they will not do it as well as you do. Delegation is hard, particularly for perfectionists like you and Don. But if you are serious about the big switch, you owe your current organizations and their boards a smooth transition, and the first thing you would both need to do is to ensure that if you leave, there is someone in place who can run things effectively."

After the dinner powwow was over, Don and Annette were silent on the way home. But when they did get home, they looked at each other and said, "Do you want to trade jobs?" They agreed that this was an idea new to them both, so they agreed to put off any decisions until they had spent some time back at work assessing the needs of their respective organizations and whether they had both the competencies and the desire that an ideal leader would have going forward.

When Annette returned to work the next day, she began to assess her direct reports, searching for a replacement, or even for someone who could do the things well that she felt she needed to improve on. But all she came up with were specialists in their own areas with no understanding of the big picture. "Well," she said, "I got what I wanted, people who could effectively manage segments of the organization. But as a result, there is no one but me able to bring it all together." She realized the need to formulate an integrated strategy that would result in a more businesslike and financially responsible organization. But this was not something she was especially gifted at. And once she stopped kicking herself for ignoring leadership development and succession planning, despite what her graduate training had told her about its importance, she resolved to ask Don if he really would be interested in taking the job. Whether or not she would fit the role in Don's organization, she felt a sense of urgency to move on.

Don was also concerned about his fit to his current role. He was great doing pitches to corporate and foundation CEOs to open their wallets so his organization could do all the good work it was capable of. But now he needed someone with the passion and the understanding necessary to mobilize dedicated employees and volunteers to refine their services and the manner in which they are delivered. Annette certainly has the passion, he thought, and she also has a way of aligning people with things close to her heart.

He also recognized that she understood the children they serviced much better than he did and that the organization needed someone who was competent in doing that. He also knew that he could do much of what Annette's association needed urgently and resolved that he would reopen the job swap possibility on a positive note.

It took five minutes for them to mutually decide to approach their organizations. And they agreed the sooner, the better.

Both boards were receptive to the proposal presented by their respective CEOs. In fact, several board members recognized that they had sensed the need for a different leadership style but had been reluctant to suggest to their CEOs to either do some high-speed development of potential successors or to get some training that would enable them to change direction. In the association board meeting, a number of the directors agreed that the boards of their own organizations were guilty of the same apprehension about attempting to redirect the leadership. Their board members were after all volunteers who had a full plate with their day jobs, and they recognized that if their pressure created a vacancy, the challenge of replacing the top person would fall into their laps. Since they were unpaid volunteers, taking on a difficult search was not an attractive prospect. Don's board had been similarly reluctant to suggest a change in style, if not direction, but they were not skilled in management and were there because their networks were instrumental in providing access to people who could fund the organization. Both boards lacked the pressure that typically exists on boards of for-profit private sector organizations. As a result, things like long-term succession planning and leadership development were often not an urgent concern.

Don and Annette both requested that Rob provide consulting assistance during the role switch to ensure their organizations did not suffer. Rob immediately contacted Howard, who he had worked for at the consulting firm he joined out of school, to see if he would look over his shoulder. "This is really tricky," he thought, since both boards knew the CEOs were close long-term friends of his. And Howard had a touch of grey hair and the manner of a wise counselor. Rob also felt good about tossing some business to Howard, who had been the source of most of his consulting work since he began his academic career.

When Rob and Howard met with the two boards, they suggested that when the change in personnel occurred, a clear understanding about succession planning should be mutually agreed to. Although the consultants did not share with the board members their belief that both Annette and Don would probably move on within three to five years, they felt it was a professional imperative that they aggressively push for succession planning programs. Both boards were receptive, and both Don and Annette had prepared written plans for identifying potential replacements and for investing in human resource development. They realized it was important to ensure that when people changed roles, they had their successors in place to minimize disruption. Don had thought about this issue a great deal, driven by his own sense of guilt about not having protected his organization against turmoil that might occur if for any reason he were to depart. He vowed to start his new role with a replacement planning orientation, then broadening it to succession planning, which was more long-term in nature and included a wider range of jobs. "We will never be able to have the bench strength of a GE," he acknowledged to himself, "but we certainly should be planning for inevitable surprises when it comes to our people."

When Don and Annette met with Howard and Rob, they also discussed workforce planning. They all recognized that the dynamic environment would inevitably cause organizations to change direction in order to remain effective. And they agreed that human resource development should not default to a "40 hours of training for everyone" simplistic strategy. This meant that they must continuously update their definitions of possible future scenarios and to ensure that they must invest in programs that would build and sustain the viability of the workforce. Annette had done an assessment of the workforce demographics in the utility industry and found the vast majority of their members were inadequately prepared for an almost certain large wave of retirements in the next few years. Don, Rob and Howard had used a workforce planning model to assess the needs of the utility Don was employed by several years ago. Don and Annette agreed to immediately add it into their management routines to ensure that they would pay an appropriate amount of attention to workforce viability when they assumed their new roles.

"We have gone from fighting talent wars to facing talent surpluses in the roller coaster environment of the last few decades," observed Howard. "But much of that is a short-sighted reaction to temporary fluctuations in the supply and demand of critical skills in the labor market. And a short-term perspective can lead to the use of quick fixes, which in the end tend to exacerbate the problems associated with balancing supply and demand." "So, I should have done replacement planning, succession planning and workforce planning, and did not even get to first base by identifying a successor," bemoaned Don.

"When your house is not on fire, it is hard to think about fire prevention and fire insurance," responded Rob, hoping to console Don without exonerating him of all guilt. "When your sole focus was on HR in the utility, you were much more aware of the need to do this sort of planning—your professional journals dealt with it constantly and someone at every professional conference reminded you of it. Then you took over an organization with a fund-raising need and shaky financial systems, so you had other things occupying your attention. But I did remember you nodding off a lot in our staffing and development course in school." "The class was held the first thing in the morning, when I was not at my best," retorted Don.

The first month after the job switch, Annette and Don seemed to be spending all of their evenings acting as consultants to each other. But as time passed, they realized the other person needed less detail about what was what in their organization, and as a result should spend the available energy deciding on what should be in the future. The one thing they mutually agreed to is that they had perhaps let human resource management issues slide too far down in their respective priority lists and that they needed to renew their commitment to the principle that their workforces were the single most important assets they had. After all, they had invested a great deal of effort in learning the principles of sound human resource management in graduate school and their prior jobs. They also knew that HR strategies and programs cannot be put on automatic pilot; they needed to be attended to continuously. "I wonder what CEOs who have come up through HR have done in the past?" Annette asked of Don. "I think the sample is too small to come to a robust research conclusion," quipped Don, regretting that this was probably truer than it should have been.

Rob and Howard had found their consulting on the job switch project to be both stimulating and rewarding. They decided to jointly write an article on the topic, thinking it to be of interest to a wide range of organizations.

18 Educating students and practitioners

Rob had assumed full responsibility for the MSHR degree program at his school and was a member of a task force looking at course requirements for undergraduate students majoring in economics or business. Kathy had also joined the task force, along with Eric, who was an HRIS (human resource information system) guru. Eric had heard about the movie *Up in the Air* and almost removed the upholstery from the arms of the chair he was sitting in when he viewed it. "Boy, I hope that firing via the internet thing was intended to be a joke," he blurted out when the topic came up in one of the task force meetings. "I cannot even imagine removing human contact from many situations involving people, particularly when there is a lot at stake both financially and emotionally. You certainly can set up a service center to allow employees to enroll in benefits programs, make changes and file claims—that's just making algorithmic transactions more efficient. But to tell someone they are viewed as inadequate or unnecessary?"

Since Rob and Kathy felt they had been the reason Eric saw the movie, they felt it was their responsibility to ensure it did not endanger his cardiac well-being. "The two of us were appalled that organizations did not have the courage to personally let people go and defaulted to bringing in hired guns," said Kathy. "Outsourcing routine transactions is fine, but interpersonal dealings should be just that—interpersonal, which means face to face." "And robotic HRM is not going to happen if we have anything to do with it," added Rob. "So, Eric, what do our students need to know about human resource information systems and how they can make HRM more effective, as well as more efficient?" Rob felt he was a Jedi Master at redirecting conversations to reduce the stress level of participants. Eric saw through it but was kind enough to pretend otherwise.

"First and foremost, they have to embrace evidence-based management, which means you define everything you should know before making a decision and then figure out how to accumulate relevant evidence and how to analyze it," Eric began. "Then you determine whether the decision can be made using a formula or known set of criteria and standards. If judgment must play a role, you have to supplement data with professional knowledge." "An example of an evidence-based decision?" requested Rob. "Sure, filing a benefits claim.

Does the person meet the eligibility requirements for coverage? Is the situation covered and to what extent? And is the filing accompanied by appropriate documentation?" "But does that not require judgment on the part of the person processing the claim?" asked Kathy. "Yes," responded Eric, "but there are decision rules that are supposed to be adhered to consistently, so it is not a subjective judgment that has to be made."

"What is an example of a transaction that does not lend itself to being made a routine using technology?" asked Rob, making notes about what he should include in his HRD class. "Appraising someone's performance," responded Eric. "When I see some of this software being offered to managers, I cringe. You just check the box that indicates the rating and the software provides commentary, plugging the person's name into the text. What message is sent to the employee when the manager cannot even be troubled to cite job-related results and behaviors that support the rating? The employees are bound to catch on to this ruse and are going to decide just how important their performance is to their manager—and even how important they are to the organization." "Yes," said Rob with a smile, "but it sure cuts down on grammatical errors and minimizes the time managers have to spend on these HR requirements that are designed to waste their valuable time." "I'll just ignore that," replied Eric.

Kathy changed the tone of the conversation by suggesting that they sort out what needs to be done, by who and in what manner: the who, what, when, where and why set of questions. "Well," offered Eric, "I am somewhat biased toward the use of systems, since that is my area of specialization, but I certainly know you don't use technology when it is clear that actions are based on subjective judgments and when there is human emotion that will certainly be involved. Some companies like Cisco have very sophisticated computerized stage-gate systems for soliciting candidates for employment and for sorting them down to the most qualified ones. But they then interject the appropriate people in the process and use interviews to really make the critical hiring decisions. Some organizations use panels of potential peers to screen candidates, such as Southwest Airlines, which is intended to find out if current employees feel that the person is going to be a good fit and if they could work with them. There is no way to turn that decision into an algorithm, although the use of a structured interview process, rather than just winging it, increases both the validity and the reliability of the results. But an action like terminating someone is going to impact the feelings of the people on both sides, no matter what kind of process is used to make that decision. It has been shown that if this is handled fairly and respectfully, it reduces the chances that a wrongful termination suit will result."

Annette recalled her experiences with the software firm when she was involved with an acquisition of an Asian firm. "And what kind of system can detect that cultural differences warrant different decisions?" she asked. "You may get away with saying it is business, not personal, here in North America, but try that in collectivist and particularistic cultures. So those systems you adopted to save time and money may end up only applying to a portion of your global operations. And it is even worse when you have a manager and an employee with different cultural perspectives—how is the system going to handle that?"

"OK, performance appraisal and final hiring and firing decisions must involve human judgment and face-to-face settings, but certainly you are not discounting the value of HRIS in making HR more productive?" responded Eric. "Of course not," Annette responded. "When employees redo their flexible benefits choices each year, there is no need to have them sit with an HR person and take up two people's time, unless there are issues. Health care claims are another example of routine transactions, although someone who has a claim rejected may need to talk to someone to explain why or to let that person know it is an action dictated by contractual constraints. That is why I think it is wise to have an appeal process in place whenever an employee feels they have been mistreated or is confused as to why something was done. Have a skilled person work with them that can understand their reaction and look for a way to have the feelings of inequity resolved."

"We had talked about the suggestion in the book *Dialogue* that sometimes poor communication resulted from HR using affective language and managers using action language, and I am beginning to see that there is a time for using one, the other, or both" Kathy responded. "If the employee feels a policy was correctly adhered to but thinks it resulted in unfair or unnecessarily harsh treatment, you need to use a blend of 'it's business' and 'it's personal' perspectives to promote understanding. An 'I know you wish your family health care premiums were not so high, but since you have five children, it would not be fair to use the limited funds to keep your premiums at the same level as those having no children or only one' kind of message. That is one message a person should deliver, not a software program. And the explanation should have both a rational component and a personal component, rather than a 'that is the policy, get back to work' kind of message." They all agreed that did not mean HR people should be the softhearted employee advocates, but rather good businesspeople who understood dealing with people requires an understanding of their responses.

"I have not had to deal with many significant cross-cultural issues, but this discussion reminds me that when organizations expand globally, they need to fundamentally rethink their policies, how they are applied and especially how they are explained and defended," Annette interjected. "That is one of the challenges I face when developing systems for global project teams," replied Eric. "Even though you can run a global relay team doing design work, it is those handoffs that are tough when crossing cultures. This is particularly true when there are differences of opinions about the right design. Trompenaars told a story at a conference I attended about Dutch engineers casually stating that suggestions proposed by Italian members of the design team were crazy. The Italians took it personally, rather than seeing this as an opportunity for meaningful dialogue, and everything unraveled. If you are all there in person, this can be worked out, but if everything is done through emails sent asynchronously, there is a potential for a disaster." Eric laughed when he recounted how he had included a piece of advice in a training program about not using all caps to communicate emphasis, since it often sends a different message (ranting). Everyone had experienced those miscommunications via email that no one intended but that resulted in high-emotion conflicts.

"The bottom line in all of this is that we are charged with developing courses for students and practitioners that will help them effectively utilize HR information systems," said Kathy, "and we want to be sure to consider that when many workforce management decisions are communicated, it is not two servers communicating but two people, possibly through servers." Rob had written a white paper (Exhibit 2) on doing HR better and had used it as a class exercise to come up with a decision model for assessing how HR was done in an organization.

Exhibit 2

"Effectively managing HR"

HR functions are being asked to do more with fewer resources and to do so in increasingly challenging environments. Doing HR differently may be necessary. This paper provides a framework to help HR practitioners decide whether changes may be required and to understand how performing HR activities differently may impact the effectiveness of the HR function, as well as its role in the organization.

What, if anything, needs to change?

If an HR function finds itself overloaded and/or not competent to perform critical human resource management tasks effectively, a series of questions should be asked:

1   *"Does this need to be done at all?"* This is the most overlooked option for dealing with work overload. Re-engineering has failed to meet expectations in a majority of organizations, and one of the principal reasons is that no one got rid of the totally unnecessary work, and the work failing a cost-benefit test. So, before HR decides whether to do some things differently, the option of not doing them at all should be considered.

2   *"Can this be done better?"* By redesigning processes and reorganizing the roles of HR staff, the work may become less burdensome and/or productivity may be improved. A question that is being asked more frequently is, "Should we automate it?" As IT capabilities increase and electronic commerce software becomes more sophisticated, it becomes feasible to perform more complex transactions and to execute them asynchronously, anywhere in the world. Employees can be provided

with 24/7 access to self-service systems that enable them to query details relating to information on benefits programs, career opportunities, how HR programs are intended to work, HR policies and the like. Another approach is to establish HR service centers, which enable employees to perform transactions such as enrollment in programs, making flexible benefit choices and updating personal information, as well as querying databases to find information. For organizations with multiple divisions and locations across the globe, corporate service centers can provide the necessary services from a centralized location, enabling the organization to enjoy benefits of large-scale business as well as being able to staff the center with trained personnel intimately familiar with policies, programs and systems. These routine activities have traditionally required the time and attention of HR staff, and if they can be automated, this workload is reduced and both efficiency and service levels are often increased.

3 *"Could this be done on a different schedule?"* Many deadlines exist due to history or inertia and changing them to better distribute workload may not result in negative consequences. If the compensation function has to use pay surveys that are well over a year old because the current year's editions do not come out quite early enough, one could question the deadlines for completing the market pricing process and updating the pay structure. Making pay actions effective February 1 or March 1, rather than January 1, may cause a one-time furor but will hardly destroy workforce effectiveness.

4 *"Should the HR organization be staffed differently?"* One of the challenges faced by HR functions is staffing and organizing appropriately. Some HR units consist of HR generalists, while others are dominated by specialists in functions such as compensation, benefits, staffing and the like. Highly technical issues (e.g., benefit program design) challenge the units composed of generalists, while units staffed by specialists often make decisions narrowly focused on one function without considering the impact on others. The appropriate balance of skills is the remedy, and the future staffing and training efforts should be focused on achieving that balance. A competency matrix for HR staff members (Table 18.1) that can be

Table 18.1 Competency matrix

Discipline Expertise	Staffing	HRD	Performance Management	Rewards Management	Employee/ Labor Relations
Basic Knowledge					
Competence					
Mastery					

(continued)

(continued)

used to determine how skilled they are in the various disciplines within HR should be developed. By determining how many people are needed at each mastery level within each discipline to operate effectively the staffing and development requirements can be determined and efforts directed to achieve them.

5   *"Should HR be doing this or should it be handed off to the line?"* Often it makes sense to distribute a high volume of work across more people/units in order to relieve the overloads during peak periods. For example, if job descriptions are all updated at the time of the annual performance reviews, it may make sense to have the bulk of the update work done by designated liaison personnel in the line units, which would distribute the peak workload and reduce staffing demands in HR.

If the answers to these questions leave HR with work that it is not staffed or competent to perform at the levels required, then one of the options that is increasingly being considered is outsourcing that work. The rest of this article will explore the outsourcing of HR activities.

Outsource what?

If it appears that some activities should be outsourced, decisions about what goes and what stays must be made. The first step is to determine what type of activities should be considered for outsourcing. At one extreme, outsourcing could mean replacing the internal HR function with an outside provider that develops all HR strategies and performs all HR-related activities. At the other extreme, it could mean having an outside provider handle specialized transactions such as payroll. Or the answer may be anything in between.

Totally outsourcing HR strategy, policy and programs is generally not advisable. No outside provider can know an organization well enough to completely take over managing its most critical resource. An intimate knowledge of the politics, the personalities and the daily details are required to be in a position to formulate strategy and to make critical decisions for the organization about how it succeeds through its people. On the other hand, performing all HR activities in-house may be a suboptimal approach. So, how does an organization make a decision as to what goes and what stays?

Some activities are algorithmic in nature. That means they can be fully defined in a formulaic manner. An example is payroll processing. An Illinois employer must deduct a specific amount of an employee's pay for federal and state tax, and there are rules to guide this activity. Therefore, the activity can be performed by a computer model, an outside payroll processing firm or an internal accountant with an abacus. Who does it and what tools are used are not important—but having the results be correct is. The accountant with an abacus may not be an efficient approach (and this may not be a rewarding career path for professional accountants), but it could be done. A decision at the other extreme is the selection of the best person to fill a key executive role. There are no specific formulas for deciding from among a group of seemingly qualified candidates. Although selection tests and other tools exist, the decision must be made by parties who know the organization intimately and who know what it needs and where it is headed.

Payroll processing is therefore more suited to outsourcing than is executive selection. The reason is that formulas/computer systems are adequate to perform the payroll work, while the selection decision demands subjective judgment. Most HR activities fall somewhere in between the specified and the judgmental poles. An example would be the decision on whether an organization should adopt a stock option plan or a restricted stock plan and who should participate in the plan. Although an outside compensation expert might be useful in identifying the plusses and minuses of the two approaches to using stock and even in advising the organization on who might be eligible to participate in the plan, decisions about how much dilution of owner equity is acceptable and how big the grants should be will certainly involve HR, the board and possibly even other parties at interest.

Given this broad range of possible involvement of outsiders, what type of model might be useful to an organization when considering outsourcing? Table 18.2 provides a guide for evaluating whether outsourcing is a good fit to the nature of the process and to the objectives the organization has for the process.

The objectives established for the process/decision should be considered, along with the impact of executing the process/making the decision well or poorly. If a process/decision that has significant long-range strategic impact on the success of the organization is outsourced and a provider is not capable of doing it well, the result is likely to be disastrous. On the other hand, if the payroll processing provider is less efficient than projected, the consequences are far less serious and the situation can probably be remedied in the short term.

Outsource to whom & how?

Providers offering to assume responsibility for HR transactions and administrative support are becoming more common. One of the reasons is that HR budgets and associated staffing levels are being cut or closely controlled and HR functions have discovered that outsourcing

(continued)

(continued)

Table 18.2 Outsourcing guide

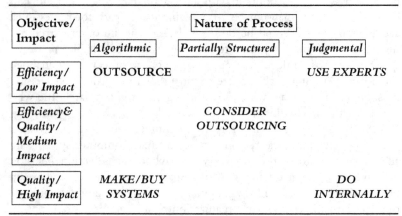

Objective/ Impact	Nature of Process		
	Algorithmic	*Partially Structured*	*Judgmental*
Efficiency/ Low Impact	OUTSOURCE		USE EXPERTS
Efficiency& Quality/ Medium Impact		CONSIDER OUTSOURCING	
Quality/ High Impact	*MAKE/BUY SYSTEMS*		*DO INTERNALLY*

can be an end-around move to stay within budget. Some organizations are obsessed with headcount control as a method to ensure there is no overstaffing or inefficiency, while others attempt to control expenditures on salaries. Both approaches are incomplete control mechanisms and can motivate dysfunctional behavior if units are able to use outside resources without having them charged against their budgets.

An example of a process that might be outsourced is the determination of the annual pay structure adjustment. If the HR staff in an organization cannot complete pay survey participation packages, analyze surveys and price jobs on a timely basis, one way to deal with the shortfall is to contract with a consultant to do the pricing. This avoids excessive overtime work during the crunch period (typically in the fall) and may improve the quality of the process as well, especially if there are no compensation specialists on the HR staff. Unfortunately, having this done outside is an expensive approach, and the organization may be better off cost wise to hire additional staff and/or provide more training for existing staff. If total dollar control (internal and external expenditures) is used, it is possible to make intelligent decisions by comparing the total costs and the benefits of the alternative approaches.

However, there is one added consideration that is often overlooked. The outside provider will operate according to a standard, mutually established procedure in doing the annual analysis of market position. Jobs will have been defined, evaluated and placed into grades. Survey sources will have been decided upon and the appropriate benchmark job matches determined. Once that is done, the provider can utilize an algorithmic process to do the pricing analysis. But jobs change subtly and the nature of the business evolves over time. If there are no qualified internal staff members to monitor these changes, it may not be apparent that some job matches are no longer valid and/or changes in the samples of companies participating in surveys used in the past make the surveys less relevant. It is possible that line management can fill the monitoring role, but it is unlikely that this will happen consistently across the organization, and local politics will often inject bias into the process.

If HR activities are to be outsourced to others, it must be decided whether a single, full-service provider will be used or if specific activities will be parceled out to several specialized providers. Payroll might be turned over to one organization while health care claims processing might go to another specialist. Although administration may be more challenging if multiple providers are used, utilizing specialist firms may result in lower costs and in the provider having more in-depth expertise in its area of practice. For example, a large payroll processing firm is apt to be able to spread costs over a larger client base, resulting in a better pricing structure. On the other hand, if a single provider is utilized, it might make the organization more important to that provider, and it may also result in the provider becoming more knowledgeable about the organization.

Another approach to using outside resources is to use internal HR staff to perform the work but to use consultants to guide efforts by providing specific expertise. For example, designing a gainsharing plan in a manufacturing organization requires considerable knowledge of operational metrics, in addition to compensation design expertise. By retaining the services of an outside expert who has been involved in gainsharing program design for a number of similar organizations, a lot of pre-study, benchmarking and trial and error experiments can be avoided. And the workload may also involve peaks of effort at specific times, which can overload existing HR staff.

Using consulting resources effectively has been covered in the literature, and an organization entering into a project requiring expertise would do well to school itself in the principles. However, there is a simple, overriding principle: *Let someone else do it (or help you) who already knows how to do it if there is little likelihood that an extensive investment in educating the current staff will have ongoing payback in the future.* Because accepted accounting practice treats training as a short-term expense and fails to recognize any benefits that result from the training, it is often hard to sell investments in developing existing staff. This pushes organizations toward using outside expertise.

However, it behooves every organization to think about the implications of not having the expertise to maintain and refine programs in-house. Once line personnel no longer look to HR for guidance, it will be difficult to sustain resource support for even a skeleton unit.

One of the lessons many organizations learned about contracting with outside providers in the late 1990s warrants discussion. A significant percentage of organizations realized that the Y2K event was just that—a one-time event. On January 1, 2000, your computers worked or they didn't. But even though hiring contractors for a one-time surge of work was the wise thing to do, many organizations that did this failed to do a good job of structuring the terms under which contractors were paid. When a contractor works on a project and is paid by the hour (the most typical arrangement) (s)he is motivated to do three things: (1) work as

(continued)

(continued)

many hours as possible, (2) never get done and (3) neglect to train the customer's staff, less a competitor be created. That sounds cynical coming from someone who most frequently works under this arrangement, but it regrettably works that way in many cases. What organizations often fail to do is to: (1) make a portion of the fees going to the contactor contingent on timely completion, (2) make another portion contingent on the quality of the result and (3) make a significant portion contingent on internal staff being fully trained and capable of operating the system in the future.

Having HR work done by non-HR people in line organizations is not outsourcing, at least not under the typical meaning of the term. But it is out of HR and may well change the nature of what is done. If line units establish their own performance management systems, compensation programs and the like with little HR oversight, there is risk of intra-organizational inconsistency and even exposure to legal liability. For example, entry-level programmers usually want to be treated like professionals and expect to be classified as exempt employees. A line manager not familiar with the convoluted exemption provisions of the FLSA may think it makes sense to accommodate the request (after all, it cannot cost more and probably will cost less, since overtime does not have to be compensated). Unfortunately, line managers often fail to realize laws do not have to make sense; they only must be complied with. Line people can be trained in the details of employment law so they make decisions that do not create legal liability. But this is expensive and is likely to be viewed as an HR plot to waste their time by those who would have to sit through training that seems peripheral to their jobs.

Mike Lotito, a prominent employment attorney and past chair of SHRM (Society for Human Resource Management), has often said his major fear when reviewing the documentation in the personnel file of a terminated employee is that it will consist of two dead moths. Upon further reflection, he made that his second worst fear—the worst was having 10 consecutive years of performance appraisals that suggested the employee "was just fine." He warns that the attorney for the terminated employee will unfailingly ask the responsible supervisor, "Were you lying then or are you lying now?" Since many line organizations lobby to develop their own systems and keep their own records, that worst fear may be all too likely to occur. Some organizations imbed HR generalists in line units to prevent major glitches, but these people often go native much like expatriates and soon see things through the eyes of their line supervisors. As a result, some consideration must be given to retaining internal expertise in the HR function to avoid these scenarios.

Also, decentralizing HR decisions so that they are made in business units or functions, rather than corporate HR, may impact how processes work. In large, diverse organizations, decentralizing HR can create inconsistencies across the organization. These differences may in fact be warranted by the specific context within which a business unit or function operates, and it is not suggested that all parts of an organization must behave identically relative to managing their workforces. Many organizations use global principles to act as control parameters and allow localized customization as long as the strategies and programs are consistent with the principles. Cultural differences often create different perspectives, which in turn lead to different HR programs and/or differential administration of the same program. An example would be how a divisional incentive fund is distributed. In one division, a fund equaling 5% of payroll may result in each employee receiving 5% of base pay. In another, the top performers may get as much as 15% and others no award. The first reflects a "shared destiny" (we did it) philosophy, while the second reflects a "pay in proportion to contribution" (you did it) philosophy.

The corporate HR executive that attempts to completely standardize practices is well advised to proceed with caution; local contexts often require different approaches. But at the same time, HR is charged with ensuring that local actions are consistent with organization-wide principles. A related issue is how strictly HR polices are followed. No policy can fit every situation, and it is necessary that provisions be made for variations from policies. Managers will make local decisions, often based on inadequate understanding of policies or based on expediency (i.e., allowing flexibility in an employee's work schedule to avoid losing a critical person). Part of the role of an HR function is to help managers make good decisions based on the full range of factors impacting them.[1]

A final approach is the use of HR service centers that are managed by the organization and staffed by employees. This enables the organization to control how services are provided and at what level more closely than it would be able to if an outside provider were to be utilized. When assessing the feasibility of an internal service center and comparing it to using an outside provider, the factors that should be considered are: (1) cost, (2) service quality, (3) flexibility, (4) timeliness and (5) employee acceptance.[2]

Multinational enterprises (MNEs) face additional challenges as a result of operating across the world. Cultural differences exist across the globe, and they often result in the need to manage performance and rewards differently.[3] Allocating rewards based on individual performance may work fine in the U.S. but not so well in certain parts of Europe and Asia. Lincoln Electric attempted to export its very successful piecework/gainsharing rewards programs to several parts of the world. It was successful in some places and a disaster in others. There is often value in having internal HR people involved in assessing cultural differences, rather than turning these decisions over to outsiders. But when dealing with issues

(continued)

(continued)

involving taxation in multiple countries, laws/regulations governing the conditions of employment and the like, it makes sense to consider consulting with providers having knowledgeable and experienced staff. For organizations that cannot justify having full-time HR staff in all locations, the use of global providers may be the only reasonable alternative.

Bottom line: outsource or not?

Managing human resources internally has advantages and disadvantages. So does outsourcing human resource decisions and processes. Table 18.3 summarizes the pluses and minuses of both approaches.

Conclusion

With the intense pressure on costs, HR functions must find the optimal way to get things done. If the work can be eliminated, done better or done by others, HR executives should evaluate the options and make the changes that will maximize effectiveness and efficiency. If work is to be outsourced, the short- and long-term consequences of doing so should

Table 18.3 Managing internally vs. outsourcing

	Advantages	*Disadvantages*
Managing internally	1 Staff dedicated full-time to organization 2 Staff familiar with culture/context 3 Easier to control staffing levels and expertise 4 Tends to be less expensive 5 HR agenda can be controlled/varied by management	1 Expertise may not extend to specialized areas/issues 2 Locked into fixed costs of full-time staff 3 Political pressures may impact professional advice 4 Harder to stay abreast of developments in the environment
Outsourcing	1 Can control resources used based on current needs/workload 2 Can use only specific skills required without incurring fixed costs 3 May be free of political pressure 4 Provider can afford to employ specialists 5 Provider can learn from experience with other clients	1 Provider not familiar with the "unwritten rules" (culture) 2 Usually more expensive 3 Organization may not be a high priority to provider 4 May result in loss of expertise in HR 5 Subject to external change

be carefully considered. Major U.S. corporations have signed contracts with providers of HR services, and some report they are satisfied with the results. Each organization must make decisions about outsourcing based on their specific context. Organizations in the same industry, of the same size and facing what seem to be the same challenges may well have different cultures, strategies and structures. As a result, it is difficult to use benchmarking intelligence to make outsourcing decisions.[4]

Totally outsourcing HR strategies, processes and decision making presents a grave danger. The ability of an organization to effectively manage its people may be eroded by hollowing out the competencies related to human resource management. Although on the surface it seems more convenient to have an outsider deny a health benefit claim rather than having the supervisor anger an employee, this situation may offer an opportunity to communicate directly with that employee in a manner that maintains a positive relationship. Strategic processes such as workforce planning should be managed at an executive level within the organization, due to the criticality of sustaining workforce viability.[5]

The bottom line of the outsourcing decision is whether the total benefits outweigh the costs. Each organization must weigh the advantages and disadvantages of alternative approaches and make its own decision. The stakes are high, so the effort expended in making that decision should be proportionate.

Rob had sent the paper to several of the people he respected, both in HR and in general management, as well as other academics, at all levels of expertise. There was such an overwhelming reaction he scheduled a day long dialogue through the school and invited all who wanted to participate to attend. The registration was even more overwhelming than the initial response to the article draft. Invitees even brought along colleagues, who had also read the article and who wanted to get their two cents in. Rob realized HR people wanted to play their roles as effectively and efficiently as possible and were willing to listen to those offering suggestions.

Notes

1 Greene, R., "Effective HR Policies and Practices," *WorldatWork Journal*, 2Q, 2007.
2 Lawler, E., *Human Resources Business Process Outsourcing*, 2004, Jossey Bass, San Francisco.
3 Greene, R., "Global Remuneration Strategies," *WorldatWork Journal*, 3Q, 2008.
4 Greene, R., "HRM Strategies: Can We Discover What Will Work Through Benchmarking?" *WorldatWork Journal*, 2Q, 2008.
5 Greene, R., "Ensuring Future Workforce Viability," *WorldatWork Journal*, 4Q, 2007.

19 The "doing HR better" dialogue

Rob had convinced Kathy to be one of the co-facilitators for the dialogue initially and then realized that Annette and Don could be extremely valuable as catalysts for the dialogue. He scheduled a panel for the second module of the day's program, with the two of them joined by Mushira and Howard, who had also volunteered to contribute their experiences. The first module would be a presentation on the key points that had been raised in the article, followed by the panel, which would involve having each of the four members provide their reactions to the article.

After presenting the main points of the article, Rob asked the group to take a coffee break and then to walk around and introduce themselves to every other person in the room. This was an approach he used in seminars to get the energy level up, rather than letting people sink into their chairs and go into listening (or daydreaming) mode. Since there were about fifty people in the room, this took some time, but it certainly generated a loud buzz and got everyone psyched up for the discussion.

"Since this is a dialogue, we need to be sure everyone has an opportunity to contribute in their own way and that we all agree we need to create a unified conversational field that can contain all views and allow people to engage in safe debate. We are not here to have our own views prevail but to create a shared knowledge pool that each of us can access in their own way. I am going to ask our panel members to make their initial contributions and then open it up for everyone to engage them in open dialogue. If views differ, we should respectfully attempt to understand why others have come to believe what they espouse and to share the genesis of our conflicting views. We may not come to consensus on everything, but it is important to leave here with stronger beliefs, which may be the same ones you came with, entirely different beliefs or beliefs that have been refined by the dialogue."

"Age before, well, here is Howard," said Rob, jokingly. "You would have been more accurate if you had said seasoned wisdom before novice speculation," retorted Howard. He began by saying, "This is a really wide topic. How to do HR better is certainly a question worth asking for every organization. But to complicate things, the answer is bound to be different for every organization. Annette has been preaching the 'what works is what fits' mantra, and

I don't think that can be said enough. We consultants are chided for our favorite 'it depends' response, but in most cases, that is precisely the right answer. I have never done 1-900- consulting. If someone calls me and asks me if their organization should have a gainsharing plan, how I answer the question says a lot about my professionalism. If my objective is to get consulting work, my answer is, "Sure, let me help you" (he said this with a broad smile). But if I want to avoid embarrassing myself, the answer is different. I would generally ask the questioner what makes them think they might want to consider a gainsharing plan. If they say that most of their strongest competitors have one, my advice is to determine why they have one and what it does for them. Benchmarking HR strategies and programs is a process fraught with peril and emulation is risky, since differences in organizational context may cause some-one else's success to be your disaster."

Howard continued, "We all want to be seen as innovative professionals. But innovation can come in the form of invention or improvement. It seems more heroic to replace a current program with a bigger, stronger and/or unique pro-gram. But you have to ask yourself how your employees are likely to respond to a major overhaul of the pay program. If you demonize the existing program, which you sold to them a few years ago as the ideal program, you have to con-sider what that elicits in their minds about your professional competence and the quality of management. That is not to say you should not change strategies and programs when the context changes—you should if it is warranted. But be careful of doing something different because it is 'new.' Most of the supposed innovations are recycled from the past. And if they are in fact unique, you might consider that another word for 'new' is 'unproven.' Striking a balance between change and stability is dilemma reconciliation, and it is very challenging."

He paused and then continued, "Let's get back to the idea of finding solu-tions through benchmarking HR practices. The practice of emulating what others do has perhaps been most prevalent in compensation. After all, you have to be competitive in order to attract and retain qualified people. And you need to motivate people to do their best. But the literature in the compensation field has historically jumped from one quick fix to another: something becomes the *next best thing* and all the periodicals are flooded with articles on how someone did it. And the articles tell of success stories, which will be of interest to people who are looking for things that work. Unfortunately, no one has the courage to write articles about their failures, so the literature is terribly biased. And it is all too easy to forget that contextual differences may make those successes the disasters of those who rush to get on the bandwagon."

After noting the occasional looks of displeasure, Howard decided to broaden his indictment of blind emulation. "And compensation is not the only discipline that has overdosed on emulation. Competency-based performance management was 'discovered' a few years ago. The problem with those who enthusiastically went down that road was that they forgot that competence was potential and did not necessarily result in performance. Again, these techniques certainly are valuable tools if applied where they fit. But they are not miracle cures."

Mushira took the microphone and suggested they focus on the *what, how and who* of human resource management. "The article Rob shared with us really got to the essence of making decisions about the organization's approach to HRM. Does something need to be done at all? Can it be done better by doing it differently? And who should do it? These are hard questions to seriously debate, given that organizations are often set in their ways and are openly committed to strategies that they have attempted to sell as optimal. But the environment of the last two decades has become dynamic and unforgiving of those that do not change to remain a good fit to their contexts. For example, if it is suggested that the organization move a significant portion of current cash compensation from base pay to variable pay, the immediate focus is on the dangers and difficulties of doing that. But if the discussion started with facing the reality that revenues are going to be variable and people costs are not sustainable if they are all fixed, then the conversation takes a different path. If there is a realization that either average direct compensation levels or staffing levels must vary to better align costs with revenues that are variable, then the focus shifts to making critical decisions about strategy. And the recognition that workforce costs must become variable also changes the nature of the conversation about questions like the composition of the workforce: Is the use of contractors a viable option and/or should some work be outsourced?"

"Are you suggesting the difficulties with making that sort of shift are not significant?" asked Ray, an audience member. "Of course not," replied Mushira. Howard supported her approach. "The real value of benchmarking is that trends could be spotted and investigations begun into why and how organizations are changing," he said. Several audience members chimed in to point out that they were getting whiplash from all the "let's do this, how about that" fad chasing, and when they suggested caution and more investigation, they were labeled as being change-resistant.

Kathy took the mic next. She suggested, "It seems that the logical approach is to first define your own organizational context and then to determine what your objectives are. Then you can decide what type of workforce you need in order to meet your objectives and what will be the best strategy for motivating that workforce to produce the desired results. Once you know thyself, you can look around at successful organizations to see what types of HR strategies they utilize and then try to understand why those particular strategies work for them. For example, if a competitor is a low-cost provider, it might make a lot of sense for them to use a gainsharing plan to focus their production people on cost control. But if you win market share by providing innovative product features, you are probably going to want to focus your workforce on innovation. So, you are not going to emulate that competitor's compensation program, no matter how profitable they are, since their program is designed to fit their context and strategy. On the other hand, the competitor that always seems to get the best design people might be an organization whose programs you want to know more about. This still does not mean you should have concierge services and extensive recreational facilities on site just because they do, particularly if it does not fit your culture." Rob asked, "*A what works is what fits you* philosophy, as opposed to *what worked for them will probably fit us?*" "Exactly," responded Kathy.

"All this about benchmarking has produced valuable insights," interjected Zahra, a visitor from the Middle East on an expatriate assignment to the U.S. headquarters of her organization. "I realize there needs to be a careful translation process when crossing organizational boundaries. Expectations about how something worked in other organizations need to be altered, to reflect contextual differences. So, the respective organizational cultures, workforce cultures and contexts all need to be factored in. Has anyone successfully done this?"

Rob and Kathy both thought a great deal about the question and Kathy responded, "I think you have to do a thorough assessment of your own context and only then begin to look outside for ideas about how to accomplish your objectives." "Absolutely," added Rob. "Going from the outside in makes you predisposed to overlook differences because you hope to find a strategy to propose to management that has been successful somewhere, since that is evidence it can work in some contexts. If you first evaluate everything based on how it might play out in your context, you are less likely to emulate when your best bet is to innovate. Doing something new or doing it differently may be the approach most likely to succeed." Kathy added, "But you also have to be careful about aspiring to uniqueness, since there is no precedent for estimating the chances for success. So, it is a balancing act between emulation and innovation."

As the dialogue wound down, a lot of business cards changed hands and Kathy offered to set up a chat group on the internet so the explorations could continue. Rob felt that they had not covered the full range of issues and resolved to keep everyone engaged. There was a lot of intellectual power in the group, and their experiences represented a treasure trove of ideas. So, the organizers committed themselves to planning for periodic sessions to keep the momentum going.

The dialogue had reignited Don's interest in the impact of organizational culture on effectiveness. He called Rob and asked for a consultation. "My first focus at the association is to define and evaluate the culture that is in place," began Don. "We have just finished a strategic plan and established our short-term objectives, working with the board. Now I want to decide if we are prepared to implement the plan and meet the objectives. Culture can facilitate or impede effectiveness, and as far as I can tell, no one has paid any attention to it."

"OK," responded Rob, "what you need to do is to develop a model for defining the current culture, deciding what it should be, identifying the 'is–should be' gaps and then formulating plans to close the gaps that will have a major impact on the organization's performance. The instrument I use to get employee input has a number of dimensions, each with a 1 to 5 scale [See pages 29-33 for an example of this instrument]. The endpoints are defined, enabling respondents to compare what is and what should be to the scale points. The critical point to be made with employees is that a 1 is not better or worse than a 5. They are just different. And employees need to know what kind of analysis we are going to do using their feedback. Our analysis will address these questions:

1   How much agreement is there on what the current culture *is*?
2   How much agreement is there on what the culture *should be*?
3   How wide are the gaps between 'is' and 'should be' on each dimension?
4   What is the impact of each gap?
5   What is our best strategy for closing the gaps?

I think we should first do the polling and the analysis, and once we have summarized the data, we should engage your employees in planning the moves going forward. We will do brainstorming sessions with groups of twenty to twenty-five, creating dialogues on what you should do, what you are capable of doing and how to proceed."

"Do you think we will identify gaps that should be narrowed but that we may not be capable of narrowing?" responded Don. Rob responded, "Usually the list of to-dos is long, but everyone has to understand that everything cannot be done, or even begun, all at once. Also, there may be implications associated with some of the changes to the culture that employees may resist." "Sold," said Don, with a wide smile.

The results of the cultural assessment were surprising. Both Don and Rob felt there would be considerable agreement as to what the culture was, given the large percentage of long-service employees. But the degree of consensus about what the culture should be was a shock. It seemed that employees knew what should change, but that there had been no forum for them to safely express their beliefs. By making the process of responding to the questionnaire anonymous, people were free to express their true beliefs without running the risk of creating conflict. The results showed that there was broad agreement about what should be changed and the importance of making the changes. There were eight or nine dimensions having large 'is–should be' gaps, and Don and Rob began to formulate plans to address them.

Employees recognized an overreliance on what customers wanted at the expense of committing to goals developed by management. Although customer/member satisfaction was important, the utility association would not be able to be effective if the day-to-day wants of the diverse membership called the shots. Don decided to use customer input when setting goals each year, but once the goals were set, resources would be focused on meeting them.

Employees recognized that they had attributed shortcomings to outside, uncontrollable forces, without adequately assuming responsibility for developing strategies to deal with these forces. Don realized that much of this was due to the management style that had prevailed before Annette had taken the lead role. He made a note to conduct an analysis in the near future to determine how the existing strengths and weaknesses impacted the association's ability to deal with external threats and capitalize on opportunities. He had intended to do this as a part of the strategy development process they had recently completed, but he now recognized that he should have emphasized how they would deal with outside threats.

The results made it clear that overconfidence in the status quo existed and that employees believed that should change. Don was a little surprised that the majority of them were anxious to challenge the veracity of their current programs and to consider making changes.

Another surprise was that employees believed that too much top-down decision making had existed and that this had resulted in insufficient delegation and employee development. Without the opportunity to assume stretch assignments, employees rarely acquired the skills to move to the next level, and this was at least partly responsible for the lack of succession planning.

Finally, results made it clear that many employees, including managers, recognized that too often decisions were made instinctively. One of Don's favorite books pointed out the need to base management decisions on the best available and most relevant evidence.[1] He resolved to provide his people with some of the principles of using evidence, although he realized that personal instinct and intuition can also play an important role, especially if integrated with evidence.

Don and Rob shared the results with the employees and asked them to input their suggestions as to how the association should begin the change process. Once that had been done, they compiled the responses and scheduled a dialogue session to agree on a process for moving forward. The session went well, and Don felt that a great deal of progress had been made toward reshaping the culture and building a consensus among employees about how the association should function.

Rob was delighted with the data he now had to begin creating a database that could be used in conjunction with other research on organizational culture, how to define and evaluate it and how to create a culture that contributed to organizational effectiveness.

Note

1 Latham, G., *Becoming the Evidence-Based Manager*, 2009, SHRM/Davies-Black, Boston, MA.

20 Transformation at the not-for-profit

Annette had been particularly attentive to the succession planning issue she had committed to addressing since joining the not-for-profit organization. Don had been successful in developing some of the managers during his time there. They at least understood that the money did not appear magically just because they were dedicated to the mission. But Annette did not want them to lose sight of the purpose of the organization either. When she was at the software firm she joined right out of school, she had resisted adopting the mindset that success equated solely to financial results, and she certainly did not want her employees here to lose sight of their primary purpose.

One of the things she had started spending her time on was conversations with employees about what ignited their emotions. If she could find out what their personal priorities were, she could avoid trying to promote people into roles that did not fit their interests or their personalities. Not everyone wants to be a manager or to run things. This was particularly true in this organization, since there were many roles that called for a singular focus on benefiting the children.

And she was beginning to realize that some of the activities should be candidates for outsourcing. The organization had been unsuccessful trying to get and keep a qualified controller, so perhaps many of the accounting and financial activities could be turned over to an organization that could perform them better. While interviewing the last short-lived controller, it had been made clear that he had felt he was peripheral to the primary purpose of the organization and well down the food chain when resources were allocated. One of the board members was a partner at a public accounting firm, and perhaps Annette could convince her that the public relations benefit from providing services to help the organization might offset a portion of the higher fees that would otherwise be charged. And since they were having problems in the IT area as well, she might ask if that could be packaged with the accounting in an outsourcing agreement.

Annette had remembered some of the principles she had learned about outsourcing: (1) if an activity is not a part of the central purpose of the organization, it could be a candidate, (2) if some jobs were hard to fill with high-quality incumbents, maybe they should be moved outside and (3) if an outside contractor is capable of performing activities at a higher level of quality and is affordable, consideration should be given to turning those activities over to them. She had heard about a similar not-for-profit charity that had outsourced fundraising with disastrous results and realized that this was no doubt due to the fact that they needed people who were committed to the primary mission doing that work. Don had taken the lead in fund-raising because he recognized the need to appeal more to corporations and foundations than to small individual contributors, but whoever was involved in fund-raising needed to be zealots about the work being done. No hard sales pitches were needed or wanted, and if a contractor was retained based on results-based compensation, there would be a danger that the image of the organization could be harmed by hard selling.

During these "what do you dream of doing?" conversations, Annette found that one of the employees responsible for delivering their services to children had aspirations of becoming the chief spokesperson for the organization and its mission. Since he had a solid business background as well as a personality that resulted in a nurturing management style, Annette realized her likely successor was already in-house and not that far away from being ready to assume the role. She realized this was a lucky find, rather than being attributable to a viable succession planning program, but it is often better to be lucky than to be good, so why argue with success?

Annette discussed the discovery with Rob and Kathy over lunch, and Kathy offered to talk to her friend Sara to see if she would act as an independent coach for the candidate that had been identified. Sara was a certified coach, and Kathy was confident in her professional ability. Annette agreed to have Sara work with the candidate and asked her to set up an eight-week program involving regular meetings and feedback reports to her. The use of outside coaches appealed to Annette, since mentoring often resulted in cloning the mentor, even when the person would benefit more from building on their current personality and style. But she had initiated internal knowledge-sharing sessions, since it was important for their people to overlap their knowledge pools. It often happened that employees had to jump in to cover for a peer, due to fluctuations in the work volume in specific programs. And this flexibility was greatly facilitated by broadly disseminating client and operational information.

She also made a mental note to discuss having Sara coach all of her managers, since most of them seemed challenged when it came to developing their staff members. Annette was fully aware of the need to have managers clearly communicate performance expectations, to provide continuous feedback and to develop trust and open dialogue. These were mandatory if performance management was to be more than just appraising people at the end of the year, when it was too late to redirect them and to develop them so they could improve performance.

Just as Annette was finishing a particularly satisfying day, Don called and asked for a powwow. He said he had something to discuss and asked Rob to join them.

21 Opportunity knocks

Don started the get-together by announcing that Howard had called him and asked him if he would be interested in an opportunity with a large private sector organization. Howard assured him that he would be a good fit in the role and that the money was big. "Is it a for-profit, money grabbing, capitalistic organization?" he asked. "Absolutely," answered Howard. Annette was where she should be for at least the foreseeable future, and being involved with helping kids was a big source of psychic income for her. So, perhaps he should be the one to step up and generate some additional income.

Don was confident that the utility association would not suffer if he left. One of their board members was the head of a major member utility and was about to retire. He had been deeply involved with the association for several years and knew its work and its people even better than Don. Since the board member's pension plan made it wise to retire at a ridiculously young age this person was certainly capable of serving 10 years at the association if he were to assume Don's job. Although Don felt a little uncomfortable making a change after switching jobs with Annette such a short time ago, he realized that "job hopper" did not carry the same negative connotation it used to. and he was confident he would not be deserting his current employer.

"So, what is this new gig?" asked Rob, a little skeptical. Annette was still in shock so was silent. "Director of HR planning for a multibillion dollar multinational," Don responded. "Is it the money, the challenge or the prestige that attracts you?" queried Rob. "Yes," responded Don, who was a big believer in the parsimonious use of words. "It would really stretch me and also allow me to apply what I learned in grad school. I have always been the planning freak in our group if you remember. And from what Howard says about this organization, they seem to have their act together and to be committed to workforce planning and development. It would give me a chance to use that workforce planning model we have developed and to take an HR-wide perspective. I also understand the VP of global HR is only two or three years from retirement and that this slot is a natural feeder into that role. And don't despair—I will still associate with you when I have reached these lofty heights." "Sure you will," responded Rob, "you won't be able to pull it off without our guidance."

Annette was still unsure about this change but encouraged Don to pursue it. After all, Don had not even met the people he had to sell the idea to, and they had not evaluated his capabilities. She wondered if she was really supportive or if she believed it was a real long shot so she could afford to be agreeable. And extra income never hurts. "Any idea how much added income you are talking about?" she asked, stepping totally out of character. "Howard said he was just guessing but figured the package would be at least 50% more than what I currently earn." That was difficult for Annette to absorb, but when they parted, the Three Musketeers had decided Don was certainly going to thoroughly explore this opportunity.

Don met with a group of senior HR staff at the multinational, and the conversations seemed to go very well. Although he initially had reservations about jumping to such a high level without private sector experience, he recognized that the new role would demand intelligence and a strategic perspective above all else. He also felt better knowing that he had Howard and Rob on call and that they were behind him. "Sort of like having both a main chute and a reserve chute when you jump off the cliff," he joked with Rob. "Yeah, but you better be sure you have enough time for the chute to open before you hit the ground," responded the veteran paratrooper. Don thought that a less than comforting analogy but let it go.

Feeling he should lay it all on the line at the original round of interviews, Don had shown his evaluators the HR planning model he had worked with. He also made it clear that the designer of the model and the process for using it would be joined at the hip with him from the get-go. The top HR executive was receptive to Don using contractors and asked to meet both Rob and Howard. "Even if they are lukewarm to me, my two advisors might pull this off," thought Don. And it was comforting that he would not be alone if he went down in flames trying to fly this risky mission.

Annette made it very clear that it was his decision, and he should rely on his head and his heart when making the decision. She offered to discuss it for as long as he wanted and to answer questions and offer her views when asked. Don called Rob and Howard later that evening to let them know where he was with the offer. He thanked Howard for initiating this opportunity and especially for the confidence he placed in Don. "Would not have done it if I thought there was any chance you would embarrass me," replied Howard. Both of them said there would be an offer forthcoming, based on his recap of the interviews. Howard suggested that unless there were major issues with the offer that he not haggle over money or play hard to get, based on his dealings with the players. "They don't play games," Howard assured him.

A half hour before he left for work the next day, the phone rang and the offer was put on the table by the director of staffing. He thanked the caller for the information provided and said he would call her back later that morning. He went back to the den and sheepishly asked Annette if she was ready for the big leap. "If you are for it, I am behind you," she responded. "Did they offer you what you expected?" "A lot more," responded Don. "The salary is half again what I am making now. If the annual incentive plan pays out at target, it will amount to 25%

of my new salary; at maximum, it will amount to 50% of my new salary. So, my cash compensation will vary from 175% to 200% of my current salary. But I am thinking about holding out for more." The pillow Annette threw at him missed, but he would not have felt it in his numbed state even if it had not. Annette suggested she should start shopping in those boutiques where only one customer is in the store at a time, but she was not able to keep a straight face, and Don looked so emotionally battered that she thought he was too easy a target.

Don had entered a very different world. He felt like Alice after she fell down the rabbit hole, but in a good way. The offices were great and the amenities overwhelming. He could grab a train two blocks from home and step off 30 minutes later a block from the new office. Once in the building, he could drop off his laundry, do his banking and stop in for gourmet coffee before going to his office. The offices were small, but there were large common areas everywhere. The walls were all whiteboards, and they were constantly being filled with half-baked ideas that others could continue to refine.

But the best part was the buzz in the air. There was a treasure trove of very bright people who were energized and focused on aligned objectives. Meetings were collegial rather than competitive, surprising Don. When he expressed his surprise to his new best friend, the director of HRD, he got a clear message in return. "You act like you are in a jousting tournament here and you will be immediately and unceremoniously disqualified," responded Francisco. "We don't have the time, energy or inclination to play games, particularly those that will detract from realizing high levels of organizational performance."

"Now I am convinced I am dreaming," Don thought to himself. He had experienced dysfunctional competitive behavior in school, at the utility and at the association. And the stakes were a lot lower there than they are here. He had quickly been made aware that he was joining a group of competent and aligned people. And he had been taught through experience that a group of competent and aligned people will outperform even the most heroic individual. He was very ready to embrace the culture prevailing in his new organization and made it clear to all the members of the HR team.

There was an HR staff meeting scheduled on Don's second day, and he was really looking forward to getting started. The top HR executive, Wayne, advised them that he wanted to develop a clear strategy for staffing the function. He started by asking them to recall their earlier experiences with jigsaw puzzles and blocks. "If you want to cover an area bounded by a border, you have a lot of options as to the shape of the blocks. You can cover it with all long and narrow blocks, either vertically or horizontally. Now think of the mile-deep and inch-wide blocks as specialists in HR disciplines and the mile-wide and inch-deep blocks as generalists. By the way, I am not suggesting you generalists are shallow or that you specialists are narrow. But the problem with either of those two strategies is that there is no overlap of knowledge or skill between the blocks. Nonaka[1] pointed out that people with no overlapping knowledge cannot effectively communicate, and they will have trouble aligning their efforts."

Wayne put a slide up on the screen that illustrated the options he had laid out (see Figure 21.1).

He continued, "What I am suggesting is that staffing at too lean a level will preclude overlapping knowledge and skill and in the long run be our undoing. But I also do not want to just double layer the blocks to get overlap, since that will just add cost. What I want everyone here to do is to become T-shaped. That means the generalists need to become deeper in one or more of the specialist functions and the specialists need to become wider by learning about functions outside their primary area of knowledge. That can be done through cross-training, developmental assignments, shadowing, mentoring and the other tools for developing people. Of course, it would be nice if everyone became a mile deep and a mile wide, but you would be in your seventies by the time you did that and you would be busy developing full time, leaving no time for work." Since the group knew the boss was an aspiring stand-up comic, with no chance of success, they suppressed their groans.

"So, Don here is going to be in charge of covering the area with blocks, by planning for the staff we need today and into the future. Alicia who runs staffing will be responsible for acquiring the raw material and Roberto who runs development will be charged with adding width and depth to the blocks as needed. Doesn't that sound simple? And Denise, our esteemed head of OD, will figure out what kind of processes we need to put into place to accomplish our objectives. Everyone like their new, concise job descriptions?" "And my role?" interjected Eric, the director of HRIS, who had joined after being recruited from Rob's school. "You keep track of all the action," responded the leader.

Don really was impressed with the plan for HR and was anxious to get started. His first step was to evaluate the demographics of the current staff. The members were fairly young, with a few exceptions. It was likely that one of the senior recruiters would be retiring shortly, and two of the trainers were in the process of forming their own business. Since there were already people in place to fill those slots when they opened up, Don realized that these losses were not going to hurt them. But many of the people in HRD were still fairly

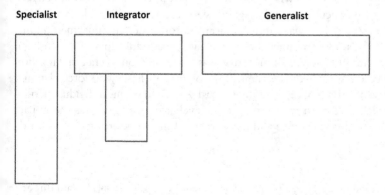

Specialist   Integrator   Generalist

Figure 21.1 Staffing an HR function

new, and they were hard-pressed to keep up with the workload, so he made a note to check with Roberto to be sure investments were being made in their development. One of the things they discussed was having the probable retiree enter into a training contract to provide focused mentoring to the younger staffing people, even after the scheduled retirement date. It was also likely to be a good move to throw a little business to the two entrepreneurs-to-be and to have them do some training for the newer HRD staff on a contract basis.

Don was concerned about their ability to implement the new enterprise-wide IT system that had been selected. This would have a major impact on their HRIS capabilities, and he needed to have a heart-to-heart with Eric to be sure he had all the resources he needed. "Although I would like a big staff so I have someone to boss around," offered Eric lightheartedly, "I think we use contractors to do the implementation and training of our current staff and those we will need to add down the road. But I don't want to repeat the same stupid type of contract we had the last time we implemented with contractors." "What was that?" asked Don. "We paid them by the hour, which motivates them to do three things." "And those are?" replied Don, playing along. "Spend as many hours as possible, never get it done and avoid training the client staff lest you create a competitor," responded Eric. Don smiled, since he had run into that same indictment of paying contractors by the hour before. "I think we should talk to our contracts people and be sure there is a whole lot of money foregone by the contractors if our people don't get fully trained," concluded Don. They were in full agreement and scheduled an appointment to review the draft contract with those responsible for its creation.

The next step Don needed to take was to evaluate how well they were developing talent sources and preventing losses of critical people. He used the planning model to identify potential sources of talent and likely losses in HR and arranged for a series of staff meetings to ensure there were plans in place to ensure the staff remained viable. Don realized he needed to expand his efforts to the rest of the organization, but focusing on HR was a good shakedown cruise, and it was a great way to get to know the people and the way in which HR functioned here. He had been invited to a meeting with the head of HR and the other direct reports to the CEO where the issue of workforce planning was discussed. Everyone in the executive team knew they were expected to give planning a high priority—the CEO had made it a significant factor in determining their annual incentive awards. Don thought that was really a masterful move. He had been gratified to find out his annual incentive was based 50% on overall organization performance and most of the remaining 50% on how well the workforce planning initiatives went. None of the incentive award was based on his individual performance, which he agreed with, since at his level, what counted was the impact on organizational performance and the viability of the workforce going forward.

Note

1 Nonaka, I. and Takeuchi, H., *The Knowledge Creating Company*, 2008, Harvard Business School Publishing, Boston, MA.

22 Work–life balance becomes a focus

Annette informed Don that she had been in attendance at a conference of local non-profit CEOs and that several of the organizations were sharing how they had adopted work–life programs to ease recruitment and retention. Don could see the gleam in her eyes, and he realized her organization should be a leader in this area but that he had never gotten around to looking at their policies and practices when there. "I want to have a team of our people look at this. It will give me a chance to test just how balanced our organization's work–life programs are." "It is a smart move," Don responded in a supportive manner, "and it is something that organization should be concerned about."

The policies at Annette's organization regarding family leave and other work–life balance issues had been developed by an organization that did consulting for many of the organizations that were cited as being the "best to work for" and "the most family friendly." They went beyond the threshold established by laws and regulations, particularly regarding time off provisions for maternity and parental leave, and she felt this was appropriate given their focus on improving lives. But she was a little concerned about key people being absent for any length of time and using the provisions for working at home. On the other hand, she remembered she had committed to doing succession planning and employee development, and one of the things that needed to be avoided is having people be critical to their operations, with no good alternatives if they for any reason became suddenly unavailable.

Annette brought in a consultant who specialized in developing work–life balance. During the initial meeting with him, Annette had been made aware of the difficulties some of the staffers had with their heavy travel schedules. Most of the issues dealt with child care, but Ralph the consultant felt they ought to be able to spread the required travel around to give these employees some relief. "Can we do it without reducing the quality of our services or significantly increasing staffing costs?" asked Annette. "I think so, but let me delve more deeply into it," responded Ralph.

Annette had another related concern. "Actually, I have always been worried that we only have one employee familiar with some of the agencies we work through and without any backup relative to managing some of our key programs. As a result, I think we ought to invest in cross-training, which would give us protection against damage caused by staff losses, and which might also allow us to spread travel without a decline in service levels."

Later that day, a staff member approached Annette about applying for the Malcolm Baldridge Quality Award. This was a real surprise for Annette, since although she had studied the award requirements while in school, she never considered that it might apply to not-for-profits, particularly those with a large dose of charitable activities. "Do you think we would have a chance?" asked Annette. "I think the intrinsic value of going through the application process is worth the effort," Arturo replied. Since Annette always thought of him as an artist at heart, his enthusiasm for taking on a process that focused on hard operational metrics seemed a bit out of character. But then she had realized quite some time ago that she was perhaps too prone to categorizing people and not looking for qualities that did not fit the general impression she had of them. Some time ago, Rob had insisted they watch the movie *Kinky Boots,* and the message that impressions too often cloud reality had touched a resonant chord in her while watching it. They all bestowed upon it the HR Movie of the Decade award, even though some of their colleagues thought them a bit daft to pick an off-beat British movie for that honor.

"Arturo, if you think it would be worthwhile to consider it, then research it and make a proposal at our next management meeting," suggested Annette, proud of her openness to new ideas. In fact, she realized that she was becoming more and more open to things that she had little or no experience with. "This has to be good," she thought. She was careful not to give herself too much credit for initiating the work–life review, since she certainly would benefit personally if the organization became more family friendly. But the other programs meant more work for her, so she thought she might be due a little credit. On the other hand, she had become a delegation zealot in order to increase the pace of employee development and to pursue her succession planning aspirations. "Would I be courageous enough to take an extended leave after developing one or more successors? Would my board and major contributors remember me after I am gone a few months?" One concern she did have related to the board. Rob had put some businesspeople on the board in an attempt to professionalize the way they functioned, and several of them were not exactly the touchy-feely types that normally celebrated the fact that the organization had become more compassionate. "But there I go again," she thought, "assuming people with a business focus are hard-hearted capitalists."

Don listened to her concerns that evening, and Rob and Kathy jumped in, since they had dropped by. "You are doing the right thing," Kathy told Annette. "The sands are shifting, driven by the demographic winds. People coming into the workforce cannot buy into leaving their lives at the door when they sign on with a company. During the industrial revolution, assembly line workers were often expected to leave their minds at the front gate, but it got harder and harder to get any takers for that deal. Now new graduates have a tough time figuring out why them taking some time off to continue their spring break tradition is ruled out by some 20-year-old vacation policy.

And commuting into work to do things that they probably would be more productive doing at home seems a bit bizarre to them. The real winner is the parental leave drill—the law says you can take time off but the career overseers frown on this demonstration of weak dedication. Come on, companies are shooting themselves in the foot with these out-of-touch policies." Rob added, "Employers with out-of-date value propositions may be able to attract people when unemployment is high, but they should not stand in front of the exits when things improve, lest they be trampled by the herd."

Annette knew she should not try to rely solely on the best work-life programs to attract and retain talent, since all the best employer awards do not necessarily impress the hard chargers who live to make a difference and to solve the most intractable problems. There is always a danger of being an employer that is not going to pay the most or provide the fastest career progression, and the resume of someone aspiring to make it big is not going to be greatly enriched by listing a not-for profit charitable organization. Annette resented the way they were subjected to stereotyping but realized it was a reality she should just deal with. After all, look at where Don was now, and he had not worked in the for-profit sector at all. Maybe what you knew and could do really did count.

23 Staffing the multinational

Don was going to need help in order to deal with the challenges he faced relative to his workforce planning initiatives. "I need a top-notch thinker who is not bound by traditional approaches," he thought. He had lunch with Kathy, who was looking for research sites, and his staffing needs came up. "Why don't you join us?" he asked Kathy, without even realizing he was going to say that. "You serious?" she responded. "You know, I really am, even though I had no idea I was going to make that suggestion. You are highly intelligent, capable of thinking out of the box, and you are not bound by a commitment to specific planning strategies." "Well," she said cautiously, "I am getting a little restless at the academic post, since I am living in the theory world 24/7, and wonder if I am increasingly out of touch with real-world issues. You pay a lot?" Don had actually been surprised how much Rob and Kathy made as faculty when Rob spilled the beans, but then realized they were among the very small minority of PhD grads that land a spot at a top school as a first job. "Yeah, I can entice you with money," he responded.

Kathy realized she might benefit from breaking out and doing something different than Rob, although that certainly was not reason enough to make this kind of move. "And just what would I be expected to do to earn this princely sum?" she asked Don. "Help me develop the HR planning strategy that will best serve my organization," he responded, sticking to his straightforward way of laying things on the line. "OK," Kathy responded. "OK, what?"' queried Don. "OK, I will take the job," she answered, being as straightforward as he had been.

"You putting me on?" asked Rob when Kathy broke the news to him later that day. "How much did he have to offer to get you to agree to enter the dog-eat-dog world?" "Not sure," she said sheepishly. "We did not talk money, but he did say I would be making a lot more than I am now," realizing a few of the details of the offer were a little undefined. "Is this a permanent break with the academic world?" asked Rob. "Not really sure, but it probably means a multiple-year hiatus at the least," she responded.

When Don talked about bringing Kathy aboard with some of the other managers in the department, he ran into a bit of skepticism. The staffing director, Alicia, was OK with the idea, but Roberto, the HRD director, had a different read. "My experience with PhDs, especially when they have spent any time in academic work, is that they love ideas but perhaps love them to death. They are willing to spend endless hours debating alternatives and are generally not in a big hurry to come to closure. Even when one is in the planning mode, there still is a bit more pressure to get on with things here," he offered. "Sounds like a bit of stereotyping, and based on a pretty small sample," Alicia responded. "Perhaps," retorted Roberto, "but we already have a bit of a low-key image in HR, and I really think we need to notch up our intensity level. That is why I think people who have been in for-profit organizations are more inclined to move more quickly when making decisions."

Don had to step in at that point. "First, Kathy is not a dreamer. She thrives on ideas but also is really good at dialogue that is focused on solutions. And fast can often border on the superficial. Since we are doing the long-range planning, our priority is to get it right rather than come to conclusions in a heated rush." Don made an effort to make his response not seem like a rejection of Roberto's concerns, but rather an attempt to set a new direction. "I certainly don't think your developmental programs place speed ahead of effectiveness, and that is something I think we should avoid in planning. I will be bringing Rob in fairly soon, and when you meet him, you will not view him as fitting your image of PhDs either. Although he had a lot more business training than Kathy while doing his MBA and MSHR work, she has really focused on research that applies to workforce management and brings a different perspective. In fact, I almost recommended that we create an HR research manager slot but thought that is something we can do at a later time, and Kathy would be a good candidate for that role once she has helped me launch our major planning initiatives."

Don knew that the research manager spot would take some selling, since the key players in HR were confident they knew what the behavioral research had to say about what will work and what will not. But Don had carefully studied the research study by Sara Rynes using over 1,000 HR practitioners and managers. The study involved administering a thirty-five-question true/false test to the HR people that covered the findings of behavioral research. And the median score had been 20! Since guessing would likely produce a score of 17 or 18, this was pretty startling—and depressing. Since then, Rob had given students the same test and found that unless they had taken the organization behavior course, they fared no better. But when Don had tried to use research findings when addressing real-life issues, most managers showed little interest. In fact, one of the managers at the utility he had gone to work at right out of school had become hostile when Don said there was no compelling support for the hypothesis that increasing employee satisfaction would increase productivity. There was a lot of evidence that it decreased turnover and absenteeism, but not that it positively impacted performance. Don had tried to convince the manager that unsupported claims, even though intuition made them seem likely, were dangerous. If executive management was promised increased productivity due to an initiative to improve employee satisfaction, there was a risk that it would not manifest, making those who justified the resource expenditure based on that assumption look bad. And even if other positive results, such as lower turnover and absenteeism, resulted, it was not what was promised.

The problem with making the pitch for adding a research specialist was that people tend to become defensive when confronted with research evidence that refuted things they believed to be true. And the more experienced and more senior folks tended to react even more, since they were used to believing they knew what was what and being confident that they knew more than those with less experience. New graduates often find their well-intentioned efforts to correct their seniors are met with limited enthusiasm, even though they often had more up-to-date knowledge. "So, we will address that issue down the road," he thought, "and perhaps my colleagues stay pretty current on research findings, lessening the need for someone to assume that responsibility."

Don had lunch with Roberto in the cafeteria and talked more about what he expected out of Kathy and how that work would help his planning efforts. He was confident that Roberto was on board with the hiring decision. He did make a mental note to have Kathy enrolled in some of their training programs early on, particularly those that dealt with the organization's businesses and its strategies for winning in the marketplace.

Kathy had spent a good deal of time with Annette since deciding to move into the for-profit arena. She grilled Annette about her experience with the software firm she had worked for and how it compared to life in non-profit organizations. "You will be fine," Annette assured her, "there are differences, but human resource planning is mostly about matching people to organizational needs. Effective and appropriate selection and development will provide the needed human capital. And how performance is defined, measured and rewarded also plays a big part in ensuring that people are focused on the things that are important and that they are motivated to expend their efforts in producing the needed results. But all of that is true in any type of organization. So, first make an effort to understand the business, the strategy and the objectives. Then figure out what kind of workforce is needed to execute the strategy and to meet the objectives, both currently and in the future. You are familiar with the workforce planning model Rob uses, and it is conceptually simple, although a little more challenging to put into practice. So, you will be fine."

The biggest change Kathy experienced when she started work was the switch from talking and teaching most of the time to listening the vast majority of the time. Listening to managers as they talked about what their workforce needs and how the current workforce measured up to their needs was the most frequent activity. She found it challenging to get them to think longer term, and she repeated the "it is hard to worry about fire insurance when your house is on fire" mantra frequently in her mind, trying to remember it was those managers who felt the pressure to deal with current issues. The other big change was adapting her agenda to the priorities dictated by the business. When doing research and developing courses, she followed her instincts as to how she should focus and sequence her efforts to produce the optimum results. The transition to the private sector where the objectives were established was very hard, but the longer she persisted, the better she felt about her choice to join the organization. The results seemed so much more tangible than she had experienced in teaching. Of course, the satisfaction with teaching had been there, but she never really got to see the results of her work with students, other than the test scores. "Gosh," she thought, "maybe this goal-driven, high-octane world is for me."

Don and Kathy arranged a meeting with the entire HR staff to initiate a dialogue about integrating the functional strategies so that they could begin to set specific objectives for the next one to three years. It was well-accepted by all the functions that staffing, development, performance management, rewards management and employee relations must be aligned if the workforce was to be viable in the short and long term. Although Don had concerns about the dialogue occurring without their common boss in attendance, the marching orders were for them to work it out among equals, achieving consensus without the exercise of any authority associated with title and rank. As Don thought more about it, he realized that even though consensus may be more difficult to achieve, it would be more lasting when it was approached this way. Common public acceptance is a powerful tool for helping people remember what they agreed to and applying social pressure to live up to their commitments. He did not believe they would consciously renege on them, but everyone has selective memory, especially when difficulties arise in living up to agreements.

During the early part of the dialogue, the managers of each of the functional areas pretty much stuck with their own areas of expertise and shied away from seeming to butt into the other managers' areas of expertise. But as the discussion evolved, each of them began to respond when asked if a strategy proposed by another area would impact them and how. Increasingly, it became apparent to those present that every functional strategy was connected to every other strategy and if they neglected to respect the interdependencies, they would not be able to produce the needed outcomes.

The real turning point had come when an analysis on a recent breakdown within HR that had been done by Kathy. For decades, one of the major divisions had hired people with potential and developed them, focusing on internal career development. But competitive pressure had caused them to upgrade their skill mix quickly, which caused them to change strategy and attempt to hire fully qualified senior technicians. They had disappointing acceptance rates, since the offers they were allowed to make were often rejected by candidates. One of the senior recruiters challenged the competence of the compensation staff, claiming that the pay ranges were not competitive and causing the recruiting failures. Not prone to backing away from a fight, the compensation staff rolled out their impressive survey data and told the recruiter to stick with what he knew something about. It took an intervention by the VP to point out that attempting to steal people from other organizations to take the same job they had would demand that a premium be offered, and that their current salary ranges were not designed to fit that strategy. A lot of bruised egos resulted, and it did not help much to reassure them that they had each developed strategies that fit what they thought was needed. And since the VP realized that the turbulent talent market was going to produce a lot of these exogenous shocks, he figured it was time to develop a new approach that had a lot more flexibility and that was responsive to frequent and significant changes. Kathy had recapped this scenario, and it helped the staff to recognize that change was afoot.

With a new respect for the need to align functional strategies, the HR staff committed themselves to increasing cross-functional participation to make their strategy formulation and execution more effective. The new process was to resemble the approach used in concurrent design of new products, all functions involved simultaneously rather than sequentially. They of course neglected to recognize that HR had borrowed an approach from another discipline.

24 Let's buy something

Don was called into a meeting with the VP of HR and the senior staff from the rest of the organization. "You are our workforce planning person, and we have some real workforce planning to do—in a hurry," he confided to Don on the way down the hall. "What is this about?" Don wondered.

The CEO announced that they were going to merge with another organization that was their major competitor in their largest line of business. "It is actually an acquisition, but we thought it would be more palatable to them if we call it a merger. Daimler got away with that for a while when they joined with Chrysler." Don thought to himself that this was a risky move. even though it looked innocent enough on the surface. A merger may call for a different workforce planning strategy than an acquisition, particularly for executives and key personnel. Mergers more or less dictated a joint agreement about who would stay, who would go, who would occupy which roles and what type of culture the new entity would adopt. On the other hand, an acquisition typically is made after the acquirer decides how the entity would be structured and bases its offering price on how much added market value would result. This was particularly true when head-to-head competitors of similar size join together. And the assumption behind the acquisition was that because the acquirer would be in control, that organization's intent would prevail, while in a merger there would be more negotiation and compromise.

Don had become aware of the track record of M&As when he studied the research on the outcomes of these marriages. Sadly, most of them were considered failures or fell short of the expected gains. And one of the principal reasons was poor due diligence on people issues. A faculty member had joked about this in a class he had taken in school, suggesting that the due diligence on HR issues was limited to identifying pending lawsuits and unfunded pension liabilities. She had gone on to suggest that perhaps issues such as staffing levels, pay levels and culture might reasonably be considered as well.

Don did not know if it was appropriate for him to challenge the CEO on the misnaming, but after whispering a question to the VP, he had a green light. "Isn't that labeling going to elicit expectations on the acquired firm that we might find difficult to deal with?" he asked out loud. The CEO smiled and acknowledged this would be a problem if they let it go on too long. "We are just trying to let people in key spots exit with dignity and expect to make the realities clear through internal communication. You will have your hands full with workforce planning, and we want to get you all the information you need. So, we need to figure out when we will have more people in specific jobs, occupations and locations so we can start to sort out the players. For that, you are going to need the cooperation of their HR people, and we have to be clear that we will be calling the shots.

"It is up to employee relations to make this process as humane and fair as possible and we are going to bend over backwards by trying to find slots for every current employee who is competent and who displays a willingness to get on board and perform. In many instances, we are going to need everyone to handle the larger book of business that will result from the combination. But we don't want to start out with excess staff, which will be hard to reduce later. And we don't want to pay people poorly just because they have not been well paid before. We will be imposing our performance standards, and if we adjust salaries upward, they will have to earn it. So, we really need to communicate honestly what we expect and what we are willing to offer for it. People should have the opportunity to sign up or sign out based on a full understanding of the realities."

Don had not met the CEO before, but he was reassured that the senior leadership was as strong as he had been led to believe. As he began to think about what the planning strategy should be, he felt this was going to be one of the most challenging things he had done. One of the trickiest parts of this was getting enough unbiased information about people so that selection and placement decisions were sound. There would be a tendency for the managers to favor the people they knew, and this may not be optimal. Just because the manager who was selected over another for a single available slot was the better choice it did not necessarily mean they would have the best people currently working for them. Don recognized the need to get the HR staffers from the acquired organization on their team and to engage them in gathering the information on employees in an unbiased manner. He recognized this would be a real challenge if some of them were not going to play a role in the merged organization. He made a mental note to use Annette's experience from the acquisition she had worked on in the software firm she had joined right out of school. Her experience had involved crossing cultures as well, and this would be an issue for a number of the jobs in the R & D function, since there were three countries currently hosting the facilities of the two organizations.

He had a brilliant idea about how to do the workforce planning for the combined organization in a manner that was consistent with what he already had implemented as a process. He would use the workforce planning model, but use the combined workforce, acting as if the merger (acquisition) was already complete. The first step would be to compare the combined workforce to the knowledge and skills that are needed and that will be needed within the next two years. He would work with the marketing and operations people to formulate revenue forecasts and estimates of the nature and type of work that must be accomplished in the short term. Then, he would compare what the combined organization had to what it needed. He immediately requested some time with the head of HR and the top marketing and operations managers, so they could verify where they were. Using that as a benchmark, he could analyze staffing levels to see if there were people who would not be needed and if there were needs that could be met either through recruiting or through internal development.

The executives were supportive of Don's approach to workforce planning, and they had already collaborated to produce a three-scenario plan for the combined organization. They had developed an optimistic, a pessimistic and a most likely scenario and had made projections about organizational needs under all three of the possible futures. Luckily, they had made an original estimate of staffing needs, which included both size and mix of knowledge and skills. Don was really enthused about their recognition that the competence of the combined workforce was critical to success of the merged entities. "No sales pitch about the importance of people needed," he thought to himself. And that would make his life a lot easier.

A summit was announced that would include the HR staffs of both organizations. The subject was HR strategy for the new organization. Don had been asked to have the operations executive present his scenario-based operational plans, and then to present the model he proposed to use in doing the workforce plans.

Don presented the model, pointing out that it would be used first to execute the merger and to put into place the workforce needed currently. It would then be used to do one- to three-year projections about what would be needed to sustain the viability of the workforce going forward.

"Once we have done the assessment of how well the combined workforce fits our needs in the short term, we will need to sort out who stays, what roles they will be assigned and what our short-term developmental needs are. We will also look for gaps that we cannot fill internally and look to staffing to get to work developing a strategy for filling them. We will be best served by really stretching to utilize all the capabilities of the people we already have and to perhaps take some risks in assigning them roles they may not be tested in. Our reputation on the street and the morale of our own people is at stake here; if we treat people as our most disposable asset, we will pay in many ways. And we are not jumping into unfamiliar territory—everything we will be doing is already being done by someone. Over time, we may choose to change the way we do things, but people are adaptable, and if we plan ahead, we should be able to help people adapt to these changes. I have Kathy assigned to evaluating alternative types of organization-wide interventions and to develop strategies for executing them."

Before leaving, the operations executive had one more request. "Try to give people the benefit of the doubt when deciding on the roles they might be capable of playing. The last thing we need is to begin our partnership with those who have been with the other organization by making them feel they will get the leftovers after we place our people in the new organization. I want a team of motivated and excited people to help me get this train moving down the tracks." Don and a number of those present reassured him that they were going to avoid terminations if at all possible.

Alicia, the staffing director, made a request. "Let's all try to forecast needs as precisely as possible, since the workforce will be in constant flux and our responsibilities in staffing and HRD require us to build in as much lead time as possible so that we can plan to meet needs. For example, if we wait too long to develop people internally, we will be forced to go into the labor markets and hire job-ready people, which has two drawbacks. First, they are going to be expensive, since we are in effect asking them to change organizations but keep the same job, which will require sizeable bribes. Second, when we jump over our own people, it gives them the impression we are not serious about career management and that their opportunities are limited. If we have the time we can hire people capable of learning and develop them. Obviously, when we require new knowledge/skills we have not had before, it may be necessary to bring in at least some people from the outside. But perhaps we can bring in fewer and use them to train our people, which will reduce the need to buy talent."

"Let me give you an example of a planning tool we used at the utility I worked for when we realized we needed to deal with an impending disaster, due to the mature population of control room operators we had," Don offered (see Figure 24.1).

"What this did for us was to anticipate the incumbent flow and to estimate the need for the next 3 years for people at the various levels of expertise. The senior/lead position required a Class IV water license from the state, and you do not create these people overnight. There had to be one of them on every shift every day of the year, so we did not have the option of having rookies fill in. By making these estimates initially and then continuously updating them as things changed, we were always aiming at specific staffing targets with timelines associated with them. The utilities that waited too long were forced to fill gaps caused by retirements by stealing senior people from other utilities. Not only was that expensive, but so many were trying to use this strategy that there were not enough people to go around anyway. This experience served as a lesson to me, and I believe we must commit to giving Roberto as much time as possible to develop people internally and to only task Alicia with recruitments that are made necessary by growth or unavoidable shortages."

The VP of operations had stuck his head back in to mention one other thing and had seen Don's presentation. He broke in, "Boy, I had no idea you all were

	Entry Level	Journey Level	Senior/Lead
Current staff	4	6	10
Current demand	2	12	6
Current gaps	-2	6	-4
Demand: 1 year out	3 (+1)	12 (-)	6 (-)
Losses projected: next year	1	-1	4
Gaps: 1 year out	0	7	0
Demand: 3 years out	3 (-)	14 (+2)	8 (+2)
Losses projected: next 3 years	4	5	10
Gaps: 3 years out	4	14	12

Progression through levels must be projected as well to determine staffing needs.

Figure 24.1 Workforce flow analysis: control room operators

so aligned with what we try to do in the front lines. Please set up some time with me so I can review some of the planning we have done. I am going to use your models here to redefine our work to date, and we can then begin to work together to be sure that we jointly update our requirements."

The grins were widespread among the HR staff, since many of them suspected the line managers of being opposed to any HR involvement in "line stuff." Several suggested this was a great start to gaining recognition that they had something to offer to the business, although the senior people knew Wayne had been at the table with senior management for some time and that his function was looked to for valuable contributions.

Rob had given Alicia a collection of articles from a research journal on overqualified employees that he thought she would find interesting. She had then approached Don. "We have always been taught to avoid hiring overqualified people, lest they become bored and disruptive until they finally leave in frustration. But the articles in the journal Rob gave me pointed out some possible benefits of people being overqualified, or at least having an overqualified workforce."

Don thought about his response for a bit. "We might be in a situation here that would lend itself to tolerating some overqualification in the newly combined workforce, if for no other reason than to avoid terminating someone who has valuable skills and who performs well. A lot of the high tech companies such as Google and Microsoft hire people who are very smart and then let them shape their roles in a way that contributes to group and organizational effectiveness. So perhaps we should have a dialogue with management about the costs of separating people and comparing that to the cost of having a workforce that is somewhat overqualified and underutilized, at least presently. Management said the combined organization will assume a dominant role in the market and that they expect rapid growth, so maybe we can ensure we have the workforce in place to handle it." Don asked Alicia to prepare a summary of the material she had read about the impact of overqualification and take the lead in the dialogue with senior management as they laid out plans for integrating the workforces.

25 Friends and colleagues join the multinational

Don got a call from the VP of HR asking him to attend a meeting along with the staffing director. When he got to the VPs office, he was stunned by the topic. The staffing director had gotten Annette's name from a search consultant as a prime candidate for the director of employee relations job that was soon to be vacant. "Well, she is certainly qualified," responded Don. "You OK with this?" asked Wayne, with his smile turning into a serious expression. "Sure," Don replied. "So, I will invite her to come for interviews with all the HR directors," Alicia said to Wayne and Don.

Don was a big believer in maintaining one's cool, but this was a test. "So, what is the professional thing to do, discuss it tonight or let it rest until the interviews?" he deliberated. He realized that he would have to face the music tonight but did not necessarily dread it. What would be challenging is adhering to the structured interview model they used for candidates, since it would be really challenging to treat her as if she were a stranger. He wished he had taken some acting classes in school, which would have been useful in maintaining a professional demeanor.

The interviews went well and Annette told the directors she would be very interested in the role she was being considered for. After the sessions were over, the directors met as a group and decided that they had just saved a search fee. Although Don had been silent throughout most of the group discussions, he did raise some issues and even suggested that perhaps they should look at other candidates. "I did that," responded Alicia, "and did not feel any of them warranted a session with the combined group." The consensus was that an offer should be made to Annette and that if she accepted, that she should come on board as soon as she could comfortably disengage from her current employer. "There are going to be some regrets on her final day," thought Don, since he knew how important the organization's work was to her.

At the end of the meeting, Roberto told the group he had an announcement to make. Everyone was aware that he had been going back to his home in Mexico from childhood through his university tenure and now went there frequently for vacations. "As a result of discussions with people there, I have become convinced I can make more of a contribution by teaching at the Technical Institute there than I can here at Alpha Corporation. Mexico needs to take advantage of our young people by educating them so they can compete globally and not just on the basis of low cost."

Roberto left to break the news to Wayne. While the rest of them were in the room, Don made a suggestion. "How would you feel about approaching Rob about the HRD role?" he asked, somewhat timidly. "What are you trying to do, take the place over?" Alicia asked with a smile. "I don't view it as nepotism in its ugly form," responded Don. "Rather, I think people who are known to you and who have worked with you on difficult challenges are a safer bet than a stranger. People are great at filling their resumes with all of their strengths, but they often fail to highlight their weaknesses. Although we are pretty good at screening people, we cannot read minds and we cannot simulate how people will react under stress in our type of environment, even by using assessment centers. I always laughed when our global HR professor, who was Indonesian by birth, challenged us to justify our negative view in America of hiring an acquaintance or even a relative. He suggested that you had more leverage with someone you could embarrass in front of the entire extended family and social network than you did with a stranger who may be just passing through on their way to the next best opportunity. We have been so conditioned to view nepotism as an evil that we cannot look at the other side of it as many Latin and Asian cultures do. But if you want me to withdraw from the deliberations over Rob, I will do so." Alicia chimed in with support by pointing out that Don was a hard-hearted, rational professional, who probably did not like anyone enough to risk making a recommendation that might reflect badly on him. Don was not quite sure how to take that, but since no one objected, he would stay engaged in the process. But he was a bit concerned that Wayne might view this hiring of Don's graduating class a bit suspiciously. "I will take the lead on this, as I should," offered Alicia.

When Rob was contacted by Alicia, he immediately wondered if Don was behind some kind of practical joke. But knowing Alicia fairly well, he doubted she would be the shill for someone who wanted to play a prank. His first reaction was to ask himself about his satisfaction level with his academic–consultant existence. He had just won an outstanding educator award and there had been a fair amount of consulting work to pad his income. There was a rumor he would be submitted for tenure consideration shortly, and although he thought that indicated a satisfaction with his work by the university, he was not focused on tenure. Maybe it was time for him to consider a change in what he did, if for no other reason than to prove to himself that he could move easily across the academic, consultant and practitioner roles. He strongly believed that it was in his best interests to have the greatest number of options available, given the turbulent environment that seemed here to stay. It was obvious to him that believing you did not have to learn anything new once you were on top of everything was a really dumb strategy. What you are on top of could turn out to be a dormant but still active volcano, one disruption away from finding you are not OK sitting still.

So, although he had grudgingly agreed to be considered for the HRD role during Alicia's call, after giving it some thought, he decided to open discussions with a truly open mind. The benefits of making the change of course included being able to work directly with his closest friends. The drawbacks included the reality that he would be working directly with his closest friends. Professionally, it would work. He respected each of them for their knowledge and their commitment, in addition to having no doubts about their ethics. He foresaw no petty competitions going on created by someone trying to look better than the others. That would be a real plus, since there is always the possibility that dysfunctional competition would occur in an organization, and especially within a function. So, he promised himself he would treat it like he would any job interview but would also know that many of the uncertainties of joining a new organization would be minimized because of the people in place.

It did not take long for the selection process to conclude, and Rob really appreciated the way Alicia had handled herself professionally. After all, she was the only person who did not know Rob well and was dealing with peers who obviously wanted to see Rob sign on. So, once the structured interview questions had been asked and answered, Rob had one question. He was skeptical about the impact of bringing a number of outsiders in at a time when the merger probably resulted in too many staff members in the new combined HR function. He knew how damaging it could be to morale if every open slot was filled from the outside, and the last thing he wanted was to start his new job with a group of subordinates who resented him.

The interviewers had discussed this issue extensively prior to Rob's interview, so they were ready with an answer. Alicia responded to Rob by sharing the decision that they needed a new start with Wayne's direct reports, and she also told him that many of the HR staff in the acquired firm had expressed a desire to leave, some because they resented the merger, and some because they knew the performance standards imposed would not be to their liking or that they thought them to be unachievable. One of the things Wayne had discovered when conducting the merger meetings for the combined HR staff is that HR had not been viewed as a business partner in the other organization, and the status of the function was reflected in the low grades their HR jobs were assigned. As typically happens, you get what you pay for, and the organization had not seen any reason to pay that much for administrative support people, which is what the HR staff was believed to be. The quick response encouraged Rob, and he violated one of his own principles: he asked where he should sign before he knew what his compensation package would be.

Don acted professionally and put a straight question to Rob. "Are you willing to give up your consulting practice?" he asked. "I thought about that a lot," Rob responded, "and I talked with Howard about it, since he channels most of the work to me. It was getting to be a bit much with both the academic activities—teaching and research—and the consulting. At times, I found myself letting research efforts slide, since there are no formal deadlines imposed, while clients are infinitely impatient and demanding. So, doing one job, even if it is an 80-hours-a-week job, will enable me to focus more."

After a few "anybody have any reservations" glances, the group ended the interview and told Rob he would receive a formal offer letter no later than the following day. "That is Saturday," Rob responded. "And you think you are starting a five-days-a-week job?" responded Alicia.

Rob started the same day Annette did, so the staffer who did new employee orientations was thrilled—one less to do. The organization had done a lot of developmental work on their onboarding process, driven mostly by Alicia, and both the rookies were pleased with the quality of the information they received and the timing of the information so that it was received when it was relevant and needed. When introduced to the manager of HRIS, Rob got another shock. It was Eric, who had taught with both him and Kathy at the school, often coming into their classes to provide a more in-depth understanding of how technology should be used in HR. "You went for the riches too," Eric said, smiling.

The first week was filled with introductions and orientations from key people from all parts of the organization. Alpha's CEO believed in teaching all employees the essentials of the business and wanted the key management personnel to be fully versed on everything that was going on. This would help to engage everyone in what needed to be done and to equip them with an understanding of how all the parts produced a whole, integrated result. Rob began to share Don's admiration of the CEO, and it really went up when the CEO joined Wayne in taking the two new staffers to lunch, which went on for over two hours. Later, Wayne indicated that there were a number of changes afoot with the merger, and the CEO wanted to get to know the direct reports of his direct reports, and anyone else who would be involved in creating the new, combined organization. There was no doubt the CEO believed that their people were indeed their most important asset.

Annette had been thrilled when she found out that the top executives were locked up in all-day (and most of the night) strategy meetings relating to executing the merger because it needed to be done, and that they were doing so on-site. "They didn't blow $300k on fancy resort rooms and meals, and they wanted to be where they could call people to join them if they needed assistance or information," she thought, "and that money could be better spent on our incentive plan awards." She marveled at what a fine capitalist she was apparently capable of being. Besides, Rob scorned at executive retreats, saying his old military division never retreated. She reminded him that his division had in the past parachuted behind enemy lines so that they were outnumbered thirty to one and then surprised the enemy by fighting their way out. "That would be a questionable competitive strategy in business," she thought, but she did not think it worth the conflict that would ensue if she pointed that out to him.

Wayne came out of the executive sessions and called a staff meeting of the HR directors. When they had all gathered, he said that the new organization had been for the most part settled, and he wanted to share the results with them. To begin the dialogue, he handed out an organization chart. Wayne was listed as the VP of administration, which included HR, legal and IT.

"What do we call you now, your eminence?" Don blurted out. "That is if we get to talk to you at all." Wayne responded by saying that his apparent elevation was mostly a vertical position on the piece of paper because the extra money did not warrant him changing his ride to a Bentley. Don was a bit stunned by the appearance of the manager of HR research slot for Kathy that he had thought would require a long battle to get approval for. But what really got his attention was the absence of a name in the VP of HR box. "We going to be a leaderless mob," he asked, pushing his luck by assuming Wayne was in a good mood. After all, Wayne's empire had been expanded greatly, and surely he would now engage in equity plans that would produce wealth beyond imagination (assuming the merger went well).

"Who do you all think should take that spot?" Wayne responded. "It will be one of you directors," he added. "I am not going outside when I have such a wealth of talent right here." "Alicia has the most in-depth knowledge of the organization," Don responded. "Forget it," Alicia jumped in. "I don't have the broad knowledge of all the functions and honestly I love staffing. Besides, I have always viewed subordinates as dependents that you could not deduct on your income tax filing. And looking at this collection of characters, there is no way I would assume responsibility for them." "That is an interesting viewpoint for a manager," Rob noted. "Don't get me wrong," she said. "I love my recruiters and the folks who do testing and run the assessment center. But they pretty much do their own thing and are not that much of a bother. Having employee relations report to me is something I can do without." "Now I feel bad," said Annette.

"OK," interjected Wayne, "what do you all think? Do you want me to do a search for that spot?" "No, put Don into it," responded Alicia. "He won't do a lot of harm and that HR planning function is not a full-time job. He is already on the verge of sitting in the park feeding the pigeons in the afternoon, when he runs out of something to do. And if caught, he would claim he was doing long-range planning." After the laughter died down, an eerie silence descended over the group. "Going once, going twice," said Wayne. "No objections and Don is it." He looked at Annette as if to say, "Can you work for this guy?" and Annette just nodded affirmatively. Don jumped in with a mandate. "If I do take it, I don't want any silos within HR. We all get involved in everything, and major decisions within each function will be by consultation with the other directors, managers and the staff members affected. And one more thing: I want the performance criteria for directors in the incentive plan to be tied 100% to organization-wide performance—no HR-specific criteria and no functional or individual criteria. We allocate the resources available to HR in a way that optimizes organizational performance. We rise and we fall together. (He used that rather than his favorite quote from revolutionary times, "We must hang together or we surely will hang separately"). "Deal," Wayne responded. "Any other issues?

Wayne continued. "Now that we have created this traditional organization chart to satisfy the people who are obsessed with order and control, let's talk about how we really are going to function. HR is not going to be a bunch of functional silos. We have all agreed with that. So, let's define our key HR processes, map them and then have people sign up to participate in those they can contribute to. The chart may look something like Figure 25.1.

Staffing

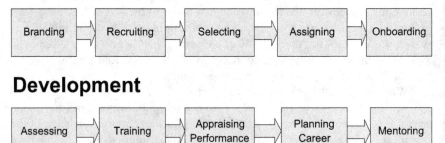

Development

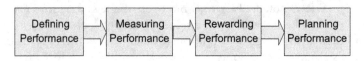

Performance and Rewards Management

Figure 25.1 HR processes

"Everyone should start thinking about where they will contribute and how to each of these processes. If you have something to contribute in one of these boxes, then sign up to participate on the team that will ensure what needs to happen happens. Employee relations, HRIS and HR research will be involved to varying degrees in each of the processes, and I ask the leaders of each of those functions to take a system-wide perspective. Also, those of you reporting directly to Don should act as an integrating team to ensure each of you respects that how you manage your function will often impact the other processes. And since 100% of your annual cash incentive plan is based on overall organization performance, it is in your best interests not to compete for resources, but rather to work in concert to be sure they are used in an optimal fashion.

"Any comments? If not, we are all going to go to lunch at my favorite over-priced restaurant, and the event will be funded out of my newfound wealth."

Before leaving for lunch, Wayne corrected the organization chart, putting Don in the VP of HR slot and taking out the separate HR planning function. He thought to himself that it was mostly luck that he was able to bring a lot of new perspectives into HR at a time when the merger called for a clean slate at the director level. Alicia was the only old-timer, and she had spent a lot of time finding spots for the people from the other organization who wanted to stay and who had the needed knowledge and skills, so she was already acclimated to the new organization. Wayne realized that they might have to thin the HR staff a bit more once the flurry of activity made necessary by the merger was past. But he had bigger plans for HR.

Don asked Wayne at lunch why he had created the HR research function, which had only been the subject of casual conversation. "I have been giving a lot of thought to that test you shared with us about what behavioral research has found, the one Sara Rynes had done in conjunction with SHRM. And I realized if HR people only answered twenty out of thirty-five questions correctly, that managers would probably do a lot worse. So, we have people making decisions based on questionable assumptions while, at the same time, we have this mountain of research that is available to correct those assumptions. There just needs to be a bridge built between research and practice, the evidence-based management thing that Rousseau[1] and Latham[2] have written about. Wayne had become friends with the CEO of a gaming corporation that had built a reputation for rejecting the use of raw intuition or past assumptions (the stuff "everyone knows"). When someone told him something would not work, his response is, 'What is the evidence supporting that?' So, I do not want to manage using practices that are not supported by evidence. Therefore, given Kathy's ability to serve as that needed bridge and to provide us with evidence that will make our human capital decisions better informed, I figured it was time to acknowledge the need by giving her that responsibility."

Don was also curious that nowhere on the HR organization chart did the responsibility for performance management and rewards management show up. "Yes," responded Wayne, "our manager is going to go to work for their family business, and those areas were grossly underemphasized in our partner organization. So, you figure it out, but let's talk about it." Don was ready to dive into this issue but figured he ought to let Wayne enjoy the lunch, since he was out of pocket for it, particularly after Don had looked at the prices on the menu. "Later," he said, "after I give it some thought." Don looked around the room and smiled, thinking this was like a class reunion for several of us, and the others who did not go through the graduate program with them were a welcome addition to the clan.

Don spent the evening after the luncheon wrestling with the alternatives for assigning the responsibility for performance management and rewards management. Performance management was something that often went unassigned to any specific manager in HR. Sometimes it was assumed to be the responsibility of an OD function, if there was one. It was much too important to be an orphan, and Don had always been concerned about that in his prior jobs. He had read with great interest the proposition that performance and rewards were inextricably linked and, after thinking about it, had adopted that viewpoint.[3] Rob and Annette had been shocked that one of the certification programs for rewards management practitioners had dropped performance management as a required course, since it was unlikely someone could design and administer a merit pay or incentive program without knowledge of the subject. How could you reward performance if you were not able to define, measure and manage it?

His deliberations led him to conclude that both performance and rewards would be the responsibility of one manager, in order to ensure they were integrated. But no candidates came to mind, and he thought he might need to have Alicia test the market. He was really saddened that no one from the organization they were merging with was an apparent candidate, since they had promised themselves that their current employees would be seriously considered. "Well," he thought, "how much of an effort are you willing to make to find someone who would otherwise be leaving the new organization but who might be qualified, even though they might be stretched?"

Don called Howard and asked him if he would meet with the other HR directors to discuss this issue. Howard was in town and willing, even anxious, to have a powwow. Since Howard had built rewards management practices in several consulting firms and had managed both performance and rewards systems in large organizations, he would be the perfect source for advice. The first question out of Howard was, "Are you sure that since you will be teaming on all major issues that there is not someone in your organization that could be stretched into a manager of rewards, as well as taking on benefits?" Wayne had walked into the room and offered his opinion. "Would that include performance management as well?" Wayne asked. Howard thought about that and then asked Don, "Could you have Rob and Kathy work on performance management for a time, gathering all the relevant research on the topic and proposing alternative strategies and systems?" "Sure," responded Don, without bothering to consult those who would inherit the task. "I wanted them on that team anyway, no matter who managed it, and I can manage it for a time. Everyone agreed that this would be the approach, and they turned back to Howard's question about someone who could step in to the C&B role.

Wayne offered a possibility. "You all have worked with Pete, one of the senior analysts. I know you all think he is a Peter Pan type who believes in that rot that you should have a life and that you don't have to be deadly serious about everything that happens at work. I looked at his file and he is really smart, as well as having the professional certifications. Would you think it a good idea to do an assessment on him? If he looks like a good candidate, Rob could partner with him, with Kathy providing some research to guide your evaluation of the current system. I don't think anything is broken, but we could use some guidance on things like reconfiguring the packages for executives and managers assuming new roles. Don and I are particularly interested in that activity, as are some of you."

Alicia said she would take Pete's file and find out if he was a diamond in the rough. If he was, she would outline what would be required to polish him. Alicia also noted, "Even though some of you are getting promotions that move your box vertically on the organization chart, I am inheriting an awful lot of extra work—remember to keep some project and spot incentive award budget for people like me." Don said they would all be rewarded based on organizational performance in the annual incentive plan, but that they would be looking at increasing the pool for outstanding contributions on projects and special assignments. He envisioned a lot of those awards being team awards, given the fact that they would be functioning much more as teams and less as individuals. "That sounds like creeping socialism to me," Eric shot back.

"What happened to the 'John Wayne won the war single-handedly' approach?" Don suggested that he had seen too many movies and that he believed the biggest mistake pioneers made is not handing out Wagon Train of the Year awards, to promote the cooperative behavior necessary to make it across uncharted territory. Don thought to himself that they might not always accomplish a lot in some of their meetings, but that working with this crew would certainly be entertaining. "Give me a group of individuals who do not take themselves too seriously every time," he thought.

Notes

1 Rousseau, D., "Evidence-Based Management," *Academy of Management Review*, Vol. 31, No. 2, 2006.
2 Latham, G., *Becoming the Evidence-Based Manager*, 2009, Nicholas-Brealey, Boston, MA.
3 Greene, R., *Rewarding Performance: Guiding Principles; Custom Strategies*, 2011, Routledge, New York.

26 The merger materializes

Despite some bumps in the road on the way to a combined organization, the merger was pretty much a reality 3 months later. The lessons learned session with senior management had been held, and one of the lessons that had been emphasized is that people issues should be under the microscope the first day an acquisition or merger possibility becomes a gleam in the eyes of executive management. For Wayne, one of the most encouraging developments was that senior management did not make this a simplistic "get the HR function involved early" thing, but rather was focused on the human capital issues that were critical to the success of the effort. Of course, HR would play a major role in addressing some of the issues, but responsibilities would be shared among all who had something to offer. Finance should be involved in evaluating issues such as the probable magnitude of unfunded liabilities for pension or retiree health benefits, supported by legal, but HR should evaluate the probable impact on the workforce if benefits were to be cut back or terminated. In fact, key management personnel came to realize that few critical concerns belonged solely to one function. The CEO made it clear to all that the next time they evaluated strategies for growth, they would be more realistic about the potential downsides of a merger or acquisition and weigh them against the benefits, as well as against the option of growing internally.

The HR function settled down a bit, or at least a majority of the key roles had stable membership. Pete had been given the nod and had taken the rewards strategy challenge to heart. In fact, a few weeks after ascending to the throne, he presented a long list of things that should be redesigned, abolished or implemented. His presentation reminded Don of the aggressive recommendations he had made in his first job at the utility, which had put his future status with the organization in question. But he had been dealing with people that were used to a stable state or at best glacial-speed change. Here, people would also respond to a recommendation with "are you crazy?" but would follow up with "had you thought about this instead?" It really was an honest dialogue when the key managers got together, and that atmosphere was increasingly evident when the rest of the staff addressed an issue. Don had made one of the conference rooms an open dialogue room, where anyone walking by could ask what the occupants were working on and join in if the topic was of interest to them. "Runs like a bloody ad agency," Eric observed, being the only one who used email for any communications with someone in the same building anymore.

Don got a call from Howard, who had been thinking about the C&B function. He was familiar with Ed, a retired C&B director who had been at a national research laboratory for years. He was a veteran of a number of major innovations during his tenure. Don asked if Ed could work with Pete more as a coach than a teacher, helping him anticipate the consequences of changes to strategies and programs. When Howard indicated that would be a perfect role for Ed, Don said he would discuss it with Pete. The discussion was pretty short when he met with Pete. "Let's see, I get all sorts of expert advice and I don't have to share my paycheck. Gee, I don't know," Pete responded to Don's suggestion. Don remembered that he had been told nothing was easy with Pete, so he treated it as an attempt at humor and the deal was sealed. Don added Pete's box to the organization chart and ran it by Wayne, who supported his approach. "Just be careful he does not push changes that would only serve to challenge and amuse him," Wayne requested. "We have had quite enough change for a while, and until we digest that, people are not going to have an appetite for another course, no matter how good it is. On the other hand, if something needs changing, then let's do it if we are sure it will positively impact organizational performance."

The organization had changed in several ways after the merger. One of the disappointments was the outflow via voluntary turnover by some of the most entrepreneurial and innovative software designers. Although they had no reason to believe that the new organization would not continue to design leading-edge products, they felt a sense of loss when they felt what they had built had been submerged into a larger entity. This was a lesson that Don had taken away from the process. People don't have to believe they are going to lose out relative to rewards or position status in order to feel a sense of loss. Identifying with an organization is much like belonging to a family, a club or a social network, and people often rebel when the boundaries of the entity they identify with are blurred. Of course, some of the blurring was a necessary outcome of a merger—having two distinct entities would not have produced the economies of scale or the larger pool of knowledge that were much of the reason for pursuing the merger in the first place. There still were pockets of culture that sometimes bumped into each other, but by mixing people on project teams, they had diminished the intensity of the conflicts.

Don was still concerned that with the close relationships that existed between many of the staff members within HR that groupthink was a constant threat. Taking on a close friend is an action fraught with peril, even though everyone understands this is not personal—it's business. Sometimes people erred on the side of caution and spent too much energy trying not to agree too easily or too quickly. But better that than lapsing into a semi-automatic routine where one person suggested and the others signed on without adequate due diligence.

One of the issues that Pete had raised rang true to the team when it was presented. That was to get rid of retiree health programs. Pete had suggested the liability it created was a problem, but a much bigger issue was that some key people had accumulated considerable wealth and were inclined to retire in their mid-50s. His recommendation is to immediately raise the premium to 100% of the cost for all future retirees and to raise them for current retirees to 50% of the cost now and to increase their share by an additional 10%, 20% and 20% of the cost over each of the next three years. Don experienced a high-voltage flashback to a similar recommendation he had made at the utility. "This guy Pete is pretty smart," he thought.

The group backed the move, although Alicia pointed out that this could impact her. "You all are lucky that I love my work and that you will have to force me out when I no longer am able to function. But let's be careful that we don't create the same problem that can occur with restricted stock grants—you build in a lot of retention power into a program and then find out you are keeping some people you wish would leave." Pete noted that most of the people in the age group this would impact were earning six-figure salaries and that the cost of health care would not be a significant determinant of how long they wanted to work. "Besides," said Pete, "if people should not be here, we should see to it that they are not here. This is not a home for the unofficially retired." Although the rest of the group thought that he might have expressed that point somewhat differently, they agreed with the principle and realized that this was not an organization that would suffer non-contributors for long. Have them exit with dignity and respect, but exit.

When Pete, Don and Wayne presented the retiree health recommendation, one of the concerns the CEO had expressed was that it seemed that all news was bad news regarding the merger when employees were informed of changes. "There are people who were moved out of the organization, leaving their colleagues and friends upset, and there have been major upward adjustments to performance expectations. If we now look like we are cutting employee benefits anywhere we can, the employees are going to believe that the merger was all about reducing costs and increasing profits. It is going to seem to them that the cost reductions are all at their expense."

"I would rather explain the reasons we have for cutting, or even eliminating, retiree health benefits in business terms," responded Wayne. "We have to make it clear that incenting people to retire when we actually want them to stay five to ten years longer is a questionable strategy, and retiree health is that incentive. We had replaced the defined benefit pension plan with a defined contribution plan several years ago, and we tied the company match formula to organizational performance. That broke down the idea that the longer you stayed, the more benefits you received. It also stopped rewarding people for leaving and taking retirement benefits at such an early age that they might receive benefits longer than they worked. That type of reward is dysfunctional, and it was one of the best moves we have made. The other reason for retiree health changes is that we have to charge the liability the plan creates against our performance, and that just distorts our results."

"OK," the CEO responded, "put together a communication plan and let's move on it. Now I have a challenge for you all. Wall Street just does not value us in proportion to our real value, and that is hurting our investors and limiting our resources. I have been studying some research on valuing intangible assets, and I think that is an area where we are not receiving credit for what we have. The work on valuing intangible assets[1] and on intellectual capital[2] really opened my eyes to the fact that assets can be more than what the accountants will recognize as such. Assets are things that have broad acceptance that they are of value. And that includes intellectual capital (our workforce), intellectual property (our patents and proprietary software), social capital (our culture) and operational capital (our ability to deliver products efficiently and effectively). That, the analysts don't see. There has been a change—some recent research shows they do consider things like sound management in their valuation. But we don't have much in the way of tangible assets. We don't keep a lot of cash, we don't own much of the infrastructure we utilize and we lease the computer equipment. Ninety-five percent of our true assets walk out the door at the end of the day, and we hope they come back sometime later. I agree we don't own our human capital, but we do a pretty good job of getting our people engaged in the business of the organization and in making them want to stay and to contribute their best."

Don was excited by the CEO's positive view of the culture and the value of their workforce. The merger had produced some bumps along the road to a combined organization, but they had not blown any tires. The general counsel had stood tall when a few employees started hinting they were considering discrimination suits. He responded simply that the organization was treating them fairly, respectfully and in a businesslike manner. If they did choose to sue the organization and if the organization believed the suit was unfounded, it would fight the case and ask to be reimbursed for its legal expenses when the case was thrown out. He had jokingly responded to another executive, suggesting they settle these things out of court by suggesting, "Let's put a sign right next to the corporate sign that has a target painted on it, along with the words 'nuisance suits welcome.'"

After a good bit of discussion, it was decided that Wayne's direct reports would identify all the things of value to the organization that the accountants would not let into the financial statements and recommend how they could present a case that these "assets" were not being adequately considered. "I remember reading the book *Intellectual Capital*[3] and also heard about the intangible asset statement that Skandia Insurance had used. Creating a statement like that would serve as a good marketing tool," Wayne suggested.

Rob had been in the latter part of the meeting and offered that the average market value of U.S. corporations was about seven times their book value, which was a pretty good indication that something the accountants ignored was valued. "So, we need to brand ourselves to the investment community as an organization that effectively utilizes our intangibles, much as the way we brand ourselves as a desirable employer to potential and current employees," Rob suggested. "Better call marketing and have them send over a few of their most influential con artists," he jokingly said to Wayne.

Everyone present realized they would be merchandising a new product to the analysts, since the merger had materially changed the organization. An obvious strategy would be to show the combination had not cost them customers and that total costs had gone down. Reconfiguring office leases, selling some excess building capacity and combining the computer capabilities had all produced cost savings. And the people costs had gone down also. But they would have to be careful to show that people cost reductions were not the result of mindless downsizing that would cut into their capacity for developing and selling products over the long run. Investment analysts had been fooled too many times by restructurings that left organizational capabilities hollowed out, resulting in poor results in the long run, even though costs had been cut and profits increased in the short run.

When Don started accumulating information that might be useful in their quest to gain appreciation for the real value of their intangible assets, he considered using statistics on turnover, employee job satisfaction and acceptance ratio for job offers. He realized he would have to be careful to factor out involuntary turnover driven by poor performance and resignations that had resulted from the merger. The more he thought about how to separate desirable from undesirable turnover, the more he realized that he could not make the distinction believable to someone who does not have an in-depth knowledge of the skills and knowledge their organization required in order to be successful. After extended deliberations, he decided that turnover numbers calculated close to a major restructuring event were not meaningful, at least for demonstrating the organization was able to retain its valued talent.

"Metrics, metrics—everyone says the more the better, but when they are meaningless, it is time to use good judgment and shift to focusing on results," he mused. "After all, if we can show we ended up with a capable workforce as a result of the merger, that should be evidence that we are capable of selecting the people we need and to reshape our human capital to match our needs." He then shifted to acceptance ratios, which he realized would also be unusable, since they were not doing as much recruiting as they normally would. And he would be reluctant to do an employee satisfaction survey until things settled a bit more after the merger process. When this thought process was finished, he decided to recommend they not build a case using the normal statistics, but rather sell others on the performance the newly combined workforce was producing.

Don shifted direction and decided to look at their intellectual capital, which along with social capital constitutes human capital. He had extracted a model of intellectual capital that he felt they could use to frame their explorations.[4]

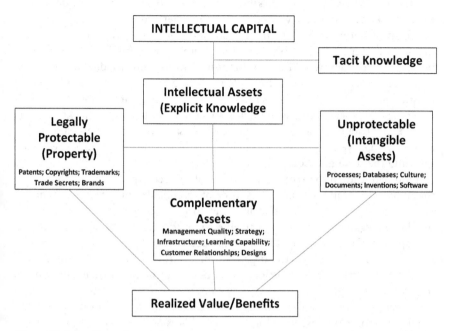

Figure 26.1 Intellectual capital

Don had found that social capital is defined by the World Bank as "norms and social relations imbedded in social structures that enable groups to coordinate actions and achieve desired goals." He believed that culture is the software that allows social capital to be created and used to further organizational effectiveness. Don felt that their culture was strong, appropriate and flexible and that it enabled the organization to function as a viable ecosystem. And when adequate social capital exists, it makes it possible to fully use the available intellectual capital. Don found the cultural assessment they had done not long ago to be very helpful in helping them fine-tune their culture and in increasing employee understanding of the type of organization they wanted to be, especially after merging the two organizations.

Nonaka's distinction between explicit and tacit knowledge[5] was useful in his attempt to evaluate their intellectual capital. Explicit knowledge was accessible, since it was defined in writing and/or was imbedded into policies and procedures. Tacit knowledge was carried around in people's heads but difficult to transmit to others quickly. The use of apprenticeship programs in the skilled trades was an example of a process intended to facilitate tacit knowledge transmission by the possessor to others. Tacit knowledge is generally acquired as a result of extensive experience doing something or repeating a mental process long enough to make it almost instinctive. The tacit knowledge is lost to an organization if someone leaves without rendering it explicit, which is why you try not to have only one person who knows how to perform critical activities.

Don had several people working on a project that was focused on identifying the knowledge that was critical to their performance, whether it be in the form of knowing how to modify software or in knowing how to keep a major customer from deserting to a competitor. Once this critical knowledge was identified, they would determine who had that knowledge and whether it was or could be codified into explicit knowledge. Then they could decide on strategies to disseminate critical knowledge, explicitly if possible or through initiating apprentice-type assignments so others could access the knowledge and act as a backup to avoid turnover being disastrous. They could also create a "knowledge yellow pages" to enable people to find out who knew what, speeding the dissemination process.

Don had studied the work of a number of respected people who contended that intellectual capital is the only source of sustainable competitive advantage. However, they pointed out that in order to be a competitive advantage, the intellectual capital must be: (1) valuable to customers, (2) difficult to imitate, (3) superior to that of competitors, (4) produce needed products, (5) capable of being diffused throughout the organization and (6) useful in the future.[6] One of the unfortunate characteristics of accounting principles is that investments in intellectual capital (e.g., training) are charged as current expenses, and the organization is never able to offset that charge with an addition to its assets when preparing statements. Don realized this is why when revenue drops, organizations subject to pressure to produce short-term profits often cut investments in training, research and advertising. After all, these things are certain costs in the short term, and there is no guarantee they will result in future revenue or benefits of any kind.

Legal had done a review of the intellectual property and found that many of their patents could have value but were not being used effectively. Other patents were not being used at all in current products and were unlikely to be useful in the future. There were organizations who could benefit from licensing agreements that would enable them to use the organization's intellectual property and who would pay a fee to do so. They would of course be careful not to put proprietary information into the hands of potential competitors, particularly when entering into joint ventures in other countries where intellectual property protection was weak. But the review disclosed a revenue source that had been underutilized. Legal also shared information with the R & D function on patents that could be useful in protecting new products being designed.

Eric had suggested their IT function be involved in the evaluation of intangible assets as well. He believed they had developed computer-based systems that could generate new software from established routines and even fix defects in very complex programs much more quickly than could be done by people. Eric suggested that even if all these initiatives did not result in hard evidence that impressed the investment community, that they would know more about things that were really valuable to them and that they could make more intelligent decisions about what to invest resources in. Don thought about that for a long while.

Certainly, they would benefit from the intrinsic value this effort offered. "That geek Eric is pretty business savvy as well as being smart," he concluded.

As the evaluation process continued, Don realized he was building a strong case that their people were indeed their most important asset. They had invented processes that could be patented, they had designed the expert systems that enabled their computer systems to increase productivity and they had acquired and maintained their customer base. Knowing that he did not need to convince the HR staff of this reality, he wondered who he needed to sell it to. Not the CEO; he was on board, as was Wayne. And the other executives certainly had made the people their focus during the merger. "So, I guess I only need to write a book that gives ammunition to the HR people in organizations where senior management does not get it." He made a note to talk to Rob about partnering with him, since he could add some behavioral research that might make the message more compelling. "But then when would he have time to write a book?" he wondered. He could wait until he retired, but by then maybe the skeptics would have had an epiphany and would have accepted the proposition that people were key to success. "Sure," he thought, "and maybe I will be 6'4" and svelte by then."

When the project team met to review their findings, Wayne was extremely pleased with the results of their efforts. "I agree with the notion that we have gotten a rich payback in the form of learning, whether or not our findings influence our market valuation. I have asked the CFO to work with us to find a way to get tangible credit for some of the assets we believe have been ignored or undervalued. The review of our patents and proprietary systems has opened the door for licensing agreements that can generate revenue. And while that subject is on the table, I want Don to see if we should develop an incentive plan that rewards people who create marketable intellectual property. We have to be careful not to overlook those who invent new ways to design and implement systems just because the benefits are internal and do not materialize in the form of revenue."

"I had a discussion with Pete about our project incentive plans the other day," Don responded, "and he had suggested that we add a component to our project incentives for new products that would share market success with the folks who design, create and roll out the products. This was a really good insight. Giving project staff a stake in product performance for a couple of years would really make it clear that though the product designs are brilliant, someone has to be willing to buy the stuff in order for the organization to benefit."

It was becoming increasingly clear to those involved that HR, legal, IT and finance should begin to play a major role in setting the R & D agenda, if only to provide input on how great ideas could be turned into revenue and into Alpha's capabilities in the form of intellectual capital. People who had in the past identified with their function or occupation were realizing that boundaries between functions were obstacles to effective functioning. Michael Porter had it right when observing that management is better at managing vertically than horizontally and that many management systems contributed to the creation of dysfunctional silos.[7] Don and Wayne committed to ensuring that HR strategies for staffing, development, performance management and rewards management should encourage integration of functions, an aligned focus on meeting organizational objectives and optimizing the application of its core capabilities.

The CEO set up meetings with influential members of the investment community and for a few weeks was a missionary. Apparently, the message took, since the stock price nudged up and the rating services were publishing more optimistic assessments of Alpha's future. Now they all had to turn their great ideas into realized gains.

Notes

1 Lev, B., *Intangibles*, 2001, Brookings Institute, Washington DC.
2 Edvinsson, L. and Malone, M., *Intellectual Capital*, 1997, Harper Business, New York.
3 Stewart, T., *Intellectual Capital*, 1997, Currency Doubleday, New York.
4 Boisot, M., *Knowledge Assets*, 1998, Oxford University Press, Oxford, UK.
5 Nonaka, I. and Takeuchi, H., *The Knowledge-Creating Company*, 2008, Harvard Business School Publishing, Boston, MA.
6 Leonard, D. and Swap, W., *When Sparks Fly*, 2009, HBS Press, Boston, MA.
7 Porter, M., *Competitive Advantage*, 1985, Free Press, New York.

27 Improving HR service levels and productivity

Eric had been energized by his participation in the review of intellectual capital, and while his little grey cells were agitated, he decided to pursue a pet project that had not been moving forward because of the other activities they had all been engaged in. He was dedicated to creating an HR service center, where employees could get 24/7 advice, handle routine transactions themselves and do queries and research. This would help them make decisions about things like making fund allocations within the flexible benefits program and allocating their defined benefit plan fund balances. Eric had taken a transactional analysis course from a psychologist at a local institute and had been intrigued by her suggestion that the last two cohorts entering the workforce had grown up necessarily more self-reliant, due to the increased numbers of households with two working parents. As a result, the parent-child type of transaction became increasingly problematic and these Xers, Yers and Millennials did not accept being fed the information someone in authority was willing to provide. Social networking tools had put the young people in touch with each other, and they already were in control of the information they sought via the internet. So, Eric concluded, the HR service center seems to be a good way to recognize these changes.

This was partially an IT project, but it also was very much an HR project. and minimizing HR involvement would increase the risk that a robotic system would result and employees would have been done a disservice. He also planned to build in a module that would help staffing connect with potential candidates and to brand the organization as an employer. Alicia had marveled at what companies like Cisco had done to their recruitment and selection process to both provide information and service to people inquiring about opportunities, and to screen candidates so the best qualified would be given the appropriate amount of attention.

He asked Don for a go-ahead on a feasibility study. Don agreed but told him he should evaluate outsourcing HR activities where it made sense. Eric agreed and got approval to put Alicia, Kathy and Annette on the project team. "This will be exciting," he thought.

Eric first decided to use a technique developed by Kurt Lewin called Force Field Analysis. He had attended a seminar on effective decision making in workforce management, and an example of a force field analysis that was both humorous and illustrative had been used (see Figure 27.1).

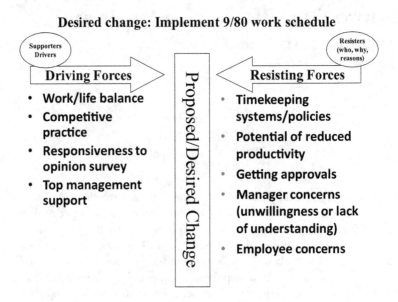

Figure 27.1 Force field analysis—example

The example was used in the seminar to demonstrate that any proposed/desired change would be given impetus by driving forces but would be impeded by resisting forces. Lewin also found in his work that removing or lessening the severity of resisting forces had more of a positive effect than increasing the pressure to move forward. The real lesson was that one should control or change those resisting forces that can be changed (as opposed to realities like genetic traits) and to focus efforts on doing that.

When Eric got the team together, they decided they would try this approach to determining whether they should outsource any or all of the HR service center activities. They started by doing research—talking with managers and employees. Their objective was to identify all of the driving and resisting forces so they could make a decision based on reality.

The next thing they did was to determine how strong both types of forces were. There could be some forces that were so strong that they overwhelmed the others; just counting the number of forces of each type would be simplistic. One of the things they noted while doing their research was the emotional intensity on the part of both managers and employees about how outsourcing could allow the organization to use the "The Devil Made Me Do It" excuse when rejecting health care claims or other decisions that would impact them. Those interviewed believed most of the decisions could be made using purely objective criteria. And if outsiders used subjective judgment, they would be inclined to please who was paying them, which would result in a bias towards minimizing costs. None of the team knew enough about the providers of outsourced services, and they realized they would be in no position to do psychological analysis on all of the provider's staff to ensure they would act in a manner consistent with the organization's culture.

Eric suggested they separate the outsourcing decisions that could be made using algorithms and keep the decisions internal that were based on heuristics. That sparked an immediate response from Alicia. "Are you studying a foreign language? If so, try doing a translation back into English." Eric gulped and realized he was not talking to his techy buddies. "A decision that is algorithmic is one that can be turned into a formula or specific routine that does not require subjective judgment or interpretation. A heuristic is a kind of rule of thumb that helps one make a better-quality decision but that does not fully specify the answer. And I apologize for using terms you all might not use daily when picking up your cleaning and deciding what kind of car you want to buy. On the other hand, the use of this distinction might help with at least the latter." "Think I will pass on that," responded Alicia. "Most of the service providers I deal with have trouble with English."

"It seems to me that we would be best served by laying out a project plan to design a service center and then make a decision on who does what once the plan is fully specified," interjected Eric. "I did some research on the satisfaction level among organizations that have outsourced HR activities and the results are all over the map. The satisfaction on processes that can be turned into specific routines is much higher, which is to be expected. When you look at processes that are largely undefined, requiring decisions that are almost totally subjective there is a much greater incidence of disasters. But things that are a bit of both, like processing health care claims for self-insured organizations, are often a problem as well. For example, providers take the heat for being heartless, but in their defense, they are using the specified protocols for making determinations. After all, insurance companies adhere to the rules specified in their policies when they process claims, so a provider of the outsourced service must adhere to whatever decision rules the customer provides. So, the answer I got out of all my research is, it depends!"

Everyone agreed they would develop a project plan for the creation of the service center, assuming all activities would be performed by HR staff. Whether all of the staff members were part of HR would be determined later. "We have a huge data-gathering task ahead of us," Eric suggested. "We really need to do an exhaustive evaluation of every activity performed by HR to determine whether it should be routed through the service center. But I was given some advice by a very knowledgeable consultant who did not have a horse in this race that HR strategy should be an internal activity. No outsider will know enough or care enough to set the direction and the priorities relative to how we manage our workforce." On that the team agreed. They then sketched out a very rudimentary process they would use, which would be turned into a detailed project plan once they had accumulated the feedback and the data (see Figure 27.2).

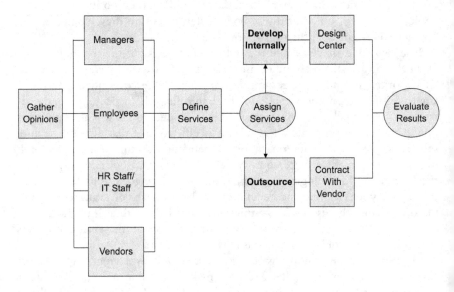

Figure 27.2 HR service center: design process

Don was amazed when the he got the feedback on all the services HR provided to employees. He had also asked Kathy to go out to a sample of employees to find out what their satisfaction level was and whether they would rather do some things themselves if they had a user-friendly system and if all the information they needed was available. There were some employees with what seemed to him a perverse interest in their $401k balances, and there were others who for some unexplainable reason were actually interested in what HR policies said about things (he wondered if that was to ensure they were toeing the line or if they were looking for ways around them). "Well at least they acknowledge policies exist," he thought.

But he did find that having access to the system 24/7 was important to a significant number of employees. He realized that they might want to make decisions about allocating their flexible benefits funds when someone was available to answer questions, while others probably wanted to research options at their leisure, probably at home. Don had already decided that HR would be putting out a lot of information on the system that had been transmitted by word of mouth before. Overworked managers were probably not the best transmission links, particularly if they did not think the information was critical. So, one of the benefits of the service center would be that the HR staff members could have their own blogs and might derive a great deal of satisfaction out of taking the initiative to tell employees what they felt was of interest in their respective functions. Don realized they had an opportunity to not only create more consistency in what employees received but also would be able to take some of the pressure off managers by delivering not so great news directly.

Eric managed the service center project, working with his IT partners and the HR staff, and seemed to be thrilled with the opportunity to do so. HRIS is often a thankless responsibility, since the only things you hear about are the system crashes and the complaints about why the system was not designed to fit the preferences of every manager and employee. But Don had been pleasantly surprised with the care Eric had taken not to make the system principally an IT thing focused on the technology, but rather a communication tool focused on the users. It had become apparent that the user satisfaction was very high within the first few months after implementation, and Don told Eric to partner with others of his choosing to write an article for the magazine published by the HR association they all were active in. "Might as well get him some psychic income," thought Don, although he realized that making your key people visible to other organizations might not be the best retention strategy.

Eric had used a publication of the SHRM Foundation entitled "Transforming HR Through Technology"[1] as a guide for outlining the key issues faced when deciding on developing IT capabilities that would support HR. The first issue was whether to acquire an enterprise-wide resource planning (ERP) system or to develop individual modules. The ERP system would have a framework within which individual modules would be available and typically integrated systems were found to be more efficient when cost and ease of implementation were considered. But these systems provided much less flexibility in customizing the individual modules and doing modifications internally was impractical, due to the enormity of the effort and the difficulty in designing them to produce integration between the modules. It they were to develop their own system, the modular approach could be accomplished incrementally, and even after the systems were in place, individual modules could be added, deleted or modified. The key decision involved in the modular approach was the make-or-buy choice. Shrink-wrapped modules were available for many HRIS applications, and the challenge would be to install and integrate each of them.

But Eric had been watching the emergence of cloud technology and realized that there was the option of using vendor computer capacity and software systems on a sort of lease basis, paying for what you use. Portals could be made available to HR staff, managers and employees so that each could access information that system controls allowed them to either view or modify. Some information would be available only to some parties and some to all employees and even the outside public. The organization would have to ensure that any information that was intellectual property was carefully protected and that proprietary and confidential information was accessible only to designated parties.

Another concern he had was ensuring data on employees in Europe was collected and administered according to the EU regulations on data privacy. There were data protection principles that must be adhered to. The principles included requirements:

- Notice had to be given to employees about data that was collected.
- People had to be given a choice about what would be collected.

- The conditions for transferring data to other files must be defined.
- How access would be controlled must be specified.
- How data security would be ensured must be defined.
- The controls to ensure data integrity must be established.
- How administration guidelines would be enforced must be communicated. Finally, under what conditions employees would be allowed to add, change or delete information would have to be made clear.[2]

The team evaluating the HR requirements developed descriptions of what the HRIS capabilities would be for each HR application: workforce planning, staffing (sourcing and selection), development, career management, performance management, rewards management, employee relations. They then defined the system requirements for each of the processes, who would be able to access what and how the system would be evaluated and refined when needed. They realized after completing this task that the modular approach would suit the defined needs better than a single, enterprise-wide system.

Don and the payroll department selected a new vendor for payroll processing, and he found a small boutique outfit to do their health claims processing. An RN had started the health claims processing business and had several large customers that Don had talked to prior to making the selection. He told the vendor that any interpersonal problems, such as outraged employees, should be immediately referred back to HR, rather than shutting the employee down by stating that "those are the rules." Annette had two people who were particularly good at helping employees understand the need for consistent policies and in conveying to them that the organization still wanted to look for a solution to an employee's problem that was the best one available. "Wonder how they convince employees that every time a kid got a scrape that it did not require a frantic trip to the emergency room," he thought.

The staff had learned a lot about project management while creating the service center. In fact, they were all amazed at how many of their activities could benefit from better project planning and administration. Most of what they did was far too complicated to do on the back of an envelope or to wing it. So, Don decided that it would be wise to have Eric and some of the other staff members attend a seminar on project management or to have someone in to conduct one. He also decided everyone in HR needed these skills in the current complex environment. There were numerous books on the topic however, so he decided to let Eric and Kathy take the lead to determine if they thought staff members could do self-study after the two of them boiled the available information down to a manageable amount of reading. They also encouraged staffers to pursue the certifications in program and project management developed by the Project Management Institute,[3] since one of the local universities offered courses to assist people develop these skills. Several of them had joked about HR practitioners no longer having a job—their lives had become a series of overlapping projects.

The HR service center project plan for the portion the HR staff was involved in was created. But the IT part of it was more complicated and required a much more rigorous plan. Eric suggested to Don that they design a project incentive plan for the IT staff involved in the project, since he felt it would help motivate staff members to focus on this endeavor. Don agreed, but when discussing this with staff, Annette contributed some of the lessons learned when the software firm she had worked with had used project incentive plans for IT staff. "The first lesson we learned is that you have to be careful that the incentive opportunity does not result in a disproportionate focus on this particular project at the expense of their other work. The other lesson was that having rewards on offer tended to make people anxious to participate, even if they were not the most qualified. And when they are not selected, they feel it is unfair because the work they are doing is just as important as the project work and the incentive can create an income inequity." This was something Pete needed to address, and Don suggested he be assigned to figure out how they would determine if a project was suitable for an incentive plan and how earning opportunity could be kept equivalent throughout the IT function.

Rob had been evaluating their human resource development needs and had come to the conclusion that they needed to significantly upgrade their capabilities in three areas: (1) skill training, (2) career management and (3) competency assessment. Their skill training needs were principally in technical areas, and he wanted to make better use of online training, to cut down lost work time and to put employees in the driver's seat when it came to scheduling the training times. Career management was far too uneven across the organization, and no one was responsible for ensuring that employees knew what career opportunities existed and what they would need to do to take advantage of them. Competencies needed to be assessed for all critical jobs to ensure the qualifications section of their job documentation included all of the competencies required for each job.

Rob talked to Eric about loading all of the job documentation onto an "opportunities warehouse" file, which would be accessible to employees and which also could be used to entice potential employment candidates. Alicia and Rob had worked together to develop system features that would enable shoppers to visit their website and get details on open jobs but also to explore "what next" career paths that existed in the organization. Alicia was convinced this was a big winner, since potential employees could be energized by the mobility that the organization provided to people who were willing to contribute and to develop themselves. Eric had told them that inventorying the job documentation including qualifications was a simple task, but that someone would have to define career paths so links could be built into the database that would take someone from the job they were currently considering to the jobs logically accessible in the future.

Alicia and Rob readily committed to that goal and agreed that they would do research on how employees had progressed in the past, as well as linking career ladders. They wanted to know not only the paths that had been taken but the ones that could be taken. Rob saw this as an opportunity to create developmental programs to open up new avenues through which employees could progress. The organization had not been aggressive in doing developmental assignments and had often recruited from the outside rather than making an intensive effort to move someone internally. The positive impact of internal promotions was enough to offset the cost of making an investment in a current employee. And Alicia had pointed out a defect in the selection process. People knew of current employees' imperfections, but the resumes of outside applicants suspiciously lacked statements about limitations. Employees had suggested that when a choice between an internal candidate and an external one presented itself, that the organization should bend over backwards in favor of the current employee. External hires lowered morale and ambition and often resulted in a top performer leaving to further their career when they could have done it internally had the organization committed itself to doing what it took to develop its people.

As the wish list grew, Don felt the need to have a Delphi session to set priorities. They could not build in all the system features at once, although they did need to ensure the framework that was designed could accommodate the other features at a future date. He had Eric list all of the services and the information that people had suggested be provided through a service center and/or the website. All HR staff members and a sampling of employees and managers were sent the list and asked to submit their top ten, in order of preference. Eric then sent out the twenty-five items that had gotten the highest scores, in order by their weighted vote total (10 points for a 1 ranking, 9 for a 2, etc.). Each participant then had the opportunity to list their top five items from that list. The result of that second round gave the HR team a rank-ordered list of the items based on the votes. It had been made clear that this was not a democratic election and that HR reserved the right to give higher priorities to those items that would provide the greatest value to both the organization and the users. Once that was done, they looked for synergistic benefits by bundling items together. For example, in order for career opportunities to be represented realistically, the qualifications for jobs had to be updated and lines of progression defined.

As the design work progressed, Rob was getting requests to do technical training for the help desk staff, since many of them had not come up to speed on a number of the new software products and new design features that had been added to existing products. Rob asked Eric to make online training available to these staffers as soon as possible, since the technical material was available and the manuals could be converted to online modules fairly easily. This was an opportunity to fill an immediate need and also to test the system to ensure it was user-friendly. The volume of changes to product features meant conventional face-to-face training would have to be conducted almost continuously, and it was difficult to do the training for large groups because their locations were far-flung geographically. Rob still had plans to do managerial training as well, but most of that training would have to be face-to-face and could be planned well in advance, making it easier to get people in one place. Given his background in developing courses and degree programs, Rob was more confident in his ability to design what they needed in this area, as opposed to relying on technical people to produce the content and to clearly specify what the learning objectives should be. He also had Kathy's capabilities available to him on educational programs.

As the first features were implemented, Alicia realized the service center could be a very important recruiting, selection and onboarding tool. Shoppers could look at the offerings the company had defined, using the job documentation and career opportunities modules. She had pushed Rob to put the online training course catalogue on the system and make it available to potential candidates. The current generation was very focused on keeping themselves up to date (and marketable) and wanted to be in control of managing their development and their careers. Candidates would also be able to look at the benefits package and policies that conveyed the organization's commitment to making compensation a function of employee competence and contributions. Might as well be honest about their "you get what you earn" philosophy and run off the people looking for a comfortable place to do just enough. That would save the expense of processing candidates who would not be hired or who would not fit if they somehow got hired.

Alicia and Rob came up with a brilliant screening tool for the help desk jobs, which constituted the highest volume of new hires. They often would get a large number of people applying when they had openings, but they had experienced a considerable amount of turnover in the first 6 months, mostly due to the work not fitting the expectations of the new hires. They made a video entitled *30 Minutes at a Help Desk*, using real-life footage. When they had a large number of employment candidates who had cleared the first screening hurdle, they invited them to view the film online. By compiling data on the number clicking through to the next phase, it became clear that they were seeing more than 50% of the people drop out at this point. "Better to lose them that way then three to six months later after we have trained them," Alicia told the help desk manager, who was upset the film was running people off. "Don't use the film thing for software designer candidates," pleaded David, who managed their design activities. "The film will show people thinking a lot, staring intently at the wall, scribbling funny symbols on paper and drinking a lot of lattes—everyone will apply for that job." But there was broad acceptance that realistic job previews were not only a relatively inexpensive and very effective tool for reducing unwanted turnover, but also an honest way to deal with potential employees.

Rob had mixed emotions about letting managers completely control who could take the on-line training courses. Since the cost to the company was minimal, he could see no reason why administrative support people could not take courses that did not relate directly to their jobs. He and Don had talked about this and Don pointed out that not only did they allow office personnel at the utility he had worked at take courses relating to field work, but they rewarded them for doing so. The organization would also pay for licensing exams if the employees wanted to obtain a license. The CEO believed that the more each employee knew about their business, the better they would be at their job. Don had been surprised that some employees had become interested in the work done in the field and had made career moves that the organization would not have expected. He had realized that if someone was not engaged in what they were doing, they were prone to leave, so enabling them to explore other options internally had often saved a good employee. One employee wondered if there were courses that would enable her to become CEO, but the CEO light-heartedly suggested you did not have to know anything specific to do his job, so courses were not needed. You just have to have a well-developed sense of humor and the skills of a zookeeper.

Don called his direct reports together to review the HR service center project and was a bit surprised to find out that it had evolved into a complete rethink of HR's role. The service center was being designed jointly by HR and IT, with Eric acting as the liaison. It had been recognized that the project consisted of several elements. The first was a system design project, which would create the technical capabilities that would allow electronic communication for all who needed access to information. IT was directing that element. The second was a model of a center staffed by HR that would respond to employee requests for action or information. The third was a system that would enable staffing and HR development to find, recruit, screen, select, place and develop employees. It became apparent that a project manager or project management team should be responsible for each of these elements, since although they each had an IT and an HR element the requirements were different and those with the greatest knowledge about and stake in each should be given the responsibility. "So, do we need a project manager to manage the project managers?" asked Don, obviously looking for a role in this endeavor for him. "No, replied Eric, "it would be better if the project managers work as a team to ensure the projects are integrated and to ensure staff utilization is optimal.

Systems had already been designed and implemented that enabled employees to access benefits information based on system requirements created jointly by Pete and Eric. Employees could do their annual allocation of their flexible benefits account funds, make investment choices for their 401k and get information on any of their benefit programs. Pete had led the design of employee compensation statements, which included individual information on pay, benefits and paid time off, and instead of printing them out once a year, they were updated continuously and accessible to employees at any time. Rob had also implemented a training inventory, which showed employees which courses they had completed, and, if appropriate, which additional courses were needed to meet their career development goals.

Alicia told the group that the new recruitment module was working brilliantly and that she had never felt as satisfied in her ability to effectively and efficiently recruit as she now did. "We waste virtually no time interviewing and processing candidates who are not qualified and who were disinterested in the specific roles they are being recruited for. We also are getting hits from university students who are assessing organizations and looking for places to begin their careers. And I am going to initiate a co-op program that will enable us to do a better job of finding future employees, as well as utilizing students that already are capable of contributing well before they complete their studies. With this system in place, we can run a continuous dialogue with candidates and keep track of them, as well as socializing them into our culture and ensuring that future employment is conditional on the organization and the person being compatible."

"So, in effect you all have taken over HR?" asked Don. "No, we just helped you make it better and freed up your time so you can spend it with the politicians in the executive suite," Rob responded. Rob had felt he had erred in not keeping Don humble by pointing out to him that he was not as indispensable as he thought he was, so he promised himself that their interactions would be more like those they had experienced when they were graduate students and went for their periodic strategy sessions at the pizza palace.

Don and Rob had recently been contacted by two of their classmates from graduate school, Nina from India and Eddie from Hong Kong. They wanted to get together to discuss something they were doing, and since Don and Rob both thought they were top-flight thinkers, they agreed. That evening the meeting took place at an Indian restaurant where Nina, put in charge of ordering, showed them just how varied and exciting the cuisine could be.

Nina and Eddie had formed an alliance after each had returned to their home countries following graduation. They had created a start-up that developed a full HR service center capability, including software systems, help desks and customer call centers. Although they had staffed the help desks and call centers aggressively, they believed they would be able to attract large organizations as customers if they had full-service capabilities in place. Eddie had been a whiz at expert systems even before graduate school, and when Nina had taken an interest in HR, they realized that very sophisticated systems could be used to do transactional work related to workforce management. Nina was blessed with interpersonal skills, and Rob had always said she spoke English better than he did, although his slang vocabulary certainly outdid hers.

"Can we make a sales presentation to your organization?" asked Nina. Don was wondering if he should admit their capabilities were exactly what Alpha was seeking and that he had doubts that creating all components of the HR service center from scratch made sense. They all agreed that Eddie and Nina would come to their offices and give them a demonstration of what they were capable of doing.

The presentation went very well, and even Eric realized that much of what they were trying to create internally, at great cost, was already available and being offered to them by Eddie and Nina. Wayne had invited the CFO to the presentation, and the two of them were impressed with what the entrepreneurs had done. After the meeting, Wayne asked Nina and Eddie if they would be interested in being acquired, since both he and the CFO thought their services were a complement to what Alpha's software division did and that they could turn this into a business.

"We are not interested in being acquired," Nina said, "partly because we are not a legal entity, but rather an alliance between two organizations. We share the organization name Zen, but we do not combine financials or operate in a manner that requires we do filings in multiple countries." Wayne had been interested in alliances as a way of extending an organization's capabilities globally, particularly since mergers and acquisitions presented enormous legal, logistical and cultural challenges. "This is something we definitely should discuss further," Wayne offered, and the CFO agreed. Nina and Eddie said they were happy to meet and discuss it further.

Wayne and Tom, the CFO, both agreed that they could have a shot at large government contracts available outside the U.S. if they could staff up their software division's capabilities. This made the alliance idea even more interesting. "We would have to find out how much software development and implementation horsepower Nina and Eddie have and how much of it could be used on work outside their HR service center activities," Wayne suggested. "Rob, Don and Annette have a lot of respect for those two, and apparently they have built a solid reputation across Southeast Asia." Tom was in agreement that this was a fascinating opportunity but pointed out they were not experienced at alliances.

"Alliances can be a lot of things," replied Wayne. "They can be very much like outsourcing to a contractor and at the other extreme can be fully integrated almost as if they were a division of the organization. Nina and Eddie may be interested in merging into Alpha down the road, or they may continue the alliance, which leaves them open to remaining private or going public. No need to press them for their view of the future because I suspect they do not know what will evolve." Tom realized that the original arrangement would involve the use of proprietary software offered by Zen and they would utilize Zen centers and personnel in order to run the HR service center. Zen would be free to provide the same services to other organizations, although Nina and Eddie did feel they could co-develop some services with Zen that they might jointly offer to others.

Don told Wayne he was confident that his past classmates Nina and Eddie would contribute mightily to the HR service center project and to the development of service offerings they might market externally. One of the problems encountered in many alliances is that one partner might put their best people on the joint effort while the other engaged in free riding by assigning people they could most easily spare. There were of course going to be issues relating to cultural differences when developmental teams were formed, but as long as they followed Trompenaar's advice to recognize them, to respect the rights of others to hold different beliefs and to reconcile them, there should be no insurmountable obstacles. Eddie and Nina had employed a number of people in India who had studied in the U.S. and had worked there for technology firms, so their English was good and they knew a good bit about Western cultural traits. Most of their location managers had done graduate work in Western universities, either overseas or by participating in extension programs at home.

"I am more worried about our individualistic employees who engage in linear thinking fitting in to the mixed teams, rather than Zen's people," Don said, in a slightly sarcastic manner. "Some of our folks drive me nuts with their short-term orientation and their insistence on strict adherence to the detailed project plan, even when conditions might warrant consideration of a fresh approach." But Tom defended the organization's approach, pointing out that they were financed by equity markets, and the attention span of Wall Street types was measured in nanoseconds. "Don, you have to recognize that many Chinese and Indian firms are either family organizations or parts of networks. Because of that, they have a lot more latitude to make decisions that consider the long term, since analysts are not downgrading their stock's outlook based on quarterly statements. I have always said the U.S. is so focused on quarterly statements that people forget they are gross approximations of current conditions, with little consideration of external trends or appreciation of investments like R & D and workforce development. I can make our quarterly statements say almost anything without fear of being indicted, and the pressure is for me to make them fit the expectations of the investment community rather than reality."

Don decided that when your CFO says something like that, you should drop the subject, medicate for stomach upset and go on to something else. "Do we need to get legal involved in this?" he asked Tom. "Absolutely, so when we contract with Zen, we must consider all the potential pitfalls," he responded immediately.

The new alliance produced an HR service center that made all of the HR staff proud. Early feedback from employees was overwhelmingly positive, and many of the employees who preferred e-training were utilizing their courseware far more than in the past. Annette cautiously approached the CEO and Wayne about two responsibilities she felt HR had not assumed and that in fact had not been assumed by anyone. One was the design of workplaces. She had dealt with an expert in ergonomics when she was managing the association who had told her much of the expense associated with treating vision problems and carpal tunnel syndrome was due to poor workplace design. Human factors engineering was a field that she knew little about, although she had read about designing cockpits for aircraft and spacecraft so humans could perform efficiently. She remembered at the time that she wished the car manufacturers would take a course in instrumentation design and location, since every time she rented a different kind of car she hoped it would not rain or get dark, because she would have to find the devices that enabled wipers or lights—each in unique locations of course. And she had driven almost an hour in one car on a freeway not knowing how fast she was going, since she could not locate the speedometer.

The ergonomics expert told her that some employees worked on computers all day in locations plagued by glare on the screens and poor positioning of the keyboards and monitors. This led to both vision strain and susceptibility to carpal tunnel problems. Annette had the expert do an audit of all their work locations, correcting problems. The positive impact on employee morale more than made up for the small expense associated with professional fees and corrective actions. "I think we should add workplace design to HR's job description and mandate that all managers have some training in the design of employee workplaces. And we should rethink having employees chained to a chair and screen for the full work day. If it cannot be avoided, we should educate them on how to take breaks and interject movement into their routines." Wayne responded by suggesting they have employees sing the company song while performing rhythmic exercises, but the look in Annette's eyes put a quick end to that feeble attempt at humor.

"Agreed. And the second responsibility?" asked the CEO. "Preparing a disaster recovery plan," responded Annette. She told them about an incident that had occurred at her association a few years back. "One of our employees who had been terminated for sexual harassment told a few of his friends he was going to come back to the office and demonstrate how the automatic weapons he had in his collection could provide payback for termination. We had never prepared any kind of plan for that type of event, or for an earthquake, flood, terrorist attack or riot either. I had read the book *Leading People Through Disasters*,[4] and it was a real wakeup call for me. When considering the natural and people-made disasters that have occurred in the last twenty years, I realized it was unbelievably shortsighted to think any organization was impervious. Recognition that many things can happen is the first step. The second step is formulating a plan to deal with alternative scenarios that could materialize. The third is to decide how to execute the plan and who is responsible for what. Although it was pretty basic, I went ahead and put a plan together and did substantial training for all of our employees on the roles everyone needed to play if stuff happens."

"That is a really great idea," responded Wayne, "and our safety/security manager is a volunteer for the Federal Emergency Management Agency (FEMA) and would welcome the opportunity to put a plan together and to ensure we are prepared for anything. We are not apt to create an oil spill or experience an earthquake, but I do know all of our plans for events like fires and power outages are focused on business continuity, with no real consideration of the people issues that would arise during a disaster. Thanks for bringing this up, and I will be sure both issues are addressed immediately."

Notes

1 "Transforming HR Through Technology," Effective Practice Guideline, SHRM Foundation, 2011.
2 www.export.gov/safeharbor.
3 www.pmi.org.
4 McKee, K. and Guthridge, L., *Leading People Through Disasters*, 2006, Berrett-Koehler, San Francisco.

28 You can look too good

The CEO called a meeting of his direct reports and their key management personnel to discuss a rumor that Alpha was the target of a takeover, which could be friendly or not. A group of large investors had been working through a venture capital firm to see if there was more value in Alpha than was being realized. Although it had not been said there was suspicion that the investors felt the pieces could be worth more separately than they were when combined in a single organization, the rumor triggered a hard look at that possibility by Tom the CFO, and based strictly on financial considerations, the answer was unclear. Don and Wayne met with the CFO and the CEO and offered a very different perspective.

"Our review of the intellectual property and capital had shown us that the value of both patents and the capabilities of the workforce is greater when they are used seamlessly across all their lines of business and products," Wayne began. "So, taking things apart could result in lines of business that looked profitable in the short run, but the absence of adequate support function capabilities would make it difficult for them to sustain their financial performance for long. It would therefore make it necessary to duplicate R & D efforts and to create licensing contracts across the new entities if the organization were broken up. The biggest loss would be incurred by subdividing the workforce. We are finally motivating our people to work together in an aligned manner and to aim at common overarching goals. Tear that apart and you lose economies of scale, as well as cause unwanted turnover of people with critical skills and knowledge."

Tom pointed out that it would be tricky to do a reverse sales job on the interested investors but that they could craft carefully worded explanations in the annual report and 10-K of how their large recent investments in developing human capital would pay off in the next few years. The message could be that the payoff would be magnified by the synergistic strategies across the businesses. Everyone in the room was amused that they were trying to discourage interest from some investors yet paint a rosy picture of Alpha's future for everyone else. "Kind of like keeping two sets of books," Tom suggested, careful to smile to indicate irony was intended.

Wayne and Don had been exchanging meaningful looks, and Don added, "And the kudos we have gotten in HR publications about our brilliant improvements in workforce management probably have not worked in our favor.

In fact, now that you have named the potential aggressor, I realize that at a recent Society for Human Resource Management conference one of their people approached me after the presentation I made about our HR service center. He showed particular interest in our HR organization and how we had managed to pull off the design and implementation of the center. I should have been tipped off when he popped for lunch at a very overpriced eatery down the street from the convention center." The CEO asked Don if he had concluded that the only reason the investors were interested in Alpha was the brilliance of the HR staff. "Mostly, but maybe not totally," Don responded, trying to control his facial expression to indicate that irony was intended. Wayne jumped in. "That is not as far-fetched as you might think. If this organization is in the 'divest and devour' business, they want to be able to do effective due diligence on the human capital of organizations and to pull off acquisitions without suffering the loss of critical talent. They study the research on M&A experience and understand that the people problems experienced in the majority of M&A cases have significantly lessened performance going forward."

"Great," interjected Tom, "we get a little credit for our workforce management expertise, resulting in a boost to stock price and investor interest. Then we alert the barracudas that we would make a tasty meal." The CEO responded, "Then we should be lousy managers so no one wants us?" The group silently accepted that there were downsides with every upside, and in this case, they would not change anything.

Within a month of the conversation, the shareholders in Alpha were made a stock purchase offer they would have been foolish to refuse, and the deal was imminent. The CEO called together the entire senior management group and made it official that their lives were about to change. "We have done the shareholders a great service by managing well, even though the result has interrupted our quest to do even more. I will be retiring, since the only reason I would have stayed on past normal retirement age was to continue what we have started. I encourage each of you to decide what you want to do very soon, so when you are approached by the new owners, you can make good decisions about your future."

Wayne called his management staff together after the CEO's meeting and informed them that he was also going to move out of corporate work. "There is a lot to be done out there, and I am serious about volunteering to contribute my management skills to disadvantaged schools. The next generation needs guidance, and I need to feel like I am contributing to something worthwhile, rather than making strangers rich."

Don followed with a meeting that included the entire HR staff. "What we have built is a team that is capable of managing the human capital of even the most complex organization effectively. Rob has been in touch with Howard, whom many of you know. He has continued to consult with major corporations, although he has done so with a network of skilled people, rather than in a large consulting firm. Rob, why don't you fill us in on what Howard suggested we consider."

Rob began by extolling Howard's professional expertise and by pointing out that he had an impressive collection of Fortune 500 clients. "Howard does not want to be in the HR outsourcing business, at least if you define that as taking over HR for the client. What he does aspire to do is to understand the client's HR strategy and then to work with that organization to determine what should be done by permanent internal staff and what Howard's team could do better or more efficiently. For example, he does the annual market pricing for almost 100 organizations and then recommends adjustments to the pay structures and incentive plans. Since the routine for performing this work is fairly well prescribed, and since it represents a high volume of work compressed into a short time period, it makes sense for organizations to have outsiders do it. And Howard has people in his network who can jump in and do the work and who can go on to do something else when it is finished. This means he does not have to worry about people who are drawing salaries working 80-hour weeks for a few months and then sitting on their hands.

What Howard suggested is that we leave as a unit and join his network. I am all for this, and Don, Annette, Kathy, Eric, Alicia and Pete are as well. But many of you have to be certain about your income stream, given that your children have acquired that eating habit and your mortgage holder has a strong preference for prompt payment of your monthly obligation. And I know some of you really prefer to be a part of something ongoing, so consulting may not fit your preferences. You learn early on that one of the realities of consulting is that you don't get invited to the celebration after a project goes well, and you do not get to form the close relationships with your peers. So, if you want to find new homes or even stay here, you may be happier. You might be shocked to find out how much you know and can do if you explore other options. We have done some great things here and others have attempted to replicate our success. So, you might even be able to move up a rung and manage HR functions in another organization. If you were not great at what you do, you would not have been here, so give yourself some credit and merchandise what you have to offer aggressively."

The new consulting entity was named Epsilon, and its mission was defined as "Helping Organizations Succeed through People."

29 Reconciling research and practice

Ironically, the first big assignment for the HR unit that had left Alpha involved acting as the HR function for Alpha during the acquisition. The venture capital firm had been left with little in the way of HR capability after the resignations of the team and felt it prudent to retain them on a part-time basis for six months. When Howard told the group of the assignment, they began to argue about who got what office back at Alpha. They were gratified that they were given this opportunity, since the cash flow would be stable. But even more, they would have a chance to finish implementing some of the systems they had developed and would be able to refine them during an acquisition. They realized that M&A environments place heavy-duty pressure on HR systems, and this could be a real shake-down cruise. Also, since several of the team members had planned on drawing down their $401k balances during the start-up phase of the HR network, this instant revenue made that unnecessary.

Rob had the most consulting experience among the team members, so he acted as the project leader for the team initially. There were no more reporting relationships between them, but rather assigned areas of responsibility, so it was not a matter of who people reported to. Rob would handle the administrative side of the consulting, including staffing projects. Howard had a controller of sorts who had worked with him for years, so Rob was not burdened with a lot of accounting detail, which was good because he assumed responsibility for running some training classes for the team on how the new consultants should discharge their responsibilities. The project management lessons the group had learned while at Alpha came in handy, and it had become obvious to all of them that HR practitioners should develop project-related skills as a part of their core knowledge base. Since less and less of HR work was transactional and repetitive, practitioners were finding their professional lives to be a series of overlapping projects. Everyone who planned to rise to leadership roles had to understand how to plan and manage projects, even if they did not manage people.

Don and Annette had contracted with the non-profit both of them had led in the past to oversee their HR activities. The organization really did not want to commit to adding HR professionals to their payroll, given the pay levels that would be necessary, so Don and Annette would assign more junior members of their HR network to projects as they became necessary and would direct the work. Pete did not find it necessary to look for work, since Howard had a large number of compensation consulting clients who could keep him busy full time. And Eric was finding that HRIS consulting was plentiful, since organizations were adding more and more services that HR was providing, as well as moving to service centers to increase productivity by handling routine transactions using IT systems. Alicia had also found a booming practice in staffing and frequently worked with Eric to provide clients with efficient systems for processing inquiries by potential candidates and streaming them into the recruitment, selection and employment process. One of the things she added was an onboarding system, which helped organizations ensure that new employees were integrated into the organization more effectively. By providing the newcomers with information directories and assigning mentors to guide them, organizations were finding they were acclimating much more easily and feeling less disoriented and overwhelmed with fitting into a new environment.

One of the questions the consulting team often got was, "How do you impartially and objectively measure HR's performance?" To that question, there was no simple answer. One of the problems was the difficulty people had in accepting that quantitative measures could be based on very subjective judgments and that personal judgments could be the best measures, even if they were made by the right parties and done using a sound decision model. One of the examples was how the results of a customer satisfaction survey were compiled. If a sample of employees responded to the question, "How satisfied are you with the answers you get from HR representatives when you have questions?" on a 5-point Likert scale that ranged from "very satisfied" (5) to "very dissatisfied" (1), and the average response was 3.2, what did that mean? It was a quantitative compilation of subjective responses. But if the responses were compiled over time and compared to each other, it could be determined if satisfaction were moving in the right or wrong direction. And if the surveys were done before and after a change, the impact of the change on satisfaction could be inferred.

Alicia had been using the longitudinal surveying approach to test the effectiveness of the information center staffing had been using to help employees plan and manage their careers. And Eric had used the approach to determine whether the HRIS was believed to be both accessible to employees and usable by them. Don had also provided clients with this process, which they could use to evaluate the effectiveness of training and development programs for clients.

Don had faced another challenge recently when asked to help a client determine the effectiveness of training programs. He utilized Kirkpatrick's four levels of evaluation to assess HRD initiatives. The first, and least helpful, level was to ask employees how satisfied they were with training. Even though this could be made more informative by not only asking how well they liked the program but specifically how they planned to apply the knowledge in their work, it did not get at the ROI of training. The second level was to test the actual learning that resulted from the training. This was certainly more helpful when the objective was to impart specific information or to improve specific skills. But the third level was much closer to what the organization needed to know: Did the training change job-related behavior and result in performance improvement? HRD practition-ers were generally well aware that new knowledge that was acquired may not end up being applied. The killer responses by co-workers, "we don't do it that way here" or "that will never work," often resulted in the newly trained person lapsing back to prior behaviors. The true test was the fourth level, which was to measure the real payback to the organization resulting from the training. And that level of evaluation was very difficult to achieve. But it was the gold standard for deciding on the effectiveness of investments in training, and relentless pursuit of metrics that would provide an ROI was necessary. The research on calculating ROI continued, adding to an abundance of past efforts, but much more needed to be done. In the meantime, the consulting team persisted in doing the best they could to help client organizations make good decisions.

If Rob had not taken seriously Kathy's commitment to helping HR prac-tice take advantage of research, he was mistaken in not doing so. He found that his evenings and weekends would be dominated by working with her to build a presentation she would be doing at a regional seminar for members of the Academy of Management (primarily academics), the Society for Human Resource Management (primarily practitioners) and the Society of Industrial & Organizational Psychology (mixture of organizational psychologists, organi-zational development practitioners and human resource management practitioners). In fact, without remembering to mention it, she had listed Rob as the co-presenter. The theme of the conference was evidence-based HR management. Rob had done a good bit of work in this area when he was a full-time academic, and the subject was very important to him, so he did not throw too much of a fit when he saw the brochure with his name on it.

Kathy had started with a model that showed the manner in which each of the two groups (researchers and practitioners) operated in parallel universes (see Figure 29.1).

She planned to show that the disconnect between what was researched and what was applied was due to a lack of alignment between the two groups. She started by listing the reasons for practitioners not using the available research evidence: (1) they don't know it exists—they don't read the journals academ-ics publish in, (2) they don't understand it—they cannot decode the way it is presented in research journals, (3) they don't see the research findings as being relevant to their challenges and (4) they don't know how to apply research findings to their work.

The next step was to figure out how to get the separate columns to form a bridge (arch). She graphically portrayed this and titled it The Ideal Road to Evidence-Based Management (EBM), as shown in Figure 29.2.

The obstacles to creating practice that was informed by research existed at each of the levels. At the first level, the obstacle was getting researchers to come up with research ideas that were related to the challenges faced by prac-titioners rather than what they felt would be accepted for publication by the journals. At the second level, the obstacle was that researchers were focused on whatever findings emerged, while practitioners wanted alternative solutions to

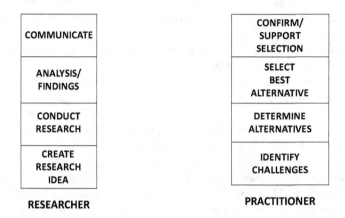

Figure 29.1 Are there two parallel universes?

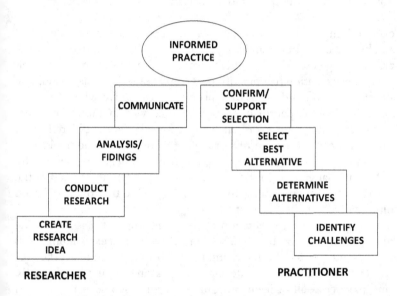

Figure 29.2 The (ideal) road to evidence-based management

their challenges. At the third level, the researchers were focused on performing the analysis their craft prescribed, while practitioners wanted decision models that would lead them to the best alternative. And at the fourth level, researchers were focused on communicating their findings to their peers in the research community, while practitioners wanted solid support for the alternative they selected.

Kathy had listed some of the things that would have to happen to ensure the gap between the two communities was bridged. Rob added some more and they came up with a wish list that would help close the gap.

1   Increase communication between the two groups by encouraging each to present at the conferences attended by the other, or run joint conferences like this one.
2   Have the members of each community broaden their reading by monitoring the publications created for the other.
3   Perform joint research projects supported by practitioner organizations and conducted by researchers.
4   Have researchers write articles for both research journals and practitioner publications on their research findings, taking care to explain how the evidence produced can be applied by practitioners.
5   Teach practitioners to be more discriminating in the "evidence" they extract from popular books and articles, as well as benchmarking against other organizations. This would require training in areas such as: (a) understanding what makes research valid, (b) understanding how to determine if research done in one context will be valid in different contexts and (c) how to interpret the quantitative analysis used by researchers.

Both Rob and Kathy knew the obstacles were not easy to overcome. They had operated in both the researcher and the practitioner roles and understood how different the language used in each differed from the other. Although there was some truth in the accusation that practitioners could not resist the latest fad, one must realize that it is often difficult to explain to an executive why something adopted by a leading competitor might not work as well in another context. And practitioners were a bit short on being allowed "thoughtful reflection time," which made it hard to justify struggling through more journals, particularly ones they are not trained to decipher. It would help if academics did not use an obscure language and statistical techniques they only learned in the advanced stages of a PhD program. But the gap needed to be closed, and both communities would benefit greatly if it were.

When they made their presentation at the conference, it was heartening to see the buzz that went on between sessions. Practitioners exchanging cards with academics, members of both communities debating what impact the cultural characteristics of the cohort entering the workforce should have on HR policies and practices—all of it encouraging. But what would happen when the conference is over and everyone went back to their world? That is what concerned Kathy and Rob.

They collaborated with Annette and Don after the conference and were encouraged by the observations of their friends. "People really got the message that it is too easy to stay in your own world and to measure success by how well you do in that world," Annette observed, "and the only way people are going to take the risk and venture outside the friendly confines is to recognize that they can make a greater contribution by doing so." "I agree," added Don, "for an academic to focus his or her research on something that will solve a practitioner's problem could be risky, especially if it is a problem the journal editors are not particularly interested in. Rob, you are unusual because you started as a consultant and recognized you had an obligation to inform practitioners of the available evidence. And when you entered the academic world, you were not particularly concerned about your publication record in the top research journals, since you did not buy into the tenure track race. So, you could speak the academic lingo and understood the principles of doing good research, but you also were most interested in research that had application, rather than just filling journals for other academics to read."

"Let's be balanced in our criticism," Rob responded. "There are a lot of practitioners in the HR field who skipped the math and quantitative methods classes in school and who do not feel obliged to learn the basics of research methodology. Understandably, they read the literature in their own field, since they have full-time jobs and are not looking for something to do. And the problem is magnified by the reality that their professional associations will certify that they know what they need to know without requiring that they possess even the basic knowledge about how to evaluate research, how to analyze research results and apply it and how to sort through the pop literature and differentiate what is sound and what is someone's unsubstantiated opinion."

"So, both communities need to find a common ground where researchers understand the practical problems and the practitioners are competent to identify relevant research and apply it to their challenges," Annette added. "Now, there was progress made here at the conference, but I think there are two real steps that need to be taken. One is for journal editors and deans to value research that addresses real needs, assuming it is done credibly. The other is for practitioner associations to recognize the need for their members to acquire skills that enable them to use research—they must require that these skills are tested when they certify people and also should include research findings in their publications."

"Could not have said it better," Kathy responded. "That is going to be one of my principal goals when I start teaching again. I am going to hook up with the HR associations so we can offer seminars and focused certificate courses through the school. They will be taught by both our faculty and practitioners who have seen the light and who are willing to convey the need for more practitioner education. I will of course shamelessly drag Rob into this as well, and Don and Annette should not think they will escape my net either." After the conversation, everyone was pleased that the needs had been recognized. Now they had to strive to meet them.

Kathy had kept her focus on the bridge-building issue after the conference. She had studied the book *Retooling HR*.[1] The retooling suggested was a conversion from a specialized discipline into a decision science, much like accounting becoming financial management and sales becoming marketing. This would necessitate the use of metrics and quantitative analysis techniques to make better talent management decisions. One of the speakers at a conference she had recently attended stated that HR needed to convert from being perceived as a cost center to being a profit center—by assuming a risk management perspective. An example used was succession planning. Rather than setting an objective as having two qualified successors identified for each key position, HR should formulate a strategy for achieving that result in a cost-effective and timely manner, after analyzing all alternatives. Another consideration would be the effectiveness of each strategy in a variety of possible futures, defined through scenario-based planning. The author also addressed risk-value analysis for key jobs and how to use that analysis when designing those jobs. He used the example of McDonald's, whose strategy was to specifically define tasks to be done and how they were to be done, the end objective being predictable and homogenous. A contrast was Starbuck's, whose strategy was to allow for more freedom and independent judgment by baristas, which encouraged innovation and the delivery of an individual experience. The key payoff from the McDonald's strategy was cost efficiency and predictability, while for Starbucks it was a satisfying experience that warranted the higher prices and built customer loyalty.

Kathy did find solace in the fact that some of the books written by people with strong research expertise had enjoyed some popular success. It was true that they chose not to write the same way they did for research journals when attempting to reach the practitioner community, but this did not dilute the quality of the messages they communicated. One of the campaigns she would undertake is promoting the idea that researchers should be rewarded by their academic institutions for making research findings accessible to the practitioner community, even if that meant writing a translated article based on journal publications. Research that only informs other researchers tends to have little impact on practice, thereby lessening its total value. Yet, Kathy did believe that students, particularly at the graduate level, must learn to access and use research from the academic literature. That would make her real popular, "Today we are going to enter the magical world of quantitative analysis." Certainly, that would make them sit up and display broad smiles. The more she thought about her decision to go back to teaching, the more she felt she was not leaving HR, only finding where she could contribute the most to those who managed the most important asset of their organizations.

The consulting team had taken on a project for an organization with a CEO who was a born skeptic, but in a good way. One of the things he hated was the premature assumption that because two things were related, one caused the other. For example, his HR leader had recommended they retain the consultant to implement a program to increase employee satisfaction, claiming it would increase productivity. The CEO challenged Annette, who represented the consultants during the first client meeting. "Is there evidence that increasing satisfaction will increase productivity?" she asked Annette. "Well, there is solid research evidence that increased satisfaction leads to less unwanted turnover and improves absenteeism, but there is not strong evidence that it alone makes people more productive," Annette responded. "But your HR staff has run focus groups with a sample of employees, and they have uncovered dissatisfaction with the current all-employee incentive plans, which we plan to evaluate and fix. And there is strong evidence that tying rewards to performance has a positive impact on motivation. Your employees are committed to the organization according to the focus group findings, and they want to make it successful, as long as they experience positive results as well."

"My HR group seems to have a poor understanding of how to frame a hypothesis and then test it," the CEO responded. "You now have given me a more believable hypothesis about how we can improve productivity, but I want you to run a mini course on how issues are defined and how alternative strategies can be evaluated against the desired results. I believe our staff confuses correlation with causation, which makes me nervous when they claim an intervention has produced the results that materialize. Can you do that for me?" Annette assured the CEO that her staff would be equipped with a better understanding of how to determine the causes of outcomes. When she left the meeting, she called Kathy, who was a real pro at teaching others how to do hypothesis formulation and testing.

The first reaction of some of the HR staff attending Kathy's tutorial was, "And we need to know this why?" Kathy did not want to use the easy way out and tell them the CEO said they needed the information. So, she promised them they would be more successful in requesting resources for HR interventions if they presented them in a more formal fashion, in business terms. Her first point was that often recommendations were not put into a "If we do A, there will be a positive impact on B" format. For example, if the current incentive plan were modified so that employees better understood how their efforts impacted the measures of performance that determined the size of the incentive fund, they would be more motivated to put forth their best efforts and focus them on the defined objectives. This is plausible, since behavioral research, specifically expectancy theory, supports it. But Kathy made it clear that they must be careful to design the implementation process in a manner that limits the possibility that the outcomes could be caused by something other than the incentive plan modifications. The improvement could be due to an improved focus on the organization's objectives. Or it could be due to the linkage we establish between what people do and the impact that has on their units and the organization. Or it could be a Hawthorne effect: just by involving them in the process could increase their belief that management valued them. But all of these factors do not diminish our belief that the intervention had a positive impact.

"So, you could frame this as a hypothesis and identify your underlying assumptions:

Hypothesis

- Modifying the incentive plan as proposed will positively impact performance.

Assumptions

- Clarifying the performance criteria and standards will increase employee focus.

- Defining the linkages between individual efforts and group/organizational performance will increase employee appreciation that everyone's efforts are important.
- Ensuring that employees believe they can perform at the required level will give them the confidence to strive.
- Ensuring that there is trust on the part of employees that performance will be rewarded will increase motivation.
- Rewarding employees based on outcomes will increase their motivation to perform.
- Ensuring employees positively value increased compensation or other rewards will give the organization confidence that they are offering the right things."

Kathy continued by cautioning attendees about potential issues. "Now, even though management may question your assumptions, it is better to get them out into the open and have a dialogue about them. For example, occasionally a pop literature book claiming that external rewards can diminish intrinsic rewards will convince some that monetary rewards should be used sparingly. It gives you the chance to share the enormous body of research that clearly supports the contention that rewards can motivate improved performance, assuming that rewards are tied to performance. This is a much better scenario than one where you promise a result that will be forthcoming and, for whatever reason, the results do not meet expectations. If the assumptions have been vetted, this enables you to attempt to find the causes for the disappointing results without management just assuming this was another well-intentioned HR thing that was ill-conceived."

The HR staff attending the session seemed to be pleased with the guidance on how to better frame their proposals to management. But several were still dubious that they would be given the opportunity to make their case. One staffer identified the reason for their skepticism. "We just are not there when the annual business plan is conceived and decisions are made on allocating money and resources. How do we get the chance to make our pitch?" Kathy assured them that their CEO was ready for HR to step up and propose things that would have a positive impact, as long as it was made clear that HR had thought through what was being proposed, why and how it should be done and that it was presented in a structured fashion. And making the business case was of course critical—the incentive plan project was aimed at improving organizational performance, which was hard to argue with. But HR would have to be careful not to justify investments of resources with the intention of achieving vague results. For example, employee satisfaction might be expected to increase, but although that may be thought to be desirable, it still left the door open for a business-oriented decision maker to say "So what?"

After the session, Kathy reviewed what her perceptions were about the results with Rob, Don and Annette. She told them it was OK to tell the CEO to watch for improvement in the way the HR staff brought forth recommendations. Kathy had gotten a great deal of satisfaction in sharing something from her repertoire of knowledge with practitioners who would be able to put it into practice. She also realized she was on the cheerleading squad for the HR profession and was ready to contribute to its status in the business world in any way she could. And not because all of those in her in-group were HR zealots.

Kathy and Pete had been asked to do a seminar on the use of quantitative methods at a conference for rewards management professionals, and Pete suggested they make the presentation to the HR staff. This would both serve as a shake-down cruise for the material but also help the staff better understand how quantitative analysis can contribute to sound HR decisions. Since the session Kathy had done on hypothesis testing was still recent, it would be easy to make this presentation an extension of what the HR staff had learned. They chuckled about how clever some of the staff members had been in school, finding innovative ways of avoiding math and statistics courses. Of course, this gap in their education hindered their ability to frame decisions based on quantitative analysis. And this deficiency made it more difficult for these ill-equipped practitioners to convince the hard-nosed businesspeople in the C-suite that their conclusions were more than subjective judgments.

The training course

Applying quantitative analysis to HR management

The concepts and techniques for analyzing quantitative data and evaluating the quality of research findings are relevant to human resource management (HRM) decision making. The types of quantitative measures and how they can be applied by HRM practitioners must be understood if sound decisions are to be made. Judgment based on past experience must also influence decisions, particularly when they involve subjective measures, but when analytic tools are utilized, they help convince those affected that they are as objective as possible.

Types of measures

Central tendency measures

Many statistical applications used in rewards management are aimed at finding "the number" out of a data set. Average rate is probably the most commonly sought value when using competitive market surveys. But when using an average, it is important to ask, "Average of what, calculated how?"

For example: A survey reveals the pay rate average of reporters in American newspapers is considerably higher than the average rates paid by each newspaper reporting in the survey. However, metropolitan newspapers have more reporters than community papers, and large newspapers

(continued)

(continued)

pay higher, explaining this seemingly puzzling result. The higher number (calculated by adding pay rates of thousands of reporters and then dividing that total by the number of reporters) is often called the weighted average or the incumbent-weighted average. The other number, calculated by adding the average pay rate reported by each newspaper and then dividing by the number of newspapers reporting, is called the unweighted average or the company-weighted average—called that, as it provides equal weight to each newspaper.

No right answer exists as to which of these two averages an organization should use to set targeted pay level for reporter jobs. The person selecting the measure of competitiveness must understand the statistics, understand the application, and have some labor market knowledge to make the right call.

Another measure indicating central tendency is the median—the middle rate in an array placed in ascending or descending order. For example, if seven rates are reported, the median rate is the fourth (from the top or from the bottom of the array placed in descending or ascending order by value). The median rate is determined by dividing the number of rates (n) plus 1 by 2, or

$$\text{Median rate} = \frac{[n+1]}{2}$$

in this case, the fourth rate in the array. As it is in the middle, the median is often considered the best rate to use to represent the competitive going rate. Also, the median is less affected by extremely high or low rates than is the average (mean).

However, the median is also a distributional measure, and an uneven distribution can cause nonsensical results. For example, if a survey reports seven monthly pay rates ($3,000, $3,100, $3,110, $3,125, $5,600, $5,800 and $5,900), the median is $3,125. The average is $4,234. Users should be concerned about *why* a big difference exists in the two clusters.

With four rates clustered around $3,100 and three clustered around $5,800, apparently a large difference of opinion exists about how this job should be paid. It could be argued that no going rate is determinable in this distribution. Was the job description too vague? Are newspapers reporting two levels of reporters into the single survey benchmark job? Does the sample consist of four small and three large newspapers?

This example illustrates that statistical measures may not produce a relevant answer but only trigger examination of the measurements. Users must understand the nature of what is being measured and what does or does not make sense. Making sense of the data may require splitting the sample by newspaper size and/or refining the survey benchmark description to reflect skill/responsibility levels within a job family. The reality is sometimes survey results only provide a computed average, without information about the distribution of rates or the mix of organizations reporting those rates. In this case, if the surveyor decided to report the median, it would be $3,125; if the average had been the choice, it would be $4,234. If the surveyor decided to report both, the knowledgeable user discovers something amiss in the sample and that further examination of the details (if available) was necessary. Regardless, the user should consider replacing the surveyor with someone who understood statistics and market surveys.

A third measure of central tendency exists—the mode. This is the most frequently reported rate, with little application in analyzing data relating to pay rates or other data involving the aggregation of discrete values.

Averages or medians can be used to compare two things as well. For example, most tourist books contain average monthly temperatures for destinations to alert the traveler going to Chicago to pack either cotton shorts or down parkas, depending on the month. Averages and medians have wide application in pay administration as well.

When selecting the median or mean as the going rate, the user should be aware that the mean is usually higher (typically by 3%–5% in large samples of pay rates in surveys). This is caused by the non-normal distribution of pay rates—the highest rates are often much further from the average or median than the lowest rates. The practicality of having a minimum wage impacts the distribution in hourly jobs by constraining how low rates can be, while no offsetting cap dictates how high they can be. As with selecting the type of average used, selecting between the median and the mean should be done based on which the practitioner feels is most appropriate. It is important though to ensure that once a measure is selected, it is used consistently in all related analyses.

Distributional measures

Distributional measures are used to describe how individual values are distributed. The median (just described) is the most commonly used distributional measure. Quartiles and percentiles are other useful distributional measures. *Quartiles* break a distribution into quarters, while *percentiles* break it into hundredths (terciles into thirds, deciles into tenths, etc.). If a student graduates in the second quartile of the class, it means that student's grade point average ranks below 50%–75% of his or her classmates and above 25%–50% of them.

Market surveys often report quartiles so the user knows generally how individual rates distribute between the lowest and the highest rate. The lowest and the highest rates are often outliers and useless to the user, but quartiles have a purpose. The quartiles enable the user to treat the interquartile range (the range between the first and the third quartile) as the middle half of paid rates, and to use this as a test of competitiveness. A market median or a market average is a single point, and it is known

(continued)

(continued)

to those with market pricing expertise that these numbers are at best accurate within a band plus or minus a percentage, generally 5%–10%. Given the reality that a computed point is probably subject to considerable error, an organization could adopt a philosophy that pay rates falling within a reasonable range should be considered to be competitive. This reduces employee perceptions that they are underpaid if they are not at least right at the market average rate.

The other distributional measurement tool is the frequency distribution (aka histogram). This tool is typically in the form of a table or chart and describes how individual values cluster in predetermined categories. It shows the distribution of reported salaries across a series of predetermined brackets. The vertical height represents the number (or percentage) of rates falling within each bracket and provides a picture of the nature of the distribution.

The histogram's graphic nature enables us to see patterns not evident in a numeric table, and a quick glance at the example indicates that this is not a normal distribution. It looks like two normal distributions side by side. This pattern is called a bimodal distribution (two modes exist, one around $600 and another at the $750–800 bracket). An experienced survey analyzer would suspect that the job being surveyed is viewed as being two jobs by participating organizations, one with an average pay of about $600 and the other about $775. This is consistent with the discussion about the possibility that two levels of reporters should have been surveyed, rather than one, as participating organizations are making the distinction. A frequent surveyor error is to select the middle level of a job family to include in a survey, while omitting the other levels, in pursuit of simplicity.

Participants want to be helpful and to report as much data as possible, so they squeeze the rates for entry-level people and for senior-level people into the one survey job, thereby producing an enormous range of reported rates. An experienced surveyor armed with individual pay rates

Table 29.1 Frequency distribution: number of weekly salaries in each bracket

Below $500	$500– $550	$550– $600	$600– $650	$650– $700	$700– $750	$750– $800	$800– $850	$850– $900	$900– up
						X			
						X			
		X	X			X			
		X	X		X	X	X		
		X	X		X	X	X		
	X	X	X	X	X	X	X	X	
X	X	X	X	X	X	X	X	X	
X	X	X	X	X	X	X	X	X	X

can detect this problem by using a histogram to analyze each organization's rates, and then admit the mistake and refine the survey or ignore it. With the graphics built into the simplest analytical software, practitioners have the tools to evaluate data in this manner without much effort and expense. But to do this, HR practitioners must understand what they are looking for and what they are looking at.

For example, if one did not understand that professional/technical jobs are best represented as job families (jobs performing work of the same nature, but differentiated into levels of skill and responsibility), it would be easy to look at the data for the single job programmer and be dismayed by the wide range of reported rates. Armed with a frequency distribution, the picture becomes clearer and the user could still use the overly combined data. By using the huge samples in the IT survey mentioned earlier, the author found that a family such as programmer typically had either three or four modes, and they were 12–15% apart, useful information for understanding how a pay structure for this family should look. Supported by knowledge of how participating company pay structures were constructed, it was possible to test the correctness of the number of levels within the job family defined in the survey. This type of analysis resulted in defining four levels in the programmer family but only three levels in the computer operator family.

Relationship measures

Relationship measures can be used to reflect the nature of relationships. The most common measure is *correlation*. For example, the weight of adult males is correlated to height (correcting for age). This does not suggest one thing *causes* the other, but only that they tend to co-vary. The coefficient of correlation is a widely understood measure directly measuring the degree to which two factors co-vary: from 0 (no relationship) to 1.0 (perfect correlation).

The nature of the relationship between two or more variables can also be explained by using *regression analysis*. Single factor regression is a technique attempting to explain one variable using one other variable. For example, a salary structure is typically built by relating the relative internal value of jobs to the competitive market averages for those jobs. If the point values for benchmark jobs, determined by using point-factor job evaluation plans, are used as the X-axis values on a graph and the market averages for those same jobs are used as the Y-axis values on a graph, the result is a *scattergram* showing the relationship between the two variables. The example in Table 29.2 illustrates the distribution of paired values for benchmark jobs.

Although the relationship is imperfect (it would be perfect if all X's were on one straight diagonal line), it can be seen that the relationship between market averages and point values is positive (the higher the

(continued)

(continued)

Table 29.2 Relationship of points and market averages

```
$                                                      X  X
60,000                                                 X
                                        X  X        X  X
                                     X  X  X
50,000                                  X  X
                              X         X  X              X
                              X  X
                           X  X  X  X
40,000                     X  X  X
                  X        X  X        X
                     X  X        X              X
                  X  X  X
30,000      X        X  X  X
                  X        X
               X  X  X
            X
20,000      X  X  X
         X  X

Points  200           400           650           950           1,300
```

points, the higher the market values) and probably could best be simply explained by drawing a straight line through the cluster, inclining as it went from left to right.

The single-factor linear name for this regression is derived from the fact that one factor (relative internal value) explains another factor (market value). Software producing this chart also reports a coefficient of correlation enabling the user to determine what percentage of the variation in dollars is explained by the points. The number varies from 0.0 to 1.0, and for this type of application, the norm for acceptability probably ranges from .50 to .90.

If the relationship between points and salary is not linear, but rather some form of curve function, it requires the use of a nonlinear formula. This is frequently experienced when analyzing executive salaries, as the rate that salaries increase is often faster than the rate at which points increase, creating an upward turning curve. Today's curve-fitting software selects the formula that produces the best fit between one variable and the other and provide a rank ordering of formulas based on how well they explain the relationship. Test all data sets using such software, as operating under the assumption that a relationship is linear forces it to be so, as that formula will be applied. And if a straight-line assumption is used on a non-linear data set, the results are distorted.

Unfortunately, in a complex world, one variable is often insufficient to explain another's behavior. In this case, one enters the world of multi-factor (multiple) regression analysis. If an organization is attempting to determine what best explains pay rates, it may use multi-factor regression to test various possibilities. If pay is entered as the variable to be explained, several variables might be entered as possible determinants. The range midpoint for the salary range would be a leading contender. Time in job/grade might be another. Performance rating might be another. If those three variables are entered and the multiple regression model results show that they explain 95% of the variation in pay rates, all is well. The contribution of each of these factors should also be examined, which is possible using the regression analysis output. It may be found on further examination that performance ratings add virtually no explanatory value and that grade level and longevity explain pay. This would be the time to take a hard look at the performance management and merit pay systems.

Another common application of multiple regression is to test the impact of HR programs on protected classes. Given today's legalistic environment, this is a good defensive technique, but it also is an opportunity to test for maladies such as racial bias or glass ceilings before trouble arises. In the previous example, the objective was to explain employee pay. If factors relating to age, gender and race were added to the equation, the results may provide more usable information.

As grade level, time in grade and performance are probably the ideal drivers of pay, one would hope to see no added factors have explanatory power. The regression would not indicate obstacles to career progression, however, as the assumption is that people are in the grade they should be (rather, as regression models do not make value judgments, this simply would not be measured). So, if minorities, for example, were paid appropriately for the grade they were in, how long they had been there and their performance, the regression results would not tell us they should have been in higher grades if selection and advancement processes were operating in a bias-free manner.

Research methodology is even more obscure to most HR practitioners than quantitative analysis methods. To determine if findings from a research study are believable and usable, there are two tests of that study: its internal validity and its external validity. Internal validity relates to how well the study was designed and therefore whether the results can be believed. External validity relates to where and under what conditions the findings hold.

The classic test of internal validity addresses how well various threats to the veracity of the results were controlled for. For example, we assume HR proposes a hypothesis that if people were given more responsible jobs with appropriate amounts of latitude, that their job satisfaction would increase and they would become more productive. One way to support that contention is to look to research results indicating the desired results

(continued)

(continued)

occur when the proposed actions are taken. If one could find one or more studies to support the hypothesis, the strength of one's conviction would be contingent on the confidence in the studies on two fronts.

First, were the studies designed in a manner controlling against threats to internal validity? Second, were the studies conducted in a context sufficiently similar to that of the subject organization such that it is logical to assume the results would be similar? This requires some findings on external validity, meaning that they would transfer to other contexts. What is important is to determine whether a similar result would be likely to occur in the context within which the practitioner means to take the action.

The internal validity threats include:

1   Events taking place during the study that might have caused the results (for example, benefits were improved during the time jobs were being enriched, positively impacting satisfaction).
2   Conducting the study when satisfaction is low relative to typical levels (for example, a layoff occurred before the study and morale is low enough that any change might be expected to improve satisfaction scores, particularly paying attention to employees and their needs).
3   Changes in the employee sample (for example, malcontents may have been encouraged to leave or chose to leave while the enrichment was going on and their satisfaction levels were among the lowest).
4   Expectations as to what jobs and the workplace will be like after the study might have inflated job satisfaction on a temporary basis.
5   Satisfaction might have improved, but there has been insufficient time to tell if this will positively affect productivity.

The threats to external validity are well known to those versed in sound benchmarking. A study that resulted in improved satisfaction and productivity in one organization might not translate to the same results in the organization embarking on a similar job enrichment program. The management style might differ from the organization(s) in the study (for example, supervisors might be more controlling and insecure about giving subordinates more latitude). The workforce might be from cultures that discourage employee initiative, which would be disrespectful of the supervisor. The workforce may lack the knowledge, skills and abilities to effectively perform the jobs in their enriched form. And so on.

The safest haven for the organization trying to determine if research supports the hypothesis they are putting forward is numbers. If numerous studies resulted in similar outcomes, the confidence level can be assumed to be higher. A *meta-analysis* is a study of multiple studies and can provide more confidence in research results. The reporting of these findings is often in research journals, which may be opaque to those untrained in research methodology. But an advisor with academic training can often locate and synthesize research findings and guide the organization in developing a hypothesis supported by research. The advisor should also be capable of ensuring the desired change to an HR program or practice is designed in a controlled fashion, maximizing the likelihood of successful implementation.

Increasingly, HR research is being reported in books that are accessible to those lacking the training in research methodology. The SHRM Foundation supports a research program examining the role of HR in mergers and acquisitions and what factors seemed to explain success and failure. Watson Wyatt developed three human capital indices for measuring the effect of HR strategies and programs on shareholder value. The Gallup organization has developed an enormous database to explore factors influencing employee satisfaction and effectiveness. The Conference Board does in-depth research reports on current issues. Models for measuring the HR function's effectiveness have been developed, tested and reported in several popular books.

Perhaps none of these research programs would meet the test of an academic research journal, but the studies just cited meet the test of admissible evidence and provide practical guidance to practitioners. It is this type of practical guidance that can help HR be more scientific in its application of research and quantitative analysis methods.

A dangerous tendency is the inclination to believe evidence that is consistent with their currently held beliefs, while rejecting or avoiding evidence conflicting with their beliefs. Everyone is subject to this form of distortion, and professionals must make a conscious effort to remain open to research findings that bring into question the practices they have used with apparent success.

The behavioral research done during the past 3 or 4 decades has not demonstrated a strong causal link between employee satisfaction and motivation to perform at high levels. Even though this linkage seems to be consistent with common sense and with experience, the evidence is lacking. Evidence indicates that employee satisfaction influences absenteeism and turnover, however, so employee satisfaction is still a worthwhile goal. It is important for professionals to be clear about the effects satisfaction is shown to have, lest they mislead decision makers. Too many HR initiatives have produced positive results but have been viewed as failures, as they did not produce the promised results. Research evidence can help guide HR to the correct path, but it is important not to try to force research to support desired results by stretching the conclusions it can support.

Although seeking employee opinions through surveys and other research techniques is a common approach to seeking understanding of how employees feel, it is also fraught with peril. As attitude surveys must frame questions in a technically sound manner for the results to be valid

(continued)

(continued)

and actionable, this is not a technique to be undertaken by amateurs. A more fundamental concern is that sometimes results may not be actionable, as what employees report and what they act on may differ. Ed Lawler, a renowned researcher, reported recently on an employee attitudes survey performed by colleagues, and it concluded that the most-desired feature of the work environment (work–life balance) had no significant correlation with the desired outcomes (commitment to the organization and retention). Most attitude surveys would have looked at the high rating of work–life balance and assumed that achieving it would have the desired results. The survey pointed out, according to Lawler, that having people rank the importance of things that are likely to be at least somewhat important to everyone has limited value, unless the researcher is willing to go the extra mile and determine if providing these things had any tangible value.

Conclusion

Even in this complex world, there is still hope for the practitioner who does not have the inclination or the time to go back for a master's degree in statistics or a PhD, so sense can be made of the chaotic environment. Adequate published information enables one to gain adequate knowledge of research and quantitative analysis methods. Advanced software performs all statistical tests mentioned in this article without demanding that the user understand the underlying equations. Finally, an increasing number of researchers are making their results accessible to people without advanced training.

There is, however, a problem for practitioners that lack basic skills in this area. The "let's try it and see how it works" approach is too slow and too costly today. The effective practitioner will take the time to find out how it has worked or is apt to work by accessing research results and evaluating all relevant evidence. The effective practitioner will demand that data be turned into information and will be capable of examining the quality of that information as it applies to the context within which it will be used.

In a staff meeting following the two training sessions, most of the attendees admitted that they were better equipped not only to understand research and the tools of analysis, but to find applications for them in their work. A few actually confessed to feelings of guilt about avoiding quantitative courses in school, and they expressed thanks for the upgrade in their professional knowledge and skills.

Note

1 Boudreau, J., *Retooling HR*, 2010, Harvard Business Press, Boston, MA.

30 The ten-year reunion

As the quartet entered the building where the ten-year reunion of their fellow MBA and MSHR graduates was taking place, they realized that Kathy had not graduated with them. They had become such a tight-knit group that this fact did not occur to them. Kathy assured them that she had met a number of people at the five-year reunion and knew who to seek out and who to avoid when the other three got into their "Remember when . . ." sessions with their fellow graduates. She also remembered that the school apparently did not have a wine steward who selected the offerings at the bar, so she was prepared to spend the evening with sparkling water and a twist, rather than bargain wine.

Time and experience have a maturing effect on most people. Some of the critics who questioned the trio's decision to acquire the MSHR in addition to the MBA were not now so certain it was a waste of time. As their own most intractable problems were generally to do with people and how to effectively manage them, they conceded that they had learned more about workforce management. They did not call it "HR," since that was often the name given to the function that consistently told them what they could not do and that imposed rules and processes that detracted from their ability to manage. Ralph had been one of their most verbal critics during their program. He had both BS and MS degrees in engineering and had gotten the MBA to prepare him for ruling the world. But he surprised the trio by asking some advice on a problem he was having with his subordinates. He approached them sheepishly at first, but they assured him that all past criticisms were forgotten. Annette graciously committed to not saying "I told you so."

Rob consoled Ralph by telling him about their efforts to convince HR practitioners that they should develop their quantitative analysis skills and confessed he had recognized that the MSHR curriculum was far too light in this area. Ralph was pleasantly surprised by this admission and offered to help in any way he could. "Actually, I had dated a girl who was taking the compensation course and tried to convince her that knowing how to design structures had an application in pay administration. She of course looked at me as if I had just arrived from another galaxy, so I let it go, but I could have helped a little." "You have just hit on what is wrong with the artificial division between the hard stuff and the soft stuff," Annette contributed. "There often is a need to employ quantitative rigor when doing workforce management, and there should be a recognition that managing technical work can be done better if one understands the principles of behavioral science." Ralph seriously requested that if Rob and Kathy were doing the seminars they were planning that he would like to attend. He was an avid proponent of evidence-based management and felt he could bridge the gap between research and practice in his field but was limited in his understanding of behavioral research. Rob took his card and wrote on the back, "Invite line managers as well," running the seminar marketing plan through his head.

As the evening progressed and Rob ran out of people he wanted to chat with, he sought Ralph out again to continue their discussion. "Can you give me an example of something HR people should know that engineers do?" Rob asked. "Well, I am pretty much playing the role of project manager, rather than engineer, or even engineering manager, so my perspective may be somewhat different. But I will tell you a story about a battle I fought with HR. We had a large project come up that was unique for us and that was probably going to be a one-time thing. I needed to staff up for the project and called HR to ask how I brought in outside consultants to do the unique things and to handle the peak workload. Their response was that it was too expensive to use consultants, since the consulting firms charged three to four times the salary of their people to us. I pushed back and said that I did not want to staff up to meet a peak workload and particularly did not want to hire employees with specific skills that we probably would not use going forward. The battle over this issue went all the way up, and finally the VP of operations and VP of HR agreed to bring in consultants. This alerted me to the fact that the HR folks did not understand the concepts of path dependence and lock-in." "Not sure I get the connection," Rob responded, joined by Kathy, who indicated she did not either.

"Decisions can lock you into a path going forward," Ralph responded, quite pleased that he had an audience with HR types. "This can happen without you recognizing it if you do not plan an entire project. For example, choosing a unique technology limited some of the computer manufacturers back when mainframes were the game and IBM did not rule. Competitors like Honeywell were handicapped in competing later in the game, since organizations found that programmers who build systems to run on Honeywell hardware were limited in number, so choosing IBM was a safer path and IBM prospered. Apple chose a different path with the Mac rather than following the PC and they survived, but the individual computer market functions differently than the mainframe world. So, your early decisions can limit your alternatives down the road. The same principle holds when staffing a project. If you select an esoteric technology, will you be able to find enough talent to work with that technology? And even if you can, is the cost palatable? Look at the way the Y2K event was handled. Almost everyone junked their legacy systems rather than reprogram them, and they created a huge demand for network people that could not be met by the supply. Apparently, no one thought about that when they made their decision. And HR went out trying to hire people to do all the work rather than bringing in contractors."

Rob responded, "But you are not being fair to the people who had to find the talent. What about the people that decided they were going to replace their existing systems without considering the obstacles?" "OK, I concede that," Ralph answered. "But let's go back to the hire versus lease talent decision to staff one-time events. I could have sent my engineers to crash courses that would give them the esoteric skills that were needed for the project, but they would have had to work 100-hour weeks to get the job done and would not be as productive as consultants who would come in with those skills. And although HR argued that using our people would challenge them and give them new skills, we probably would have to pay them for having those skills, even though they would be rarely used in the future. Now, if I rent outside consultants, what happens when the project is done? They go home. I have not expanded my employee headcount or locked myself into paying them for additional capabilities I will not need. In fact, I probably have increased the odds they will go to work for the consulting firms I should have hired in the first place, so they can use those skills."

"You really have something," Rob conceded. "I know technical people make decisions about the technologies they will use without adequately considering the consequences for staffing that will result from the decision. And I am sure that few technical managers invite HR in to discuss the potential workforce implications (his wry smirk gave away the irony intended)." "You are correct, it does not happen and I plead guilty to this oversight," Ralph responded, with a less-than-happy facial expression. "I think we have just helped each other out here," Rob concluded. "So maybe the bridge building should not be limited to the research and HR practitioner communities but be extended to the line and staff communities. Boy, that would make an interesting article, but I am not sure who would publish it. The HR publications would if the message was that line needed to listen to staff, and the general management publication would if the message was that staff needed to listen to the line."

Late in the evening, a large number of the attendees informally gathered in a circle, probably not realizing that it looked like a scout camp get-together around a fire. People had begun asking each other the "what next, what do you want to do with the rest of your career?" questions. Most of the group was fairly satisfied with where they were. Some were frustrated with their progress, probably due in part to the suggestion by a few faculty members they had in their degree program that they would rule the world in short order. Some had problems in their personal lives, but few wanted to take the conversation in that direction. But most of them were wrestling with their plan for the next ten or twenty or thirty years of their careers. A few admitted that the question they dreaded the most when interviewing for a new job or with a new organization was, "where do you want to be ten years from now?"

There were several suggestions made to the HR delegates that recruiters and staffing people should strike that question from their structured interview list. Given the turbulence in the world and the reality that stuff happens, the general feeling was that this question created unnecessary angst for them.

Zahra and Mushira, who had been two of the international students, both suggested this was a question people should ask themselves, but it should be something personal. "Besides," Zahra offered, "are they going to tell a recruiter or the HR person that they only want to hang around this dump for a year or two, until they can get some experience and go out to find a decent job?" "We have honesty tests we can use to catch the liars," Annette jokingly interjected.

The evening ended with this question foremost in the minds of those in attendance. What constituted a *worthwhile* life? What was a *successful* career? What should one be satisfied with? Rob, Don, Annette and Kathy knew that managing the people in the organization in a mutually beneficial manner gave them all the meaning and satisfaction they needed in their professional lives. They were convinced their work was centered around recognizing and rewarding the organization's most important asset.

31 Let's be strategic

Don, Annette, Kathy and Rob had attended a program offered by a professional association. They decided to collaborate after the session to discuss what they had heard. "What was the message you all got?" asked Rob. Annette shot back, "Be strategic and not transactional or tactical—for the thousandth time." Don was a bit taken aback by her sharp tone and gave her the raised eyebrow message that suggested she could explain what was behind her response. "Well," she said, "I have been hearing that same message for a decade or more, and those sending it seem to think that HR practitioners will be transformed by being more strategic. I wonder if they even looked up the definition of the word."

"I just looked it up on my smart phone," responded Rob, "and Webster says it is defined as follows: 'of, or having to do with strategy.' Since that did not help much, I looked up the definition of strategy and that is: 'the science of planning and directing large-scale operations.' It differentiates strategy from tactics, which are more related to execution of strategy." Don reacted by suggesting they needed to consult a respected book on business strategy, which would be more relevant to their discussion. "Well, I don't have any e-books by any of the strategy wonks on my phone," Rob shot back, "but I think we could agree that what the presenter this evening was suggesting is that HR strategy should be derived from and should support the organization's strategy. And in our university studies and subsequent experience, we learned that strategy should be formulated after the mission was defined, the culture understood, internal and external realities considered and alternative approaches to competing evaluated. But then the presentation failed to go past the trite appeal for HR people becoming more strategic."

Kathy had studied management history and pointed out examples of instances where a business strategy was formulated and then HR strategies were experimented with to see what contributed to attaining the organization's objectives. "I was really interested in one of the lessons that Sloan learned when he had developed the unique strategy for General Motors that created a number of cars targeted at income levels, from Chevrolet to Cadillac. When it came to producing the cars, they discovered an interesting thing about the workforces. They could not easily convert a Cadillac plant to a Chevrolet plant even when the demand for models dictated a shift in production capacity. The Cadillac employees had been trained to work at close tolerances and high-quality levels, with equipment designed for that purpose. They could not easily adjust their way of working, making it too expensive to make Chevrolets in Cadillac plants. This was a lesson in ensuring the workforce fits the work. And IBM had to go through a complete reassessment of the type of workforce strategy they needed when they moved from big iron to services."

"Yes," Rob responded, "but so many organizations change slowly, and like the frog in water brought slowly up to boiling, they don't appreciate the need to refine their HR strategy. So, their mix of knowledge and skills becomes less and less appropriate given their evolving business strategy. That is the reason I have always believed HR should be involved in strategy sessions intimately, so that the workforce implications are discussed when strategy changes are decided on, rather than waiting until a problem is evident."

"So, does everyone in HR have to be strategic?" asked Annette. "Sure, to varying degrees," responded Rob. "Being strategic to me means being future oriented, planning what you do, as included in the Webster definition. The future for an entry-level HR generalist may be a few months out, while for the CHRO (top HR executive), it may be five to ten years. And even the novice should think about the long-term implications of what and how things are done in the short term. A short-term focus can lead to solving a problem in what appears to be the best way but does so in a manner that limits options going forward. Something as simple as approving a special work arrangement for an employee often sets a precedent and results in an avalanche of requests for other deals by co-workers. Once a policy is shown to be flexible, it opens the door to individual negotiations, and consistency can go out the window. We typically don't think about someone as behaving strategically just because they think about the future implications of current actions. But encouraging this type of balanced focus on both now and then prepares people to continue that kind of thought process as they develop in their careers."

"I think the term strategic has been used so often in so many ways that it has become useless for any type of classification," offered Don. "I prefer the 'think about the long-term implications of everything you do' mindset Rob just described—it avoids hard classifications. For example, both the Human Resource Certification Institute (HRCI) and the Society for Human Resource Management (SHRM) have two levels of certification. No one seriously believes one level is 100% strategic and the other 100% tactical. Yet, some people assume if you hold a management role in HR that you should be strategic, and if you are an individual contributor, you should be tactical. Everything is a matter of degree. A CHRO at GE has said he would be at the most risk of getting fired from something as tactical as payroll systems going haywire. So, everyone, despite their level, needs to get things that are necessary done and done well. CHROs do not spend all of their time being strategic, but they certainly should consider the long term when making short-term decisions."

Annette chimed in. "I remember our favorite *Dilbert* cartoon when we were cutting them out and taking them to our classes at school. The pointy-head boss says he used to think their people were their most important asset, but he was wrong—they ranked eighth. When Dilbert asked what was seventh, he said carbon paper. And since then, we have run into senior-level executives that might even rank the human capital lower. That just blows my fuse." "Yes," Don assured her, "people are important and we should love them. But the real issue is whether executive management can be convinced that the workforce can be a strategic competitive advantage. A classic study that is cited frequently found that in order to be a strategic competitive advantage, an organization's human capital must be: (1) valuable/critical to the business, (2) rare and (3) difficult to imitate.[1] It would be a stretch to believe that all types of talent in all types of organizations would fit those criteria. So, the CHRO of one organization is being strategic when recognizing that the workforce or parts of the workforce may not be a potential source of advantage and that cost minimization is the best approach. On the other hand, a competitor may believe quality of service or some other advantage can be gained and recognize that having a different kind of workforce would be needed." Rob added, "Lester Thurow has said that the only sustainable competitive advantage is a competent and committed workforce . . . all other resources can be obtained by competitors under similar terms. And he said a workforce like that cannot be bought—it must be built and its viability sustained."

They broke up their discussion that evening, agreeing that being strategic was good, and that thinking both long-term and short-term was necessary. HR being strategic is when HR strategy was well-aligned with the business strategy. Rob had sarcastically said that reaching so many conclusions in one meeting should make them proud.

Kathy had gone back to teaching for a while but rejoined her three friends at Epsilon after taking a leave of absence from her faculty position at the university, and along with Don, Rob and Annette formed a core team. The foursome was about to begin a consulting project for an organization that had been a start-up only a few years ago but had experienced dramatic growth and success. Their assignment was to help the organization formulate an HR strategy that would serve the organization going forward and to design the structure for the HR function. And they were to assist with finding a CHRO who could implement the strategy. One of the first things they realized is that they did not want to wait to find an executive to run the HR function until after they formulated the strategy. That would tie the hands of the newly hired executive and would also inhibit their recruitment efforts, since a qualified candidate would want to be able to participate in the strategy formulation process. The discussions about "strategy" and "strategic" had resulted from their discussions about the qualifications of an ideal candidate for the client organization.

Chris, the CEO of Gamma Corp., the client organization, had given the consultants the firm's history and had expressed a concern about making the transition from a "management by enthusiasm and brilliant insights" to a "manage professionally" philosophy. She had told the consultants that they were still struggling to find the right strategy for defining, measuring and rewarding performance and knew that a "good fit" strategy would help them attract the right people and motivate them to do the right things. She was also having difficulty aligning the senior staff. Each had been hired as one of a kind. The CFO handled Finance, the COO handled logistics and production, the R & D exec called the shots on design, and so forth. Rob pointed out to her that this was typical in start-ups, given their small size at the time, and that since none of her direct reports had general management experience, it would be necessary to align them by putting into place integrative systems.[2] He suggested that the first step was to develop an organizational performance model that defined what was needed for success at each level (organizational, functional/unit and individual). He showed her a model that provided a framework for doing this (see Figure 31.1).

The critical success factors were those things that had to happen in order for the organization to use its core capabilities in a manner that supported the organizational strategy. The key performance indicators (KPIs) were the metrics that were used to measure results, and these would be defined at each of the three levels. Objectives established at the organizational level would be cascaded down through each level. Each of the business units/functions would have to meet their own objectives in order for the organization to meet its objectives. Then the business unit/function objectives would be cascaded down through the intervening levels, all the way to individual or team objectives. This process would enable lateral integration at each level and enable the CEO to ensure everyone was in alignment.

Another challenge that would have to be addressed first was identifying the core competencies of the organization and how they could be turned into capabilities that would provide a competitive advantage. They might be able

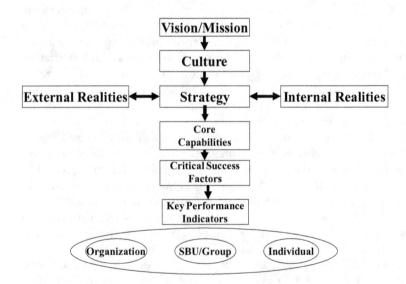

Figure 31.1 Performance management model

to invent and design a superior product (good or service) that would be welcomed by customers, but they needed to turn the design into a product that could be sold and delivered. They did not want to repeat the experience Xerox had with the Palo Alto Research Center (PARC), which had invented many of the products that enabled computers to advance technically. Doing the research and inventing things was a core competency of PARC. But the entity did not turn this into a capability that enabled Xerox to benefit commercially, since the innovations were given away or sold at rock-bottom prices, to the delight of organizations like Microsoft and Apple. Xerox had been unable to incorporate the innovations into the mother organization. General Motors had developed New United Motor, Inc. and Saturn but was unable to import the things that made those ventures viable into the mainstream organization.

Rob suggested that the executive group work together to develop the performance model by identifying the key performance indicators and establishing objectives—first at the organizational level and then working through subordinates to complete the cascading process. He offered to sit in on the sessions, specifically to understand what type of incentive programs would help to promote lateral management as well as vertical management. By aligning the economic destinies of people across functions, they would be able to motivate cooperative and supportive behavior by focusing on the overall results, rather than on each person's objectives. The organization had used stock options heavily since the founding, both because there was a shortage of cash and because it was believed that people with aligned economic outcomes would operate in the best interests of the organization. Employees who are owners are more likely to behave like owners—people don't wash or maintain rental cars. Although this strategy had worked reasonably well, the annual cash compensation levels were well below competitive levels, and there was a danger that some of the key people would be targeted by other organizations. "This is a critical time," Rob told Chris. "People will realize they have contributed to rapid and profitable growth and they will begin to wonder what their true market value is." Chris agreed to Rob's suggestion that they run integration sessions and said they would begin soon.

When Rob met with the rest of the consulting team, he stated with assurance that he had been "100% strategic" in his discussions with the CEO. Annette suggested that focusing on acquiring more billable consulting work so they could pay the rent next month probably was tactical, but conceded that the subject matter of Rob's meeting was indeed highly strategic. Don pointed out that her take on Rob's work was pretty cynical and bordering on the sarcastic, but she was undaunted. "I can remember when he thought any planning beyond next week was strategic," she responded.

During their next meeting, Chris asked Rob about a book she had found to be extremely thought-provoking about designing an organization in a manner that would enable it to change.[3] Rob had followed Lawler's work since he entered the university and was prepared to discuss the book. "What were the ideas that you felt to be most relevant to your situation?" he asked. "That if we wanted to make the transition from a great idea and hard work to a viable entity for the long term that we should shape our mission, culture, structure and strategy in a way that would enable us to change when the environment changed," Chris responded. Rob had been taken by the way the book had described the mindset that would lead to sustainable success. It required committing to continuous strategizing, not to a specific strategy, and to ensuring environmental scanning is done continuously so necessary changes to strategy could be identified in time to adjust to the emerging environment. It also required committing to a process of continuous organizing rather than settling for a specific structure.

Rob had dealt with organizations that spent a lot of effort trying to find the right culture, strategy and structure that would enable them to perform at high levels for a long time into the future. But the more that they focused on a single strategy and structure, the more they were locked into one way of operating. This made each future decision path dependent, which meant it needed to be consistent with the road prior decisions had put them on. When someone takes a wrong turn in a maze, they can retreat and reroute when they met a dead end. Unlike the maze, an organization that is operating in the commercial rerouting may result in a just-too-late response. Speed and agility have become critical capabilities in the competitive environment and being too late was very costly.

Rob suggested that they focus on the HR strategy the organization would adopt. "I am suggesting we use a scenario-based planning process that defines three possible futures: an optimistic scenario, a pessimistic scenario and a most likely scenario. We can then formulate a business strategy that will work reasonably well in a variety of possible futures and base our HR strategy on that strategy. At the same time, we put into place a process that incorporates continuous environmental scanning and plans for revising the strategy when environmental change alters our scenarios." "Sounds like a lot of work that never is done," Chris said, with a pained look on her face. "Yes," Rob assured her, "it means you are doomed to be eternally strategic."

"Once a strategy is in place, the continuous feedback from environmental scanning should signal the need to change something," continued Rob. "It will be necessary to decide whether the strategy should be adjusted, reoriented or replaced. That is, you may elect to stick with the strategy but change the emphasis, say from premium pricing that is made possible by technical superiority to less aggressive pricing to reflect the diminishing gap between your products and those being rolled out by competitors. Or you could reorient to providing high-quality service. Or you could transform yourself into the lowest-cost provider when production has been scaled up in a way that gives you a cost advantage. And as these modifications are made, consideration should be given to realigning your HR strategy to ensure you continue to maintain workforce viability."

Gamma Corp. had an R & D director who was a true scientist, and she had created a way to use 3D printing to manufacture their most important products more quickly and more cheaply. Although this had given Gamma the early adopter edge competitively, it was unclear how long it would be before competitors caught up. What was most important currently for the organization was its ability to scale up production and to penetrate markets before their products were commoditized. After long discussions with Chris's staff, it was decided that the most immediate need was attracting the highest quality of production people who had the required knowledge and experience to outperform competitors. It would also be necessary to finance the infrastructure required in an effective manner. But infrastructure was useless if the right people with the right capabilities were not on board to utilize it. The executive team was confident that their technical advantage could be maintained for the foreseeable future, but it was critical that the skilled production people were able to provide the product quality required and do so at an acceptable cost.

Since the existing rewards strategy included a heavy reliance on stock options, Rob alerted the executives that this might not be the ideal approach for attracting and retaining the most qualified production people. "Although executives and senior managers can often accept that their contributions will have a direct and significant impact on overall organizational performance, the rest of the workforce may feel that they only control their own performance and have a more limited impact on their unit's performance," Rob told the group.

"Given the turbulent environment and the pace of technological change, it could be unrealistic to think most employees will accept that a large part of their rewards should be based on overall performance, which can be impacted significantly by uncontrollable external factors. Therefore, you should consider shifting a portion of the equity-based rewards to cash compensation for much of the workforce. It is still important for the executives to function as a team and to focus on delivering organization results. The extensive use of stock as a source of economic rewards makes sense for you, at least for your key management people. I believe it makes sense for you to have a shared destiny incentive plan in place for all employees, but perhaps that should be a cash profit-sharing plan for the majority of employees. In the production function, a gainsharing plan may make sense, since this type of plan focuses on productivity and quality, and would use metrics employees recognize they can impact."

Several of the executives questioned the us-them mindset that might be created if the use of stock were used for some and not others. But Rob countered that with a rationale. "In addition to the uncertainty on their part about how much impact these employees can have on stock price, we must also consider how much value they would place on different types of rewards. Many of them are trying to improve their standard of living, and cash is the key to doing that. Even though they could exercise options and sell the stock to produce cash, they might be concerned about how that would reflect on others' view of their commitment to the organization. And the tax treatment of stock purchases and sales are probably a mystery to them, exposing them to the possibility that they will make errors that penalize them financially. Besides, stock options are not a free lunch—the ownership dilution they create should be considered."

Darren, the CFO, added his perspective. "I am glad you brought up dilution of ownership as an issue. There is also the reality that an opportunity cost is involved. If the organization in effect turns over control of stock that would have appreciated, it is foregoing the financial benefits it might have realized. I know we say this is in lieu of cash awards, but I wonder if we are really calculating the tradeoff between the true long-term cost of giving out options and the current cost of rewarding employees with cash. Despite my hard-hearted, rational financial perspective, I love the idea of employees having stock. It seems a tangible way of recognizing their critical contributions and of aligning everyone's interests. I know I am less concerned about the well-being of a rental car than I am of my own car, and making our employees owners can promote an owner's perspective. But the number of options required to give everyone a significant earning opportunity is really large, and I wonder if there is some middle ground."

Rob thought about that and made a suggestion. "What if we designed an annual profit-sharing plan that paid out in both cash and stock. Employees would be taxed on the stock portion as well as the cash portion, but we could take the tax out of the cash portion and deliver owned shares that had already been taxed. This would over time build ownership without having employees exposed to the need to make sophisticated decisions about exercising options and selling shares. It also would significantly reduce the number of shares required, as well as linking them to tangible results produced. Too often, stock options are issued when someone is feeling generous or when it seems things are going well, without any direct link to specific outcomes. This makes them more of a holiday bonus than a reward based on performance. Also, when an egalitarian approach to distributing options is used, it can result in some types of employees experiencing a significant benefit as a percentage of pay and others less of a benefit."

Chris jumped in. "I love the idea of the profit-sharing plan paid out in two parts. That allows us to reward when we have the results to justify it and to forego rewards when we are not doing well—for explainable reasons. But how do we make decisions about how much each level of employee gets? Do we tie it to their grade in the pay structure? To their level on the organization chart? Or how well we like them?"

Rob had dealt with this same issue recently when designing a cash incentive plan for a large investment company. "Annual incentive plans almost always have target awards tied to a level, however defined. You all will have to decide how the level is determined. For example, we could establish a target award as a percentage of base salary or pay range midpoint for each level. This might be a target award of 100% of base and a maximum award of 200% for the executive level. The next level, perhaps defined as managers and key individual contributors, might have a target of 50% and a maximum of 100%, and so on. The amounts need to be decided and integrated with your competitive posture. You might decide to set base pay levels at market average and incentive targets at market average. Or you might set the base at 85–90% of market and provide a larger incentive opportunity. The decision should be a good fit to the culture and the value proposition you use to attract and retain talent. The profit sharing plan could be designed in a similar fashion, although you have to decide if there also needs to be other annual cash incentive plans as well. But if you use the profit sharing approach, you should include everyone to provide that shared destiny image."

Ray, the head of production, had been raising his hand during Rob's suggestions and used the gap to have his say. "In production, we will need several types of incentives. I am sold on the idea of a gainsharing plan for the plant people, including plant management. We can develop a baseline of productivity and reward everyone for gains. This is what I would call a shared destiny plan. We may also have individual and team/unit incentives where they make sense. But if we are rewarding our people with those plans, do we really need to include them in an incentive plan based on overall organizational performance?"

"I think so," answered Rob, "but you certainly need to decide on a balanced approach when deciding how much of their potential rewards are based on plant and how much on organizational performance. Remember, we want to have everyone remember where their pay comes from and how rewards are determined. But you also need to teach employees the business of the organization and educate them on what contributes to results, both in the short term and over time. They will figure out that the better the plant performs, the better its gainsharing awards will be, and the better the organization performs, the better its profit sharing awards will be. That is in the short term, but the fact that it will also have stock will help to link its economic well-being with the longer-term performance of the organization."

"There is an additional concern. If you do use individual and unit incentives as well, they need to be integrated with each other and with the plant and organizational plans. For example, if one part of the plant uses teams, you might want to provide incentives based on team performance, in lieu of individual rewards. For employees who focus on and control their individual performance, you might want to base their rewards on their performance. You have to be careful that having any employee rewarded for individual, team/unit, plant and organizational performance is not overcompensated or undercompensated in aggregate. And you must also be concerned about the complexity of the value proposition you offer someone. There is an old joke about sales incentives that says if you make the plans overly compensated, the participants will perform poorly. Figuring out how much they might make will take so much of their time that they will not be able to make sales calls."

Chris suggested they close the meeting and schedule another late the next day. In the meantime, she told everyone to think about what had been discussed and to email Rob by midday tomorrow with their views, concerns and questions. She committed Rob to compiling their input and to coming to the session tomorrow with an outline of what the collective views are. Rob volunteered Don and Pete to help him make sense out of the feedback he had gotten from Gamma executives by the end of the day. Since they would be going well into the evening, he even offered to pay for some first-rate food.

While sitting around a table in their favorite Spanish restaurant, Don and Pete asked how close the respondents were to agreement. "They agree on some principles," Rob began. "The idea of cutting back on the use of stock for people below the executive level is seen as a good idea, particularly by the CFO who was worried about ownership dilution. And a profit sharing plan that is paid out partially in cash and partially in stock is seen as a great move. But several of them think there should be a one-third stock and two-thirds cash mix, since by the time the deduction for the tax on the full award is taken out of the cash part, there won't be much spendable income left. This is seen as a bigger problem for support personnel and less so for the management folks. I think what I am going to recommend is that a mandated ownership level be established for each different category of employee and that the stock/cash mix out of the profit sharing differ by category. The ownership level will be expressed as a multiple of base pay range midpoint: perhaps 300% for executives, 200% for managers and professionals and 100% for support personnel. Once that mandated minimum is reached, an employee can elect any mix of cash and stock in their award."

"You sure this complex, sophisticated framework is going to be understandable?" asked Don. "I think so," Rob responded, "since I am going to pressure them to conduct extensive training for all employees when this framework goes into effect. And I am going to recommend that individualized compensation statements be prepared each year so people know what they got and where they stand." Rob had a great deal of confidence that the workforce at Gamma consisted of savvy and serious employees for the most part, and they were used to open and extensive communication.

Rob showed them the framework he had roughed out to communicate the overall philosophy and strategy (see Table 31.1).

"This is really neat," Pete said with great enthusiasm. "I could question some of the details of the proposed plans, but it is really a nice device for getting people to think about total compensation and where it comes from. By the way, where are the direct salespeople?"

"I left them as a separate group," Rob responded, "but perhaps I should also put them in as a separate category, in addition to sales management. I had a side conversation with the executive who has marketing and sales, and he felt strongly about including his people in the profit sharing plan so they remembered they actually worked for Gamma. I was relieved to hear that, since sales executives often want to run their own show and feel they should not confuse their people with issues like how well the organization or business unit is doing. You could see that with the bankers who used failed concepts like guaranteed bonuses even while their organizations were melting down in 2007–2009, due to their misguided efforts. It was one of the problems with conquering armies and pirates—if they got a share of the loot then pillaging other's property was the rational behavior."

"And what are your initial disagreements with the matrix entries?" Rob asked Pete, who was quick to respond. "You did not include a provision for

Table 31.1 Performance management model

Form--→ Ee. Type	Base Pay	Individual Incentive	Group/Unit Incentive	Org wide Incentive	Stock
Executives	Merit pay	None	None	Exec inc. plan profit sharing	300% min. ownership
Managers	Merit pay	None	None	Mgt. inc. plan profit sharing	200% min. ownership
Professionals	Merit pay	None	None, but some project incentives	Profit sharing	200% min. ownership
Support – Admin.	Merit pay	None	None	Profit sharing	100% min. ownership
Support – Operations	Skill-based pay	Output-based incentives for some	Plant-wide gainsharing	Profit sharing	100% min. ownership

team incentives being offered to some professionals and support personnel. And there is no mention of a long-term cash incentive plan for executives, although perhaps you think the stock plans would motivate them to consider both short– and longer–term results when making decisions." Rob raised his eyebrows and admitted that was an issue he needed to surface with the executives the next day.

During the second meeting, the general reaction to Rob's strategy framework was positive. Most of the executives had requested more detail on "how much" since they generally agreed with the "how" of rewarding employees. But they realized that would be worked out once a strategy was agreed on. Chris suggested that the executives discuss the proposed framework with their direct reports, to get their personal reactions and a sense of how they felt this would be received by all employees. "The thing I like the best about this approach is that we can change the specifics of the plans we use for different categories of employees as dictated by environmental change," she offered, "and it is consistent with the concept of custom strategies that are consistent with guiding principles. Rob shared one of his favorite books with me that proposed that concept,[4] and I believe it is appropriate for today's diverse and complex workforces. So, we go on record that we will pay people differently—not only how much but how. And we explain the philosophy behind the approach and support it with a business-oriented rationale."

When Rob went back to Gamma, Chris advised him of the strategy meetings they had been holding and wanted to be sure they were able to fashion an

HR strategy that fit the business strategy. What was interesting to Rob is that they had gone through an exercise that questioned what they would adopt as a source of competitive advantage. In the book *The Discipline of Market Leaders*,[5] the authors had presented a model that listed three sources of competitive advantage. The first was operational excellence which was based on being the low-cost provider. The second was the product leadership, which was based on having the best goods or services. The third was customer intimacy, which was based on developing strong, enduring relationships with customers. Chris admitted they initially wanted to be all three, but they realized no organization can be a leader in all three. They had to be sufficiently competent in all three of course, but an organization's focus should be on the one that would provide a competitive advantage. Rob had been through strategy assessments using the model before and asked Chris which they had chosen.

"We got our initial advantage through product leadership and that is still the source of our principal advantage today. We also realized that unless we continued to stay ahead of competitors through significant innovation, that our advantage could be overcome by lower-cost providers. When customers do not recognize a meaningful difference between brands, they view the products as interchangeable commodities and will buy based on price. So, we have at least for the present decided that we will focus on rapid prototyping and other techniques to get the best and most innovative products out into the market and enjoy premium margins. When competitors catch up with one of our products, we will probably abandon that product, either replacing it with something better or leaving that market segment to others. What this means is that we are in effect an R & D/innovation-focused organization and need to operate as such."

Rob was pleased. "The clarity will help us in formulating an HR strategy that will be a good fit to your business strategy and contribute to success. Innovation-focused organizations should have staffing and development strategies that will get and keep the kind of workforce that can execute your chosen strategy. It will also help us decide how to define, measure and reward performance. Organizations often neglect to realign their HR strategy when their business strategy changes, which can result in a workforce that is not competent to execute the new strategy and not focused on the new key performance indicators. So, we should develop the performance model that supports your chosen strategy. Using a balanced scorecard approach is still valid, but there will be changes in the way we measure things. For instance, it will make sense to continuously evaluate the percentage of revenue and profits that accrue from new products and from products that still can support premium pricing and be competitive. This will enable you to focus your R & D efforts on things that are needed to replace the sales that will be lost when commoditized products are dropped or when they can only compete with low-margin pricing. It will also be necessary to motivate the sales force to focus on specific products, rather than just selling whatever is easiest to sell. That will require focused incentives and perhaps even a shift in the type of personnel you select and how you develop them."

Each of the functional executives at Gamma prepared their own plans for operating in a manner that was consistent with the product leadership strategy and the performance criteria and standards that had been developed. They also used the workforce planning model Rob had provided them to evaluate their current workforce considering current needs and to project what would be needed in the future and how the workforce could be reshaped to meet them. It had not been necessary to point out to the executives that their jobs were not only to manage the present but to ensure the organization was positioned to operate well into the future. They knew they were in a precarious situation—choosing to lead through innovation put them in the position of a Western sherriff who hoped he would not meet anyone faster on the draw than he was. Disruptive technology was being created virtually everywhere, and the products they relied on for revenue and profits could be leapfrogged by a competitor who was not known to them or who did not even exist today. Several of the executive team began to question the wisdom of abandoning markets that became competitive, since there were examples of organizations who continued to be successful even when lower-cost competitors had emerged, offering somewhat comparable products.

Chis ended the meeting by thanking Rob. She said, smiling, "I hope you can spend your time helping other organizations see the light, as long as they are not our competitors. Now the rest is up to us."

Rob hated the thought of the assignment coming to an end, but he felt the positive response meant Gamma would pay the invoice on a timely basis and be a source of referrals in the future. He remembered what Howard had told him about one of the things about consulting that many found disturbing— you did not get to stick around to see the benefits of the work or go to the party celebrating success.

Notes

1 Barney, T. and Wright, P., "On Being a Strategic Partner," in *Human Resource Management* (1998), 37(1), 31

2 Greene, R., *Rewarding Performance in Emerging/Start Up Organizations, World at Work Journal,* 2d Q, 2012.

3 Lawler, E. and Worley, C., *Built to Change,* 2006, Jossey-Bass, San Francisco.

4 Greene, R., *Rewarding Performance: Guiding Principles; Custom Strategies,* 2011, Routledge, New York.

5 Treacy, M. and Wiersema, F., *The Discipline of Market Leaders,* 1995, Addison-Wesley, Reading, MA.

32 Motivating and rewarding sales personnel

Annette and Don had gotten a call from Lambda, a provider of software to engineering firms and engineering functions within all types of organizations. Their concern was that they were not compensating their sales personnel correctly. They had to take a long flight to get to the client location and had a chance to recount Annette's experience at her first employer out of school, which was also a software firm.

"All the time I was there I don't think HR ever got a call from the sales executive. He just did not think HR knew enough about the products, the customers and the sales process to be of much use in the design of the compensation package for his people. And although I found that to be somewhat offensive, I was told by our compensation manager that there was some truth in this accusation. He said that measuring performance of the direct sales representatives was a very tricky proposition. All volume was not of the same value to the organization, all the products have different profit margins, sales of packages were a one-time deal, while getting service contracts provided a revenue stream, and so on. So, HR was probably better off not trying to impose a compensation package for the sales staff. The sales executive seemed to know what he was doing, since turnover among high producers was low and revenue and profits grew, at least until the economic downturn changed everything. HR did monitor the package to ensure it was reasonable relative to market rates and that it did not raise equity questions relative to other functions. Of course, the design engineers thought too much was being paid to a bunch of fancy-dressing, fast-talking peddlers but I guess you run into that everywhere."

Don had spent a considerable amount of time studying sales compensation over the last few years and had worked on a number of client assignments that had equipped him with at least the right questions to ask, if not always with the right answers. "The one thing I learned was that what is best will vary across organizations, even if they are in the same business and competitors, and often variation makes sense within an organization but across business units and product lines. So, walking in the door with a hammer and treating every situation as if it were a nail needing to be driven will almost certainly end in disaster. What we really have to start with is an in-depth evaluation of the context within which Lambda sells its products and also of its culture. I worked with a research laboratory that did contract research for major corporations. It had developed a leading-edge information retrieval system for a client under a grant and ended up with a commercially viable product it was free to sell. But the leadership of the lab felt it would violate their culture to use individual incentives for anyone, since that would conflict with their values. After telling them that sending their researchers out into the field to compete with software salespeople would be a failed strategy, they decided to license the product to one of the software firms who could then use its sales force to sell it. I have no idea how much money they walked away from, but if the right compensation program would have been in conflict with their values and culture, I guess they did the right thing. That's when I realized sales compensation strategy was about more than just motivating people to sell as much as possible."

Rob had also shared with Don the lessons learned when the operations executive at Gamma discussed the ideas he had gotten from one of his colleagues about sales compensation. The principles were: (1) reward what you want, (2) don't distract the sales personnel from what you want by rewarding something they did not produce and (3) don't provide a comfortable income when you are not getting enough of what you want. Don kept that in mind when he prepared for the Lambda project.

The meeting with the Lambda CEO, CFO and chief marketing officer started slowly, since it was evident the marketing executive was suspicious of some outsider telling him how to compensate his people. This became obvious when he gave them their first question: "When is a sale a sale for purposes of compensating the person who generated it?" Annette responded quickly, "When the organization realizes a benefit. For example, if you 'sell' someone something that can be returned, is that a sale? Or if the customer doesn't pay for the something, is that a sale? Or if you 'sell' something that has a value only when they use it, how do you determine the value of the sale?" Annette had done her homework and found that the software provided by the client was in the cloud, and customers were charged on an as-used basis. So, she figured they were being pressured by sales representatives to pay them when they licensed a new customer and hooked them up. This had led her to ask the last question.

The marketing executive was a bit taken aback when Annette cited the very issue that had been plaguing them. Their salespeople had been running from presentation to presentation, dazzling the engineers who were the potential users of the software with the technical wows that had been built in. But they did not seem motivated to do the missionary work, which involved regular visits to see how much and how the customer was using the software and to show them how to use it for different applications. He knew enough about motivation theory to know that you can influence behavior, especially that of salespeople, by how you measure and reward performance. So, he had evaluated the commission earned when a new license was purchased and the customer went live and found it to be substantial. But he then looked at the earnings potential tied to usage that had been built into the commission plan and found that, even though this is where the real profit potential for the company was, it was not the best avenue for the salespeople to maximize their income.

"OK, you passed," he told Annette. He then shared the volume and earnings figures for their sales representatives for the last three years and asked them to suggest how they could best focus behavior by using incentives that were aligned with the desired performance. Their analysis showed that the "run around and do new licensing" approach was more rewarding than balancing new customer hookups and revenue from usage. After adjusting the commission rates, they were able to arrive at a sales incentive plan that provided the most income to reps that produced the optimal result. But Don suggested they might be missing something and moved away from metrics to competencies of sales personnel. "Some people are better at selling new customers, which involves establishing a quick rapport and motivating people to make the desired decisions. Others will tend to be more effective at developing relationships over time and at working with customers to expand their utilization by demonstrating how the product can be valuable in a broad range of applications. All of your salespeople have some technical background, but not all of them have the knowledge to identify the full scope of potential product application. So, perhaps by evaluating both technical competence and interpersonal competence, you might be able to sort the sales force into two groups, the hunters and the farmers. This would make it easier to find people, since you would not require two sets of competencies that may be rare in a single person."

"That is a brilliant suggestion," the marketing executive responded, "and something I had not given any thought to. It would make it so much easier to ensure that regular visits to existing customers are happening and that we are building the current customer revenue base appropriately. We could also focus our sales training more effectively by making that distinction. But I don't know if all of the reps should only sell new customers or only grow the base from existing customers. That could lead to new customer sales that were made by overstating product capabilities or by overselling a new licensee, not a formula for maintaining customers for a long time."

They decided they would have their staffing and their development functions within HR look at developing two competency models. They would then work with management and the current sales staff to sort people into the newly created roles. Marketing staff would work with Don and Annette to develop a new sales incentive model that would fit the new sales force structure.

"One more pressing issue," he interjected before the meeting broke up. "I am not sure we are compensating sales support and sales management personnel correctly. The sales support people are salaried, and I wonder if we should be attempting to create some type of incentive plan for them as well. And sales management folks, including yours truly, have their own incentives that may not be ideally linked to overall organization performance."

Don began his response by stating what he viewed to be a sound principle. "Salespeople, if they are employees rather than contract personnel, should understand who they work for and should have some of their income based on overall performance. You have a cash performance-sharing plan for all employees to provide a shared destiny that motivates them to be interested in making the organization successful. The sales support and sales management folks participate in that plan and that is as it should be. Some might argue that direct sales representatives have their commission plans and that they should not be double dipping. That I believe to be a mistake. If they are participants in the performance sharing plan, they are rewarded for individual performance *and* for organizational performance, both of which are important for them to realize."

"Makes sense to me," responded the marketing executive. "I do think the field people sometimes believe their results are solely attributable to their own brilliance, and they even push back if they have to do something that does not necessarily impact their sales this month, what is often called missionary work. I have a tough time to get our booth at conferences staffed if it is more of an institutional advertising effort rather than leads generation. But if we make them eligible for the organizational incentive, we could at least tell them it is part of their job, and they will be rewarded for it if the organization performs. Of course, they will blame someone else for poor performance in a down economy or will cite misallocation of resources when profits fall. They forget they would have nothing to sell if the R & D folks were not keeping us on the leading edge of technology, so they don't see the need to allocate revenue to something with a longer-term, uncertain benefit when we could be giving it to them."

Erin, the CEO, shifted the topic to compensating sales management. "Let's start with the top functional executive in sales and marketing, and he can stay in the room and offer his opinion. A considerable portion of his annual incentive opportunity is based on sales performance. We had a tough year profitwise last year due to prudent investment in new products and product features. As a result, he did better than the rest of the executives, since sales were up. Another of the execs asked how he could have had a good year while they were having a bad year if the executive team made the strategic decisions and determined what investments were made. I did not have a very good answer to that because I had not asked myself if his role was to run sales or if it was to be a member of the executive team who happened to be responsible for sales. I believe it should be the latter, but I guess the way we have rewarded people did not align well with that role definition. So how do I develop a model that defines what each type of employee is rewarded for?"

Annette laid out a framework on her laptop. "This is not final, but here is a typical way to define performance for different roles people play. At the extremes, you could base executive team incentives totally on organization-wide performance, and for support personnel, you could base the majority of rewards on individual performance. This is for you to use in developing an overall model for rewarding performance. You may need more role definitions. Some support people may have a smaller percentage of their income based on organizational performance—perhaps only 10%—and that might come from the performance sharing plan, rather than a separate annual cash incentive plan. And you could tie a portion of an executive's incentive to the

Table 32.1 Model for rewarding performance

Based on → Role	Organization Performance	Unit/Function Performance	Individual Performance
Executive	100%		
Manager	25%	50%	25%
Professional	25%	25%	50%
Support	25%		75%

performance of their function. The CEO, COO, auditor and perhaps Legal might be based 100% on organization-wide performance, and I believe the CHRO should also be in that category. The executive responsible for human resources should be motivated to allocate efforts to produce the best overall result, rather than focusing on HR metrics that often are of limited relevance and difficult to measure objectively. The marketing executive could have a portion of his incentive tied to sales performance, and the amount should be determined by what you want his focus to be. When you reward performance, you have to get the definition of performance right. George Odiorne once advised, "If your people are headed in the wrong direction, don't motivate them." And Steve Kerr pointed out that "rewarding A while hoping for B was ill advised."

"Shouldn't the sales support people also have some incentive opportunity tied to sales performance as well as participating in the performance sharing plan?" asked the marketing executive. "I am thinking out loud, but I have heard people in regional sales offices suggest they do everything they can to make the people in the field successful, but only the reps are rewarded for success."

"No reason why they could not have a regional incentive plan so their rewards are tied to regional performance," responded Annette. "It could be a fairly small percentage of their salary, since they do not have a significant impact on regional sales, but it would reinforce the 'we all make it happen in this region' mindset. Or, you could use spot awards and/or celebrations throughout the year, so successes in February do not go unrecognized until the following January when regional results are finalized. And we have not talked about sales management people between the top executive and the individual reps. It is common practice to base sales manager incentives on performance of their area of responsibility, be that region, district, product line or customer segment. The matrix would suggest perhaps 25% of their incentive be tied to organizational performance, which would be consistent with other managers. Then 25–50% could be based on their unit's performance and the remainder on individual performance. The reason you might vary from a fixed 50% is that less-tangible measures such as development of their sales personnel may be very important in some cases and less so in others. Actually, it might be wise to modify the matrix to reflect that variation across all managers. This is a much better approach than what is commonly done, which is to calculate sales management incentives by equating performance solely to what their people sold. This is dangerous, since some managers will have larger management challenges or customer base issues and it is important to ensure that what is measured and rewarded is important to the organization."

"This has been great," said Erin, accompanied by head nodding all around the room. "Let us do our homework, and we will get back to you with a tentative plan."

33 Defining core capabilities

The consulting staff decided to have a day-long session exploring the scope of their services. They did not want to keep jumping from one type of assignment to another just because there was a customer asking them to do. As a result, they felt it was necessary to define their practice. When Don's mother had recently asked him what it was that he did he responded, "Give advice." She retorted, "Your father and I did that and we never got paid for it—we still had to have a job." Don realized it was a bit challenging to describe his professional role and thought it would be a question to pose to Epsilon's staff.

Don began the dialogue by suggesting they list the services they wanted to provide: the topics they consulted on and the products they offered. The increased popularity of the HR service center system had clouded the boundaries between products and services, since a strategic assessment of a client's needs was required before a decision could be made as to what portions of the system were to be used. They knew they were not in the business of supplying shrink-wrapped software. The software that enabled the system to function was just that—an enabler. What was really important was the identification of what the client needed and the development of a system that would meet those needs.

"Let's look at this from the client's perspective," Don began. "Effective workforce management should begin with environmental scanning, scenario-based planning and workforce planning. We consult with the client to develop strategies for conducting these critical processes, but they are the ones with the in-depth knowledge of their business and what they need in the way of human capital to be successful. I think our role is to convince them to do the scanning and the planning. We have all dealt with companies that wanted to make it up as they went and then were surprised when their reactions to crises were always just too late. So, this is the heart of what I would call our HR strategy consulting service. We help them compare what they have to what they currently need and then to plan for future needs using workforce planning."

Eric interjected in a rather hesitating manner. "I have been working on a presentation to the annual conference of my association that deals with information systems technology. While doing it, I began to realize that it is necessary to acknowledge that big data, artificial intelligence and machine learning is upon us.

The literature in my field is dominated by the subject, and even the popular press is on it. TV shows about robots that are humanlike and movies about replicating the human brain with machines sell well, and not just to kids. Google, Amazon and others are utilizing AI tools to help you decide what you would like to have so they can sell it to you. And there is angst relative to the possibility that millions of jobs may disappear, replaced by intelligent systems. This development in the technology is going to impact workforce management in a big way, and I think we need to alert HR practitioners that they need to have the knowledge to stay abreast of the technology. I overheard some of your HR folks at that local association meeting admit they had skipped courses in math and statistics they now wish they would have taken. I would like to suggest we run some seminars on the emerging technology and how it can be used. We could partner with your HR association or do it on our own. We have both the technology and the HR knowledge and could do a bang-up job."

Rob responded. "I did a presentation on the impact of cognitive bias on workforce management recently and had initially titled it 'Cognitive Predisposition: Lessons from Neuroscience and Behavioral Economics Research.' I showed it to a friend who is more of a marketing type, and he said the presentation was great but the title would ensure that I could safely rent a broom closet to accommodate the audience. I took that subtle advice to mean that I should tone the title down a bit. So, what do we call this seminar to ensure we actually have an audience, 'All the Advanced Quantitative Analysis Tools You Did Not Know You Needed'?"

Eric was a bit taken aback by the sarcasm but felt Rob had a point. "Perhaps we could focus it on applying technology to workforce management and demonstrate how it can inform strategies and decisions. You all have said your clients know they need to better use evidence in making decisions and recommending strategies so they are credible. The marketing field has moved forward on tools for data analytics and the value they can contribute to better gaining customer acceptance of their products. The finance field has been using sophisticated modeling and operations practitioners have incorporated technology into production. They all make recommendations to senior management with a lot of evidence supporting them, so your HR people need to catch up."

"I think you are right on," Kathy interjected. "But we need to be careful not to criticize our audience for not being up to speed on the more advanced versions of multiple regression and causal path analysis, even though it would be helpful it they were. I have been asked to present a hot topic to a class of HR practitioners working on an MSHR degree at nights by a friend and client. Why don't you and I work on a presentation with you providing the technology stuff and me suggesting the potential value of applying it in workforce management? Then, you could use it for your presentation, offering suggestions as to how the tools can be applied to the real world."

Eric agreed and Rob suggested they keep in mind the potential as a line of business. "We could put together a white paper and put it on our website, then turn it into an article and submit it to a publication read by HR professionals. But the more I think about it, I don't know if we can think of this as a separate line of business. Maybe its real value is to demonstrate that we incorporate the latest technology in all that we do, especially when it informs workforce management decisions and provides support for HR when recommendations are made to senior management."

"Bravo," said Don. "I am happy to contribute what I can and I am sure the rest of you will provide your perspectives. This could serve as the basis for a series of social media postings as well. We have not been as active as we should be in doing those."

The group disbanded and Eric and Kathy went to a secluded spot to begin their work.

The White Paper

The Potential of Technology in Workforce Management

Decision makers should use both data and intuition/judgment as evidence to support their recommendations. Advances in technology have provided new tools that can inform decisions and perform analyses that have not been possible. Big data is in the news. Organizations are using data analysis to determine what we are likely to buy and to make sure we get the chance. Workforce management is an area that can benefit greatly from technology. There are tools that can identify the characteristics of people who are likely to perform well in a specific role and that can help to identify people who are prone to leaving the organization. This enables the organization to do a better job of selecting the right people and minimizing the loss of critical talent.

There are two approaches to using evidence to inform decisions. One is to develop a hypothesis and then to use data analysis to determine whether it is supported. This is the deductive approach. An example would be to hypothesize that increasing employee satisfaction will increase productivity and performance, which seems logical. Research evidence could then be accessed or created to test whether this is true. There is a large body of research that has already been conducted on this hypothesis, and the results only weakly suggest that increased satisfaction has a positive impact on performance. However, there have been recent research studies that suggest good performance increases satisfaction. So, there is a *correlation* between satisfaction and performance, but the *causal path* is in the opposite direction from what is predicted by the initial hypothesis. This improved understanding enables management to understand that working on helping employees enjoy early success, even though small, will be likely to positively impact satisfaction. And there is strong evidence based on four decades of research that increased employee satisfaction positively impacts attendance and tends to reduce unwanted turnover. So, the logical assumption that satisfaction and performance tend to go together is supported. But using the appropriate evidence enables management to identify what might increase both satisfaction and performance. In this case, it is more effective to focus on performance management rather than initiatives to directly improve satisfaction.

The other approach to using evidence starts with data analysis. This is called the inductive approach. The first step is to accumulate relevant data. The second step is to analyze the data to identify patterns, which can then be used to create a hypothesis. So, when an organization selling products on the internet amasses millions of transactions involving the purchase of a particular brand of mobile phone, it can search for characteristics of the people making the purchases. Were they high- or low-income? Young or mature? Did they live in cities or rural areas? Based on correlations between the buyer profiles and the purchases, the seller can identify who is a likely buyer and then focus their marketing on the most productive niche. An example related to workforce management would be to analyze the characteristics of hires that were successful and the characteristics of those who performed poorly or left the organization. The results of the analysis can then inform staffing personnel and enable them to screen applicants more effectively.

Inductive is in the news today. And it is often hard to form hypotheses in today's chaotic environment. It is much easier to troll large databases to find relationships of interest, particularly because of the computing power available through the cloud for even small organizations unable to afford big iron.

But although big data is being heralded as a cure-all, danger lurks. Without using a hypothesis to guide the search for relationships, there is a danger that spurious discoveries will abound. The suggestion that sufficiently tortured data will confess to anything may be dismissed as low humor, but there is an element of truth in it. There is another danger, caused by cognitive biases that everyone has. Neuroscience and behavioral economics research has identified a number of biases that can cause evidence to be misused.

For example, we are predisposed to accept evidence that agrees with what we already believe or that we think should be true. We also sometimes see things in clouds when there are really only clouds. So unguided fishing expeditions in large databases can both inform and mislead. The bottom line is that decisions should be based on both human intuition and relevant information. If a strong preference for quantitative, objective evidence crowds out anything viewed as subjective (like judgment), the data-driven decision can be wrong. Football teams often use objective data (based on measures of speed, strength and the like) to make

(continued)

(continued)

decisions about who to recruit. But sometimes things like a personality that is a good fit to the team will have the largest impact on success. The movie *Moneyball* illustrated the quantitative side, while the movie *Trouble with the Curve* suggested that experienced scouts can see things that cannot be turned into hard data that will have an impact on success. Both/ and thinking is a better bet than either/or thinking. And Ryan Leaf was selected ahead of Peyton Manning in the NFL Draft (Ryan who?). Leaf was the right choice based on all the quantitative measures dealing with physical ability, but his personality was out of synch with the team, and other players would not play for him. Personality and someone's match to a culture are much harder to quantify, but knowledgeable people can make judgments based on experience. Another example of both/and.

There is so much data easily available today that a practitioner has to select the data to be used based on a cost-benefit analysis. Using data is not free, even if there is no charge for the raw data. It still must be analyzed using computers and/or people's time. So, it is necessary to select the raw data that will be used. The data must of course be accurate and timely. It must also be cost-effective. If an organization wishes to find the causes for turnover, it may limit the analysis to data relating to top performers in high-value roles to reduce the effort required. It must also be relevant to the issue at hand.

For example, if an organization is trying to determine the compensation paid to CEOs by direct competitors for executive talent, it must acquire data from direct competitors. The analysis in Figure 33.1 compares the compensation of the organization's CEO with what is paid by other organizations. Initially the data had been aggregated into an average

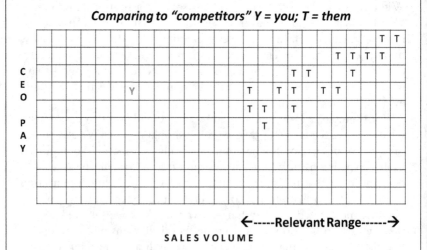

Figure 33.1 Data outside the relevant range

of all reported rates, but the results showed an enormous variation. A further analysis was made, plotting the individual rates by the size of the organization.

Once the analysis was presented this way to the compensation committee of the board, the chair voiced a concern that all the competitor organizations were much larger. Since it has been established by many studies that executive compensation is highly correlated with the size of the organization, it was not unreasonable for the chair to ask for another analysis, based on relevant data.

It may be necessary to break the data down into differentiated samples that avoid important differences from being obscured by over-aggregation. An example of the dangers associated with prematurely aggregating results is the analysis shown in Figure 33.2, which was based on an employee survey of satisfaction with their employee benefits package.

If the average of all responses is used, the conclusion would be that employees think their benefits are OK, but that is misleading information. When a frequency distribution of the responses is arrayed, it is apparent there are two sets of opinions. It could be that the benefits are great for one group and not meeting the needs of another. But in order for this information to be of real value, one needs to know what the groups are. Is one long-service, older employees, while the other is newer, younger employees? One males and the other females? One highly paid managers/professionals and the other lower-paid support personnel? If the data does not include markers that enable the analyst to understand what the characteristics of the two groups are, it is of little use. This example illustrates that the raw data must include enough information to enable the analyst to provide the more in-depth analysis that will be of value.

									AVG									
																		X
																X	X	
			X						**A**						X	X	X	
			X						**V**					X	X	X	X	
			X						**E**				X	X	X	X	X	
			X	X	X				**R**			X	X	X	X	X	X	
		X	X	X	X				**A**			X	X	X	X	X	X	
	X	X	X	X	X	X			**G**			X	X	X	X	X	X	
	X	X	X	X	X	X	X		**E**		X	X	X	X	X	X	X	
X	X	X	X	X	X	X			**A**	X	X	X	X	X	X	X		
X	X	X	X	X	X	X	X	X	**A**	X	X	X	X	X	X	X	X	X

Figure 33.2 Employee satisfaction with benefits

(continued)

(continued)

Another application of data can be testing the impact of an intervention. An example would be the adoption of a gainsharing plan in an organization's plants. Even though it had been hypothesized that rewarding improved productivity would motivate employees to work toward being as productive as possible, management wanted to know if the implementation of the plan made a difference. In order to make that determination, it is necessary to know what

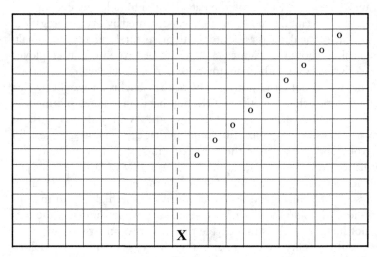

Prior periods----------------→ Post-implementation----------→

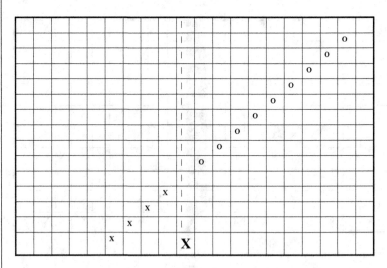

Prior periods---------------→ Post-implementation-------→

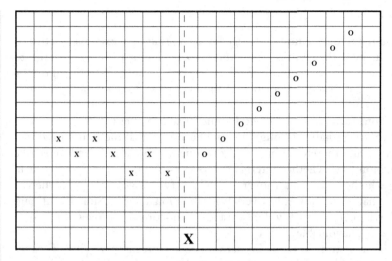

Prior periods--------------→   Post-implementation------→

Figure 33.3 Did "X" make a difference?

happened before and to compare what was to what is once the plan is implemented.

The analysis in Figure 33.3a involved measuring post-implementation productivity, which showed a positive trend over time. However, no data on past results was included. When asked whether "X" (the plan) made a difference the analyst was unable to answer.

By using pre data as well as post data as in Figure 33.3b, it was determined that the implementation seemed to not disrupt but also not to improve the trend already underway.

If, on the other hand, the analysis showed the pattern in Figure 33.3c, a strong case could be made that the plan had an immediate and continuing positive impact on results. It could be argued that other factors might have had an influence if changes occurred at the time of implementation, but a reasonable conclusion would be that the plan worked, or at least had a positive impact. Whether or not it met the standard hoped for would depend on expectations.

There is danger in using quantitative data if all the criteria mentioned earlier are not met. Inaccurate, out-of-date, overly costly and irrelevant data cannot produce sound evidence, no matter how good the analysis of that data is. Human judgment is required in the selection of the data, just as it is when interpreting the data.

The intuition of a professional can often lead to formulating sound hypotheses that evidence can be used to test. And often judgment is

(continued)

(continued)

required to decide how to categorize data results. An example is a turnover analysis that breaks down total turnover into the various types to enable the organization to focus on unwanted and dysfunctional turnover. The results of the analysis in Figure 33.4 still leave much to human judgment.

Total turnover is 29%, but dysfunctional turnover is 12% (4% internal and 8% external). Although it could be argued that the analysis is quantitative and therefore objective, someone has to make several subjective decisions: (1) whether internal turnover is functional or dysfunctional, (2) whether external turnover was voluntary or involuntary, (3) whether external voluntary turnover was functional or dysfunctional and (4) whether external, voluntary and dysfunctional turnover was avoidable or unavoidable.

Internal turnover can be harmful to an organization, but if career choice leads to mobility that not only increases employee contribution but also avoids losing a valued employee to a competitor, it may be positive. Managers will sometimes rationalize the loss of a valued employee by suggesting it was no big loss. But if there is a sound performance management system in place, it can help to determine if that is true or just a way to avoid criticism or scrutiny. Harmful losses can sometimes be explained away by contending that they were unavoidable. But if the organization had accommodated family issues by allowing telecommuting, the employee might have been retained.

Artificial intelligence is a potentially powerful tool, but someone needs to create the software. Machine learning can allow complex analyses to be done faster or even better. But the technology must have relevant data to analyze. If an organization is attempting to invent that which has never

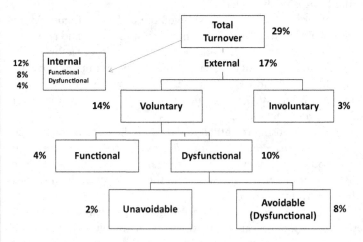

Figure 33.4 Evaluate turnover: is it too high? What are the implications?

existed, it is difficult to think that any software will be effective in replacing human creativity—there is no data on that which has never existed. Technology is able to do more, but if it is not effectively combined with human judgment, its impact will be limited. Both inductive and deductive approaches are needed. Objective and subjective evidence should be combined when appropriate. When an integrated approach is used, professionals charged with developing workforce management strategies and programs will be able to increase the quality of decisions.

Kathy and Eric presented the white paper to the entire staff, and the reception was gratifying. Although there was unanimous support for the concept, there was still uncertainty about whether this was another line of professional practice for the firm. "I don't think it has to be, at least not a separate line," offered Kathy. "But it is critical that we clearly identify that the services we do offer are state of the art. For example, if the service center is more about quantitative analysis of data, without the integration of professional judgment, I think its value is diminished. If we oversell the benefits of automating processes I think we are in danger of being criticized. Automate transactions are performed using a set of rules, of course, but also make it clear that analysis must be based on human as well as machine processing. And I do think a lot of folks out there who had their last training in quantitative methods years ago are not in possession of valuable knowledge as to what is possible today. So, the seminars may not make us a lot of money, but they can clearly have a positive impact on our brand as a consultancy."

The group was unanimous in agreement. Line of business—maybe not. A new dimension in all of their services—absolutely.

34 Evaluating executive compensation strategy

Don had received a call from Lori, one of his classmates from his university days. She had risen to be the COO of a manufacturing firm and had also been appointed to the board of another manufacturer who supplied products to her firm. She had overheard some of the conversations Don was engaged in at the 10-year reunion and wanted to know if he or his colleagues would be willing to consult with the board she served on. "Seems to me that the way we compensate our top executives is not aligned with our objectives very well," she confided in Don. "And I don't think we are doing the organization any favors when we compensate board members the way we do."

Don was intrigued by the latter comment and arranged to meet with Lori, figuring he would take Rob and Pete along. At a staff meeting, he asked the group about whether they really should engage in executive compensation consulting as a part of their practice. Pete was all for it but Rob cautioned them that it often involved a good bit of tax and accounting work and that they did not have those capabilities on board. "We can always stick to developing the conceptual models and have the client organization do the detailed implementation work," Pete suggested, realizing that the topic is highly charged with emotion and can be political, and that often adopting the best strategy is not feasible because of that. Don proposed that they bring Howard in as a sage advisor and have him counsel them.

Howard met with the staff a week later and gave them a primer in executive compensation.

"First, there is much that is different than compensating the rest of the workforce. Whereas executive management determines how much and how employees are compensated, it is typically the board that is responsible for managing executive compensation. But they are charged with pleasing a number of constituencies when they formulate the strategy and the programs. How much the CEO and other senior executives of an organization should be paid is an issue upon which different constituencies are apt to differ, given their different perspectives. It is important to understand the perspective of each party and how they are likely to answer this difficult question. It is also helpful to anticipate that the 'right' perspective will be the one held by the party addressing the issue. Each constituency will be evaluated from the perspective of equity theory, which contends that any party will evaluate reasonableness based on a comparison to others, considering the relationship between what they contribute and what they reap as benefits. How differences are to be reconciled is a much more difficult question and one which has no ready answer. But understanding the differing perspectives is a big step towards reconciliation.

The executives themselves. Executives compare their earnings primarily to other executives with similar roles in similar (size and industry) organizations. Some will view their compensation in light of how much shareholder value has increased during their tenure, but since they do not typically risk their own funds in the way that investors do, this argument is not compelling, since the value of the organization can be determined by economic factors and things outside the control of the executives. Prevailing compensation levels in the marketplace are determined in a number of ways: proxy information, surveys, board members (who are predominantly executives themselves), analysis done by HR and/or outside consultants and even the newspaper and magazine reporting. The specific comparison group chosen is often based on organization size (sales and profits), industry and in rare cases, performance measures (ROI, stock price performance, total shareholder return, image and the like). And the question of how compensation is paid is also important. The mix of current cash, deferred cash and equity must make sense to both the company and executives.

Other employees. Other employees will have a different perspective when it comes to evaluating the executive pay levels. They typically compare executive pay with their pay. Although they will also consider their employment stability and advancement opportunities as being valuable and part of their rewards package, the most direct comparisons with executives will be based on current income. Employees typically do not have direct access to compensation surveys, but summaries are readily available in magazines and in the newspaper. The articles in the press have their own bias (the bigger the numbers, the greater the reader interest) but employees typically are not making detailed comparisons. When they read the CEO to average worker multiple used to be 30 times and is often 400 times today, they are not required to make calculations using higher math. The degree of resentment among employees is greatly impacted by how they feel about their treatment by the organization. If they enjoy relatively competitive pay and benefit levels and have a reasonable amount of employment security, the amount of angst they might feel when they see comparative data is apt to be lessened.

Government and society. The public has the most difficulty with large executive compensation packages when the organization paying its executives well is doing poorly or is laying people off/cutting wages and benefits as the first option for pursuing profits. Closing down plants and offices in the local area is sure to incur criticism as well, although the public has been surprisingly accepting of what has been portrayed as the "price of remaining competitive." When organizational performance is poor and yet senior management pay levels do not suffer, there is apt to be criticism. But even though the government and society at large are unhappy with what has gone on, they have done very little about it and are not likely to do so. On the other hand, the federal government created say on pay so shareholders could express their opinions about executive compensation in publicly traded organizations, so government is not without some influence.

Board of directors. The board is charged with (and paid for) evaluating executive compensation levels in comparison to other similar organizations and for ensuring they are reasonable according to whatever philosophy they adopt. The SEC disclosure guidelines include a requirement that the compensation committees of the board develop and articulate a compensation philosophy and demonstrate that the programs they approved were consistent with that philosophy. But giving organizations great flexibility is consistent with the economic system and political environment that has prevailed in the U.S. And since most compensation committees are composed of outside directors who have knowledge of compensation principles, there is some basis for confidence that this board responsibility is in capable, or at least knowledgeable hands. But poor board oversight is often blamed on the lack of member independence, since most members owe their position on the board to the CEO of the organization, or to the network within which that person operates. Having boards populated by CEOs of other organizations can be criticized (on the basis that they are biased) or lauded (on the basis that they know what they are talking about). But at least their mandate has been clarified somewhat of late. Also, the compensation for being a board member has shifted substantially from being mostly cash to being mostly stock options or other devices whose value is determined in a manner similar to that of shareholders, which should encourage alignment with shareholder interests.

Shareholders. The people who provide the capital for publicly traded organizations are very diverse and are huge in number if vested stakeholders in pension funds are included. As a result, their interests are varied and their perspectives relative to executive compensation are hard to characterize. Since most are not involved in the management of the organizations they own, the prevailing viewpoint is typically focused on total shareholder return (dividends plus stock price appreciation). If the return is better than they believe they can get anywhere else at an equivalent level of risk, they will tend to hold the stock. They are also free to divest themselves if they believe otherwise. Shareholders may use the same information available to anyone else to decide whether executive compensation expense is excessive. On the other hand, if the shareholders are experiencing returns that exceed their wildest expectations, it is unlikely that they will worry as much about their executives being paid more than market levels. However, when that changes, views can change as well.

Human resources. HR is charged with formulating compensation strategy and programs. This involves determining competitive compensation levels through the use of surveys, their contact networks and outside advisors. HR represents management and the board/shareholders simultaneously, and though this dual allegiance may result in conflicting direction relative to the nature of the market comparisons, most compensation professionals can develop their findings in a manner viewed as credible."

"So, which of these perspectives is 'correct' and who decides?" asked Kathy. Howard smiled and responded, "Each constituency believes the perspective they hold is correct. So, reconciling them is the responsibility of the compensation committee of the board, according to legal/regulatory mandates. Many boards retain outside advisors to provide that expertise. HR may be viewed as biased, given that the CEO and other senior executives outrank the top HR executive and they make decisions impacting the employment and compensation of the HR executive. Still, it is critical that HR demonstrate its ability to consider all perspectives and to advise the board on how the differences can be reconciled."

Howard went on and described the characteristics of an effective and defensible executive compensation strategy:

"First, executive compensation should be based on performance criteria and standards that are related to the organization's strategy.

Second, it must be the case that shareholders are paid a fair return on their investment before the programs reward executives generously. Incentive thresholds that ensure shareholders receive a fair return before any award pool is generated are very effective in convincing parties at interest that executives must "earn their salary" before cashing in on additional incentives. The same principle holds true for stock-based programs. If executive options increase in value when stock price appreciation is average or even below average, the shareholders are justified in viewing this as a sort of give-away program. Shareholders should also understand the potential costs of all programs in advance of approving them. They should know what the costs would be under multiple scenarios, ranging from optimistic to pessimistic projections of results. This enables shareholders to determine if there is an appropriate amount of downside given bad performance in addition to knowing what executives will be paid if things go very well. And the board and shareholders should know how the executive total compensation package compares to that of a sample of competitive organizations.

Third, programs should be designed to efficiently deliver after-tax income to recipients relative to the after-tax cost to the organization.

Fourth, there should be open and continuous communication about objectives, strategy, what is earned and why. Explaining to all parties why a particular program was adopted and how it will work is the first step in ensuring that people understand why income is or is not realized from the program. And then there should be continuous communication of interim results and their impact on the value of the program to participants.

Finally, there must be adequate oversight and governance. Compensation committees of the board must be impartial."

Kathy was fascinated with the concepts being presented and asked, "So, what are the characteristics of programs that should be avoided?"

"There are characteristics of programs that will not stand up under scrutiny and that will breed suspicion that the playing field has been tilted in favor of executives," Howard responded.

The first is programs that provide high upside potential but little downside risk. High base salaries, incentive programs with low thresholds, stock plans that do not require sustained ownership, repricing stock options and programs that are modified when they do not pay out; these are sure to attract criticism. Base salaries over $1,000,000 are not tax deductible to the organization in the U.S., since they are not performance dependent, and it is difficult to understand why they exist at all. Cash or stock-based incentive plans that begin paying out at very low levels of performance are also indefensible; the objective is to pay for *good* performance. And repricing stock options and lowering incentive plan performance requirements during the year to ensure a plan pays out when it otherwise would not have cannot be justified.

The second is programs with elitist appearance. Perquisites that are not business-related should trigger an investigation into the governance structure to find out why well-compensated executives felt they could obtain reimbursement for personal expenses. Abuse can lead to the erosion of trust of other stakeholders. Even when perquisites are technically legal and within established policy, they send a message that there are different rules and principles for different people, which can erode the social capital within the organization and impact employee motivation.

Another characteristic that should be avoided is rewarding something other than performance: Golden parachute programs that protect executives in the case of a change in control have their place. But excessive termination/severance arrangements that pay out no matter what the circumstances can easily increase the cynicism of the public about executive compensation. If total failure on the part of senior executives is rewarded, with the shareholders providing the funding when their investment is probably diminished in value, there is bound to be criticism.

Perhaps the most damaging characteristic is poor communication. When executive compensation is managed out of the sight of shareholders and other employees, there will be more skepticism among employees and investors about how fair and how appropriate programs are."

The group took a break and Don asked Howard to talk about the role HR should play in executive compensation. The board member that had approached him about consulting with their organization had suggested that HR did not seem to be able to provide the board with enough input to enable them to make informed decisions. Don had not seen much written about the role of HR and really wanted to make that a part of the consulting assignment.

Howard started up again by admitting he had often asked, "Where was HR?" when executive compensation abuses became public. "But HR is in a tough spot—telling your boss (s)he is paid too much or paid incorrectly can be career limiting. In fact, I counseled a newly appointed HR director recently, providing him with a survival guide for HR. I suggested the following actions:

1   Develop a clear compensation strategy in conjunction with the board, providing the function's technical expertise to those charged with developing

a strategy. HR has an obligation to become competent in the principles of executive compensation and to maintain staff support for the board.

2   Embrace defensible and avoid high-risk programs, as described earlier. The fact that other organizations are using programs that breed shareholder criticism does not justify their use. If there is some doubt, shareholder approval should be sought, even if it is not legally required.

3   Communicate freely and continuously to all parties, even going beyond legal and regulatory requirements when it is information that is relevant to shareholders and the investment industry.

4   Monitor adherence to policies, and either deal with infractions or report them to the board. If the board does not address illegal acts, HR has an obligation to report them to the SEC and other regulatory bodies. If the HR executive loses a job by adhering to ethical principles, the chance of getting another one is many times greater than if that executive went along with actions that violate policy, ethics or the law. HR should attempt to convince the board to develop ethics guidelines that ensure parties reporting policy violations are protected and that it is those who do not report violations that will suffer.

5   Maintain a professional posture, avoiding advocacy and considering the various perspectives about what constitutes reasonable rewards. Points of view should be supported by empirical evidence, such as market data and competitive practice benchmarking results. If outside consulting assistance is used by HR and the executive management, the same support should be provided to the compensation committee of the board. It has been argued that the board should have a separate consultant, but this often leads to 'my consultant can beat up your consultant' confrontations that accomplish nothing except to positively impact the revenue of the consulting firms."

The consensus of the consulting staff was that Epsilon should accept executive compensation assignments but should exercise caution when the CEO, rather than the board, retains them. They felt it was critical to protect their professional reputation and not answer, "What do you want it to be?" when the CEO asks them, "What should my compensation be?" They laughed about this attempt at humor but were serious about the principle involved.

Don, Pete and Rob met with selected members of the board of the manufacturing organization to explore how they might be of assistance to them. The lead director, who also chaired the compensation committee, told them they wanted to align how executives and board members were compensated. Pete asked him to clarify what he meant by "aligned."

"We should be contributing to the success of the organization in our respective roles and should be motivated to do so by our compensation package. I do not mean we would have the same mix of compensation elements, since I have looked at the survey data and know there is a trend recently to pay board members less in the form of fees and more in the form of stock options or other types of stock programs. And that makes sense to me, since we want to represent the investors and take a long-term view of performance. And it does not necessarily argue for increasing the mix of stock in the executive package."

Pete had analyzed the company's stock price performance for the last 5 years in anticipation of the meeting and had found the stock to be very volatile, impacted by the general condition of the economy. He recognized that the high volatility should be considered when the company decided how to use stock in rewarding executives and board members but believed stock should be a long-term reward vehicle. He shared his views with the board representatives. The lead director responded, "We on the compensation committee do think the recent economic downturn has overly depressed stock prices, since the value of the organization is not that impacted by business cycles. We seem to benefit when the economy is good, but the extreme volatility of the stock price is still discouraging."

Don asked if the stock price performance had so impacted the competitiveness of the executive compensation package that it had resulted in unwanted turnover. "No," the director responded, "but it certainly has caused some of our people who are near the end of their careers to question how it will impact their retirement income and estate building capability. This could result in some key people leaving when the economy is good, even though it is sooner than they had planned or we had expected."

Rob asked about how they handled the stock when an executive retired. "Does the executive vest in options upon retirement, and are they required to exercise and/or sell the shares at that time?" "That is an issue we had to face last year when our long-service CFO retired," the director answered. He left when we all expected him too, and we had been careful not to grant options that would not vest until after the planned retirement date. But he had accumulated a lot of stock, both in the form of owned shares and vested options. He exercised the options and sold the stock as soon as it made sense taxwise and there was no concern about how things turned out. But it raised another issue. Several of his peers were taken aback by the number of shares he had accumulated when they compared it to their own holdings. When I looked at the list of holdings by executives, there seemed to be no pattern that made sense. After doing some investigating, it became clear to me that options had over the years been handed out with no real plan—those that benefitted the most were just in the right place at the right time. So, that is something I definitely want us to evaluate."

Pete requested a complete record of the stock held by each of the executives. "We need to look at the dates of option grants and the conditions: vesting provisions, value of the shares upon grant and so forth. We also need to look at all option exercise events: date, price of stock upon exercise and so on. Finally, we need to look at all sales of shares, whether they resulted from option exercises or outright purchase. Once we have that, we can figure out the relative holdings and benefits realized. Since you pointed out that no one knew of a model that controlled the use of stock, it is likely that there are some significant differences among executives, so we should figure out what the implications are and what, if anything, would produce a more rational pattern of holdings."

Don requested information about the stock held by board members as well. "Give us a similar summary for the current directors so we can look at their holdings." "I hope you will find a lot more rational pattern," the director responded. "We have really focused on establishing rules for using stock for board members. There have been option grants and stock bonuses that have occurred on a planned basis, typically every two or three years. And we made sure to distribute stock in a manner that was similar for all directors. But you should look at our holdings and evaluate what we have done."

Pete had been given a complete listing of the various compensation plans in place for executives, and he had briefly looked at the information. "You have used long-term cash incentive plans in addition to the annual cash incentive plan," he noted. "Did you attempt to integrate the long-term plans with the annual plans and the stock plans?" The director smiled and responded, "Interesting that you said 'attempt' rather than 'integrate.' We really struggled with how to balance the three plans with each other. The market survey data gave us average base pay and average current cash compensation figures for most of our jobs, so we felt we had balanced those pretty well. Our strategy was to set base salaries at 90% of market average and to provide an annual incentive opportunity that was about 20% larger than what was typically offered by competitors. We wanted the executives to be paid below market if annual performance was below target, at market if it was at target and above market if we did better than the competition. Read that in a book on the subject,[1] and it made a lot of sense to us. But we had a tough time figuring out what market average was for long-term incentives, both cash and stock."

"You and everyone else," Pete assured him. "Long-term cash plans vary in their measurement cycles and in their provisions, and it makes it tough to assign a current value to them when assessing annual compensation competitiveness. In some industries, the measurement cycle can be five years or more, while others commonly use three or four years. You can try to calculate a present value for plans that do not pay out until the end of the cycle, but that is fraught with peril. What most analysts do is to take a multiyear view and use the cash income received in each year for comparison purposes. And when you get to stock plans the variation in practices is bizarre. Nonqualified stock option grants, stock bonuses, restricted stock grants, performance shares—they all need to be evaluated differently. And what really presents a problem is the tendency for the media to report headlines like, 'Joe Smith made 15 million dollars this year while laying off employees' when what really happened is that Smith recognized income from a ten-year stock program."

"We are very concerned about optics," one of the other directors pointed out. "We have some stockholders who seem to get up on the wrong side of the bed every day, and their chief form of recreation is to complain about how our executives are paid." "Don't forget their interest in how the board is compensated," added another of the directors. The compensation committee chair took a more positive view. "One of the best things that happened to us was the regulatory requirement that mandated we state our philosophy guiding executive compensation and provide tables of information that demonstrated we were following the philosophy. We spent a lot of time formulating our philosophy, and it helps to keep us on track when we make decisions about our plans. Thought I would never say 'thank you for imposing that regulation,' but it really did help us crystalize our thinking. And the proxy disclosure regulations are reasonable as well."

"We need some time to process what you have told us and to analyze the information you have provided," Don said, closing the meeting. "Let's try to schedule another meeting next week to see where we are."

When the consultants got back to the office, they were optimistic that this assignment would benefit greatly by having the type of board members they had met with calling the shots. They had all read about the horror stories that were caused by poor governance and/or boards that were not competent or who were not committed to representing the shareholders rather than the executives and themselves. That did not seem to be the case here.

During the next meeting, the rest of the board compensation committee membership joined in, along with the chair of the finance committee. They had met to discuss just what their philosophy was and came prepared to provide guidance to the consultants. "We really are concerned about developing a framework that will enable us to gain more consistency among executives as to how many options they have and what the terms are," the compensation committee chair stated. "We are agreed that we don't want to continue issuing options going forward and will work with the executives to clean up their current holdings. It seems that restricted stock grants make more sense to use as both a motivation and a retention tool. The executives close to retirement are not likely to leave, so perhaps we will allow them to close out their careers with options, which we will adjust so they make sense for them. The remaining majority are at least ten years from normal retirement age, so the retention objective is more relevant."

"Have you explored the financial implications of restricted stock, such as the charge to earnings that will be required?" asked Don. "Yes, and we really think we want to use restricted stock in a way that enables us to build in performance criteria as well," responded Earl. Don and Pete laid out a ten-year framework for using restricted stock, similar to what they had used in prior assignments, and presented the model.

1   Five-year restricted stock grants to be issued in Years 1, 4 and 7. The value of each grant (number of shares times the current price at issue) would be a percentage of each executive's salary range midpoint.

2   Each year the performance of the organization would determine if none, one or two years of credit against the five-year restriction period would be applied. This would cause the restrictions to lapse in five years if performance met target in each of the five years. If performance met the outstanding standard in a Year 2, two years of credit would be applied to the five-year restriction, and if it did not meet the target, there would be

no credit applied. As a result, the restrictions on a single grant could expire in as few as three years and may not expire at all, although if they had not expired after ten years, the grant would be canceled.

3   If an executive left the organization voluntarily, all shares that still carried restrictions would be canceled. If an executive retired with restrictions still active, they would receive a pro-rated share based on what portion of the restriction remained.

4   Once the restrictions were lifted from the shares associated with a grant, the executive was free to sell the shares as long as their total holdings of owned stock remained at a minimum of three times their salary range midpoint.

Earl started the questioning process. "And you base things off the salary range midpoint rather than the current salary because it results in similar grants for people at the same level?" he asked. "Yes," said Don, smiling. "Are you a consultant in disguise? That is a pretty sophisticated insight." Earl pointed out that flattery would have no impact on how quickly their invoice would be paid.

Several of the board members looked as if they had just tried to take a sip of water out of an open fire hydrant. Don could see that some of them had puzzled looks, so he took care to point out why they had suggested this model. "Restricted stock can serve as a retention tool, but sometimes people make it through the restriction period even though the organization is performing poorly, which delivers a reward for longevity, not performance. That is why we suggest you lapse restrictions more slowly or more quickly if performance is far below or above target levels. This aligns their interests more closely with investors. And, of course, the eventual value of the shares depends on stock price performance, which also aligns the economic fate of the executives with those of the shareholders. And we recommend having overlapping grants, which provides executives with a long-term view of their potential rewards, as well as discouraging exits when restrictions on one grant expire. The rather erratic way you have issued options left executives confused as to when additional issues might occur and what the terms might be. Finally, we think mandating a minimum ownership level contributes to engagement on the part of executives." Rob pointed out that the restricted stock approach they were recommending was also linked to annual performance. "If the organization has a great year, it will result in a large annual incentive award, as well as the potential for accelerated lapsing of the restrictions. That really links total compensation to organizational performance."

The vice president of human resources joined the meeting after being invited by the board. He had proposed to the board that they make two changes to their employee benefits programs, and while the consultants were there, he wanted to present the proposals. "The first is that we implement flexible benefits. We offer very little choice to employees as to what their benefits are and, as a result, we are not maximizing the perceived value of the total benefits package. We have a very diverse workforce, and having an inflexible package means we probably satisfy no one fully. We do have three options for health care coverage, but that is about it. For example, I would like to make it possible for employees to sell vacation days back so they could purchase better health care coverage. They would have to take two weeks but could sell the additional days back at 1/260th of their salary. And then there would be no carryover."

All of the consultants expressed their support for adding flexibility to the benefits package, based on their positive experience with the approach and their knowledge of research findings. "And the second change?" asked Don. "I recommend we provide individualized total compensation statements annually." The consulting team was very much in favor of this approach, but Don felt they should discuss its value for the sake of the board members.

"We have become avid supporters of individualized statements," he said, "based on a good bit of research that shows how employees undervalue their benefits. The typical guess by an employee as to what the benefits cost the employer is about 40–50% of the true cost. That is a disaster—spend a lot of money and only get credit for spending only a little bit of money. But just designing and providing the statements is much less effective than making them a part of a comprehensive communication program. For example, even though the high cost of health care is in the press all the time, employees have a hard time believing that applies to their coverage. So, by providing the true cost, the employer should get more credit for their expenditure. There are also sophisticated techniques that enable organizations to compare the present value of all their benefits to those of their competitors. This can help an organization to know how competitive their package is but also how balanced it is. The shift away from defined benefit retirement plans to defined contribution plans has resulted in a mixed bag: some organizations using one type, others using the other type and some using both types. With the available technology, both cost and benefit comparisons can now be made. This provides tangible measures that enable the individualized statements to be used with confidence. But they still have to be explained to employees."

Although there was no decision on the two recommendations immediately, it was clear that the strong support demonstrated by the consultants would carry the day, and the HR executive left satisfied the changes were forthcoming.

"One last topic," Earl said. "We would like you to evaluate how the board is compensated. One of the principles we want to follow is aligning our financial interests with those of both the executives and the board. We had discussed the different mix or rewards that would be suitable—less cash for board and committee meetings and more stock-based rewards. It seems misplaced to tie compensation to the number of meetings; these are not hourly employees. If they feel the needs of the organization are met by more or fewer meetings, that should be their guide. The surveys we have seen do show a trend toward heavier use of stock, and there seems to be a trend toward using restricted stock and restricted stock units rather than relying primarily on options, and I wonder if that is the best approach for us. What would it look like if we were to use restricted stock grants instead of options?"

Rob frowned, which seemed to indicate he was struggling with the question. "Are you interested in motivating retention of board members, or do you want to be free to initiate changes to the membership, based on performance and current needs? Since board members need to be elected each year, that approach probably would not work. But you could issue options based on performance. The stock price will be impacted by organizational performance over time, albeit imperfectly, so the value of the shares will be tied to performance. The number and value of options granted can be similar for all board members, which makes the stock program function like an organization-wide incentive plan. You should also deliver some cash compensation tied to activity level, including board and committee meetings and project work, but only when unusual demands cause a significant amount of work. An example might be during due diligence relative to a possible merger or acquisition. Overall, then, this strategy will compensate members for the time and effort they invest, but the major determinant of the value of the total compensation package will be stock price performance. This aligns board compensation with shareholder returns."

"OK," we will invest some time deliberating this and let you know where we stand," Earl said, closing the meeting.

Note

1 Greene, R., *Rewarding Performance; Guiding Principles; Custom Strategies*, 2011, Routledge, New York.

35 Formulating a global workforce strategy

Eddie called from Hong Kong to ask Rob if they would be interested in developing a global rewards strategy for one of Zen's Asian customers. Eddie and Nina had installed their service center system for an organization based in Singapore with operations throughout Asia. Now, Dragon Enterprises, the potential client, was setting up North American manufacturing and distribution operations in Vancouver, Canada, and European operations in Prague. Their CEO, Ron, had approached Eddie for help in formulating a global rewards strategy that would enable them to move executives and critical skill professionals around the world easily. He admitted to Eddie that it was difficult for them to trust people they did not know well to set up and run the new operations, so they would be using expatriate assignments and business commuting to put their people on the ground on the two continents. Eddie assured the client that they could help them, using partners who were experts. He had crossed his fingers under the table, hoping Rob and the Epsilon staff would be interested in taking the lead on this engagement. Otherwise, he would be reading a lot of books on the subject.

Rob came to the rescue and offered to come over with Annette and Pete to meet with the client. Pete had been working with some of their transnational clients to evaluate their compensation programs for expatriates, and Annette had gained experience in the subject as well. Pete asked Eric if their systems were capable of administering foreign assignment programs and had been assured that they were, as long as the policies and procedures were well-defined. "Actually, the system could keep track of individual packages even without a clear and consistent set of policies," Eric told him, "but that is really not ideal." Pete promised him that they would focus on developing a coherent strategy and the policies for executing it before the system would be used.

Curt, the client's chief of operations, welcomed the consultants to Singapore and outlined their plans for setting up the facilities in Vancouver and Prague. "We are not building infrastructure from scratch," he said, "since we have bought out existing facilities in both locations. There will be people there who know how things work, and the actual manufacturing and distribution capabilities will transition to our products fairly easily. But we purchased the operations because we knew we could apply our expertise to improve productivity. This requires that we use technology we have developed and also that we train employees to do things our way. The workforce in Vancouver has a substantial number of people who came from China and Hong Kong, so we think the cultural issues will be manageable. In Prague, we may face more challenges, since most employees are locals, but we were very impressed with the work ethic and the educational level. We hope that our expatriates will be accepted in both locations and that our methods can be taught fairly quickly. So, our chief concern is selecting the right people to go from here to the foreign locations and to be sure they are compensated appropriately. Kim, our human resource director, will work with you to explore how we select a strategy and create policies."

Pete and Rob met with Kim to develop a profile of employees who would be selected for assignments in the two new operations, while Annette analyzed the company's HR policies for employees throughout the Asian operations. "We will be sending a country manager and senior finance and operations staff initially, probably for three-year expatriate assignments," Kim told Pete and Rob. "Technical people will go as needed, probably on shorter assignments as project leaders. They can probably be treated as if they are doing extended commuting. The three-year assignments will involve family relocation, although we will not require expatriates to sell their residences in their home country. Our chief concern is to develop strategies and policies to ensure we treat people consistently so we don't have to face endless individual negotiations." Pete asked about their plans for bringing people from the two new operations to Asia as inpatriates. "I have not heard that term before," Kim answered, "but I guess that would be someone who came in for extended assignments, a reverse expatriate of sorts. Well, would that be much different than what we do for people going out, assuming the purpose is to send them back?"

Pete agreed that the philosophy governing the compensation packages would be similar for inpatriates and expatriates. He then explored their treatment of employees across Asia to determine if they needed a separate policy for third-country nationals. "It could happen that someone from China or India could be sent to one of the new locations, but at least for now we plan to only use employees based here in headquarters."

Over lunch, Rob, Pete and Annette were educated by Kim relative to company philosophy, culture and policies. "We recognize that by having a headquarters in Singapore and other major operations in Dalian and Mumbai that we could develop consistent regional policies, even though some would argue that would be more of a megaregion approach. There are major differences between the three locations—laws, culture, logistics and economics. So, we have maintained local policies and have not been obsessed with consistency across countries. And we will probably continue that philosophy in Vancouver and Prague, at least for current employees. What we really need to focus on is a strategy for compensating people on international assignments. Perhaps in the future we will think about having a global cadre consisting of people that are not considered as having a home base, but I doubt that would work well for us. Home is home for most people and we think that should be respected.

Taking someone's roots away by moving them continuously for extended periods is not an approach we would accept easily."

Rob sketched out the three alternatives an organization can adopt for people on international assignment. "The first is to leave their compensation as is. This would be most common for your business commuters. Of course, you might reward people with some sort of differential while they are away from home if you feel that is appropriate. And you must be careful to provide expense reimbursement that is reasonable and consistent across employees on assignment. People can get worked up over someone having better quarters or allowances than they do. The second approach is the one most often used for expatriates and inpatriates—continue to administer compensation consistently but use differentials to make the employee equally well off between being at home and being on assignment. There is a long list of things that need to be equalized: taxes, housing, children's education, spousal employment, living expenses, home travel and so forth. This approach is the most time-consuming to administer, and some organizations contract this out to a provider. The third approach is to localize the assignee. This is most common for assignees who are not likely to return to their home country, but to stay for an undefined time in the host location or to go on to another international assignment. Some organizations use this approach for new hires and early career employees who have not established their lifestyle in the home country."

Kim said that they had talked about all of these when conducting due diligence on the two new foreign operations, and they had concluded that their culture precluded localizing the management personnel who might be in one or both of the new locations for the foreseeable future. The technical personnel on project assignments would surely be returning, even though they might spend much of their time bouncing around, so they would be treated as commuters. So, the real issue was how to treat expatriates so they were equally well off when on extended assignment.

Rob showed Kim a model he had used in his university course on global workforce management (see Figure 35.1).

"This is a way for whoever does the administration of the differentials to be consistent across assignees. There are of course other issues, such as currency exchange rate variation, hardships, home leave expense, perquisites provided and assistance with the home country residence. One of the challenges that companies do not give enough thought to is how the expatriate will live compared to how local nationals live. If you send a manager to another country and that person is able to live in a residence that is clearly superior to his or her local peers, you can create resentment and feelings of inequity. On the other hand, if the expatriate faces hardships that locals do not, such as restrictions on the employability of a spouse or access to good schools or medical care, it may be the expatriate who feels unfairly treated. You certainly don't have to consider physical danger in Prague or Vancouver, but in some parts of the world, foreigners are not welcomed gladly. There may be suspicions on the part of locals that the assignee is benefitting financially, due to salary

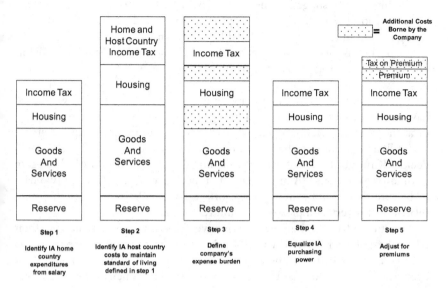

Figure 35.1 Home-country-based balance sheet approach

differences or cost differentials, but as long as your policies are reasonable, that should not be a major concern."

Kim asked if they should retain someone to administer the expatriate programs and if Epsilon was the right provider. Rob suggested they consider firms that did this work globally, since it entailed monitoring currency fluctuations, familiarity with local laws and taxation regulations, and the like. "What's this?" Kim asked, "a consultant turning down business?" "Yes," Rob answered, "we try not to extend ourselves beyond our competence, and there is no way we could be as efficient as providers who do this on a large scale. We are happy to work with you when we are confident we are the right choice. For example, the HR service center system we offer may be something you should consider, given your far-flung operations. One of the things you should do is to assess the knowledge and skills people have in your new operations and to evaluate how you might develop people and manage career opportunities. And Annette is talking with your staff about some of the HR strategies and policies you might look at."

"I am happy to buy lunch." Kim responded, smiling. "You have been very professional in providing me with the advice I need at the moment without turning it into a big consulting project."

Annette informed Rob that the HR staff had some work to do getting all of the current policies and employee data collected from the two new operations and that they would contact her when they were ready to develop an overall HR strategy and policies that would integrate global operations, to the extent they would be integrated. Annette had suggested they use the term "aligned," since "integrated" suggested the result would be homogenous. Global principles and local strategies was the approach that would probably be adopted, though it was unclear how global and how local things would be.

All of the visitors wanted to get to bed early, since they had 5 a.m. flights out and that meant getting up at 3 a.m. At 11 p.m. Annette got a phone call and it was Kim. "I am so sorry if I woke you," Kim said sheepishly, "but we are still at the office and we have another issue that the CEO told us we should have explored with you. Can you change your flights to a day later and stay, or at the very least, can you and whoever else you think necessary?" Annette was still groggy but said she would need to know the topic before she could decide. Kim shot back. "We want to define the ideal profile of our leaders in our global operations." Annette suggested they delay their return for two days to be sure they could gain at least a surface-level understanding of the issues related to this very complex subject and Kim agreed.

Annette called the travel representative back home and requested their return be put back by two days. "In this case the time difference works in our favor—their staff is in the office," she thought. But now she had to roust everyone so they could be told they could sleep in. When making the calls, she got Rob and he said he would reset his alarm and cancel his wakeup call. "But I need to send out some clothing because I only overpacked by one day," he moaned. "And I hate paying hotel prices for laundry." Annette suggested he had a sink in his room, but since a dress shirt was involved, he made it clear his ironing skills were not up to making a shirt presentable. Annette then called Pete and got his voice mail. "Here we go," she thought, "now I have to find him." The hotel they were staying in had a casino associated with it and she had a pretty good idea where to locate him. Walking up behind him at a video poker machine, she snapped, "Planning to sleep on the plane rather than work?" Pete shot back, "I am doing an anthropological analysis of the local culture." Since Annette was pretty sure the video poker machines in Singapore were culturally identical to those back home, she could have rebutted that specious claim but decided to let it go. Pete smiled at the news and said, "Great, now I have time to get my money back." "Oh well," thought Annette, "he was a good consultant."

The next morning, they were introduced to Grace, who was a professor at a prominent local university. She was doing work on global leadership and had served as a staffer on the GLOBE research project that studied the effectiveness of leadership styles in different cultures.[1] She began the meeting by discussing what research has found on this topic. "An academic named Fiedler developed a contingency leadership theory that proposed multiple style alternatives that might be effective, based on the context. Then the GLOBE study looked at this in more depth. What we found is that different cultures viewed leadership differently, based on a number of characteristics. They were very close to those used by Trompenaars and other cultural anthropologists."

The first principle to be derived from the research is that you should know what seems to work well and not work in each region. The second principle is that mobile leaders must be able to adapt their styles to the cultural context, and if they cannot, you should select people for assignments that best fit their style. As with most things, there is no best or worst style—it is all about what fits the context.

"So, what is it that you want us to look at?" Kathy asked. Kim laid out the issues. "The CEO wants to quickly develop a selection model for expatriate assignments for people in leadership positions. And Ron's real question is whether leadership style can be assessed and whether it will be necessary to use different styles in our different locations. I believe we have enough accumulated knowledge about our key leaders to know in general how they lead and I am comfortable using biodata to get a handle on them. Of course, this only tells me how they have led in the past, and there is nothing to tell us how adaptable they will be to different cultures. So, can we get more predictability about how individuals will probably do on a specific assignment?"

"Is there no way to measure adaptability?" Kim asked. "Sure," Rob responded, "we can look at personality characteristics and get a rough idea about adaptability, but the measures are pretty crude and might not get at what is really at issue here. You have to decide whether you are going to continue doing things the way you do here in your new locations. If that is the case and if the leadership style fits the workplace culture you now utilize, then you might think about changing the cultural profile in the new locations.

"The GLOBE study looked at both the leadership style that is prevalent now in the countries but also asked about what study participants thought the prevalent style should be in order to succeed. There were a lot of gaps, I suspect mostly caused by changing cultural profiles. For example, even though a self-protective leadership style might have historically been accepted in the Middle East and parts of Asia, it does not mean that is what people want or that is what will be effective in the changing environment. The awakening of a desire for democratic systems in some regions will almost certainly result in people preferring more participative leadership, at the countrywide level and perhaps at the organizational level. So, sending a participative leader into that type of context may result in the old guard hating the style and others welcoming it.

"And no leader is purely one type; there are shades of grey. The best work on leading people out of dysfunctional states like entitlement or fear into a more suitable frame of mind was done by Bardwick.[2] She suggests actions that can be taken to move people to a better place, but she also suggests that how leaders do this is critical to their success. I don't think anyone has concluded that there is one way to lead in a specific type of culture. Trompenaars analyzed the success of twenty-one global leaders in unique situations, unique from the organizational point of view and unique from the cultural setting point of view.[3] So, the bottom line is 'what works is what fits.' And if a leader you are planning to send into a context has a style that does not fit the context, then you can try to change the leader's style, try to change the cultural context or select someone else."

Notes

1 House, R., "Cultural Influences on Leadership and Organizations," in Mobley, W., *Advances in Global Leadership,*Vol. 1, 1999, JAI Press, Stamford, CT.
2 Bardwick, J., *Danger in the Comfort Zone*, 1991, AMACOM, New York.
3 Trompenaars, F., *Twenty-One Leaders in the Twenty-First Century*, 2001, Capstone, Oxford, UK.

36 Focusing the professional practice

The consulting staff reconvened after everyone got back to the office. There was a lot of discussion about the discomfort some of the people felt when jumping from one assignment to another. Eric said that he loved the variety and the stimulation it provided, but others said that was because he did pretty much the same thing no matter the nature of the assignment. "That is the way it is with us IT types. We keep running the same set of programs until we have to revise them or replace them." Everyone knew he had been stretched as much as they had, particularly because the HR service center system was more of a concept than a single homogenous product and it required reconfiguration to meet each client organization's set of needs. Don assured him that he had been frustrated when trying to reuse consulting reports, since each context demanded a relook of the strategies and programs to be sure they were a good fit. "So much for having a hammer and being able to treat each client issue like a nail, or just changing the company name and date on consulting reports," he thought.

Several of the staff members had worked in private and public sector organizations, and they constantly were comparing life as a practitioner and life as a consultant. Rob and Kathy had also served on university faculties and as a result had three different types of experience in their backgrounds. "HR is HR some people would say," Annette offered. "You staff the organization, develop the people, define, measure and reward performance and manage employee relations. But I have yet to find a repeat experience after doing HR in for-profits and not-for-profits and in consulting firms. They all were different, based on the mission of the organization, its culture, the internal and external realities and the strategy of the organization. Every project required defining the organizational context. From that, a structure was designed and an HR strategy was formulated that was a fit to the context and the objectives. And I don't know if the variety has lessened when staying with the same organization. If you don't coevolve with your environment, your viability erodes and eventually you cease to exist."

Don seconded Annette's theme of eternal variety but did concede that there were similarities and things that worked across contexts. "I guess it is principles that transport, rather than specific strategies and programs," he mused.[1] "Yet a well-designed gainsharing plan can work in multiple production plants if there are not significant differences in the contexts. And structured interviews are more valid and reliable for selecting the right people than ad hoc procedures pretty much everywhere. The real difference between the competence levels of HR practitioners is the richness of their knowledge and skill base, which can be used to figure out what fits. When you become more competent in the field, you tend to have a wider perspective and are better able to consider the long-term implications of actions. But there are people that have been practicing for many years who have been doing pretty much the same things the same way, and it is those cases that refute the idea that more experience necessarily results in a higher level of confidence. Malcolm Gladwell once observed that one must *organize* one's experience in order for years to equate to expertise level."

Pete thought the conversation had become overly theoretical and suggested they focus on a marketing plan that would result in more business, since more business would result in more pay. "Did you overspend when shopping in Singapore?" Annette asked. "No," responded Pete, "I am just materialistic." Don and Rob redirected the conversation to the marketing plan. The firm had been responding to opportunities as they came up, rather than pursuing a strategy based on targeted markets and specific products and services.

Kathy suggested they try to sort out what they should be doing for clients and what clients should do for themselves. "That is a challenging distinction to make," Annette responded, "but it might help to focus us on what our offerings should be." The group contributed one by one around the table, providing opinions. Several of the members felt it was up to the client organization to decide what consulting assistance they wanted, while others felt that would leave the door open for them to stray far afield from their core capabilities. "I get worried when a client asks me to set performance standards for an incentive plan," Pete offered. "There is no way I know enough about an organization to be able to decide what reasonable targets are. Besides, the more I take a position on something that requires knowledge of the culture and context, the better the chances I will err. And if I am making those kinds of decisions, how does HR ever gain respect in the organization?" Don responded with a question: "Have we all not had HR plead for us to recommend something they have not been able to gain acceptance for? Why we can say the same things as internal staff yet be more influential has always disturbed me, but I guess there is no choice if that is the only avenue to gaining acceptance of something that is needed."

"Some of the deference to the outside consultant is explainable," Annette said. "We generally have the benefit of having worked with a large number of organizations and have experience with strategy execution and program implementation. If the client is doing something for the first time, they will not have that base of knowledge. I have worked with two organizations recently that had top HR executives who had spent their entire career with the organization. It is pretty hard for someone without some breadth of experience to be confident something they have never done will work. You can read all the case studies and books yet still be reluctant to do something you have not done in a similar context. It makes you a little leery of coming on strong with a specific recommendation. Like it or not, we are the scapegoats when something does not work well if the internal staff is clever enough to deflect any blame for a failure. And in a way, that is acceptable because we are the ones that supposedly had the knowledge needed to make a strategy or program work."

Kathy decided to share some thoughts about consulting she had been having lately. "The worst thing about consulting is that you have to be confident and aggressive in your recommendations. The best thing about teaching is that you can say that research findings do not provide a clear answer to a particular issue without seeming evasive. You can explain the theory and convey what is known about things like the relationship between job satisfaction and unwanted turnover and do so honestly. But when you adopt the role of consultant, you are generally expected to make firm recommendations. Certainly, you can say that it is uncertain if increasing satisfaction by involving employees in goal setting will necessarily lead to improved retention, but if you are a successful consultant, you probably have buried that information in a footnote or certainly de-emphasized the uncertainty. If you wait for certainty when dealing with people issues, you will be frozen in place and won't do anything. I really empathize with HR practitioners who have to make recommendations when the likelihood of a decision being the best one is unknown. We sometimes accuse the internal staff of doing a poor job of implementation and administration when a program we recommended does not result in success. And internal staff will probably believe it was our error that led to poor results. This is human nature. All of us tend to attribute success to our own efforts and failure to external causes that were not controllable. The trouble with that is an employee's supervisor will tend to do the opposite—attribute success to environmental factors (or the supervisor's brilliance) and failure to the employee."

"I still often think about being back in a practitioner role," Don confided. "You can build on what you have accomplished and stick around to enjoy the celebrations of success. You also get to mourn when things do not go well, but that is an opportunity to improve." Pete retorted "Mark Twain once said he seemed to be surrounded by insurmountable opportunities, and I think you forget just how miserable things get when failures occur. And when nothing seems to work, you can get downright pessimistic." "Yes," Don replied, "but I wonder if we consultants don't get to hear only about things that go wrong, since if a strategy works, the client is instantly convinced it was due to their brilliant execution and forgets to give you a call to thank you."

Kathy pointed out that teaching was even more lacking in feedback. "You never hear about how an idea you gave a student worked out, good or bad. Actually, you never know if they even bothered to try to turn theory into practice. So, it seems everyone—practitioners, consultants and academics—all have their own brand of frustrations." Pete suggested the conversation was so grim that the only antidote was to go to lunch, an idea which everyone welcomed.

Alpha, the corporation that most of the consulting staff had worked for prior to its being acquired, reappeared on the radar screen. Don had gotten a call from Andrea, the corporate VP of HR, who asked him if they could meet to discuss an assignment. Don agreed, largely out of curiosity, although they did have consulting staff operating at less than 100%. When he arrived, he was glancing at an internal phone directory in the lobby and was amazed to find that some of the senior management was still in place. But the more he thought about it, the more he realized that the HR staff members who ran out the door did so principally because they felt their environment was going to change for the worse and that they would be constrained by policies formulated by some higher power. The other factor that entered into their decision is that they were still in the early to middle part of their careers and could afford to take a chance. Some of the managers whose names he saw in the directory were less than ten years from expected retirement, and the stakes are much higher if one chooses to walk away from a decent job, even when uncertainty about the acquisition was present. On the other hand, he asked himself where there is certainty in this free agent world.

Andrea had attended a presentation by a systems guru who specialized in stirring people up to get them thinking about using advanced techniques in all parts of the organization. Oddly the presenter had selected HR as "the stodgy administrative function" that used stone-age processes to do their work. He had asked if anyone was in HR, and several hands went up, so the presenter hit them with a series of questions.

"Have you looked into using any of the following techniques in your HR world? Scenario-based planning? Kaizen? Lean processes? Business process reengineering? Total quality management? Six Sigma? Causal path analysis? Fishbone diagrams? Delphi approach? Brainstorming? Share point? Benchmarking? Social media? Data analytics? Artificial intelligence?

The taunting nature of the presenter irritated Andrea, and she shot her hand up when brainstorming and benchmarking were mentioned. Some of the other HR people did not bother to raise their hands at all, and she wondered if they were intimidated or if they felt this stuff was only suitable for other functions. A number of them rallied when social media was mentioned, although some of their frowns were probably attributable to their uncertainty as to what constituted the use of social media in HR.

Andrea decided to do a little taunting of her own. "What do you mean by use?'" she began. "Is evaluating your pay levels using surveys benchmarking or do you mean using benchmarking to evaluate processes or programs? And does tweeting among staff members meet your use criterion for social media?"

The presenter was a little taken aback but did refine his meaning by specifying the use of the techniques to refine the operational processes within the HR function. "I guess what I was after was whether you continuously evaluated your processes to ensure they were effective and efficient. There was a recent study of HR practices that showed there was little progress being made in the function becoming more strategic and less tactical or being seen as a strategic business partner [2] In order to be seen as a business partner, any staff function should be using all the available tools to improve processes, to include strategy formulation and execution. It is of course necessary to improve efficiency in order to respond to the ever-greater demands being placed on all parts of the organization. But only using tools to be more efficient is not enough. For example, using advanced social media applications to improve an organization's brand and to attract better applicants should result in cost-efficient staffing, but even more importantly should increase the quality of the organization's human capital over time. And using causal path analysis to establish what impacted the success of a strategy rather than just to generate cost-saving fixes to current operations makes the tool more valuable and impactful on organizational success."

"I read that same study you cited. What was of most value to me was their LAMP (logic, analytics, measures and processes) model for driving strategic change and organizational effectiveness," Andrea had responded. "During my formative years in HR, I was taught to measure important things like turnover, cost and time to fill a vacancy and employee engagement. I was not alerted to the need for an overarching logic for selecting the measures that would be focused on, and I was not sensitized to the need to consider the impact on the organization when setting priorities and allocating resources. Since my student days, I have come to realize that having 100 HR metrics can be dysfunctional, even if all of them are worthy of monitoring. But tracking too many things can take your eye off overall results. Working on reducing time to fill vacancies can result in realizing at a later date you have not ended up with the best mix of people for future success. And using techniques like causal path analysis just because they are put forth as the 'next best thing' can result in a short-term focus."

Andrea shared this recent experience with Don and asked him if they would take a look at the tools and processes HR was currently using and to recommend how they might improve. "I really like the phrase 'practice informed by science,'" she said, "and I want to be as confident as I can be that when I make recommendations I have based them on all the relevant evidence that is of high validity. For example, our people are really into benchmarking against competitors and successful organizations. I buy that for operational processes like logistics, but when it comes to strategies for managing people, I worry about emulation as being the right approach. I think the presenter I told you about was enamored with using all the 'new' (really?) techniques, whether or not they applied to human capital management. Sure, our work needs to be managed so the quality is first rate and our processes need to be efficient, but what I am really after is the utilization of scientific methods when they make sense."

Don suggested that Andrea read a book on strategic human resource management written by two prominent academics in the field[3] and that they meet again once she had a chance to think about what role she wanted HR to play and what they needed to do to contribute to organizational effectiveness. Andrea agreed, and they set a second meeting for the next afternoon, given her need to decide what she would present to the CEO at the end of the week.

When Don arrived for the meeting, he was surprised to find the CEO and CFO were joining them. Andrea set the stage. "After reading the book I got at the bookstore after we met—until 2 a.m. the next day by the way—I had a discussion this morning with these two about risk management and how the organization approached it. They immediately grabbed the book, and I believe they have had an opportunity to at least give it a quick look. But I definitely wanted to pursue this topic and I want to share a SWOT analysis I did on human capital. One of the issues that had come up during a management meeting is that we seemed to get undercut on our pricing of mature products by lower-cost competitors. We have a truly outstanding R & D staff, which has resulted in a number of significant innovations and patents, but we have a difficult time turning the innovation into commercially viable products quickly and at a reasonable cost. So, we did a SWOT analysis, and after injecting truth serum into the arms of R & D and engineering management, they admitted to having real challenges. The R & D function had been staffed with the best and the brightest who were capable of breakthrough innovation but suffered from two unfortunate tendencies: (1) they could not stop refining a prototype until it was as good as it could be, rather than just good enough and 2) they were a very expensive workforce. As competitors used techniques like crowdsourcing among a wide range of contributors and using contractors rather than full-time employees, they created a workforce cost structure that was lower and more flexible than ours.

That analysis then disclosed what we in HR might do to help us escape the trap we had fallen into due to using a staffing strategy that did not really consider its implications over the long run. Lacking a strategy, it is easy to recruit the top 1% of graduates and then only later wonder how you are going to keep them motivated and to afford the large payroll costs."

Randy, the CFO, offered his perspective. "I never thought about risk management being a concern of anyone other than those who are assigned that responsibility full time. But now I realize that legal, HR and even line functions should be more aware of the implications of any strategy for managing our risks and liabilities. I remember complaining about our generous vacation policy, which includes carryover, since it was building up large liabilities we have to book, but I guess we talked about whether to change the policy from a 'right thing to do' perspective, rather than from the financial liability perspective. And it never occurred to me to challenge anyone about getting the best of the best from graduating classes—I celebrated those 'successes' along with everyone else. Makes you feel outsiders are confirming what a great organization you are. Well, live and learn."

The fact that his CFO had become almost philosophical gave Carter, the CEO, a bit of a shock. But then he realized that having a philosophy of management

	Strengths	Weaknesses
Opportunities	*Capitalize*	*Increase capabilities or minimize impact*
Threats	*Deal with vulnerability*	*Deal with problems*

Figure 36.1 Human capital SWOT analysis

was something they all had and needed to have, and this discussion was opening them up to new opportunities. Randy had read a book by a leading academic on the future of management[4] some time ago and had considered suggesting to the executive team that they challenge the fundamental assumptions underlying their management style. The author had pointed out the fallacy of the top-down control approach and argued for a culture that created a democracy of ideas. This would enable emergent discovery to occur, due to the encouragement of anyone at any level to put forth ideas for improving the organization. He suggested that the further down in the organization someone was and the more unconventional their ideas, the less chance there was that those ideas would get a fair hearing.

The flexible continuously changing organizational structure that was recommended in the book did not scare Carter, even though much of his professional training had biased him toward structure and stability and against anarchy in any form. He had often thought earlier in his career that if he was to become a CEO, he would have to welcome turbulence that was functional and uncertainty that was unavoidable. A book on leadership he had used at an executive development course the prior year had mesmerized him, since it opened his eyes to the new science of chaos and complexity, and its relevance to organizations.[5] He was excited by the new perspectives offered in that book and had asked a group of his colleagues at a CEO conference if they had considered the implications of viewing organizations as adaptive complex systems. The reception he got was what he would expect if he had announced he had the plague and was in the contagious period. He reacted to the chilly reception by convincing himself he was ahead of the crowd and decided he would not regress to the popular views.

Don suggested that Andrea's SWOT analysis was a good start in using systematic approaches to evaluate the organization's human capital strategy. And he suggested they consider having an open dialogue with the management population about the organization's mission, internal and external realities, strategy and structure. One way to do that is to have a "what would you focus on if you were in my job" dialogue, using an iterative Delphi approach that would summarize input and feed it back to respondents to initiate another round of input. "You could ask them to list the three things you should do to improve organizational performance," Don suggested to Carter, "and then send the top ten back out and ask people to prioritize them and send their rankings in. This could go on for as long as necessary to generate a consensus about what people felt the CEO should work on. Then, after the executive team wrestled with the issues, they could formulate a strategy and have the managers evaluate that. Andrea could then take ownership of HR-related issues, Randy could address the financial issues and so on. IBM did this with over 100,000 employees, suppliers and customers in an Innovation Jam seeking ideas for improving performance. What it accomplishes at the same time is to engage employees in the business and in the well-being of the organization."

Andrea thanked Don for stirring them up and promised they would get back to him, probably to serve as a facilitator of a process that would get a lot more people involved in evaluating strategies, programs and processes, and not just in HR.

Don came rushing into a meeting of the consulting staff back at the office and threw a gauntlet down. "Are we missing a fundamental characteristic of organizations?" he asked the group. After looking at the research on adaptive complex systems done at the Santa Fe Institute and increasingly by scientists elsewhere, I think we are forgetting that organizations are adaptive complex systems and that change comes from emergent behavior, rather than top-down control." Annette thought a cold compress on Don's forehead might calm him a bit but knew when he was fired up like this it was best to let his adrenaline level subside before resisting. "And this impacts our planning meeting how?" she asked.

Don knew he had perhaps skipped some introductory comments to frame the dialogue he hoped to create, so he backed up a bit. "We are increasingly working with clients to help them gain strategic advantage through their people. And they almost always understand that management needs to identify a mission that employees can sign up for and to develop a strategy that will facilitate fulfilling that mission. But how they structure the organization and how they engage their people is critical. The critical behaviors emerge from the bottom up, top-down control might force people to toe the line, but it will never bring out the creativity and the passion that is necessary for organizational success. Think about this meeting. We always have an agenda, including a schedule. It never turns out that way, so why do we bother creating an agenda? Wouldn't we be better off letting everyone know what the pressing issues are and ask them to bring their best thinking? And should we not welcome someone interjecting an issue or opportunity that was not mentioned? I am not arguing for anarchy but merely a recognition that what happens in a group will be determined by the relationships between them, what they individually bring to the party and how aligned they are in their focus on organizational objectives."

Rob jumped in to support Don's point. "I also believe we have an opportunity to abandon the structured approach taught to us when Newtonian physics was dominant. In the world of fuzzy logic and quantum mechanics that has replaced much of the previous thinking, things are different. And Don has identified the fact that organizations are complex adaptive systems that do not do the bidding of anyone no matter what their title. I suggest we talk about this among ourselves and then figure out how we can de-traumatize it when we go to clients. It is funny that I was recently rereading *Leadership & the New Science* by Margaret Wheatley and extracted the following questions from the introduction to the book":

What are the sources of order? How do we create organizational coherence, where activities correspond to purpose? How do we create structures that move with change, that are flexible and adaptive, even boundaryless, that enable, rather than constrain? How do we simplify things without losing both control and differentiation? How do we resolve personal needs for freedom and autonomy with organizational needs for prediction and control?

He continued: "These are of course not the questions you throw out at a client meeting, but they should be in our heads when we try to help clients understand how to better design organizational structures and define the roles employees play. And I think all of our clients are concerned about how to better engage employees, motivate them to give their best effort and to take the initiative to innovate, and to align their efforts toward achieving the current objectives. This mindset, emergent behavior rather than top-down control, will not be popular with some, particularly those whose authority comes from the title and position they have. But employees just aren't willing to slave away to make nameless shareholders rich, even if they are paid to do so. Look at the research—increasingly, people want to increase their satisfaction in their work. This is particularly true because what you do for a living and your formal status have largely replaced community and even family in defining one's self."

Annette, being the resident advocate for meaningful work and concern for people's quality of life, joined the fray. "Well, you are correct in acknowledging the concern employees have about experiencing some meaning in their work, as well as wanting to feel they are being justly treated. And we know we cannot use the old models to predict what happens when people form into groups or teams. Emergent behavior can only be understood by considering the relationships between the people. It is risky to assume that if the required knowledge and skills are possessed by team members, the performance of the team will meet expectations. Look at how poorly quality circles performed when imported from Japan to the U.S. The differences in the cultural orientation of the participants was overlooked, and the results expected did not often materialize. How foolish it was to think something that worked well in one of the most collectivist societies would work as well in one of the most individualistic societies. But business schools have traditionally focused on getting the structure right and managing the people effectively so people bring their training with them when they begin to manage. I give more credit to managers than you, since I doubt most believe people are going to be effective with top-down direction if they are not engaged and committed to meeting organizational objectives. Yet, we need to at least offer alternative approaches to structuring work mechanically and we should continually market the advantages of having people self-actualize and take the initiative to figure out how to do things the best way possible."

"How about people like us?" asked Pete. "We are supposed to provide professional counsel to clients, but how does it feel when they do not take our advice? I suppose the same feeling of frustration is experienced by our contacts within client organizations. They are probably even more frustrated when we tell management the same thing they have been saying, yet management ignores them and listens to us. I never have been able to figure that out, but I sure see a lot of it. Let's take Andrea, the HR exec at Alpha. She is supersmart, totally engaged in making the organization successful and is very knowledgeable about the people, the politics and the current realities. Yet she confided in me that some of what we are successfully selling management on is not that different than a lot of what she has tried to do. Is this because we really know more, have a broader experience base or are smarter? Or is it because the executives feel we don't have any particular agenda? All very puzzling."

"The same tendency exists when organizations recruit personnel," Kathy jumped in, slightly out of breath after her hallway jog. "And sorry I am late. A conference call ran long, and amazingly it was relevant to this issue. One of my clients is trying to choose between two finalists for a key finance job and is perplexed. One finalist is an internal guy who interviews like a top used car salesman but with a limited track record and references that are not glowing. The other is a lady from Laos who just got permanent resident status. Her resume is so-so and she represents herself well but seems a lot less qualified and aggressive while interviewing than the other candidate. But when we checked her references, they portray her as a dynamo with an amazing track record of accomplishments. So, what do they use as the basis for selection?"

"I would suggest there are two things going on here," Rob answered. "One is probably cultural. There is a tendency for people who were socialized in Asian cultures to be modest about individual capabilities and things accomplished by themselves, while over here we take credit for everything we have done and some of what others did. I know that is a stereotypical analysis, but it probably is contributing to the disconnect between the Asian candidate's resume and what she really has accomplished. The second is the 'I know people I know are not perfect' effect. This impacts the gap between the way the currently employed candidate represents himself and the opinions about him peers have. It would be my suggestion that they do an assessment center exercise in the form of a simulation using work similar to that required in the job. People doing financial analysis work do not succeed because they are good at marketing themselves—it is about how well they do the work."

Kathy nodded and returned to the prior conversation among the team members. "The tendency of management to accept our recommendation is understandable, and we should not feel guilty about it. When someone like Andrea is not listened to, it may be a form of insurance for decision makers. If something goes wrong, they can deflect blame by pointing out they got expert advice from people with no agenda. We should not apologize to the Andreas we work with but rather treat them as partners and welcome good decisions, no matter who gets credit for them."

Pete nodded, still convinced management often paid a price for not valuing the input from internals adequately. He had never bought into the principle that operating/line management made decisions and staff functions provided advice that could be taken or not. "I know every manager thinks they are an expert on their people and their operations, but the reality is that they know a lot more about the operations stuff and a lot less about the behavioral aspects of managing. Why they view taking guidance from HR professionals who do know a lot more about the behavioral stuff to be diminishing escapes me. Let me give you an example. One of our clients uses project teams extensively, and they get frustrated when they change the membership of a team and find the performance is different, even though the new person has the same knowledge and skills as the departing member. Back to your complex adaptive systems concept—outcomes are dependent on the relationships between members as well as the presence of the required knowledge and skills. You cannot take fixed-shape pieces out of a system like that, since it is more like a field than a tangible entity. If you remove part of a hologram, you still get the same image, but it will be less focused. And in an ecosystem, if you remove a species, you may find that the results are largely unpredictable. Turnover in a social system is probably going to change its functioning, but you are going to be hard-pressed to predict exactly how."

Andrea broke the silence following Pete's comments. "This is what is wonderful about working with a bunch of smart, thoughtful people who are not in competition with each other for the next promotion or pay increase. I wish we could do 'after action reviews' like the U.S. Army and do them right after each client engagement that has the potential to teach us something. We are stronger when we share what we know with each other and when we listen to each other. We all agree that the functioning of any policy or program stays the same when context changes and that leads us to be cautious when trying to reuse a Company A success at Company B without considering the differences between the two contexts. But we surely can accumulate stories and form patterns that lead us to better analysis and decisions."

"Let's go back to your point about us not being in competition with each other," Rob added. "I have always respected the potential for merit pay and individual incentives to elicit competitive rather than cooperative behavior. The fact that we don't have managers here who have to allocate a fixed-sum pay increase budget among subordinates or allocate incentive funds based on a subjective 'who did the most' basis lets us cooperate and support each other. Yet, we know performance-based rewards are effective in providing motivation, and we certainly eschew egalitarian rewards distributions when there are differences in what is deserved across individuals or units and will continue to recommend this valuable management tool. So, how do we help clients not frustrate their attempts to have employees share their best ideas with their peers, rather than using them to gain credit and prosper economically?"

"Edward Lawler has long said one of the critical requirements for effective incentives is to get the level of measurement and reward right," Kathy added. "I think that is such an important idea. Yes, we want employees to perform well individually, but we also want them to do so in a way that makes others effective, the unit effective and the organization effective. One thing Rob has taught me about rewards management is that selecting only one level at which performance is defined, measured and rewarded is typically a mistake. Yet there are exceptions. The sole sales representative in Utah may be in total control of individual performance and the organization may want to focus the rep on performing as well as possible through an individual commission plan. On the other hand, it might be a good idea to have sales reps participate in an organization-wide performance sharing plan and the benefits program, to remind them who they work for. And a machine operator in a production unit may be in control of output but still be at the mercy of the availability and quality of material, so we may have a major part of their earnings based on physical output but build in mechanisms for adjusting rewards formulas for variations that the incumbents cannot control. And we also may use unit incentives like gainsharing plans and organization-wide performance sharing plans to give operators a sense of community and remind them how their performance connects up to the larger picture."

"Should we look at the detailed agenda we had for this meeting to see if accidentally we actually touched on one or more of the topics?" Don snapped. He was not displeased with the dialogue but realized that they might cuddle each other into financial insolvency if they did not take care of business. Yet, how does one overlook the benefits of having this type of open exploration of ideas?

Rob quickly responded, "Our resident capitalist cries out for reason and a focus on material matters." Since he was smiling, Don did not consider verbal retaliation. "But Don does bring us back into the real world—we are not senators in the Roman Forum. I did glance at the agenda and would remind everyone we were supposed to look at our current practice definitions to see if we wanted to target specific services in our marketing plan for the next quarter. I, for one, believe we are not erring in responding to a wide variety of inquiries from existing and potential clients. We do not seem to have dissipated our focus or stumbled into areas where we lack expertise. That is my view and I would like to hear from everyone else."

Kathy, Pete and Annette signified agreement with a thumbs-up response. Don was not so sure. "I think we have done pretty well, but I get a sense that we are in a totally responsive mode, without a destination in mind, other than prospering economically. Given my lavish lifestyle, I am good with that, but are we investing in developing the 'next best thing'? I am not suggesting we become fad generators—there are far too many of those being propagated and peddled to unsuspecting innocents. But current advantages like our HRIS and the associated services could well be emulated, and that means we would have a commodity and would have to compete based on price alone. Been there, done that. Not a good place to be, since by the time you realize where you are, it is too late to get a jump on the competition. I would suggest we spend some effort in exploring the area of workforce/HR metrics and analytics. Management wants their decisions relating to human capital to be optimal, and measurement systems are the key to that. We certainly have helped HR functions become more *efficient* with our HRIS, but has it made them more *effective*? And more valued by the organization?"

"Our colleague offers great wisdom," interjected Eric. "We can process data with our systems, but in order to turn the data into information and knowledge, we need to get definitions and methods of measurement standardized. I love those surveys that ask questions like, 'What is your cost of hire?' With the wide variation in how that is calculated across organizations, the compiled results are meaningless. I remember an association asking, 'Are you considering broadbanding?' or 'Have you adopted broadbanding? or 'If you have adopted broadbanding, how successful has it been?' Tell me how you make any sense out of the answers.

"I think my consulting assignments have been successful but really am not sure what factors I used to decide that. And when broadbanding was all the rage, there must have been five or six definitions floating around. Engineers are trained to use standard definitions for what they measure, while people with liberal arts degrees seem to find that approach limits their creativity. Now, I know some of you believe every HR practitioner understands when you ask the question, 'Have you implemented a formal performance appraisal system?' but will practitioners be able to answer the question accurately and using the same definition and criteria? And if not, what sense can be made of the answers? The real question is whether you have performance management systems that motivate employees and contribute to organizational effectiveness. I know you are not able to use formulas in the same way an engineer determines the hardness of a steel beam, but developing standards can at least give us a Rosetta stone so we can be sure practitioners are defining and measuring things the same way. Absolutely, let's take advantage of this standards development activity and incorporate it as appropriate into our work."

The meeting closed with no regrets that the agenda had been virtually ignored. The participants all recognized they had experienced a rare event—people stepping away from the day-to-day issues to talk about larger ideas. Kathy had an insight into why she liked being in the academic community. Even though there still was some competitive behavior, many of the faculty members realized it would only benefit them to share their ideas with colleagues, as well as listening to them when they shared.

Notes

1 Greene, R., *Rewarding Performance: Guiding Principles; Custom Strategies*, 2011, Routledge, New York.
2 Lawler, E. and Boureau, J., *Effective Human Resource Management*, 2012, Stanford University Press, Palo Alto, CA.
3 Cascio, W. and Boudreau, J., *Short Introduction to Strategic Human Resource Management*, 2013, Cambridge University Press, Cambridge, UK.
4 Hamel, G., *The Future of Management*, 2007, Harvard Business School Press, Cambridge, MA.
5 Wheatley, M., *Leadership and the New Science*, 1992, Berrett-Koehler, San Francisco.

37 Compensation

Can it be a satisfier?

Annette got a call from Maria, an HR manager she had met at a local HR association meeting. "We are experiencing turnover in critical occupations and, in addition, there is an elevated level of complaining about a variety of things: pay, workload, quality of management and so on. I would like to get at the source of dissatisfaction so we can figure out how to deal with it. But I first have to establish that there is a problem before management will seek solutions." Maria's tone suggested desperation and frustration. She thought about her response and decided to suggest a process that Maria might initiate.

"Let's start by moving up to a strategic level. Does management recognize that the turnover and apparent dissatisfaction is impacting organizational performance? If so, then you have a business reason to explore what is going on, rather than just another HR initiative to make the workforce happier. Then, there is a need to ask if poor performance is a result of turnover, lower productivity, inability to hire the people you need or other causes. That needs to be sorted out working with line executives, since they will have their own explanations for declination in performance. If turnover within key roles is the cause, then you can explore the reason(s) for it. Is it that rewards are not competitive? Is it dissatisfaction with the work being done? Is it the workload/stress level? Or is it the result of aggressive action by competitors to fill slots in short-supply occupations? If it is the result of competitors upping their game, then you may find that just being competitive is not enough."

Maria offered her views. "We have thoroughly surveyed compensation levels for the occupations that are turning over and we are actually paying somewhat above market levels. So, I think we are competitive externally. I did some focus groups in design engineering, one of the hotbeds of discontent and untimely exits, and the opinions about what was causing dissatisfaction seemed to point to lack of training and development that was necessary to keep our people competent in using the leading-edge technology. Several of the employees were spending nights and weekends attending courses or studying, all of which was on their own. Our training budgets had been slashed because the CFO pointed out training expense was a short-term certain cost with an uncertain future benefit, if any. In fact, she suggested any investment in development would just prepare our people for better jobs elsewhere. I have had my challenges with her on similar issues before and have pointed out that although they could not book any return of investments in training, the lack of it was causing other problems that certainly were creating liabilities."

Annette responded to Marie's despair. "I am not going to say I feel your pain, but I certainly understand your frustration with people who view the costs related to the workforce differently than they do when purchasing capital equipment. But they are right in suggesting you cannot own your people or even be certain they will be willing to use their knowledge and skills to contribute to organizational effectiveness. Unfortunately, if every organization thought that way, there would be far too little investment in human resource development and a subsequent shortage of critical skills. A pool of human capital, no matter how rich, must be managed well and must produce the required results. But the lack of an adequate pool renders the rest of the organization's assets useless, so this accounting mentality that precludes adequate investment in human capital development can be fatal."

"Well," Maria asked, "is assessing employee satisfaction the place to start?" "I think so," said Annette, "but perhaps so is a dialogue with management about what a survey is intended to discover and what management is willing to do in the way of a response. You know you will probably be unwilling to raise pay levels even further, so perhaps you focus the survey on non-monetary issues, such as the nature of the work, the workload, whether performance expectations are reasonable, the quality of management and the ability of employees to realize a work-life balance. Once you determine what is detracting from satisfaction, and perhaps contributing to voluntary turnover, you will have to be willing to openly share the findings and be ready to discuss what the organization might do to improve satisfaction. If the survey discloses issues that management is unwilling or unable to fix, you will at least be able to recognize these issues and enter into a dialogue with employees that lets them contribute ideas about how to minimize dissatisfaction. For example, if technical personnel feel the technology they are working with is not state-of-the-art, there may be ways to remedy that. If they feel there is insufficient recognition for accomplishments, you might work with managers to learn how to catch people doing things right—they probably are adept at *catching people doing things wrong*. Finally, you must focus on the most critical people and how they feel. Perhaps the way you are allocating reward funds is not adequately differentiating based on relative contribution. If you try to please everyone, you will not succeed. One of the findings from research is that if you increase differentiation based on performance, you will be likely to increase dissatisfaction with marginal and poor performers, but if that is who is going to leave, that might not trouble you."

"I don't have that much faith in our performance management system," Maria responded. "Or I guess I don't have a problem with the methods or processes but rather with the ability of managers to administer it well. We have managers who do year-end 'blame allocation sessions' after remaining silent all year about employee performance. I know continuous measurement and feedback is critical in order to do this well, but how do you convince managers of that?" Annette smiled and responded, "You know how—you train them. But then getting the budget and time to do adequate training is going to run up against that 'certain cost with unknown benefits' mentality that is blocking your assessment of satisfaction. We can propose a management training program, but I think we need to convince management there is a need for it to have a chance of selling it. To do that, I suggest we have Rob and Kathy prepare a summary of the research dealing with motivation, satisfaction and performance and see if that provides your decision makers with a compelling case for making the investment."

"Well," said Maria, "at least you have convinced me I am not alone in this. Perhaps I should go to a meeting of fellow HR professionals so we can all participate in a group whine. I smile as I say that because the last thing HR needs is to act like a hapless victim. We need to put together our business-related case for investing in our people and sell it. If we cannot, then at least we have done what we should. Let me go back and see if we can get an audience for a presentation that will inform management about what might be going on and what the implications might be."

"Is the CEO available now?" asked Annette. "Perhaps I could be of some help to you in getting the ball rolling." Maria called CEO Cameron's assistant and found he was about to go to the cafeteria for a quick lunch. He agreed to meet the two of them down there. Maria cautioned Annette that he was very intellectually curious and probably would grill her mercilessly. "Is he big on execution as well as on accumulating information?" Annette asked, and a vigorous nod from Maria gave her hope that this meeting might prove to be fruitful.

"So, why is my HR executive bringing in a consultant to work me over?" Cameron asked. "I presume it is a pitch for doing a satisfaction assessment." Since Cameron said this with a smile, Annette felt comfortable answering. "Not necessarily," she said. "I think there needs to be a clear objective for doing an assessment first, and you and your executive team need to define that objective."

Cameron clarified his position. "I am not at all against finding out what is driving turnover, and I certainly would like to turn down the frequency and volume of complaints. I am just reluctant to find out we have issues we cannot address after raising expectations by doing a survey. Maria and I are convinced we do not have a pay problem, at least not the level of pay and other rewards. But we do think we have some challenges when it comes to defining, measuring and rewarding performance. Some of our managers got to be managers by being the greatest contributors, especially in design engineering, without any regard for their ability or desire to manage the work, as opposed to doing it. That is not necessarily a problem as long as we can convince them that managing performance is one of the critical responsibilities of those in leadership positions. I know a few of our engineering managers don't think you can measure performance if people are doing creative work and that they think they should trust professionals to do their best. Noble idea, but it does not always work."

Maria reviewed what she and Annette had talked about and asked his support in convincing the executive team it was in their best interests to get on top of the turnover and dissatisfaction issues. "Done," Cameron responded. "Let's have Annette get her folks in to explore this, and if they convince our team that there is a way we can get a handle on the causes and deal with them, I will support it." "Done," Annette responded. On the way out, Maria thanked Annette and said she was optimistic that they could make some headway.

The following week Rob and Kathy regaled the executive team with all of the relevant behavioral research findings. The operations executive made it clear that he found their presentation to be informative and relevant. He went on to ask, "Why is it that so many of the articles I read in the professional literature are contradictory about the relationship between satisfaction, rewards, turnover and engagement? I have read claims that improved satisfaction improved productivity, that rewarding people with money reduces their intrinsic satisfaction from doing the work and that performance appraisals should be abolished, since results are most often impacted by things employees cannot control. They all cannot be correct. How do the authors get these things published, and what do they base their conclusions on? Seems the literature is unreliable, at least the pop literature. But I cringe at the thought of trying to get anything out of research journals, even though I suspect they are more science based. My neighbor is an academic and at a barbeque he insisted I read this 'fascinating' article about a study on motivation. It was more opaque than the Enigma machine used in World War II, and I did not have hundreds of code breakers to make sense of it."

Rob and Kathy both laughed out loud and Kathy remarked, "I hope it was not one of my articles. We are forced to write in our own language so those not within the inner circle cannot access the enormous body of knowledge we possess. The only ones who can decipher our publications are fellow wizards, and we are punished if we translate them so outsiders can learn anything." All of the executives had a good laugh, but one asked, "But are there no double agents who can give us access?" Rob answered, "That is what we consultants are for."

There was little doubt in the room that turnover and dissatisfaction were critical issues that needed to be addressed. But several of the executives were reluctant to stir up the beehive with a formal survey that would raise expectations and focus employees on the issues. A consensus formed after further discussion assured the group that an assessment of the root causes could be done without agitating the bees. They agreed that Maria would work with the consultants to dig into what seemed to be causing the turnover and what was contributing to the dissatisfaction.

Over the next week, Maria worked with the consultants to gather and organize data on the distribution of performance ratings across divisions and the relationship of ratings to rewards. The executive group met, and they were given a copy of the analysis of rating distributions (see Table 37.1).

Table 37.1 Distribution of performance ratings

Rating	Admin	Opns	Mktg/Sales	Finance	R&D/ Engrg	HR/Legal	Public Affairs
Outstanding	22%	2%	55%	19%	5%	42%	67%
Significantly Exceeds Standards	35%	8%	35%	31%	15%	28%	33%
Fully Meets Standards	40%	81%	10%	45%	80%	25%	0%
Does Not Fully Meet Standards	3%	8%	0%	5%	0%	4%	0%
Unsatisfactory	0%	1%	0%	0%	0%	1%	0%

The public affairs and marketing executives considered leaving the room, particularly after Cameron suggested that he would adjust performance expectations for the divisions based on the rating distributions. If a division did indeed have numerous employees who were outstanding performers, it was reasonable to expect great things from that division. Alternatively, if the division did not perform at a spectacular level, it would be assumed that the standards in that division were far too low relative to other divisions.

Not a lot more needed to be said to establish the need to find a process that would better align distributions to make them equivalent. Annette suggested the calibration approach at each level. "Each manager will have his or her supervisors rate their people and also rank them. Then the manager will convene a calibration session with all the supervisors, and no one leaves the room until the supervisor ratings and rankings are merged with each other, producing an equitable result. This process is then repeated at each management level. This not only will align ratings better, but it will also give management much better information about the employees in different units, as well as being able to offer their perspectives on them. Once employees understand this is the new normal, they will be able to express their views and perhaps appeal their ratings using substantive data."

Brian, the head of operations, responded. "Sounds like a bunch of work, but I know you are going to tell us there is a high return on investment, particularly since this has to help employees believe they are being treated fairly and being measured against equivalent standards. And that should help lessen dissatisfaction. I am going to be labeled Attila the Hun, but I am open to learn and to adjust."

The second chart showed the results of an analysis of performance ratings by level within the organization (see Table 37.2). "This one is also a bit troubling," Maria offered, "since it appears all of the best ratings are reserved for the highest-ranking individuals, which is probably the result of a failure to raise expectations for people at the highest levels."

Table 37.2 Performance rating distributions by grade level

Grade	OUT	SES	FMS	DNFM	UNSAT
50	100%				
49	100%				
48	90%	5%	5%		
47	75%	15%	10%		
46	19%	22%	58%	2%	
45	12%	17%	65%	5%	1%
44	6%	19%	69%	4%	2%
43	2%	15%	75%	5%	3%
42	1%	18%	75%	4%	2%
41	1%	15%	76%	6%	2%

"Management jobs start at grade 47, and I seem to see a discontinuity in the pattern below and above 47," Cameron observed. Are we all guilty of assuming that people in key roles are performing at a higher level without consideration that the expectations should be adjusted upward?" "Probably," responded Charles, "I guess I have this pattern across the levels in the engineering career ladder, and much of it is probably due to not having clear standards established at each level. And right now, I want to change the subject until the redness leaves my face. How are we doing tying rewards to performance?"

"Hard to tell," said Maria, "since the performance ratings are all over the place. This is a lesson I learned from Rob when he did a seminar for our local HR group—that you have to have the foundation (performance) soundly measured before you build a skyscraper (rewards) on top of it. And we have some work to do. But to answer your question, there seems to be a correlation between pay increases and performance ratings, such as they are, but the differences between meeting standards and being outstanding as far as base pay increases go are minute. Going the extra mile for an additional 1% or 2% in one's salary increase is not likely to provide strong motivation. Yet our budgets have been small during the economic downturn, and we all probably made the mistake in thinking we had to give something to everyone."

Cameron furled up his brow and shared a revelation he had just experienced. "We should have been using a part of our meager budgets to do cash awards limited to the best performers. By spreading the money around, we just raised our fixed cost via adds to payroll and ended up sending the message that performance counts but not that much. So, we add to already above-market salaries and end up causing dissatisfaction and disappointment on the part of the best performers. What a brilliant strategy."

Annette let the silence after Cameron's very clear message linger. She figured there was learning going on and that it was time for them to think about what path they would follow going forward. There was mutual agreement that everyone should reflect on the findings and suggest how they might best move forward. Annette was happy that the meeting adjourned and assured Maria that they were headed in the right direction.

Rob and Kathy suggested to Annette that they prepare a brief report letter reiterating all that had gone on at the client's office. They felt the process should proceed according to a defined plan, which included the following steps.

1   Obtain approval for a management training program dealing with performance appraisal, goal and standard setting and conducting calibration sessions. They felt some background information on the motivation theories underlying sound performance management should be included, although the presentations should not sound like a college class, rather a practical, interactive discussion about the challenges faced when doing appraisals.
2   Conduct the training and do a dry run on appraisals, analyzing the results once they were completed. Since they knew not all appraisals had been done in the past and many of them were done late, there should be a firm schedule for doing appraisals and analyzing the results before managers talked to employees.
3   Formulate a direct compensation strategy that established principles governing base pay and variable pay management. This would require discussions with the executive team to zero in on a desirable balance between increases to base pay based on merit and individual cash incentive awards. Guidelines governing the relationship between performance, position in range and pay increases would be established prior to the next round of increases and manager recommendations would be reviewed against the guidelines prior to finalizing decisions.
4   Conduct employee training sessions to inform employees about how the new performance and rewards management strategies would impact them and to convey management's commitment to equitable and appropriate rewards based on employee performance.
5   Create a process for evaluating performance and rewards programs and for enabling employees to appeal decisions when they believed they had not been treated fairly or appropriately.

Annette added another item to their list. "We are going to also have to help management decide on how much differentiation should exist between appraisals and rewards, considering the nature of the work performed. Some tightly controlled, low-discretion jobs might warrant a pass-fail approach to appraisal and less differentiation between employees who were performing at or above a satisfactory level. Others might warrant the use of group/team appraisal and rewards, such as members of research teams. Pay for performance should be limited to rewarding true variation in performance, and only when it makes a difference. Once we have this all straightened out, we can perhaps do an employee satisfaction study, although I think focus groups would work better than mechanically scored survey questionnaires. While we are straightening out the performance and rewards management items, we also might dig into the turnover to see if there are patterns and what might be going on to cause dysfunctional voluntary turnover among key people." Rob and Kathy drafted a report, ran it by the entire consulting team, incorporated suggestions made by colleagues and gave it to Annette to transmit to Maria.

When Maria got the report, she recognized that this was a much better approach to addressing their issues than a full-blown survey would have been. A chat with Cameron reinforced that conclusion, and she felt HR had stepped up a notch relative to the respect it commanded in the organization. She promised herself that in the future she would address issues by focusing less on symptoms and more on underlying causes that would explain the symptoms. She also had recognized that asking employees why they were dissatisfied is likely to be more fruitful after exploring the things that might be leading to dissatisfaction. Finally, she pledged to herself that she would increase her understanding of what behavioral research can help understand about the relationship between satisfaction, motivation, behavior and an organization's workforce management policies, programs and processes.

38 Reflections on careers

The staff of Epsilon had been invited to a meeting of consulting firms intended to explore the creation of an association for consultants. There had been associations that consisted solely of consultants as members, and a few of the largest HR associations had attempted to provide forums for their members who were consultants. The Academy of Management had long served the academic community and the Society of Industrial and Organizational Psychology had existed for those academics and OD practitioners within organizations. But no entity was currently focused on the consulting profession. The organizers of the meeting were from large consulting firms and their stated goal was to provide a forum for people in the profession, whether they worked for firms or were individual practitioners.

Don, Annette, Rob and Kathy considered attending the gathering but had their reservations. "Is consulting a profession with definable boundaries?" asked Rob. "What about HR practitioners within organizations who are specializing in organizational development? And what about academics who do consulting as well? Aren't all of those people served by SHRM, ASTD, SIOP, the Academy of Management and other associations with established missions and long track records? And although one might have to belong to several associations if they dabble in several roles or make career changes that change the roles they play, is there not adequate opportunity to affiliate with others who do similar things? It seems the only people not directly served are full-time employees of large consulting firms."

"Well, look at our staff," Don responded. "Rob and Kathy cannot make up their minds month to month if they want to be consultants or academics. Annette and I have been HR practitioners within public sector, private sector and not-for-profit organizations before becoming consultants. And we all may cross bridges again to assume new identities. I may consider an internal HR practitioner role again if I tire of the travel and of bouncing from one client organization to another. I am sure Kathy will go back to teaching as soon as she tires of being a capitalist and has her beach retreat and her villa paid for. And Annette is probably going to be drawn back into the nonprofit world to fulfill her desire to help others who cannot help themselves. Careers parallel lives. Be a student, get a job to pay back your student loans and to fund your lavish lifestyle, go back to school to get an advanced degree, try consulting, take a teaching position, retire and volunteer for charitable organizations. This is not due to the inability to make decisions but to fit your professional role to where you are in life."

Annette added in another perspective. "When is an HR practitioner within an organization more like a consultant than a practitioner? How about when they teach part time as an adjunct while working as an HR practitioner? Is someone a consultant when they are between corporate jobs and need some income? Is a professor who spends 25% of her time consulting a hybrid? I think for me the big question is where does an HR practitioner turn when the person needs to develop advisory skills. Most start as doers in a specialized function or as generalists, responding to needs as they emerge. Over time, that practitioner becomes a sort of applied researcher, trying to uncover the causes of issues and ways to resolve them. As that person rises in level within the organization, the need to become an expert who advises management on workforce management strategies becomes more important. So, tell me at that advisory level what the difference is between our client Andrea and our consultants. Not much, except she has to stay put and live with the decisions she makes while we move on to the next client without really knowing how things played out at the last one."

They were all familiar with the extensive research on careers and understood that people had become more mobile across what had historically been more like career silos. You come out of school, pick a career (or take the job that is available) and work in that career until you retire—that was the old normal. But as the environment became more turbulent and the skills required for success in any career shifted, people attempted to find roles that were a good fit to their capabilities and their desires. As the employment contract increasingly became 'you stay here as long as you want to and as long as we want you,' the need to retool oneself became more pressing. Going back to school and pursuing professional certifications can help people to credential and to build their own intellectual capital. The pressure to make fixed costs flexible has increased as globalization and technology have made revenues and market position more uncertain. This has caused organizations to make greater use of part-time personnel, consultants and contractors. These new realities made it necessary for people to consider different roles as their careers evolve if they want to have a stable income. And the recognition that the organization was not going to commit to a forty-year career arrangement made people less willing to pay their dues by becoming committed to a single employer, with the hope that they would have security and stability and not need to broaden their capabilities.

"One of the career strategies that has become less viable is deep specialization in one discipline or function," Don suggested. "Becoming a 100% HR professional may seem to be a good strategy, since managing the organization's human capital has become increasingly critical and complex. But there is pressure for HR practitioners to become better businesspeople understanding the different perspectives across functions. HR people are often criticized for not sufficiently understanding financial and operational issues, leading them to embrace strategies that are not economically feasible or that do not lead to increased operational effectiveness. Yet the same concern should be extended to the financial and operational practitioners. Finance can focus on short-term cost control and choke off funding for critical workforce development initiatives that are necessary to keep the workforce viable. Operations can focus on efficiency without considering the impact of using top-down control to improve performance on motivation, satisfaction and engagement."

He continued. "Theoretically, people at the executive level have a broad view of strategies and recognize a variety of measures needed to define performance. Look at the increased usage of the balanced scorecard approach. But what about the middle management folks? Is anyone educating them about financial and people implications of making operating decisions? Or the operational and financial implications of workforce decisions? It seems unlikely that people promoted to executive-level positions will have a divine visitation and all of a sudden be able to consider the broader implications of decisions. Even though their peers from other functions are supposedly available to counsel them, there is often intense competition rather than integrative cooperation going on. Operations wants the funding for technology or infrastructure that they know is critical for ongoing success, but finance believes it will negatively impact the quarterly and annual statements and lead to punishment by investment analysts. And the HR executive is waving his or her arms, crying, 'what about the implications for employees created by limiting funding for development?'

Rob pointed out that historically it was common for up-and-coming managers to do a tour in HR, often as the head of the function, before moving on to bigger and better roles. "That may have had some negative consequences in that they were probably not knowledgeable enough about technical aspects of HR, but at least if they reached the top, they would have a clue about what the issues are relative to workforce management and perhaps value the organization's human capital."

"Are we going to that meeting or not?" Annette chimed in. "We need to decide so we don't have to sleep on park benches." "Probably not," Don responded. "This discussion leads me to believe we don't need yet another professional silo when people are moving so often between roles." Kathy voiced her support for that view and Rob and Annette agreed.

Before they parted, Kathy made a suggestion. "The three of you have your twentieth college reunion coming up and I had an idea. Why don't each of you write a letter to yourselves with the title And That Was the Way it Was, but do so as if you had just retired. All this talk about careers and meaning must have stirred up reflections on the paths taken and those not taken, the satisfaction and the disappointments. It seems like this kind of exercise can tell us a lot about what we would like to have accomplished, particularly when we still have time to deal with unfulfilled agendas. I am still fairly early in my career and I am not suggesting you all dye your hair to cover all the grey and have purchased rockers. But I believe it would be intriguing to write the letters and then to share them with each other. I plan to accompany Rob to the reunion, and as an outsider, I would be interested in what this exercise might prompt you to discuss with your fellow graduates while there."

Rob suggested that he planned to work to the very end, so he might not be at more than mid-career, and it would be difficult to anticipate how he might feel when he hung up his spurs. Don thought Rob was mad, since he planned to get out of the game as soon as he had the resources to sustain his lavish life-style for the rest of his years. Annette was intrigued with the idea and wrote the two of them off as left-brainers. After a bit of thought and further discussion, the three of them decided to give the letter a try.

Reflecting on our careers

> To: Rob
> From: Rob
> Subject: And that was the way it was
>
> As I close out my career as an academic and consultant, I believe I have made a positive contribution to my field and to my students and client organizations. This brings me considerable satisfaction. I finished my basic education while working to support myself and then served in the military, fulfilling what I viewed to be an obligation of citizenship. While serving in an elite airborne unit, I learned to balance discipline with self-reliance and became confident in my ability. While attending graduate school to earn master's degrees, I recognized my interest in understanding the scientific method and in developing my intellectual capabilities. Yet I also wanted to apply science to practice, to better face challenges.
>
> Upon graduation, I entered consulting with a large firm and began to develop an interest in applying behavioral science to management. After several years in consulting, the desire to finish my education and to try teaching let me to completing my PhD and to enter the academic world. Since I had continued my studies while consulting and then continued consulting while teaching, I began to realize that there were enormous benefits to be enjoyed if one could use science to inform practice and to use practice to inform science. Consulting continued to be a source of challenge, growth, excitement and satisfaction for two decades, but then I realized that going back to teaching would enable me to not only share my academic knowledge, but also my experience in practical application of principles. Kurt Lewin's observation that "There is nothing more practical than a good theory" resonated with me, as did the knowledge that theory for theory's sake alone does not benefit people or organizations.
>
> *(continued)*

(continued)

Along with my close friends and colleagues, I became convinced that an organization's most important asset was its people and committed myself to promoting a willingness among decision makers in organizations to value that asset and to invest wisely in it. I came to understand that people's academic training and their functional orientation led them to view human capital differently. Whether one looks at the workforce as a cost, as an asset, as a tool to get things done or as a collection of people with different values, beliefs and needs will shape one's view of human capital. I came to believe no one view—finance, legal, HR or operations—was the correct one. Rather, it is necessary to consider all of those perspectives and to reconcile them when workforce management decisions are made. My own perspective became that of a business–oriented human resource management practitioner. That is, I recognized cost efficiency is required when considering investments in human capital. Legal compliance is mandatory, even when laws appear not to make sense—they still must govern actions. Operational effectiveness is a prerequisite for organizational success, even if employees must sometimes be subjected to stressful demands, make monetary sacrifices or live without job security. Yet each organization must continually find a way to attract, retain and motivate a workforce capable of doing what needs to be done—now and in the future. This means each organization must take care to brand itself as an employer in a manner that enables it to have the workforce it needs.

My decision to reenter the academic world in the latter part of my career resulted from two realizations. One, the perpetual uniqueness of the challenges faced when going from one client assignment to the next can be offset by the lack of satisfaction to be gained by being a part of building something over the long run. As my consultant colleagues pointed out, consultants don't get invited to the events celebrating successes and you don't have the opportunity to see the results that an architect would have when the cathedral he designed was completed. Second, the academic world challenges you to create new knowledge and to help others develop their own capabilities, and you often have the luxury of exploring ideas without being subjected to a project schedule and budget. Yet, I came to realize that living in one of those two worlds without at least an understanding of the other can result in tunnel vision. Practitioners joke that academics don't create knowledge—they just cut and paste what they read in a lot of books and journals. Academics joke that practitioners don't read books and journals but rather copy other organizations that seem to be doing well at the moment. Both are half right and half wrong.

My work as a consultant/practitioner was informed by my formal education and academic research/teaching. My work as an academic was informed by organizing my consultant/practitioner experience. Most people do not have the luxury of the knowledge that living in both worlds brings. Yet I did not serve in the role of a full-time practitioner within an organization and wonder how doing that would have changed my perspective. Walking in someone else's shoes mentally is not the same as dealing with the day–to–day politics, interpersonal conflicts, budgetary constraints and continuous emergencies. Although I probably did not fully appreciate the difficulties others faced in taking my advice, I hope that I was able to respect their position and not write them off as being incapable of seeing the wisdom of what I recommended.

In retrospect, I wonder what the ideal career path is. Coming out of school and becoming a consultant without living in the practitioner world can cause one to believe that the right answer is apparent without understanding the obstacles of implementing recommended actions. Staying in school as an academic can lead one to focus on what theoretically will work without facing the challenges associated with turning theory into practice. Becoming and staying a practitioner can cause one to live in the realities of today, buffeted by continuous challenges and obstacles to implementing what one believes to be the correct strategy. The ideal seems to be spending time in each of the three roles, although there is rarely the opportunity or the time to stay in one role long enough to become proficient at it. Yet there are opportunities to gain all of the perspectives by making an effort to step back and consider options from another angle.

I implored academics/researchers to make the effort to understand the challenges being faced by practitioners so they could focus their research efforts on practical issues and to make their results accessible to those who were not schooled in research methodology. I tried to convince practitioners to better prepare themselves to understand how to access and analyze research and to apply usable results in their decision making. And I tried to help fellow consultants appreciate the necessity to incorporate theory into their work and to understand that practitioners were not free to decide on their own how to implement consultant recommendations.

Having lived in the academic and consultant worlds, I believe I was able to understand practitioner issues and to apply research evidence to my consulting recommendations. But I don't know if I suffered from tunnel vision relative to the challenges faced by practitioners. I hope not. I was often frustrated by what seemed to be the reluctance of practitioners to pause and engage in thoughtful reflection. I was also critical of their lack of investment in dialogue with their management and their employees about alternative courses of action. This was probably unfair, since I went from client to client and rarely had enough information about what went on day to day in the organizations. I was also disappointed that practitioners did not write and speak about what they had

(continued)

(continued)

learned so that others could benefit from their experience. But I had the luxury of enough time to write and speak and was often rewarded for doing these things, both in the form of new business and both economic and psychic rewards. Most practitioners did not have that luxury and rarely were encouraged to do so. I was also a critic of the bias in the literature within the field. Successes were written about, yet failures were not, even though both could be sources of learning. I understand it takes courage to write about failures, but many fads start because readers are seduced by the overwhelming success of the "new best thing." And many of the claims made in books and articles are based on opinion rather than on sound evidence.

That was the way it was, and it was for the most part pretty good. Having survived the ups and downs without becoming a manic depressive was an accomplishment. It was frustrating to at times have so much work that there was no time to market. Then it seemed the work was all done and it was necessary to market full time so more work was available. It was also difficult not to exaggerate one's abilities when marketing, particularly during competitive bidding. Being honest about limitations sometimes lost consulting engagements. Yet, the nature of consulting is that you become an optimist, convinced you can resolve any issue and overcome any challenge—this is the mindset that keeps you going. I sometimes probably was unrealistic about what I could do for an organization or about the effort and resources required to complete a project. I justified the conservative estimates by committing to spend whatever time it took to deliver. And when I was told that what I believed to be the right answer was not feasible, I might have assumed it was due to the lack of client competence, rather than facing the reality that it just was not going to work.

If I was provided with a do-over, I do not think I would change much. My mission was to convince organizations that their most important assets were their people. If that was accomplished, it would become possible to convince management to invest heavily in their human capital, but to do so in an optimum manner. It was often difficult to overcome the reluctance to invest in human resource development because it was treated in the financials as a short-term cost, with no offsetting tangible benefit, or at least one that could be booked. It was frequently challenging to convince management to focus on the intangible aspects of managing, such as creating a culture that enabled and encouraged all employees to focus their efforts on the success of the organization. And in spite of the fact that I had extensive psychological training, I sometimes believed that change could be sold using rational arguments, without appreciating that individual self-interest always plays a part in deciding whether individuals accept that change. But it is not reasonable to think one has always analyzed situations correctly, made good decisions as to what recommendations would be presented and understood fully what it would take to implement those recommendations. But since batting over .300 keeps you in the major leagues, I think I exceeded that and probably did a pretty good job of deciding what my career should be and performing at a major league level.

To: Annette
From: Annette
Subject: That was the way it was

When I invested in graduate–level education in human resource management, my expectation was that I would work in organizations that helped people, helping them do a better job of managing themselves. Short of becoming a direct provider of assistance to those in need, as a nurse, teacher or counselor would do, making organizations providing these services more efficient and more effective seemed to be a fulfilling and valuable mission. For a time, I heard the siren's song and became a capitalist and found that money could probably not make you happy, but the things you could buy with it made it easier to be happy. Joining the HR function within a software firm introduced me to making shareholders and employees rich as a mission. Although one could argue that this was consistent with my objective of helping people, including myself, it certainly was not how I saw myself moving through my career. I learned a lot about business while there, but I also saw the "our people are our most disposable asset" mentality emerge when the economy turned sharply downward. It seemed as if management viewed employees as vehicles for generating financial results, with little attention being paid to their needs. After exiting the software firm, my time at the utility association seemed an improvement, and I was able to think about how to make utilities more effective in managing their people. And utilities were organizations that impacted the quality of life of those they serviced. Even though financial pressures precluded them acting as charities, they tended to focus on employee benefits and the well-being of their people. Ratepayers often suspected them of taking care of themselves a little too generously (with someone else's money) and sometimes exerted pressure on them to be more like for–profit organizations. But one could argue that if it were not for investor pressure, that private sector organizations would be more concerned about employee health and security and less on profitability.

When I took the job at the association, Don had originally been the obvious candidate, while I was on the surface the best fit to the charitable

(continued)

(continued)

organization Don joined. But after recognizing the nature of the roles we would play in the organization, it became apparent the best answer was the reverse. I loved what Don's organization did for children, but its challenge was to do well financially so it could do more good. And he was a better fit at that time. The fact that we traded organizations at a later time taught me that the type of leader an organization needs at any time can change as its needs change and that long service by leaders who do not change their focus can keep the organization from responding appropriately to environmental change and changing internal priorities. When I swapped roles with Don, I was a much better fit to the charitable organization, since Don had put it on a firm financial foundation. And I was desirous of focusing more on staff development within the organization I led, which was consistent with what that organization needed. Don was also a better fit to both organizations when he served them.

Both Don and I had the luxury of our relationship with Rob, who frequently brought academic research to us. I believe any practitioner or consultant should build a network of relationships with the academic/research community so they have someone who can notify them of research findings and also who can challenge the rigor of the analyses we do. It is unlikely that research will ever be made widely available in layman's language, due to the nature of the tenure track focus on publications that are aimed at other academics, rather than practitioners. And both Don and I eschewed the temptation to read research journals for entertainment—they suffered from poor plots and limited character development. But we benefitted from knowing what behavioral research could tell us about the issues we dealt with in workforce management.

The decision of the three of us to join a consulting firm was fortuitous, since between us we had a pool of wide-ranging knowledge and experience. The staff at the firm further broadened and deepened our knowledge and skills and helped us in working with client organizations to address their human resource management issues. We gave ourselves credit for being futurists and for knowing our MSHR degree program would provide us with valuable credentials and knowledge we could apply in our consulting work. Actually, it was more blind luck that we followed our interests in choosing our educational pursuits and then finding that it was valuable. Consulting was intellectually stimulating, and the wide variety of clients and issues provided an opportunity to develop individually and as a team. It did not provide the sense of being a part of the organizations we worked for, since client engagements were often brief and focused on the problems at hand. My decision to go back into the not-for-profit sector late in my career gave me the opportunity to really engage in the direct provision of needed services to those not able to function without them. (I realize while writing this that this is an assumed path, not yet taken. But the fact that I feel the need to do this before the end of my career makes me believe the probability is high, verging on certainty. If I do not make that choice, I believe it will cause me to feel that I have not done what I needed and so wanted to do.)

Throughout my career I realized that I was in HR, even when I wasn't in HR in the traditional sense. It occurred to me that the most important thing executives and managers manage are the people who do the work of the organization. Sure, finance folks manage money, operations folks manage technology and infrastructure, R & D folks manage the creation of knowledge and products and marketing folks manage the process of getting the products to the customers. But they all do this through their people, and without those people, all the other resources are useless. HR is a defined function within most resources, but human resource management is the responsibility of all managers. How the development of HR strategy and programs is divided between HR people and line management may vary across organizations and across time, but at no time does the HR function have the exclusive responsibility for initiatives related to workforce management. So, our mantra we continually repeated, that people are the most important asset, is something that comes from a deep belief it is true, albeit often ignored or forgotten.

To: Don
From: Don
Subject: And that was the way it was

I was competitive from an early age—at school, at play, at sports and even with my siblings. In college, it was made clear that performance was relative and that your class standing would mean a lot when you looked for a career. When in graduate school, I found out everyone was smart, and some even smarter than I was. And everyone seemed to have a different perspective and a somewhat different inventory of knowledge and skills. Courses at the graduate level often required working in teams, and although I originally despaired at the idea of being given the same grade as my team members, it slowly came to me that results manifested at a team level, requiring the collection of individual contributions. This realization did not reduce my competitive adrenalin, but channeled it into competing against challenges and goals. Winning became getting the job done, efficiently and effectively.

My first job at the utility was a near disaster from the start. I went into this public-sector entity believing the people there were civil service types looking for great security and a rich pension and focusing on surviving

(continued)

(continued)

rather than excelling. When I first looked at the total rewards package, I heroically presented an agenda for transforming the organization by totally reconstructing the existing programs. My recommendations were met with horror, but luckily a seasoned operations executive took the time to help me understand that much of what was in place was intentionally aimed at producing workforce stability. He made me realize that the primary objective of the utility was reliability—safe water provided when needed. He recognized that some of the programs I challenged were costly and perhaps outdated and admitted this could create an upward pressure on rates, negatively impacting the community. But he made a compelling case for a seasoned and knowledgeable workforce—people who knew where the pipes were really buried and how they were hooked up, often contrary to what the records said. That was my first 'what works is what fits' aha moment relative to workforce management strategies and programs. And it certainly would not be my last. In fact, it became the fundamental principle driving my decisions relative to strategy.

When I took the reins at the not-for-profit, I became a CEO, which opened my eyes to another perspective regarding workforce management. I was now challenged to get the job done through people, rather than recommending strategies and programs. Because of my training and work experience in HR, I recognized human resource management was a very large part of a CEO's job, even though my board thought raising contribution levels should be my dominant concern. I found I could address both of those challenges and used my business knowledge to convince large and corporate donors that their contributions would be used to their best advantage by a competent and focused staff. In effect, I was selling them that I had a workforce capable of effectively and efficiently doing the work everyone was convinced was worthy of support. Once the funding issues were addressed, I began to realize that Annette would be better suited to reshaping the services provided and developing the staff to provide them. So, we switched roles.

While at the utility association, my first efforts centered around shaping a culture that would enable the association to perform well but also to respond to the needs of its member utilities. Rob gave me tools for defining and evaluating culture, and this initiative made me a believer in the criticality of having the right culture. It was clear that there was no one best culture, but only a best-fit culture. During my tenure at the association, I came to appreciate the value of a board that understood the constituency they were representing. Since all board members were executives at member utilities, they were a source of insight into the challenges faced by members and what they would most benefit from. So, I had plenty of guidance, even though sometimes it was a little too much and too varied.

My decision to enter consulting was partly attributable to my desire to work with my close friends, but mostly due to a desire to do something on my own. The competitive streak reemerged, in the form of a "can do" attitude. Some of the client challenges put that optimism to a test and there were times when I realized I needed my peers to help. So, what might have initially been intended to be a solo hero type of endeavor turned out to require a lot of collaboration and cooperation. And the biggest challenge was admitting to a client that what they were doing was fine or that I just did not know how to solve their problems.

In some cultures, managers are expected to have answers for all problems and to admit they do not negatively impact their standing with subordinates. But even though the U.S. has one of the most individualistic cultures in the world, it is often acceptable, and even preferable, for a manager to respond "I don't know—let's figure it out" or "give it your best shot and we can evaluate the results." Rob taught me a lesson when it came to performance management by adding "contribution to the effectiveness of others and the unit" as a factor in appraisals, the need for individuals to not only succeed at their work but to do so in a way that positively impacted others. The bottom-line principle is that performance must be defined, measured and rewarded at the organizational *and* the unit/team *and* the individual level if an organization is to be successful in meeting its objectives and fulfilling its mission.

Consulting was satisfying, challenging and lucrative for 20 years, but I found I could retire at an early age and that I wanted to, so I did (pinch me if I am delusional and anticipating a future that cannot happen). What I did with the rest of my life was satisfying, and although I occasionally relapsed by telling war stories to old colleagues and anyone who would listen, I no longer felt the need to justify myself through what I did rather than who I was. Helping disabled and infirm veterans get to their medical appointments and deal with daily life was a source of considerable satisfaction, even though there was intense competition for air time when it came to telling stories about military experiences.

The bottom line is that I am satisfied with what I did and accomplished in my business career and in my second life. There is little I would change, save being less arrogant and brash early in my journey. It still embarrasses me to reflect on how naïve I was, but since I see the same mistakes being made by those going through that stage, I guess I wasn't that stupid after all.

After the three friends had written, they shared their letters with the others and with Kathy, who agreed to make observations about them. Although Kathy was not an outsider, having partnered with the three for several years, she was in a position to adopt a neutral perspective.

She began by sharing her amazement at how similar their perceptions about their careers were. The three letters emphasized different experiences and perceptions, but they displayed a common view of what was important in business and in life and the two guiding principles they had repeatedly called upon to guide their actions: (1) what works is what fits the context and (2) the people in any organization are the most important and yet often the most undervalued asset. She also thanked them for the opportunity to work with and learn from them.

She went on to make a suggestion. "At the twentieth reunion, why don't you have some of the people you know best and respect most write their letters extemporaneously? That would undoubtedly lead to a fascinating and enlightening discussion."

Annette frowned a bit and responded to the suggestion. "People would have to feel emotionally safe to consider this level of soul-searching and that kind of revealing exercise. We all have bared our souls, our fears, our dreams and our opinions with each other for so long that we don't realize just how threatening that could be to someone who is uncertain of the people who become privy to things generally thought to be very private."

Don agreed. "A couple of our classmates who think they conquered the world in venture capital and investment banking don't appear to have souls to bare, and if they ever did, they successfully exorcised them. We might try a simple question like, 'If you had a do-over, what would you change?' That would be interesting and we could go on to ask why they would change something. But much deeper than that and I think we would be the only four left in our chat group after a few minutes."

"Don is probably right," Rob responded. "And what would we learn anyway? Not many people have the luxury of a do-over and just thinking about how they would have liked to go back for graduate studies or to have spent more time with their kids while they were growing up could be punishing. A lot of suppression goes on in people's lives in order to protect their sense of well-being. Besides, I just want to establish that some HR geeks were able to succeed financially, contribute professionally and find happiness. I know that aspiring to that does not display the highest level of mental health but I want revenge for being called The Three *Mousketeers* rather than The Three *Musketeers* by all those superior classmates figuring out how to become CEOs rather than worrying about the well-being of others."

"Wow," Kathy blurted out, "What did you have for breakfast? It is not like you to go for the low road and to seek revenge." Rob came back instantly, "I guess I should have had a broad smile on my face to indicate I was skillfully employing irony in my comments. Sorry. And you don't have to go into the yellow pages to find me a therapist. Some of what I suggested did have a grain of truth in it. We were a bit skeptical when peers beat us up for focusing so much on human resource management and I am glad our subsequent experiences justified our decisions. So, I really don't have a need to get even by rubbing our success in the face of the skeptics."

"Whew," Don responded. "I thought you were kidding, but you should not be so convincing. We all live on the razor's edge and life has a way of trying to push us over at times. I still regret that so many of our intelligent classmates thought the path to success was all about maximizing profit and the return to investors. But I think we all have created some converts to the 'people as assets' way of thinking. But let's go to the reunion and just reconnect with people on a social level."

39 The twentieth reunion

As expected, the ranks had thinned further since the tenth reunion. Annette had been involved in summarizing the responses to the invitations and found a significant number of classmates were posted to foreign assignments. She thought to herself that globalization will increasingly make that a reality. Some had probably declined because they did not have success stories to share and were unwilling to listen to the accomplishments of those who did. She reflected on the reasons why the four of them had automatically assumed they would go. What did they expect to get back? She had not asked the others but hoped that she was going just to catch up on the lives of those she knew at another time in a different setting. Anniversaries can serve as checkpoints at which progress and success might be evaluated. But she promised herself that she would not let the gathering turn into a competition to decide who had done the best. If it became that, she would not participate.

Don observed that people were wearing classier attire than they did at the tenth reunion. But that could either be a signal that they were more prosperous or that they felt they had to try harder to impress others. Kathy commented that few of them wore what they wore to work, since virtually no one showed up in business casual attire. She longed for a return to a better time when people dressed more formally for work, for travel and even out shopping at the malls. If she had to sit in an airplane seat next to someone in a tank top and shorts one more time, she felt she would lose her cool. And when she saw faculty members show up to teach looking like they might just have been recruited off a street corner, she really lost it. People could wear their cutoffs, or even their pajamas, when they were telecommuting. But when coming in contact with other people, it seemed to her to be disrespectful to dress as if one was in the backyard tending the garden.

Rob kidded Kathy about her sensitivity relative to dress, but he shared her views about dressing to fit the role. He too felt teaching warranted a certain level of formality, since faculty members were not one of the gang. In places like Indonesia, he saw people lose respect by not dressing and behaving in a manner that fit the role they were playing. And he felt it to be a reasonable expectation for students and trainees to have respect no matter where an event took place. It was not a façade in his mind, but rather a recognition that the person was willing to fill the role being filled and was respectful of the obligations that went with it.

Not much occurred that was consequential or surprising, and the crowd thinned out at an earlier hour than it had at the tenth year reunion. "Guess it was getting close to people's bed time," Don quipped. "Know I am tiring a bit. Starting at 7 or 8 p.m. makes things run late, much like Monday night football games." "Save me," responded Annette, "you will get home and stay up for hours replaying your college's athletic victories. Guess that is more stimulating than being around people like us." Rob and Kathy rolled their eyes and pretended they were focused on something else.

Several days after the reunion, Don announced that he was moving to half-time for 6 months and then retiring after he finished up the projects he was participating in. None of the other staff members made a big deal of it, not knowing if he was serious or just thinking about it. Most of them were convinced that as long as they kept him busy and challenged, that he would forget about cutting back his hours or moving to feeding the pigeons in the park full time. Annette had made it clear that when Don went, she would also, to ensure there was someone to watch him and to save him from himself. Kathy and Rob had been talking about yet another reentry into the academic world, and the other staff members began to realize that the senior tier of the firm could well be gone in short order.

Some of the key players were not interested in leadership roles. Pete enjoyed consulting on compensation and showed no interest in babysitting a bunch of highly paid dependents you could not claim on your income tax. Eric was a techie and acknowledged the only management he was interested in was in digital format. It seemed that the time had come to consider selling the firm and for staff members to decide whether they were doing what they most wanted to do or if they should consider moving into jobs within organizations. If they put out feelers now, perhaps a buyer could assume control while everyone was still in place to smooth the transition. Yet they knew that outside of intellectual capital, a consulting firm consists of office leases, a small amount of capital equipment and a client list. The intellectual capital was mostly in the form of human capital, which was mobile and could not be owned. Some of the systems and processes could be turned into intellectual property, with legal protection making it valuable. Yet, there was value in the name, and clients often accept changes in the personnel providing services to them. The staff members were for the most part willing to sign noncompete agreements if they decided to leave the firm so they could be viewed as valuable by the buyer.

Surprisingly, two potential buyers went into a bidding contest for Epsilon, and the sale was finalized quickly. All of the senior staff were made offers to remain with the newly merged firm, and everyone agreed to stay for a minimum of six months. Don, Annette and Rob received stock in the new firm in the same amount as the equity they had accumulated. Kathy, Pete, Eric and several others were given restricted stock grants equal to 150% of their salaries, with a five-year certain vesting that could vest earlier if firm performance exceeds plans each year. Don and Annette committed to not leaving current clients without the support they were promised and agreed among themselves that even though they still planned to depart in six months, that they would not desert people who had placed their faith in them. Rob and Kathy got permission to leave early to begin their teaching term but also committed to finishing work they had started.

The four of them met at what over the years had been their primary source of nourishment, in the form of pizza in the early days, but with salads playing a more significant role as they were forced to decide between dietary change or expenditures on clothing alterations. Bittersweet was the feeling surrounding their table, even though they knew they would see each other regularly. Annette pointed out that their meetings could now be purposeless and frivolous, rather than trying to mix socializing with business. Don admitted he was glad he was pretty much done with slaying dragons and welcomed the opportunity to discover what really made him happy. None of the four had regrets and felt blessed because they had been able to make a living doing what they loved and rarely woke up dreading the day ahead. So many people work because they have to, and the foursome realized that was one of the major challenges inherent in human resource management. Creating widespread satisfaction among the workforce and motivating them to do what is needed for organizational success is devilishly difficult when the employees do not derive any intrinsic satisfaction in what they do. Feeling powerless to do anything but what one is directed to do is bound to create resentment and dissatisfaction.

All four of them, throughout their careers, felt it to be their responsibility to make the best of what was mandated in order for the organization to do what was required. Selecting people who fit the culture; investing in their development and career progression; defining, measuring and rewarding performance fairly, competitively and appropriately; providing employees with adequate protection through benefit programs; treating people well—these were all things they had attempted to do. The cultures they shaped, the HR strategies they formulated and the programs they designed and implemented all were intended to respect employee dignity and to make the organization the best employer it could be.

This was something they could all take pride in and move on in their lives feeling good about themselves.

Printed in the United States
by Baker & Taylor Publisher Services